Contemporary Dualism
A Defense

Ontological materialism, in its various forms, has become the orthodox view in contemporary philosophy of mind. This book provides a variety of defenses of mind-body dualism and shows (explicitly or implicitly) that a thoroughgoing ontological materialism cannot be sustained. The contributions are intended to show that, at the very least, ontological dualism (as contrasted with a dualism that is merely linguistic or epistemic) constitutes a philosophically respectable alternative to the monistic views that currently dominate thought about the mind-body (or, perhaps more appropriately, person-body) relation.

Andrea Lavazza is a research fellow at the Centro Universitario Internazionale, Italy.

Howard Robinson is University Professor in Philosophy, and former Provost, at Central European University, Hungary, and senior fellow at The Center for Philosophy of Religion at Rutgers University, New Jersey.

Routledge Studies in Contemporary Philosophy

For a full list of titles in this series, please visit www.routledge.com

21 **Rawls, Citizenship, and Education**
M. Victoria Costa

22 **Objectivity and the Language-Dependence of Thought**
A Transcendental Defence of Universal Lingualism
Christian Barth

23 **Habermas and Rawls**
Disputing the Political
Edited by James Gordon Finlayson and Fabian Freyenhagen

24 **Philosophical Delusion and its Therapy**
Outline of a Philosophical Revolution
Eugen Fischer

25 **Epistemology and the Regress Problem**
Scott F. Aikin

26 **Civil Society in Liberal Democracy**
Mark Jensen

27 **The Politics of Logic**
Badiou, Wittgenstein, and the Consequences of Formalism
Paul M. Livingston

28 **Pluralism and Liberal Politics**
Robert B. Talisse

29 **Kant and Education**
Interpretations and Commentary
Edited by Klas Roth and Chris W. Surprenant

30 **Feminism, Psychoanalysis, and Maternal Subjectivity**
Alison Stone

31 **Civility in Politics and Education**
Edited by Deborah S. Mower, Wade L. Robison

32 **Philosophical Inquiry into Pregnancy, Childbirth, and Mothering**
Maternal Subjects
Edited by Sheila Lintott and Maureen Sander-Staudt

33 **Authenticity as an Ethical Ideal**
Somogy Varga

34 **The Philosophy of Curiosity**
Ilhan Inan

35 **Self-Realization and Justice**
A Liberal-Perfectionist Defense of the Right to Freedom from Employment
Julia Maskivker

36 **Narrative Identity, Autonomy, and Mortality**
From Frankfurt and MacIntyre to Kierkegaard
John J. Davenport

37 **Contemporary Feminist Pragmatism**
Edited by Maurice Hamington and Celia Bardwell-Jones

38 **Morality, Self Knowledge, and Human Suffering**
An Essay on The Loss of Confidence in the World
Josep Corbi

39 **Contrastivism in Philosophy**
Edited by Martijn Blaauw

40 **Aesthetics After Metaphysics**
From Mimesis to Metaphor
Miguel de Beistegui

41 **Foundations of Freedom**
Welfare-Based Arguments against Paternalism
Simon R. Clarke

42 **Pittsburgh School of Philosophy**
Sellars, McDowell, Brandom
Chauncey Maher

43 **Reference and Structure in the Philosophy of Language**
A Defense of the Russellian Orthodoxy
Arthur Sullivan

44 **Civic Virtue and the Sovereignty of Evil**
Derek Edyvane

45 **Philosophy of Language and Webs of Information**
Heimir Geirsson

46 **Disagreement and Skepticism**
Edited by Diego E. Machuca

47 **Philosophy in Schools**
An Introduction for Philosophers and Teachers
Edited by Sara Goering, Nicholas J. Shudak, and Thomas E. Wartenberg

48 **A Philosophy of Material Culture**
Action, Function, and Mind
Beth Preston

49 **A Philosophy of the Screenplay**
Ted Nannicelli

50 **Race, Philosophy, and Film**
Edited by Mary K. Bloodsworth-Lugo and Dan Flory

51 **Knowledge, Virtue, and Action**
Essays on Putting Epistemic Virtues to Work
Edited by Tim Henning and David P. Schweikard

52 **The Ontology of Psychology**
Questioning Foundations in the Philosophy of Mind
Linda A. W. Brakel

53 **Pragmatism, Law, and Language**
Edited by Graham Hubbs and Douglas Lind

54 **Contemporary Dualism**
A Defense
Edited by Andrea Lavazza and Howard Robinson

Contemporary Dualism
A Defense

**Edited by Andrea Lavazza
and Howard Robinson**

NEW YORK AND LONDON

First published 2014
by Routledge
711 Third Avenue, New York, NY 10017

and by Routledge
2 Park Square, Milton Park, Abingdon, Oxon OX14 4RN

Routledge is an imprint of the Taylor & Francis Group, an informa business

© 2014 Taylor & Francis

The right of the editors to be identified as the author of the editorial material, and of the authors for their individual chapters, has been asserted in accordance with sections 77 and 78 of the Copyright, Designs and Patents Act 1988.

All rights reserved. No part of this book may be reprinted or reproduced or utilized in any form or by any electronic, mechanical, or other means, now known or hereafter invented, including photocopying and recording, or in any information storage or retrieval system, without permission in writing from the publishers.

Trademark Notice: Product or corporate names may be trademarks or registered trademarks, and are used only for identification and explanation without intent to infringe.

Library of Congress Cataloging-in-Publication Data

Contemporary dualism : a defense / edited by Andrea Lavazza and Howard Robinson. — 1 [edition].
  pages cm. — (Routledge studies in contemporary philosophy; 54)
Includes bibliographical references and index.
1. Dualism. 2. Materialism. I. Lavazza, Andrea, editor of compilation.
B812.C66 2013
147'.4—dc23
2013024487

ISBN 978-0-415-81882-7 (alk. paper)
ISBN: 978-0-415-81882-7 (hbk)
ISBN: 978-0-203-57920-6 (ebk)

Typeset in Sabon
by Apex CoVantage, LLC

Printed and bound in the United States of America by Publishers Graphics, LLC on sustainably sourced paper.

Contents

1 Introduction—Dualism: What, How, and Why 1
ANDREA LAVAZZA, HOWARD ROBINSON

PART 1
The Limits of Materialism

2 Against Physicalism 17
UWE MEIXNER

3 Problems of Physicalism Regarding the Mind 35
ANDREA LAVAZZA

4 Materialism, Dualism, and the Conscious Self 56
DAVID LUND

PART 2
Dualism and Empirical Research

5 Neuroscience: Dualism in Disguise 81
RICCARDO MANZOTTI, PAOLO MODERATO

6 Quantum Theory of Mind 98
HENRY P. STAPP

7 A Dualist Account of Phenomenal Concepts 112
MARTINA FÜRST

PART 3
Cartesian (Substance) Dualism

8 What Makes Me Me? A Defense of Substance Dualism 139
RICHARD SWINBURNE

viii *Contents*

9 Naturalism and the Unavoidability of the Cartesian Perspective   154
HOWARD ROBINSON

10 On What We Must Think   171
RALPH C. S. WALKER

PART 4
Non-Cartesian Dualism

11 The Promise and Sensibility of Integrative Dualism   191
CHARLES TALIAFERRO

12 The Dialectic of Soul and Body   204
WILLIAM HASKER

13 Dualism, Dual-Aspectism, and the Mind   220
DAVID SKRBINA

14 Why My Body Is Not Me: The Unity Argument for Emergentist Self–Body Dualism   245
E. J. LOWE

Contributors   267
References   269
Index   285

1 Introduction
Dualism: What, How, and Why

Andrea Lavazza, Howard Robinson

In February 2013, the European Union earmarked one billion Euros (1.3 billion dollars) for its two flagship projects in scientific research this decade. One of them, *Human Brain Project*, involves replicating the human brain with the help of computers. In spring 2013, the US administration was also launching a 10-year research project called *Brain Activity Map*, with funding amounting to 3 billion dollars, and whose purpose is to unveil the workings of the human brain, in part with the aim of creating forms of artificial intelligence that can increasingly resemble the human mind.

We believe it is intellectually honest on our part to state from the outset that if one of these projects—whether in ten or one hundred years—will be successful in the sense we will specify later, this book will inevitably be obsolete, and many of the arguments therein will simply have to be considered mistaken. Obviously, it is equally important to specify the sense in which the project can be *successful*. And we also believe we can state that many, if not all of the authors represented here are skeptical concerning the fact that these projects can be fully successful as far as the contents of this book are concerned.

One possibility related to the projects cited before is that the *in silico* or *in vitro* reproduction of human cortical columns may shed light on the functioning of the human brain at a fine scale, thus improving the data in our possession and making them more precise and specific. This means that we may be able to discover the neuronal correlates of many superior functions and manipulate them, both for clinical purposes—for example, in order to treat neurodegenerative diseases that affect our intellectual performance, such as Alzheimer's and Parkinson's—and in order to boost the current "natural" abilities of human beings, for example by improving memory or lengthening attention spans.

All of this is of enormous scientific, health, and social importance. It is a source of pride in the progress of research and in its impact on our quality of life. However, it does not appear to be able to change certain philosophical and empirical problems related to the explanation of some of our "mental" abilities, including, for example, phenomenal consciousness, intentionality, semantics, the possibility of deriving universally valid logical laws, and the search for the "meaning" of things and of existence. All of these problems would remain inaccessible to scientific understanding—i.e., replicability—and philosophical reflections on the mind would still have room to exist.

If, instead, it should prove possible to build "artificial" brains that can simulate the previously listed abilities in a way *we* find convincing, then things could radically change. We are not only talking about the so-called Turing Test, where a machine is made to engage in a conversation with a human: if the human does not realize, based on the replies—however they are conveyed (verbal communication, written text, images . . .)—that she is talking to a machine, then the machine is said to have passed the Turing Test. In terms of pure logic and the amount of information they can handle, computers have long passed us, as evidenced by, among other things, the defeat of leading chess champions at the hands of a computer programme. What machines still generally lack is a reasonably sophisticated fuzzy-logic concept. And yet, this is not the concept that could make this book obsolete. The point is to build a machine—whether from silicon or any other new material (including a robot equipped with a brain that is exactly like ours, but is not made of living, organic matter)—endowed with phenomenal consciousness, subjective sensations, intentionality, semantic abilities, the capacity to grasp universally valid laws, and a commitment to searching for "meaning" in things and existence.

The rationale behind both the EU and US projects is that these abilities are properties that will naturally emerge (not in the philosophical sense, the abilities will literally "pop up") once the extraordinarily complex architecture of the human brain is adequately reproduced and once a dynamic system that can imitate the equally extraordinarily complex and rapid interactions between neurons is implemented. In other words, the basic simplification underlying the general outline of these projects is that materialism is real, plain and simple, and that the apparent difficulties in explaining it are related to the physical brain "type" and the "amount of computing" that takes place within it, which must be brought to bear from the outside in order to understand its functioning.

It should also be noted that the amount of funding that has been earmarked is a meaningful indicator of a certain cultural climate. Such a major investment in a project to replicate the human brain indicates a widespread consensus in the scientific community that such a project may achieve at least partial success. This consensus is not limited to the community of scientific experts in this sector; it extends to political decision-makers who are responsible for allocating a great quantity of public funds and are therefore under the obligation to steer them towards projects with a realistic chance of producing results that are both interesting and useful for the collective good. That the functioning of the human brain (and consequently, of the human mind in its entirety) is replicable in the lab and that no enigmas remain inaccessible to scientific naturalism applied properly with currently available tools have thus become widespread convictions, to the extent that many believe that in the not-too-distant future, those capacities/properties that remain without an accepted explanation we hinted at before will not only have the potential to be understood in scientific terms, but also to be replicated at will, albeit with an imposing collective effort.

At that point, it would no longer be necessary to look elsewhere for explaining and understanding the capacities of the human mind (and the human mind itself), capacities which still appear to lie beyond the exclusive reach of science that follows a physicalist paradigm. This paradigm seems to propose once again—bereft of the veneer of philosophical sophistication of its early days—the view "that mental states are entirely material or physical in nature, and correlatively that a complete account of the world, one that leaves nothing out, can be given in entirely materialistic terms" (Bonjour 2010: 3). The thesis of this book is that such a view cannot by itself account for the entire mental spectrum as it appears to us, in a primitive and unquestionable manner.

Obviously, materialism in the strict sense is a metaphysical thesis, and as such it cannot be proven by even the most powerful of computers. And intentionality and primary meaning are not to be found inside neurons: much like in Leibniz's famous mill, we see only wheels, levers, and springs, and nothing than can be likened to mental contents. The ability to replicate biological brains which manifest the mental properties that most elude understanding does not tell us how these properties have become an inevitable component of the world's furniture. And yet, it seems trite to point out that every day, fertilized ova become embryos, which eventually become children and adults with well-developed brains on one hand, and persons endowed with diachronic identities and phenomenal consciousness on the other. However, this process is unable to tell us if and how bodies and individual persons are identical, and if and how phenomenal consciousness is merely an epiphenomenon of neuronal activity.

In other words, it seems that there are metaphysical and conceptual problems—the ontological status of the physical and the mental, and their relationship—whose treatment cannot ignore empirical and experimental science, but which are not in any way made insubstantial or eliminated by the latter.

Eliminative materialism simply denies the reality of the mental. Reductive materialism and supervenience materialism do not have problems with the explanatory completeness of neuroscience. They merely coat it with a conceptual mental veneer, sacrificing the mental in its original, substantive sense.

In this regard, it has been argued that:

> Many believe that the instantiation of mental properties is nevertheless determined by instantiation of physical properties, where the hypothesized determination relation is a *contingent* relation—for example, a contingent causal or contingent nomological relation (in which case

> either the physical events would cause the mental events, or it would be nomologically necessary that, if physical facts are such as they are, the mental facts would be as well). These views, however, are not positions in the metaphysics of mind; they are instead contingent scientific theories and as such are not versions of materialism, at least not on the primary use(s) of "materialism" in traditional philosophy of mind.
> (Koons and Bealer 2010: xvi-xvii)

However, in our opinion, one could also take seriously a form of materialistic naturalism which makes use of contingent relationships to demonstrate that this thesis is nevertheless a reductionist and incomplete view of reality, since it attempts to exclude the mental, which we feel instead is an integral, ineliminable part of reality itself.

Let us consider Wimsatt, Bickle, Bechtel, and Craver's sophisticated reductionist viewpoint, which speaks of "multilevel mechanistic explanations", which, based on current knowledge, seems to constitute a reasonably plausible model of how memory works (Bickle 2011). If memory can work mechanistically and if mnemonic processes in animals can be elicited or blocked at will, based on current knowledge, however, nothing of the sort is possible for consciousness, qualia, or intentionality in human beings. First-person phenomena may be declared an illusion, but this illusion is so obstinate that it must be taken seriously, and about which theories (including metaphysical ones) about these phenomena must be formulated and assessed in terms of their explicative ability and soundness. The problem of explanations through "mechanisms" is that inputs and outputs fall in different categories. The different reflectivity of light that "produces" colours is undoubtedly a physical matter, but the sensations it produces in the individuals who perceive those colours is something that no physical matter is able to fully capture, even though the eye and the activity of the brain are necessary elements for there to be qualia. When categories become the central point, the dispute is once again a merely philosophical one.

In particular, many of the authors who contributed to this volume argued in favour of some sort of dualism, namely "the theory that the mental and the physical—or mind and body or mind and brain—are, in some sense, radically different kind of things" (Robinson 2011: 1). The starting point seems to be a double realism—both ontologically and epistemically—according to which the primitive phenomenon of the consciousness through which we access the world from a first-person perspective is a way to come into direct contact with outside reality, even though numerous lines of evidence highlight the limits and distortions affecting it.

If the question asked by Descartes in his *Meditations on First Philosophy* was "What am I?", and his famous reply—"Something that thinks"—marked the foundation of classic substance dualism, this approach could be turned upside down today, in spite of the fact that textbooks in philosophy of the mind continue to take their clues from dualism, as a discredited response to the mind-body problem towards materialism as the correct answer. We cannot deny that, by shared admissions, many functions have been subtracted from the dominion of the mental in the Cartesian sense, or, better yet, that the explanation of certain components traditionally assigned to the mental have seen the scientific method prevail, giving preeminence to *res extensa*.

The point is that there are things that neither philosophy of mind (materialistic) nor empirical science have yet been able to explain (cf. Nagel 2012). For this reason, dualism can still be at the heart of a progressive research programme.

CRITIQUES OF MATERIALISM

The point is then that the materialist ontology is too parsimonious to provide the resources needed to accommodate the phenomena—a condition that must be met by any acceptable view of human experience and its place in the natural world. An awareness of the importance of being faithful to the phenomena would help account for the lasting appeal of mental-physical dualism, in one or another of its forms—an appeal that persists in the face of a full awareness of the challenges the dualist must try to meet, of a contemporary intellectual culture that seems to regard dualism as suspicious at best if not entirely misguided, and of the plethora of recent attacks upon dualist views. But the attacks are often dismissive, and the arguments are met without difficulty. Indeed, the present situation indicates that mental-physical dualism has fallen into disfavour in the contemporary intellectual scene not because the arguments for it have been found to be faulty but because it is assumed not to fit, or fit sufficiently well, with the naturalist perspective that the advance of science had made seem so irresistible. One result of this has been a widespread failure to appreciate the force of those arguments.

Dualists and others have frequently pointed out that the thoroughgoing materialist seems unable to accommodate not only the subjectivity of experience but also the qualitative character of sensation and perception. Of course, cognitive activities such as thinking, remembering, imagining, intending, and, indeed, all conscious activities present apparently insuperable problems in accommodating the subjective aspect—the "what-it-is-like" to have any conscious state. Part of the problem for a materialist account of sense qualities arises because physical science provides a treatment of only the causal-relational properties of matter and apparently has no place for the properties that are intrinsic to the content of sensory experience.

A more specific but apparently insuperable difficulty for the materialist is to provide an account of what reasoning could be in a natural world entirely constituted of matter in its various forms. Proper (deductive) reasoning is achieved when one accepts a conclusion because it is seen to follow from the premises. But what can seeing the logical relation between premises and conclusion be on an account of thinking in which the conclusion is reached entirely as an effect of the activity of the elementary particles constituting one's brain?

The problem of understanding what the intentionality (i.e., the directedness or "aboutness") of thought can be for the materialist is another of the relatively well-known problems. As Alvin Plantinga asked, how can a belief have a content (i.e., be directed upon a content) if it is reductively understood to be "an assemblage of neurons, a group of material objects firing away"? For how can such a group have a content, i.e., be *about* anything? The events constituting the group simply occur, as events in a causal chain. But causation is a non-intentional relation. If intentionality is an *intrinsic* property of belief and thought (i.e., is irreducible to anything else), then the case for materialism is lost.

Another set of arguments that present an apparently unanswerable objection to a materialist view is grounded in the fact that every item in an entirely material world would admit of third-person description. Every item would be accessible to the third-person viewpoint and would be amenable to description based on what is revealed to that viewpoint. The problem for the materialist view is that any such description will fail to capture what is accessible only to a first-person viewpoint and thus necessarily will omit the very centre of a person's world; more specifically, it will omit the self, understood as the subject of conscious states as well as much of the intentional content of those states. As David Lund maintains, third-person information about oneself (knowledge of oneself by description) seems indeed to be neither necessary nor sufficient for consciousness of oneself. It is not sufficient, for (in first-person terms) I would be unable to see that the third-person information is information about *me* unless I were already aware of myself in a first-person way. But in the materialist view, it would have to be sufficient.

A different and apparently unanswerable argument for rejecting materialism in all its forms is what we might call "the transcendence argument", advanced by Howard Robinson. The thinking subject has to transcend the physical world about which (among other things) it thinks. Only if a strong reductionism were true could its thinking be part of that physical world. But a strong reductionism cannot be true. Special sciences (which, unlike physics—the basic science that purports to tell us how the world is independent of any special interest or concern) tell us how it is from the perspective of an interest in something that affects us, e.g., the weather. These sciences and the entities that they postulate exist from certain intellectual perspectives, and a perspective, whether perceptual or intellectual, is external to that on which it is a perspective.

A final problem for materialism to be noted at this juncture is pointed out by several scholars, some doing so in the course of arguing for the simplicity of the self and for its "strict" or absolute identity through time, others by focusing on the difficulties that arise in having to maintain, as the materialist must, that the self is compositionally complex.

CRITIQUES OF DUALISM AND RESPONSES TO PROBLEMS

Some of the most persuasive arguments for mental-physical dualism are of the modal kind, attempting to establish certain possibilities or impossibilities, necessities or contingencies. To put it as succinctly as possible, these are the arguments developed by Descartes and Leibniz. The former argues that I can exist without a body or physical properties, but that no material thing can exist without physical properties, and thus the self is different from any material thing. The latter instead argues that one cannot account for the nature of mental phenomena in physical terms, and that therefore natural phenomena are not the property of physical entities. I have mental properties, therefore I am not a physical entity.

In other words, dualism takes seriously the reality of the mental, and, in its contemporary versions, it attempts to account for this in the face of the materialistic view, which either seems to fail in accounting for the mental or ends up—either implicitly or deliberately—removing it from the elements that have the ability to act in the world. The fact remains that dualism, as we stated before, has a bad reputation, which is sometimes well-deserved and often brought about by the arguments employed in its defense, which are either too weak or too ambitious.

Since mental-physical dualism is widely regarded as an untenable view, primarily because it is believed to have no adequate account of mental-physical causation and to fit poorly into a thoroughgoing naturalism, it is highly important to address these and other criticisms of dualist views. Let us characterize these criticisms as indicative of problems for dualist views and divide these problems into four general categories: (1) the "bifurcation" problem, (2) interactionism—the problem of mental-physical causation, (3) the problem of the origin of the mental, and (4) problems for substance dualism (in addition to those already listed). What emerges from this book is a quite persuasive, if not compelling, case for concluding that some form of dualism has the resources to provide adequate treatment of all these problems, that it is able to provide a philosophically adequate account of persons and their place in the natural world, and that it is in fact more defensible than any of the materialist views with which it clashes.

The Bifurcation Problem or *the Problem of Embodiment*. The dualist is frequently criticized as having sundered mind from body with mind directing the body in a way analogous to that of a pilot directing his ship—a criticism often citing Descartes. Descartes and, it seems, Eccles talk as if the body played no direct part in thinking, relying on the body only for sensory content. But thinking seems to be more deeply embodied in the brain. Robinson (1989) attempts to solve this problem, but it is probably true to say that if the dualist can prove his case against the materialist, the real 'mind-body problem' moves from being the problem of consciousness to being the problem of embodiment.

Interactionism: the Problem of Mental-Physical Causation. The simplest objection to interactionism is that, in so far as mental properties, states, or substances are of radically different kinds from each other, they lack that communality necessary for interaction. It is generally agreed that, in its most naive form, this objection to interactionism rests on a 'billiard ball' picture of causation: if all causation is by impact, how can the material and the immaterial impact upon each other? But if causation is either by a more ethereal force, or energy, or only a matter of constant conjunction, there would appear to be no problem in principle with the idea of interaction of mind and body.

Even if there is no objection in principle, there appears to be a conflict between interactionism and some basic principles of physical science. For example, if causal power was flowing in and out of the physical system, energy would not be conserved, and the conservation of energy is a fundamental scientific law. Various responses have been made to this. One suggestion is that it might be possible for the mind to influence the *distribution* of energy, without altering its quantity (see Averill and Keating 1981). Another response is to challenge the relevance of the conservation principle in this context. The conservation principle states that "in a causally isolated system the total amount of energy will remain constant". Whereas "[t]he interactionist denies . . . that the human body is an isolated system", so the principle is irrelevant (Larmer 1986: 282).

Robin Collins (2011) has claimed that the appeal to conservation by opponents of interactionism is something of a red herring because conservation principles are not ubiquitous in physics. He argues that energy is not conserved in general relativity, in quantum theory, or in the universe taken as a whole. Why then, should we insist on it in mind-brain interaction? Most discussions of interactionism take place in the context of the assumption that it is incompatible with the world being 'closed under physics'. This is a very natural assumption, but the problem with the closure of physics may be radically altered if physical laws are indeterministic, as quantum theory seems to assert. If physical laws are deterministic, then any interference from outside would lead to a breach of those laws. But if they are indeterministic, might not interference produce a result that has a probability greater than zero, and so be consistent with the laws? This way, one might have an interaction that yet preserve a kind of nomological closure, in the sense that no laws are infringed. Because it involves assessing the significance and consequences of quantum theory, this is a difficult matter for the non-physicist to assess. Some argue that indeterminacy manifests itself only on the subatomic level, being cancelled out by the time one reaches even very tiny macroscopic objects: and human behaviour is a macroscopic phenomenon. Others argue that the structure of the brain is so finely tuned that minute variations could have macroscopic effects, rather in the way that, according to 'chaos theory', the flapping of a butterfly's wings in China might affect the weather in New York (for discussion of this, see Eccles 1989, 1994, and Popper and Eccles 1977). Still others argue that quantum indeterminacy manifests itself directly at a high level, when acts of observation collapse the wave function, suggesting that the mind may play a direct role in affecting the state of the world (Hodgson 1991; Stapp 2005).

The Origin of the Mental. The common assumption is that the mental was not always present in the natural world and so must have an origin. Though many thinkers do not specifically address this matter, others make a point of doing so. Panpsychists hold that the mind is omnipresent and a fundamental constituent of the natural world. And the emergentists place the origin of the mental at the centre of their concerns, with a view in which the mental emerges as a property of material particulars as new causal powers arise on the higher levels. However, the objection concerning the origins of the mental is not conclusive, since, first of all, the fundamental point concerns the *existence* of the mental, which dualism acknowledges as a primitive and fundamental aspect of the world's architecture, while materialism, which aims to have a theory (based on the physical brain) on the origins of the mental, cannot even fully account for the existence of the mental at all.

Problems for Substance Dualism. A number of the contributors to this book are substance dualists who also maintain, implicitly in some cases, that (contrary to the "bundle" or Humean-type dualist) the self is a simple substance having no substantial parts. In addition, they hold that the self is non-physical, though some only imply this in affirming the (metaphysical) possibility of it existing in separation from the physical body. This "strong" form of dualism (as contrasted with the "weaker" property and bundle dualisms) is frequently charged with lacking an adequate basis for holding that a non-physical substantial self exists and with being unable to provide a satisfactory account of its continuing identity through time, and of how similar selves are to be individuated.

Arguments presented by mental-physical dualists for a dualist conception of mentality do not exclude a bundle dualism according to which the self is a collection of states and thus a complex entity rather than a simple subject to which these states belong. Accordingly, the substance dualists must show that bundle dualism should be rejected. It may be affirmed that unless we acknowledge the self to be simple, we cannot accommodate certain irresistible intuitions concerning personal identity, e.g., the intuition that the matter of whether someone exists must be a matter of *fact*. But the bundle view implies that there are conditions under which this is *not* a matter of fact—an implication that clashes head-on with what is evident from the subjective point of view. One can also argue that such an implication is totally unacceptable from the first-person viewpoint, a viewpoint that must be taken seriously, if not authoritatively, in such matters. The bundle theorist is committed to a criterial account of personal identity, both over time and, perhaps more crucially, concerning counterfactuals of origin. This latter, in particular, seems to be fatal to bundle theories (Robinson 2012a).

Finally, a major criticism based on the findings of neuroscience regards the cerebral location of mental functions, including the most elevated and sophisticated ones. In this case, dualists must certainly acknowledge that the brain is necessary for such mental functions to take place, yet they are not forced to admit that it is also sufficient. If focal lesions inhibit the function in question, it does not necessarily follow that thought is an activity that exclusively takes place in the brain. Consider this situation: when someone moves their vocal apparatus in order to talk, new neuroimaging techniques can empirically show that a certain part of the brain is more active than the others, and therefore that it is somehow engaged in accompanying or overseeing the movements of the vocal apparatus. Additionally, when that part of the brain is damaged, or merely temporarily deactivated thanks to currently-available techniques such as transcranial magnetic stimulation, the person in question is no longer able to adequately move their vocal apparatus, and thus can no longer speak normally. However, this does not prove that speaking is an activity of the brain or that the brain is both necessary and *sufficient* in order to be able to speak.

THE PAPERS

At this point, it may be worth mentioning that the number of philosophers currently defending some form of ontological (as contrasted with linguistic, conceptual, or epistemic) dualism is enormously dwarfed by the number of philosophers and thinkers in related fields apparently subscribing to a thoroughgoing (or ontological) materialism. Indeed, rather well-known ontological dualists are not so easy to find. Recent book publications in philosophy of mind reflect this lopsided proportion, making a concerted dualist response all the more timely and important. This group of selections would amount to a significant response of that sort. Though the different authors would advance quite different considerations and arguments for either substance or property dualism, there would be considerable agreement of a general kind. The selected articles seem to succeed in providing (together, if not individually) a compelling case for believing that a dualist view can provide an important contribution to the ongoing discussion about the mind-body relation in philosophy of mind and cognitive neuroscience as well.

The book is structured in four sections. Part 1 is devoted to the "The Limits of Materialism". David Lund, in his chapter *Materialism, Dualism, and the Conscious Self*, after offering an overview of the broad kinds of materialism, argues that none can accommodate occurrent consciousness or plausibly deny its existence. A substance dualism is then defended. Lund maintains that the irreducible reality of a subject of conscious states must be acknowledged, that it is the centre of consciousness and agency, that it is an endurer with a primitive matter-of-fact unity, and that one's initial consciousness of it is unmediated, non-observational, pre-reflective, and yet epistemic—a knowledge by acquaintance.

Uwe Meixner, in his chapter *Against Physicalism*, begins by specifying and defending a certain conception of physicalism (that is, he defends the position that the specified conception is the right conception of physicalism, *not* that the specified conception is true). After some stage setting (which already tells against physicalism in the sense specified), Meixner proceeds to the presentation and justification of six arguments against physicalism (as initially specified): the two Cartesian modal arguments, the Chalmers-Descartes modal argument, the causal argument, the argument from illusion, and the argument from perspective.

Andrea Lavazza, in his chapter *Problems of Physicalism Regarding the Mind*, argues that physicalism implies that all mental functions arise from the functioning of our material organ, the brain. In turn, this reductionist perspective implies that the human brain, in its current configuration, is nothing but the fruit of biological evolution, which is by nature casual and contingent. If this is true, certain considerations—which so far have received little attention—seem to arise from these premises. Lavazza states that one could argue for the existence of incommensurable conceptual schemes, while mental experiments on the mind would seem to lose their necessary character. Finally, logical laws themselves may be made contingent unless some form of Platonism or dualism is accepted.

Part 2 is devoted to "Dualism and Empirical Research". Riccardo Manzotti and Paolo Moderato, in their chapter *Neuroscience: Dualism in Disguise*, argue that in the last two decades, neuroscientists and philosophers alike based most of their research on the belief that the mind will eventually be explained in purely neural terms. Although many neuroscientists profess a strict physicalism, Manzotti and Moderato purport to show that neuroscience is rooted on a dualistic ontology that keeps reemerging in the form of implicit premises, experiment descriptions, and expected conclusions. The disguised dualism is mostly the result of the widespread, but seldom questioned, doctrine of internalism. The persisting difference between neural activity and consciousness generates a gray area of epistemic entities that are mistaken for ontological promissory notes. As a result, neuroscience often contradicts the alleged rejection of dualism that so many scholars profess. Thus, Manzotti and Moderato conclude that either neuroscientists venture to consider different ontological landscapes or they ought to admit they can't live without dualism.

Henry P. Stapp, in his chapter *Quantum Theory of Mind*, focuses on the theory of mind pursued by most neuroscientists which has been called "Promissory Materialism" by Karl Popper. It is characterized by a commitment to the view that an understanding of the mind-brain connection will come eventually from dogged adherence to the concepts of classical mechanics. Those concepts are known to be fundamentally false, make no mention of mind, and have been replaced at the fundamental level by those of quantum mechanics. Stapp argues that the latter theory, in its orthodox form advanced by von Neumann, is basically a theory of the connection between the minds and the brains of observers, and it involves observer free choices that can influence, via the basic quantum laws, an observer's physical actions.

Martina Fürst, in her chapter *A Dualist Account of Phenomenal Concepts*, considers the *phenomenal concept strategy* a powerful response to anti-physicalist arguments. This physicalist strategy aims to provide a satisfactory account of dualist intuitions without being committed to ontological dualist conclusions. Fürst first argues that physicalist accounts of phenomenal concepts fail to explain their cognitive role. Second, she develops an encapsulation account of phenomenal concepts that best explains their particularities. Finally, she argues that the encapsulation account, which features self-representing experiences, implies non-physical referents. Therefore, the account of phenomenal concepts that has strong explanatory power does not explain away dualist intuitions—rather, it reinforces dualism.

Part 3 is devoted to "Cartesian (Substance) Dualism". Richard Swinburne, in his chapter *What Makes Me Me? A Defense of Substance Dualism*, argues that informative designators are words which pick out properties or substances, such that if we know how to use the words, we fully understand what we are picking out. Two properties or substances are the same if, and only if, their informative designators are logically equivalent. Hence pure mental properties such as sensations, thoughts, or intentions are not the same properties as brain properties, nor are human persons picked out by each one of us as 'I' the same substances as brains or bodies. Thus, Swinsburne can conclude that each of us is a pure mental substance, a soul which has (on Earth) a body as a contingent part.

Howard Robinson, in his chapter *Naturalism and the Unavoidability of the Cartesian Perspective*, maintains that if the world is closed under physics, it might seem that all the entities and laws found at the other 'levels' and sciences—chemistry, biology, psychology—have no serious work to do. This is a version of Kim's exclusion principle. In particular, a Laplacean demon could ignore the existence of consciousness without loss. Dennett shows that this leads to paradox. Robinson argues that it is a paradox that no naturalist—even one who eschews physicalism—can avoid and that the Cartesian perspective is ineliminable. Then he also argues that, *contra* Loewer and Fodor, all the special sciences are dependent on that perspective.

Ralph C.S. Walker, in his chapter *On What We Must Think*, states that we think we are responsive to reason, which is objective and delivers "oughts" that can guide our thoughts and actions. So, we are committed to thinking of ourselves this way: our conception of the world depends on it. We cannot take seriously the possibility that we are wrong, any more than we can take extreme skepticism seriously. Drawing on that, Walker argues that our responsiveness to reason cannot be accounted for in material terms. Because the mind has non-material properties, we should recognize it as a substance, capable of existing on its own, once we have seen what is wrong with the objections brought against that idea.

Part 4 is devoted to "Non-Cartesian Dualism". Charles Taliaferro, in his chapter *The Promise and Sensibility of Integrative Dualism*, underscores that some contemporary philosophers think that materialism is more in line with common sense than dualism (the appeal to simplicity, contemporary neuroscience findings), but this is often based on a misconception of dualism, the physical sciences, and consciousness itself. Taliaferro argues that dualism can be developed in a fashion that preserves the non-identity of person and body while holding that a healthy embodied person functions as a whole, embodied person. Thus, a form of integrative dualism makes more sense of the physical sciences themselves, mental causation, and what we know of ourselves as conscious subjects.

William Hasker, in his chapter *The Dialectic of Soul and Body*, argues that while considerations of substance dualism usually begin with Descartes, the older tradition of Thomistic dualism, based on the Aristotelian view of the soul as the form of the body, also deserves our attention. The view is outlined, following Eleonore Stump's exposition, and some objections to it are noted. Hasker then considers a modified version of Thomistic dualism developed by J.P. Moreland, and he finally directs his attention at two contemporary versions of "emergent dualism", which have many of the benefits aimed at by the Thomistic view without its drawbacks.

David Skrbina, in his chapter *Dualism, Dual-Aspectism, and the Mind*, argues that for centuries philosophers have had competing inclinations toward both dualism and monism. As is well known, both views have strengths and weaknesses. But traditional dualism has failed to earn many adherents, and modern physicalist monisms cannot account for many aspects of mind and consciousness. Skrbina's path forward is to respect both intuitions and to construct something like a dual-aspect monism, one which combines the advantages of both views while still taking the mind seriously. So, he proposes a parallelistic, panpsychic dual-aspect theory that attempts to combine the best features of both outlooks.

E. Jonathan Lowe, in his chapter *Why My Body is Not Me: The Unity Argument for Emergentist Self-Body Dualism*, tackles the nature of self, its existence and identity, starting from the question that Descartes raises in the *Meditations*: "What *am* I?"—or, in its plural form, "What *are* we?" He stresses the ontological dependency of a thought upon its subject, which arises because thoughts are partly individuated by their subjects and thus have their identity determined by those subjects. Lowe's argument is that I am *nothing* bodily at all. Selves or persons, conceived as subjects of thought, are an ontologically basic category of things. They are what *we* are, in the most fundamental sense. This does not mean that we are something wholly immaterial or non-physical, as Descartes believed. But it does mean that we should reject the view that we are 'nothing but' animals of a certain kind, or 'nothing but' our brains[1].

NOTE

1. Many thanks to David Lund for important contributions to this Introduction.

Part 1
The Limits of Materialism

2 Against Physicalism

Uwe Meixner

1. WHAT IS PHYSICALISM?

The thesis of physicalism (or, if you like, the *main* thesis of physicalism) is this: *Every non-abstract individual is completely physical.* If philosophers profess to be physicalists but *deny* the thesis I just formulated (which means: assert that *some non-abstract individual is not completely physical*), then I have *no* quarrel with them (but they certainly seem to be confusing physicalism with something it is not).

The thesis of physicalism could be formulated in a way that enables it to assert (much) *more* than it does in its just previously presented version: simply replace "non-abstract individual" with "entity". If there are other entities than non-abstract individuals (for example, *abstract* individuals, or *universals*, or other non-individuals, abstract or not), then the resulting version of the thesis of physicalism would assert *more* than the version I favour—but physicalism would also seem only all too easy to refute. Are not all abstract entities completely non-physical? Are there not universals that are completely non-physical (and hence not completely physical)? The situation is only slightly improved if one merely replaces "individual" with "entity" (and thus retains the restriction expressed by "non-abstract"), for the discussion of the philosophy of mind in the last twenty years has, in the end, rather tended in the direction of accepting that some non-abstract universals—certain properties—are not completely physical.[1] The combined efforts of so many physicalists have not been able to disperse the strong impression that, say, the property of *being in pain* is not completely physical. As a result, the doctrine of, so-called, "property dualism" has won quite a foothold among the philosophers. And the sworn enemies of dualism—they would rather bite off their tongues than profess dualism in any form—have reacted, too: the thesis of physicalism has, by and large, taken on its previously presented, already rather restricted form. *This* is what physicalism now is.

However, many philosophers nowadays in fact believe that physicalism is *something else*. In reaction to critical arguments, they have gone even further than merely reducing physicalism from "Every *entity* (or alternatively, *every non-abstract entity*) is completely physical" to "Every *non-abstract individual* is completely physical". In what way have they gone even further (on the way of retreat)? The thesis of physicalism, as it is formulated here, is a thesis of *subsumption*: all non-abstract individuals are subsumed under the completely physical ones. One can also put this thesis in terms of *identity*: *Every non-abstract individual is identical with a completely physical one*. This is logically equivalent to the version of physicalism introduced in the first paragraph;[2] it is also a version that everyone who has followed the discussions in the philosophy of mind immediately recognizes as the "the token-identity theory" (sometimes the effect of recognition can be increased by replacing "individual" by "particular").

Now, many philosophers have quietly taken their leave even from "the token-identity theory" in recent decades—*but* still declare themselves to be physicalists. In their eyes, the thesis of physicalism is *not* a thesis of subsumption; it is a thesis of *dependence*. Dependence can be spelled out in various ways. In recent years it has been fashionable to spell it out in terms of (various relations of) *supervenience*. Doing so is pleasingly technical, since supervenience concepts are fairly complex and invite discussion. But what physicalism as a thesis of dependence boils down to after all is simply this: *Every non-abstract individual is either a part of the completely physical (world), or depends—for its very existence and also for the way it is—on the completely physical* (where *the completely physical*, it should be noted, is taken to be defined by *physics*). If physicalism is put *in this way*, it becomes rather easy to defend it. For, while there is hardly any evidence that, say, a particular pain-event *is* completely physical, there is ample evidence that it *depends*—for its very existence and for the way it is—on the completely physical, specifically, on the completely physical goings-on in a particular, completely physical nervous system.

But the trouble is that it is hard to see why *this*—the just-formulated thesis of dependence—*is* (the thesis of) *physicalism*. One is, quite reasonably, inclined to object that the *dependence* of the Fs on the Gs, even if it is dependence in the strongest sense, does not imply that the Fs *are* Gs. One expects, quite rationally, more of physicalism than just to be a thesis of dependence; one expects physicalism to be a thesis of subsumption. For may not also *dualists* underwrite the above thesis of dependence? Indeed, they *may* underwrite it (and I, for my part, do underwrite it); all that is necessary for dualists to take that step is a readiness to see minds as parts of nature (*albeit* as parts that are at least partly non-physical).[3] Thus, *unless* the above thesis of dependence—let it be taken to assert dependence *in the strongest sense*—is complemented by a conditional thesis of reduction (which thesis, note, would never be accepted by dualists),

> *If a non-abstract individual strongly depends on the completely physical, then the best thing to do is to consider it completely physical,*

the above thesis of dependence *is not* physicalism.

If, however, it is complemented as described and the reductive injunction is obeyed, then, clearly, the assertion of the dependence-thesis induces the assertion of the corresponding subsumption-thesis—which is the thesis formulated in the first paragraph of this essay. *Nothing* has been won. Physicalists might as well stick to that initial thesis. Indeed, they *must* stick to it—or lose their identity (i.e., the rational right to call themselves "physicalists").[4] For that thesis is *essential* to physicalism.

In what follows, I advance various arguments against the thesis of physicalism as formulated in the first paragraph of this chapter, in other words, against what is widely known as "the token-identity theory". (I have explained why I take physicalism to amount *in essence* to that thesis or "theory".) Those arguments seem to me not without some merit. But in any case, they can be considered to be arguments against physicalism *which are paradigmatic in the long run* (that is, *paradigmatic* in consideration of the relevant history of ideas *in its entirety*).[5] The general trouble with arguments, however, is that they all start with *premises*. This elementary fact renders arguments powerless *ad personam* in truly controversial cases: opponents can always counter the argument by denying its premise, or all or some of its premises. If their position is dear to them, *no costs* incurred by doing so—by denying premises—will be too high for the opponents. Consider in this connection the following rather telling quotation: "[D]ualism is to be avoided *at all costs . . . accepting dualism is giving up*" (Dennett 1991: 37, all emphases are in the original). I trust that the arguments that follow will, sometimes at least, fall on ground that is less stony (i.e., less irrational) than the ground of cognition apparent in this quotation. And note: if an argument is powerless *ad personam* (i.e., cannot convince opponents who are hardened in their position), it does not follow that the argument is *simpliciter* powerless, powerless *from the rational point of view* (an objective point of view I take to exist).

In preparation of the ground on which the arguments are to fall, the next two sections offer ruminations on my (i.e., *our*) nature.

2. IT IS (AT LEAST) DIFFICULT TO FIND ME AMONG THE MATERIAL THINGS

I cannot doubt that I exist (i.e., that I am an actual entity). In fact, doubting that I exist is not only a psychological impossibility for me, it is also a rational impossibility—because my doubting entails my existence. Long ago, Descartes drew our attention to this elementary fact (apply it to yourself). Doubtless, therefore, I *am* ("*ego sum*"). But *what* am I? This seems rather less obvious than that I *am*. Consider a particle that is now in my body. For a long time it has not been there, and for a long time it will not be there. The same is true of each and every particle in my body. The particles in my body cannot make me up, cannot be me, neither their totality, nor a subset of it. For I am there, in my body, completely, as long as I exist, they are not. None of them is, no set of them is.[6]

The organization or structure of my body is ontologically indifferent to the individuality of the particles in my body (they only need to be *of the right kind, at the right time at the right location*)—just as indifferent as I am. And that structure is there, in my body, as long as I exist—just as I am. This may suggest that I am the structure of my body. But I am not. For I am an *individual*, the structure of my body is not. The structure of my body is a *universal* (instantiated at different times by different collections of particles, even by collections that have not a single element in common). I am, therefore, not the organization or structure of my body.

But what if the structure of my body is not a universal? What if it is a *trope*? A trope is an *individual* after all. But *which* trope? For the life of my body certainly comprises a *succession* of very many structural tropes. If the structure of my body is a trope, it must be one of these successive tropes. But *which* of them is *the* (individualized) structure of my body? *Which* of them *am I* if I am to be the structure of my body?—These are questions without answers, and not because of a mere lack of knowledge. It seems obvious, moreover, that I exist much longer than any one of those successive tropes; if this is not an illusion, I cannot be any one of them. The conclusion, therefore, can hardly be avoided that I am not the structure of my body, not even if that structure is taken to be an individual, a trope.

Am I my body itself? But there is a huge multitude of candidates for the role of *my body*. There is *my maximal body*. In my maximal body, at a given time, consider item X, which is material but inessential for my existence (in the sense that it could be lacking without replacement and my existence would, nevertheless, not be impaired); consider my maximal body *minus* X. This body is *my once-reduced maximal body*. The procedure can be reiterated, and we obtain (in thought) my maximal body, my *once*-reduced maximal body, my *twice*-reduced maximal body, my *thrice*-reduced maximal body, my *four-times*-reduced maximal body, etc. *They* are many, but I am only *one*. Which of them am I if I am to be *my body*? Which of them is *my body*? So far, I have no clue.

But is there not a *constant minimal body of mine*? If so, that body would be the best candidate to be identified with *my body*, and therefore the best candidate to be identified with me—if I am to be *my body*. Suppose there is a constant minimal body of mine, Z. In Z, there is *no* X that is material and inessential for my existence. Now, if there is *no* X in Z that is material and inessential for my existence, then, consequently, there is *no* (material) *particle* in Z that is inessential for my existence. But we have already seen that *every particle* is inessential for my existence (its lacking without replacement would not impair my existence, or, at least, *another* particle—of the right kind—in its place would do as well); therefore, every particle *in* Z is inessential for my existence. It follows that there is *no* particle in Z—which is absurd. There is, therefore, no constant minimal body of mine.

3. I CANNOT BE FOUND AMONG THE PHYSICAL EVENTS

One can circumvent the problems apparent in section 2 if one does not look for me among the material *things*, but among the physical *events*, more precisely speaking, among the physical life-processes. Why not say that I am a certain physical and physically unified life-process? This has the consequence that if I say "I", I am not referring to something that exists already in its entirety (unless "I" is the word with which I die), but to something of which, to date, only a temporal part exists—which does not seem right. Or I am, indeed, referring to something which exists already in its entirety, but with temporal parts (those in the future, perhaps larger parts than are already *given to it*) which are—for itself and for others—*terra incognita*. And this does not seem right, either. Phenomenologically, I am quite something else than my life-process—whether that process is purely physical or not. Phenomenologically, by saying "I" on various occasions, I am *also not* referring to various (more or less) momentary egos in a long procession of such egos, each ego different from all the countless others in the procession, each rather similar in a particular way to the others (though the similarity decreases as temporal distance increases). Phenomenologically—that is, such as I (we) experience it—by saying "I" on different occasions, I am referring to numerically the same entity which is wholly present (no part of it is not present) on each of these occasions, and which, nevertheless, undergoes change in the course of time. If this phenomenology is veridical—and there is no good reason why it should be considered non-veridical[7]—I cannot be an *event* (extended or momentary). A fortiori, I cannot be found among the physical events.

Nevertheless, my body and its parts, and my life and its parts, certainly stand in a close relationship to me. That relationship, although it does not seem to be identity, does not seem to be a mystery, either. Are not my body and its parts *mine* simply in virtue of being experienced by me in a particular way (closeness, intimacy, agency, and, say, collocated double sensations of touch, etc, are hallmarks of the contents of that experience)? And is not my life *mine* simply by consisting of my experiences, of which I am the intrinsic subject?[8]

4. THE CARTESIAN MODAL ARGUMENTS

The following two arguments are inspired by the *Meditations (on First Philosophy)* of René Descartes (published in 1641).[9] They also have a modal character. This is why I call them "the Cartesian modal arguments".

4.1. The First Cartesian Modal Argument

Scepticism about the external world is based on a possibility: It is possible that I exist—with just the states of consciousness I had, have, and will have—and the physical world does not exist. Accepting this possibility is a *necessary condition* for external world scepticism (i.e., for scepticism about *the existence* of the external world); it is not, of course, a *sufficient* condition. There are few who *doubt* the external world, but there are many, indeed, who entertain the possibility just proposed. They are not moved to doubt by it, but, as it were, merely to dipping their toes into the waters of doubt—because, after all, the possibility in question is a *mere* possibility, as they firmly believe.

To believe that the possibility in question is a *mere* possibility is quite a different thing than *to deny it*. If the question is whether to assert that it is in the broadest sense possible that I exist without the physical world existing, *or* to assert that it is not even in the broadest sense possible that I exist without the physical world existing, then the first alternative wins hands down. I proceed on the assumption—*premise* 1a—that it is (in the broadest sense) possible that I exist and ("at the same time") the physical world does not exist.[10] If it is possible that I exist and the physical world does not exist, then it follows that it is possible that I am completely non-physical. This seems clear enough. Hence, it is possible that I am completely non-physical. Now, it seems to be necessarily the case: if I am completely non-physical, then I am completely non-physical *necessarily*. Could the property of being completely non-physical be a contingent property of mine? Is there a possible world (in the broadest sense) where I have that property but do not necessarily have it? It seems not,[11] and thus I propose *premise 2a: Necessarily, if I am completely non-physical, then I am completely non-physical necessarily*. It follows *that I am completely non-physical* (and, a fortiori, *not completely physical*).

How does this follow? In this way: Since it possible that I am completely non-physical, and since it is necessarily the case that if am completely non-physical, I am completely non-physical *necessarily*, we obtain (by elementary modal logic): it is possible that I am completely non-physical *necessarily*. Therefore (by S5-modal logic, which is applicable here since we are talking about possibility *in the broadest sense* that goes with impossibility and necessity *in the strictest sense*),[12] *I am completely non-physical*.

Thus, the thesis of physicalism stands refuted because, in addition to being completely non-physical, I certainly am a non-abstract individual (no proof needed), even an existent one, and because being completely non-physical obviously entails being not completely physical.

The best objection to this argument is that its premises cannot be correct, not both of them, because it is *obviously (glaringly, almost self-evidently) untrue* that I am a completely non-physical being. After all, do I not have hands and feet, arms and legs, and a trunk and a head? The response to this objection is this: "I" does not always mean the same. In the argument, "I" refers to the subject of my experiences; in the objection to the argument, however, "I" refers to a certain—no doubt existing—human being, comprising not only the subject of my experiences but also my body. It is indeed obvious that the human being referred to *is not* completely non-physical, but this *does not* preclude that the subject of experiences referred to *is* completely non-physical.

One is free to deny the premises of the previous argument. But this move will be convincing *to others* only if the grounds for the denial of the one premise or the other, or of both premises, are better, from the rational point of view, than the grounds for their acceptance. I, for my part, do not perceive that the grounds for denial are better than the grounds for acceptance (far from it). Note that in seeking to provide *grounds* for denying premises $P_1, \ldots, P_N$ that logically lead to conclusion C—a conclusion one happens to dislike—one cannot rationally adduce non-C *as such a ground* (although it is perfectly alright if one rests assured that those premises cannot all be true—because, after all, one does not believe that C is true, in fact, one *believes that non-C is true*).

Another attitude one might adopt in response to the argument is *agnosticism* with respect to its premises. But this, properly speaking, is not a dialectical attitude: it is the refusal to adopt a dialectical attitude. Still, one might ask: Is not all that is in play in accepting or denying the premises of the first Cartesian modal argument a pointless confrontation of mere intuitions? The thought behind this question is that mere intuitions, in particular modal ones, are baseless, and therefore arbitrary; one may just as well claim the opposite intuitions. But it is unlikely that the intuitions *in favour* of the premises of the first Cartesian modal argument are arbitrary, since they seem to be the *natural* intuitions. This indicates where the burden of proof lies: *not* with those who accept the premises, but with those who deny them. Moreover, the *insistent* demanding for reasons and grounds is epistemologically irrational, since every ladder of grounds and reasons will, if descended, sooner or later lead to where all such ladders must start (if they are to be useful at all): *to assumptions* for which no grounds have been provided. Blessed are those who have "baseless" intuitions, "mere" intuitions in favour of their ultimate assumptions! For the ultimate assumptions they make are as far away as is possible for such assumptions, in their function, from being epistemically arbitrary.

4.2. The Second Cartesian Modal Argument

Premise 1b: If I am completely physical, then I am identical with my body or with some part of it.

Premise 2b: It is possible for me, my body and every (physical) part of my body that I exist but it does not exist.

Therefore (on the basis of *premise* 2b alone): I am neither identical with my body nor with any part of it.

Therefore (on the basis of the preceding intermediate conclusion and *premise* 1b): I am not completely physical.

This argument has several advantages over the first Cartesian modal argument. A considerable advantage of it is this: it goes directly for the conclusion *that I am not completely physical*, whereas the first argument goes *first* for the much stronger conclusion *that I am completely non-physical* and reaches the conclusion *that I am not completely physical* only as a corollary. In fact, the second Cartesian modal argument is *logically incapable* of establishing that I am completely non-physical—which is no disadvantage if the aim is *merely* to refute the thesis of physicalism. Indeed, with *this* aim in mind, the logical inability to establish the logically stronger conclusion indicates an advantage, for it means that the premises of the second argument are *logically weaker* than the premises of the first, and therefore likely to be *epistemically stronger*: stronger in their status of rational acceptability.

Premise 1b is not a modal premise (and one feels tempted to exclaim: What a relief!).[13] One will certainly accept that premise if one considers oneself a *thing-like* being. But if one considers oneself an *event-like* being, then *premise* 1b is perfectly acceptable, too—provided one also considers one's body and its (physical) parts as event-like beings. In order to see just how strong *premise* 1b is *epistemically*, try to deny it. Treating "if, then" simply as material implication, the denial yields this: I am completely physical, but I am neither identical with my body nor with any part of it. Now, *what* completely physical being might I conceivably be if I am neither identical with my body nor with any part of it? I, for my part, have no idea.

Premise 2b *is* a modal premise. For passing correct judgment on the logical cogency of the argument, it is important to appreciate that this premise asserts a possibility *de re* for me, my body, and every part of it, *not* just a possibility *de dicto*. The difference between *de dicto* possibility and *de re* possibility, and the crucial importance of being aware of this difference in evaluating arguments that, like the present one, seek to establish numerical difference, can be illustrated by a simple example.

One might raise an objection against the second Cartesian modal argument by pointing to a case that is prima facie analogous. It is possible that the morning star exists without the evening star. Who would deny it? But it does not follow that the morning star and the evening star are numerically different. On the contrary, everybody knows that they are one and the same star, the planet Venus. *Response*: The possibility asserted in saying that it is possible that the morning star exists without the evening star is a mere possibility *de dicto*; such a possibility is not sufficient for inferring in a logically correct way that the morning star and the evening star are numerically different. What would be needed for inferring that conclusion in a *logically correct* way is the corresponding *de re* possibility: It is possible *for* the morning star and the evening star that the former exists without the latter. But, in fact, it is not possible *for* the morning star and the evening star that the former exists without the latter (because they are one and the same star—and nothing, of course, can exist without itself).[14]

We can now rest satisfied that the intermediate conclusion of the second Cartesian modal argument *follows logically* from its second premise, *premise* 2b (because that premise asserts a *de re* possibility for the entities it is about, not just a *de dicto* possibility). We can also rest satisfied that the final conclusion of the argument *follows logically* from its first premise—*premise* 1b—*plus* the intermediate conclusion. Since we have already seen that *premise* 1b is perfectly acceptable, the fate of the second Cartesian modal argument hinges on the acceptability of *premise* 2b. Its acceptability is boosted greatly if the possibility in that premise is taken—just like the possibility in *premise* 1a (in the first Cartesian modal argument)—to be a possibility *in the broadest sense*.[15] In fact, understood in *this* way, *premise* 2b seems undeniably true.

In this case, too, the negation-test may help one to see just how acceptable the premise in question really is. Therefore, try to deny *premise* 2b! Then, does it seem plausible to you that for you and your body, or for you and some part of your body, it is *in the strictest sense impossible* that you exist but it does not exist?[16] That, *in the strictest sense*, you *cannot* exist without it?[17] It does not seem plausible to me, or in any case, much less plausible than *premise* 2b. Even those who are unable to share my view should acknowledge that, objectively, the burden of proof lies with the deniers of *premise* 2b, not with its proponents. (In-principle objections against *intuitions* in general—and against *modal* intuitions in particular—have already been treated in the discussion of the first Cartesian modal argument.)

5. THE CHALMERS-DESCARTES MODAL ARGUMENT

The Chalmers-Descartes modal argument results from the second Cartesian modal argument if *premise* 2b is replaced by the following proposition (and everything else remains the same—except that in the intermediate conclusion, the first conclusion, "2b" must be replaced by "2c"):

> *Premise* 2c: It is possible for me, my body, and every (physical) part of my body that it exists but I do not exist.

The logical mechanism of the Chalmers-Descartes modal argument is essentially the same as that of the second Cartesian modal argument, and everything that has been said in defense of the latter mechanism (in the previous section) is also applicable in the defense of the former. The Chalmers-Descartes modal argument includes "Descartes" in its name because *premise* 2c is a *Cartesian* assumption that can be found—not verbatim but in essence—in Descartes's writings (in particular, the *Meditations*). It certainly figures there less prominently than *premise* 2b, but Descartes would not have hesitated to agree to *premise* 2c, just as much as to *premise* 2b (consider *Meditations*, VI). The Chalmers-Descartes modal argument includes "Chalmers" in its name because the anti-materialistic arguments in Chalmers (1996) also point to that premise, *premise* 2c. *If* the entire physical world, precisely as it actually is in itself, might (in the broadest sense of possibility) exist without consciousness existing, *then*, in virtue of this possibility, my body, as it actually is in itself, and every part of my body, as it actually is in itself, might exist without *me* existing (since the complete absence of consciousness entails *my* absence). The protasis of the conditional just proposed expresses Chalmers's central intuition that the physical world, as it actually is (with all these living organisms, humans among them), *might be* a world of consciousness-lacking *zombies* (in the philosophical sense); it is no bold hypothesis that Descartes shared this intuition (the gist of it, not the formulation).[18]

Today, *premise* 2c seems to anti-physicalistically inclined philosophers rather more plausible than *premise* 2b, and Chalmers's central intuition—just described—seems to them rather more acceptable than the central Cartesian intuition[19] that consciousness might exist, just in the way it actually exists, without the physical world existing (this latter intuition stands to *premise* 1a and *premise* 2b as the former intuition stands to *premise* 2c). It is an interesting fact of the history of ideas that the order of acceptability was *quite the other way around* in the eighteenth and nineteenth century. The explanation of this fact is that, *in earlier times*, there was an onto-epistemological predominance of the non-physical over the physical in the *non-physical/physical* duality (consider that the eighteenth and the nineteenth century is the age of the rule of *idealism*); *nowadays*, the order of predominance is entirely reversed, and there is an onto-epistemological predominance of the physical over the non-physical in the duality *physical/non-physical* (after all, this is the age of the rule of *materialism*, and therefore of an intellectual atmosphere that even dualists cannot quite escape).[20]

6. THE CAUSAL ARGUMENT (AGAINST PHYSICALISM)

It is agreed on all sides that there are certain completely physical events for which we have been unable to find any completely physical sufficient causes, although we have been looking for such causes for more than a century. It does not follow that there are no such causes, or that we will not find them. Still, the following assertion is an assertion which is, as far as we *now* know, very likely true:

> *Premise* 1d: Some completely physical event has no completely physical sufficient cause.

Add to this premise the following premise:

> *Premise* 2d: Every event has a sufficient cause.

It is a matter of straightforward first-order predicate logic that these two premises entail the following intermediate conclusion:

> Some completely physical event has a sufficient cause that is not completely physical.

Add to this intermediate conclusion the following premise:

> *Premise* 3d: Every cause is a non-abstract individual.

It is a matter of straightforward first-order predicate logic that this premise and the intermediate conclusion just previously reached together entail the following ultimate conclusion:

> Some non-abstract individual is not completely physical.

And therefore, the above-presented argument—for obvious reasons, it is called "the causal argument"—refutes the thesis of physicalism *if* its premises are *rationally acceptable* (for its logic is impeccable). Note that the argument does not hinge on modal notions (modality may lurk in the notion of *cause* itself, but this is of no importance to the argument); modal intuitions—thought to be very problematic by many—do not come into play in this argument at all. Note also that the causal argument does not hinge on any very specific idea of causality. This has the effect that *the nature* of a sufficient cause for a completely physical event *without* completely physical sufficient cause is left largely unspecified by the argument—except for two things: such a sufficient cause is (i) not completely physical and (ii) a non-abstract individual. The argument does not present any *example* of such a cause. But the quality of the causal argument *as an argument against physicalism* is not diminished by its relative unspecificness.[21] If it is not necessary to be specific about causality and causes in order to refute physicalism, all the better! To demand more specificness would be an unreasonable (and dialectically unfair) challenge to the argument because it neither addresses the premises of the argument nor the logic.[22]

It is more reasonable to declare that one does not understand this or that expression in the argument. As a physicalist, one cannot well declare that one does not understand "physical" or "completely physical". But one might declare that one does not understand "sufficient cause". Here is the explanation of this latter expression: a *sufficient* cause is neither a mere *conditio sine qua non* of its effect nor a factor that raises the (objective) probability of its effect; it is an item that *actualizes* its effect, *makes it come about*, either all by itself or given the scaffolding of circumstances and laws. I submit that here we have before us a truly good occasion to let David Lewis's famous quip, "any competent philosopher who does not understand something will take care not to understand anything else whereby it might be explained" (Lewis 1986: 203n), be a rule *with exceptions*.

Since *premise* 1d has already been defended, I immediately turn to the defense of the remaining two premises of the causal argument. Here it must be noted that *premise* 3d is beyond reasonable doubt. Every cause must have causal powers, but what is *not* a non-abstract individual (or particular)—because it is abstract or because it is not an individual, or because it is both—does not have causal powers. Therefore, every cause is a non-abstract individual. Note that the mainstream position on the ontological nature of *causes*—that causes are *events*—and the mainstream position on the ontological nature of *events*—that they are *non-abstract particulars*—together imply *premise* 3d. That at least some causes are *agents*, not events, has been argued by some philosophers.[23] But agents are, of course, *non-abstract individuals* (albeit of a different kind than events: they do not have the inbuilt temporal dimension that events have). That causes are *states of affairs*, not events, has also been argued by some philosophers.[24] But states of affairs are causes only if they are isomorphic to events that are causes, hence isomorphic to certain causal *non-abstract individuals*; these individuals are, in all cases, the causes in the primary, independent sense, whereas the corresponding states of affairs are causes only in a secondary, dependent, analogical sense.

The upshot of all this is that *premise* 3d stands unshaken. But what about *premise* 2d? This premise is, indeed, the hub of the argument. Everybody knowledgeable in the history of ideas in general, and the history of philosophy in particular, will immediately recognize *premise* 2d as *the principle of sufficient cause* (i.e., as the principle of sufficient reason *in its causal form*). That principle was an unquestioned principle of reason—comparable in status to a principle of logic—until the beginning of the twentieth century. With the advent of quantum physics, however, it has widely been considered to be no longer tenable. The reason for this dramatic "fall from favour" is that the principle of sufficient cause is thought to be incompatible with the—very likely true—assertion that *some completely physical event has no completely physical sufficient cause* (i.e., with *premise* 1d). As a closer look immediately reveals, there is *no logical incompatibility* between the two statements. There is, as a matter of fact, only a *conditional incompatibility* between them. This means that if *a certain other* statement were true, then this would entail that at least one of the two statements is not true. Thus, since *premise* 1d is true (it is reasonable to proceed on this assumption), we would have on the basis of that *other* statement—if it were true—that *premise* 2d is *not* true. This outcome would be fatal to the causal argument, but the question is, of course, *whether* that *other* statement is indeed true.

What *other* statement am I talking about? It is this one:

> CC1: If a completely physical event has a sufficient cause, then it also has a completely physical sufficient cause.[25]

This is a *principle of causal closure (of the completely physical)*, which, though not as old as the principle of sufficient cause, has been widely accepted (not necessarily *explicitly*) for centuries, beginning with the rise of modern physics. The same is true of the following logically stronger principle of causal closure:

CC2: Every cause of a completely physical event is completely physical.

It is easily seen that CC1 is a logical consequence of CC2. But is CC1 true? CC1 is true if CC2 is, but is CC2 true? Just as *premise* 2d and *premise* 1d are incompatible *conditional to* CC1 (or CC2), so *premise* 2d and CC1 (and *premise* 2d and CC2) are incompatible *conditional to premise* 1d. Given the current epistemic status of *premise* 1d, it is, therefore, seen that principles which were once upon a time (until a little more than a century ago) perfectly good friends—the principle of sufficient cause (*premise* 2d) and the closure principles CC1 and CC2—are now inveterate enemies: the division between them is a division between world views.

There are two ways to deal with this situation (and I concentrate on considering CC1): *either* a choice of acceptance is to be made between *premise* 2d and CC1, *or* not. If no choice of acceptance is to be made between them, then one either denies *both* propositions in question or adopts agnosticism with respect to *both* (what one *cannot* do while accepting *premise* 1d is to *accept* both). Agnosticism is no option here; the matter is too important. One has to take a stance. And denying both propositions *kills* physicalism. For consider what denying CC1 (along with *premise* 2d) amounts to: it amounts to accepting that some completely physical event with a sufficient cause has no completely physical sufficient cause, and consequently also to accepting that *some completely physical event has a sufficient cause that is not completely physical*—which is the intermediate conclusion of the causal argument. Does physicalism fare better if a choice of acceptance is to be made between *premise* 2d and CC1? The choice of acceptance is between accepting *premise* 2d (and denying[26] CC1), or accepting CC1 (and denying *premise* 2d). Which choice is the better choice?

It is quite clear that accepting *premise* 2d—accepting *the principle of sufficient cause*—is the better choice. For the principle of sufficient cause has credentials that are completely independent of the question whether physicalism is true or not. (This is clearly indicated by the fact that non-materialists *and* materialists alike have accepted that principle throughout the history of philosophy—till the beginning of the twentieth century, when new empirical facts became apparent that gave very strong support to *premise* 1d.) The principle of sufficient cause is *metaphysically neutral*. Thus, there can be no question whether the causal argument commits a begging of the question, whether it degenerates into a *petitio principii*. It certainly does not. Every single one of its premises—and what is most significant: *premise* 2d—is justifiable quite independently from assuming its conclusion to be true. CC1, in contrast, *is not* metaphysically neutral. Indeed, it is hard

30   Uwe Meixner

to see how one could justify CC1 (let alone CC2) if one does not assume physicalism from the start.

And there is also another consideration in support of the position that accepting *premise* 2d is a better choice than accepting CC1. CC1 leads to the conclusion that the events which are as described in *premise* 1d have no sufficient cause: according to CC1, *all* completely physical events that have no completely physical sufficient cause have no sufficient cause at all; in other words, their taking place is, in each case, to a certain positive extent a matter of pure (objective, ontological) chance. There is—this is the best hypothesis to date, it is far better supported than its negation—not just one event which is as described in *premise* 1d (although if there were just one such event, *premise* 1d would still be true): there are *very many*—countless—such events. Thus, CC1, if accepted as true, has the consequence that pure chance—and therefore *inexplicability*—is introduced into the (completely) physical world to a considerable extent. But now, is not the explicability of completely physical events that have no completely physical sufficient causes *by not completely physical sufficient causes* a lesser insult to reason than *the inexplicability* of such events? It seems only reasonable, only paying due respect to epistemological rationality, to admit that it *is* a lesser insult—or, indeed, no insult at all, whereas *the inexplicability* certainly is one. Thus, in the presence of *premise* 1d, the principle of sufficient cause wins in the competition of rationality against CC1 (and a fortiori against CC2). And thereby, the consequences that *premise* 2d has in the presence of *premise* 1d win against the consequences that CC1 has in the presence of *premise* 1d. Physicalism stands refuted.

And not only physicalism. The causal argument is rendered special among the arguments against physicalism by the fact that it also refutes (without our having to make any additions to it) two mainstays of physicalism: CC1 and CC2. The *negations* of CC1 and CC2 are straightforward corollaries of that argument. (It should be noted that if physicalists argue for their position, then CC1 or CC2, or a proposition rather similar to the one or the other, is very likely to show up. But usually physicalists are content simply to *claim* the *scientific* superiority of their position.)

The causal argument does not give us a specific counterexample to physicalism: the argument stays on the general level (which cannot be held against it, as I have argued). But each of the following two arguments against physicalism again gives us *a specific counterexample*, just as each of the three arguments presented prior to the causal argument gave us *a specific counterexample*. But *now* it is not always *the same* counterexample. In the next argument, the counterexample given is *not I*, but a certain event.

7. THE ARGUMENT FROM ILLUSION[27]

Visual experience is full of illusions. For example, one line appears to be shorter than the other, while, in fact, they have the same length. One need not adduce the more or less spectacular cases of visual illusion—the optical illusions—in order to accept as true that *completely physical objects appear in visual experience not as they really are*. They continue to appear so even if we have stopped to be deceived. This suggests that visual illusions have *carriers* that do not go away even if the false beliefs that, initially, attend on the illusions do go away. There must be *entities* that transport these illusions. And indeed we do not have to look far for those entities: the carrier-entities for visual illusions are our visual experiences (note the plural) themselves. Thus we have: *There are visual experiences in which completely physical objects do not appear as they really are*. What kind of entity is *a* visual experience? It is an event; it happens at a certain temporal location, it fills a certain interval of time. Moreover, as an event, a visual experience is a non-abstract individual. Consider now any visual experience in which completely physical objects do not appear as they really are. Is such an experience a completely physical event? If it is, then it must be identifiable with something that is completely physical. This seems impossible; it seems it cannot be "fitted in". What the experience presents is—though completely physical *in intention*—no part of the (real) physical world (since the experience is illusionary), and yet it belongs essentially—inseparably—to the illusionary experience. The best completely physical candidates for identification with illusionary—falsifying, distorting—visual experiences of parts of the physical world are certain brain events (in the brain of the person who has the experiences). But while these brain events stand in a causal relationship to the experiences, they cannot *be* them (indeed the causal relationship already precludes their *being* them, on pain of self-causation); they cannot be "the images created in the brain", as the matter is popularly (and misleadingly) put. For, causal considerations aside, it is no part of the intrinsic nature of any brain event that, say, a particular pencil-drawn line on a particular piece of paper appears to be shorter than another such line on that same piece of paper—whereas this is indeed part of the intrinsic nature of any *Müller-Lyer* visual experience. Thus, the conclusion can only be this: *certain non-abstract individuals*—in this case, illusionary visual experiences of parts of the physical world—*are not completely physical*. Again physicalism stands refuted.

8. THE ARGUMENT FROM PERSPECTIVE[28]

Suppose I aim a laser gun at a certain target—and make a good shot. This means that, when I pulled the trigger, the target point I aimed at, the front sight and the back sight on the gun, *and the point of my perspective* in aiming—i.e., the point from which I aimed—lay on the same straight line. Let P be the point from which I aimed. P is the origin of that straight line. It is a certain point in space.[29] *Which* point? Which point it is can be experimentally determined. Staying where I am and without moving my head, I aim the gun at various targets points, very many of them, say, one hundred (doing so each time as precisely, as correctly as possible, as if I wanted to

32 Uwe Meixner

hit, with the laser beam, the point I aim at). The line in space in which the gun lies in each act of aiming is recorded (it is externally observable). P is, or lies within, the small region of space where all the lines of aiming converge.

Now, it seems correct to say that P is not only the point from which I aimed, but also the point *where I was* as long as the experiment lasted. The alternatives to my being in P—to my precisely occupying P—are (i) that I am nowhere in space, and (ii) that I am in—precisely occupy—a region in space other than P. Both alternatives are out of the question when one considers that, while aiming the gun, I would be ready to say the following things (and we have no good reason to doubt that they are *literally true*): "The backsight of the gun is closer to me than the frontsight", "The eye with which I aim is closer to me than my hands that hold the gun", and "The inner region of the eye with which I aim is closer to me than its outer region, which I can cover by closing my eyelids".

Thus, I am *in* P (literally)—during the time under consideration: time T. But *what* am I if I am in P during T? It seems I would have to be a completely physical individual. Unfortunately, the completely physical individual that can be found to be in P during T—constituted by relatively few atoms in more or less complex arrangements[30]—is no likely candidate for being me, although it is the *best* completely physical candidate for being me (given that I am in P during T). There is no better completely physical candidate, but it is not a good, not even a satisfactory candidate, far from it. Thus, the conclusion can only be that I am not a completely physical individual after all, and that therefore (since I certainly am a non-abstract individual)[31] I am a non-abstract individual that is not completely physical.

But then, why does it seem that I would have to be a completely physical individual if I am in P during T? The impression is generated by thinking, without justification and in fact wrongly, that if proposition A is true, proposition B—which, superficially regarded, is similar to A—must be true, too. It is *true* that every completely physical individual is, at any time of its existence, a non-abstract individual *in* (physical) space. But it does not follow that every non-abstract individual that is *in* (physical) space at a given time is completely physical. In fact, the negation of this is true.

NOTES

1. Note that a physical universal must be physical in a quite different way than a physical individual. The physicalness of a universal must be compatible with the characteristic ability of all universals: the ability of being wholly present in *different* locations at the *same* time. Note also that one *might* take the stance—it is not positively irrational to do so—that already *that* ability turns all universals into completely non-physical entities.
2. It is an elementary law of first-order predicate logic *with identity* that $\forall x(Fx \supset Gx)$ is logically equivalent to $\forall x(Fx \supset \exists y(Gy \ \& \ x = y))$.
3. The further possibility of a naturalistic dualism (or dualistic naturalism) is quite outside the ken of many philosophers. The widespread *idée fixe* that the

denial of physicalism implies the acceptance of *supernaturalism*—that is, the recognition of supernatural non-abstract individuals—does much to explain why physicalism is so tenaciously held on to. But physicalism, although it entails the negation of supernaturalism, is not identical to the negation of supernaturalism.
4. Cf. Meixner (2008).
5. A rich array of anti-physicalistic arguments—including versions of those that have, in the recent decades, dominated the discussion *ad nauseam*—can be found in Meixner (2004). Recent collections of essays that are critical of physicalism are: Antonietti, Corradini and Lowe (2008), and Koons and Bealer (2010), Göcke (2012).
6. It does not already follow that I am an immaterial entity (it only follows that it is difficult to find me among the material things). For consider this: What is true of the particles in my body is, mutatis mutandis, also true of the particles in *the Ship of Theseus*. Yet, doubtless, the Ship of Theseus is a material thing.
7. Cf. Meixner (2002).
8. The details are a matter of detailed phenomenological description, as pioneered in the works of Edmund Husserl. See, in particular, Husserl (1982) and (1989) (that is, *Ideas I* and *Ideas II*).
9. For the first argument, consider *Meditations*, I and II (in any good edition); for the second argument, consider *Meditations*, VI.
10. The assertion has the form $\Diamond(Ea \;\&\; non\text{-}Eb)$, *not* the form $(\Diamond Ea \;\&\; \Diamond non\text{-}Eb)$.
11. Note that *my having a body* does not preclude that I am, nevertheless, completely non-physical.
12. The logical principle used is this: $\Diamond \Box A \supset A$. It is not only a theorem of S5 but also (already) of B, the Brouwerian system. Cf. Hughes and Cresswell (1985).
13. Why does one wish to avoid modality? Modality leads to epistemological difficulties—although certainly not all applications of modal concepts are epistemologically troublesome. The troublemakers are possibility without known actuality (of what is considered possible), possibility with known actuality of the negation (of what is considered possible), and necessity (if it is not entailed by actuality). How does one know such things? Some answers are provided in Meixner (2006a).
14. The *de dicto* possibility has the form $\Diamond(Ea \;\&\; non\text{-}Eb)$, and the corresponding *de re* possibility has the form $\exists x \exists y(a = x \;\&\; b = y \;\&\; \Diamond(Ex \;\&\; non\text{-}Ey))$. The *de dicto* possibility *plus* a = b (and nothing further) does not logically entail $\exists x \exists y(x = y \;\&\; \Diamond(Ex \;\&\; non\text{-}Ey))$ (this latter formula is logically impossible, its negation a logical theorem); the *de re* possibility, however, *plus* a = b (and nothing further) *does* logically entail $\exists x \exists y(x = y \;\&\; \Diamond(Ex \;\&\; non\text{-}Ey))$. In other words, a = b is, in itself, logically compatible with $\Diamond(Ea \;\&\; non\text{-}Eb)$, with the *de dicto* possibility; but a = b is not logically compatible, in itself, with $\exists x \exists y(a = x \;\&\; b = y \;\&\; \Diamond(Ex \;\&\; non\text{-}Ey))$, the *de re* possibility.
15. What does this mean *precisely*: "X is possible *in the broadest sense*"? It means that there is *no restriction except conceptual consistency* for the *alternatives to actuality* that are taken into account in addition to *actuality*, and X pertains to actuality or to (at least) one of its alternatives.
16. The negation of possibility *in the broadest sense* is impossibility *in the strictest sense*. The logical form of *premise* 2b is this: $\exists x \exists y[a = x \;\&\; b = y \;\&\; \Diamond(Ex \;\&\; non\text{-}Ey) \;\&\; \forall z(zPy \supset \Diamond(Ex \;\&\; non\text{-}Ez))]$. The negation of this is logically equivalent to this: $\forall x \forall y[a = x \;\&\; b = y \supset (non\text{-}\Diamond(Ex \;\&\; non\text{-}Ey) \lor \exists z(zPy \;\&\; non\text{-}\Diamond(Ex \;\&\; non\text{-}Ez)))]$. Therefore (logically): $\exists x \exists y[a = x \;\&\; b = y \;\&\; non\text{-}\Diamond(Ex \;\&\; non\text{-}Ey)] \lor \exists x \exists y[a = x \;\&\; b = y \;\&\; \exists z(zPy \;\&\; non\text{-}\Diamond(Ex \;\&\; non\text{-}Ez))]$.

17. What does this mean precisely: "X is impossible *in the strictest sense*"? It means that there is *no restriction except conceptual consistency* for the *alternatives to actuality* that are taken into account in addition to *actuality*, but (still) X pertains neither to actuality nor to any of its alternatives.
18. It is important to remember that an assertion of the form "It might be the case that A" does not necessarily indicate that the proponent of the assertion accords a subjective probability greater than zero to A. The proponent of the assertion may be simply asserting that A is true in some possible world, and he can very well assert this even if he holds that the subjective probability of A is zero. In the given case, it is safe to assume that both Chalmers and Descartes accord the subjective probability zero to "The physical world, as it actually is, is a world of consciousness-lacking zombies".
19. There is a central and a *less central* Cartesian intuition; for Descartes did share Chalmers's intuition.
20. It is not unlikely that the reversal in the order of predominance has to do with the reversal in the relative strength of two cultural forces: religion (favouring the non-physical) and science (favouring the physical).
21. If one puts it (with modifications) *to other uses*, then that unspecificness *is* a drawback. See Meixner (2009) and Meixner (2012).
22. Already in antiquity, Euclid proved that there are infinitely many primes. It is a corollary of the proof that there must be a smallest prime that is greater than 243 to the power of $10^{1000000000}$. Would it be a reasonable challenge to Euclid's proof that it does not tell us which number, precisely, is that prime?
23. For details, see, for example, Meixner (2001).
24. For details, see again Meixner (2001).
25. This is, of course, meant to be a general statement, not a particular one.
26. It must be *denying* CC1 (i.e., accepting the negation of CC1), not just *not accepting* CC1—because we already accept (as true) *premise* 1d. The same remark applies also to *premise* 2d. (Consider what the truth of *premise* 1d means for the relationship of CC1 and *premise* 2d.)
27. Cf. Meixner (2006b).
28. Cf. Meixner (2010).
29. By "point in space" I do not here mean a *geometrical point*. I mean a very small region of space. One might consider replacing "point" by "spot".
30. The atoms are relatively few because P is a very small spatial region. Due to the relatively small number of atoms in P, the degree of complexity that can be attained by their arrangements is also relatively small.
31. I am causally responsible, in the end, for (the event of) the pulling of the trigger. It follows that I am a non-abstract individual (cf. *premise* 3d).

3 Problems of Physicalism Regarding the Mind

Andrea Lavazza

1. PHYSICALIST MONISM AND MIND/BRAIN

Philosophical practise (except for cases of absolute solipsism) works with the physical expression of thoughts as transmitted through voice (sound waves recognisable by the listener's auditory apparatus) and writing (signs that can be deciphered by the reader's visual apparatus, traced with various techniques and materials on varied support media). Material media transmit contents that are understood as part of a process that is provisionally defined as the elaboration of the information coming from the mind's "black box". Compared to other aspects of everyday life, philosophical practise is characterised by respect for a set of rules for reasoning that has been honed and stratified over time. Logical formalization imposes constraints that all participants in the philosophical debate must respect. The origin of these constraints is controversial, but the "rules of thought" seem to impose themselves autonomously, and their violation is considered a blatant manifestation of incoherence and invalid lines of reasoning, thus nullifying the argument at hand. The gradual exploration of the physical world through increasingly precise and shared rules (what we call experimental science) has led to a growing convergence towards a series of constraints on those lines of reasoning aspiring to validity, whose conclusions aim to be coherent with accumulated knowledge.

The ontological statute of some of the "instruments" of this edifice of knowledge is an open question subject to broad debate. Mathematical concepts, formal logic, and scientific theories are "entities" that enter and exit our minds/brains, and prove themselves useful and efficient in helping us understand the world and our fellow humans. Nonetheless, there is no agreement on an essential definition of them, on how they have come into being, or on their relationship with the subjects that have thought them up and the objects to which they refer.

This does not prevent us from continuing to pursue philosophical practise. Nevertheless, if one considers that the so-called material basis of the mind is increasingly being linked to the higher intellectual functions, it can be inferred—as contemporary philosophy of mind does—that the latter depends closely on the physical configuration of the brain. In the wake of Quinean naturalism, some scholars are exploring the new field of "neurophilosophy", in which the mechanisms investigated by natural sciences—which are subordinate to what we call the mind—are brought to the forefront as conditional aspects of thought (Churchland 2002; Edelman 2006). This applies not only to epistemological aspects, according to which the cognitive process could be related to psychology first and then to neurobiology, but to the entire "mental life" of subjects.

We know that the development of the structure of the human brain is driven by its genetic heritage, which also plays a key role in the day-to-day functioning of the brain, since genes are responsible for launching the individual cellular processes in the one hundred billion neurons that make up the encephalon and in the enormous network of synaptic connections that support memory, language, attention, volition, empathy, and other faculties typical of humans, or which are particularly well expressed in *Homo sapiens sapiens*.

The current make-up of human DNA is the result of the evolution of the hominid branch of the tree of life over the last six million years, but it arises from a process of random mutations and selections that is not yet fully understood and dates back to billions of years ago. Based on what biological and paleoanthropological studies have empirically proven so far, this is an eminently stochastic process, in which randomness plays an important role, as do external physical conditions, which are also subject to changes over time (both endogenous changes and those caused by the impact that living beings have on the environment). The brain that supports our rational mind (let us provisionally accept this highly imprecise, but intuitively understandable expression) thus shows a structural configuration and a functional set-up that are absolutely contingent, and that are not characterised by any degree of necessity in the philosophical sense (cf. Coyne 2009).

2. THOUGHT EXPERIMENTS AND CONCEPTUAL SCHEMES

2.1. The Argument

The assumption of the identity of the mind/brain and its contingency, which arises from rigorous physicalism and neo-Darwinian evolutionism, can have various consequences, but it does not imply, in and of itself, a revision in philosophical practise. But let us now consider the thought experiments that involve epistemic and modal concepts, along with what prevalently happens in thought experiments that involve the mind and its contents. Many such experiments depict a scenario in which the assumed condition is characterised by necessity; that is, by the fact that their propositions are valid in all possible worlds. Consider, for example, the "my division" experiment performed by Parfit (1984) on personal identity or the "zombies" experiment of Chalmers (1996) on the phenomenic aspects of consciousness.

This assumption is justified both on the basis of shared logical rules and by that which we hold to be metaphysically and physically possible (although this is not subject to "mandatory consent", meaning the same type of approval required of certain generally shared assumptions. Arguments that make controversial use of the concepts of conceivability and possibility are the object of debate among members of the philosophical community, although some consider them nullified by certain types of fallacies. Conversely, arguments marred by obvious logical contradictions are usually defined as blatantly inconsistent and are generally not considered, Szabó Gendler and Hawthorne 2002).

Let us now imagine a thought meta-experiment in which a radical change in genetic heritage (artificially induced by the experiments of a mad scientist able to use extremely advanced DNA manipulation techniques, or caused by catastrophic changes in the natural environment) provokes an unpredictable and dramatic change in the way the brains of some—or all—humans are wired. The consequence of this could be a "mental set-up" (let us provisionally call "mental set-up" the software provided by our biological hardware) so different that it would render the thoughts produced by our current nervous system incommensurable with those produced by the brain resulting from the genetic anomaly. To make an analogy, incommensurability could be understood as the inability to translate between two wholly separate languages, in a context in which other tools of communications are entirely lacking, that is, where neither ostensive indications nor non-verbal representations are available. This would be a world in which nothing that can be thought with our current "mental set-up" can be projected; it is a possible (mental) world, but our minds cannot grasp it.

It should be noted that I am not questioning the fact that the contents of the thought experiment should take into account all the possible worlds that we could "reach" with our current mental/brain set-up. A thought experiment such those cited before could be valid in all "our" possible worlds (but not necessarily so). The point is that a different brain, such as the one envisaged by the thought meta-experiment, may have access to a different constellation of possible worlds. The metaphysical structure of the world is undoubtedly *mind-independent,* but we could speculate that our ability to access it—if the hypothesis of radical physicalism of the mind is true—is limited and/or conditioned by the material structure of our brain. We are thus not questioning the fact that, at least in principle, the metaphysical necessity is *mind-independent;*[1] the point is that, in accordance with radical physicalism, *knowledge* of metaphysical modalities may be limited and/or conditioned, and thus *mind-dependent.*

Thus, if we bring the effects of physicalism on mind to their radical consequences, we must say that thought experiments on the mind cannot claim to be necessarily valid in the usual sense of the word.[2] It should also be pointed out the objection of multiple realizability, and how it has been used against certain types of identity theories between mental and physical states, does not seem to be valid. Even if we admit that the same mental property can be realized or implemented by numerous possible physical properties, in the situation postulated here the variation of the physical basis is so great under all aspects as to make a manifestation of the mental states of which we are aware through our brains extremely unlikely.

It is a well known fact that radical and influential reservations have been expressed regarding the admissibility of incommensurability (Davidson 1974). Arguments against the idea of different conceptual schemes question the hypothesis that the world can be conceptualised according to different points of view, and that empirical contents (neutral and imposed by external reality) can be organized by paradigms, rules, or principles (or that the conceptual schemes fit the empirical contents), giving birth to closed systems of meaning, which can only be accessed from the inside. In such a way, a theory or a language could be impossible to translate into another theory or language. The knowledge of a given individual would thus not be compatible with that of another individual from a different linguistic or theoretical framework.

Davidson tends to identify conceptual schemes and languages. The existence of radically different languages is tied to the fact that one cannot be translated into the other's terms, and vice versa. But Davidson, simplifying his argument, holds that if someone uses a "language" that resists any attempt at translation, perhaps she is not using a language at all, or at the very least we are not able to recognise her "language" as such. It would thus seem legitimate to say that we cannot treat as a language a human activity that we cannot even minimally translate, basing our view on the hypothesis that such an activity performs the same organizational functions as our language; if it really did perform the same organizational functions as our language, it would not be completely untranslatable into our language.

Furthermore, Davidson questions the "third dogma" of empiricism: the dualism of scheme, of organizing systems and something waiting to be organized, cannot be made intelligible and defensible. If we cannot find differences in conceptual schemes, we have no reason to assert that they even exist in the first place. As a consequence, the idea that is being questioned is that there exists an outside, objective world with which we come into contact through sense impressions, and that those impressions are filtered and organized by our conceptual schemes. Indeed, if someone should have a radically different scheme from us, then he or she could experience the world very differently, although it will be the same outside, objective world. It would seem that Davidson's conclusion is that linguistic truth-value is all there is to "truth" because there is only one possible way to come into contact with reality and its parts (assuming this is a correct way to express Davidson's perspective, according to which there is an unmediated connection between language and the world, and there is nothing that stands, epistemically speaking, between language and its subject matter). Ultimately, the very idea of a conceptual scheme does not seem to provide any explanatory contribution, and indeed it may be unintelligible (much like the idea of untranslatable languages), and should thus be abandoned, as with any other concept that is "unreachable" by evidence, experience, *a priori* argument, or other sensible means.

This third dogma of empiricism is convincingly demolished if one does not consider a so-called "conceptual super-scheme", or if one overlooks—as the supporters of this position seem to—a rigorous physicalism with regards to mind. The conceptual super-scheme, as understood here, is the one that correctly considers individual nervous systems to be similar in terms of their structure and functioning, both with regards to external receptors and cognitive architecture.

If instead we introduce the hypothesis of a brain structured in a radically different way—a hypothesis that physicalism of the mind must hold to be fully admissible—it follows that for such a modified brain the same incoming "elements" might be perceived as radically "different", even though they come from the same ontological furniture of the world.[3] It is not necessary to introduce an excessive degree of "constructivism" with respect to incoming elements in order to take this scenario into consideration.[4] (We are not questioning what kinds of things exist or what is in the world. A change of conceptual scheme can modify a certain degree of organization in the way the world is arranged, namely the relationships between things, which can in part depend on how we organize things with our minds. Semantic externalism, according to which "meanings are not in our heads", and a certain degree of realism and conceptual Platonism, such as that of G. Rey (Rey 1985), according to whom a concept is that which gives an object its characteristics, whether we are able to understand it or not, do not seem to undermine the argument proposed here).

It is because our brains are similar in terms of the matters we are dealing with that we can sense that their physical basis is the condition that makes it possible to think in terms of conceptual schemes, and that such a framework can function as conceptual super-scheme. Brains that are radically different from a physical point of view would presumably produce radically different languages, unless one considers the translatability of all possible natural languages to be necessary *a priori*. But it is the condition itself of possibility regarding natural (and artificial) languages—the biological organism known as the brain, with its current set-up as derived by random natural evolution—which is radically contingent. It would thus be reasonable to define as a conceptual super-scheme the Davidsonian "universe" in which we operate, and in which we can successfully criticise the very idea of a conceptual scheme. If there is a radical change in the material support for the conceptual "universe" from which that "universe" strictly depends—if one believes in physicalism—it may be possible to talk about the possibility of another, completely untranslatable, conceptual super-scheme.

A useful analogy is the well-known argument regarding "untranslatability at the subjective phenomenology level" in Nagel's "What Is It Like to Be a bat" (Nagel 1974). It is possible, however, that someone may want to question that example on the basis of Davidson's critique of conceptual schemes: indeed, both a bat's sonar and our own sensory faculties have evolved from a shared ancestor, whose phylogenetic diversification reflects adaptations to the outside environment. Therefore, it could be argued that the two "mental languages" ultimately end up organizing similar things. The scenario can thus be further radicalized: for example, with the existence of a nervous system that cannot access the macroscopic "reality" defined by what we call wave function collapse, but rather that operates within a purely microscopic-quantum "reality", wouldn't its "language" become completely untranslatable, despite the fact that both languages—ours, which refers to macroscopic objects, and that of the "new" nervous system, which refers to the "indeterminateness" of the quantum wave functions—are "true" with regards to their own "world" (which could turn out to be the same "world")?[5] Of course, the chances that such a scenario could actually unfold are infinitesimally small, but it remains fully legitimate from a philosophical point of view, once a monistic and physicalist concept of mind/brain is assumed.[6]

We can ask ourselves whether such a situation is ideally conceivable.[7] One could object that a mind/brain such as that described before is not comparable with our own mind/brain. However, this would mean that our mind/brain belongs to a specific ontological type. From a physicalist point of view, though, a purely contingent origin would not make it possible to create univocal ontological borders, neither with animal minds/brains nor with human minds/brains made up of neurons, white matter, and cell structures similar to those currently present on Earth. Differences are gradual and quantitative, with extensive intraspecific variation. Furthermore, species themselves are not a fixed quantity, but rather the result of evolution from a shared ancestor, and they change over time. Nor does incommensurability have to do with opaqueness, inertia, or unconsciousness. Humans with such a genetically modified brain could thrive in both an environment identical to ours and in a different environment to which we also could adapt without problems.

One can object that if the "legitimate" modifications preserve the same functional relations of input to behavioural response, then it is not obvious that they would embody a different, incommensurable scheme. Could not physical flexibility constrained by the functional requirement that it copes similarly with the environment thereby be thought to restrict the conceptualization? A possible rebuttal could be that the argument seems to become teleological to a certain degree, since there are certainly limits to the functional assets compatible with the environment that a modified brain can take on in order to survive, but in and of itself this does not mean that the result must be a certain type of conceptual scheme, unless some sort of anthropic principle—or finalism—is assumed, according to which the evolutionary trajectory of the universe must produce a rational being such as *Homo sapiens* is today. On the other hand, this type of objection is possible precisely because we are currently built in a certain specific way, in keeping with Davidson's defense of the impossible existence of incommensurable conceptual schemes. In other words, finding out the result of stopping the flow of evolution at a given point and restarting it after modifying some key conditions remains an empirical question. In deference to current knowledge, the consensus is that repeating the flow of evolution even without any modifications would lead to different outcomes.

The fact that such a situation is physically possible is due to the pure contingency of our minds/brains and is shown by the (preliminary) experimental findings of neuroscience, including recent stimulation and artificial and selective interference experiments involving the higher cognitive functions. Nor is this situation incompatible with the nomological structure of the universe, at least based on current knowledge.

From a physicalist point of view on the mind/brain, it should perhaps be stressed that such incommensurability is destined to fade away in any given environment, since in this perspective, concepts arise out of the physical interactions between organisms and the physical world in which they live and from which they draw their nourishment.

This is the "*irrealism*" objection: if it depends on the contingent cerebral material basis, nothing we assert is literally true, meaning that it is appropriately connected to the actual state of affairs; instead, what we assert is merely what we can say given the way we are. A possible counterargument is that the irrealism hypothesis is based on an empirical induction drawn from a single case, namely the entirely contingent history of our universe since the Big Bang. Additionally, recent neurobiological descriptions of our mental representations of reality do not reflect total irrealism, but rather a form of *constructivism* that depends on the actual functioning of our *current* neuronal networks. For example, according to Metzinger (2009), outside of ourselves, in front of our eyes, there is nothing but an ocean of electromagnetic radiation, a chaotic, varied medley of different wavelengths. Most of them are invisible to us and will never be part of our conscious model of reality. What is happening is that the visual system of our brain is digging a tunnel through this complex physical environment, and as it does so it "paints" the walls of the tunnel in various colors. Literally, for Metzinger, *phenomenic* colors. *Appearances*. For our conscious eyes only.

2.2. A Disambiguation

At this point, a clarification is in order, since the argument as presented so far could be seen as having confused epistemology and metaphysics. As is well known, a long philosophical tradition, starting with Kant, "holds that necessary features of the world are a by-product of our conceptual scheme (or schemes): we regard as necessary what we could not experience, or conceive, or linguistically describe as being otherwise. Necessity, in that case, does not inhere in the things themselves: it is projected onto them by us"

(Marconi 2009). Generally speaking, modern philosophy authors supporting this claim did not explicitly consider the material composition of the brain, and somehow took it for granted that the mind was the black box in which philosophy was produced. Kant maintained that the conceptual apparatus is an immutable given, while according to more recent philosophers such as Carnap and C.I. Lewis the conceptual apparatus could be, in principle, radically different from what it is.

Today, instead, "many philosophers believe that things have essential (hence necessary) properties independently of how we experience, conceptualize, or describe them, and that certain facts—certain ways things stand—are necessary, i.e. common to all possible worlds in which their constituents exist" (Marconi 2009). Kripke's arguments for some truths being both necessary and *a posteriori* are commonly regarded as having established the latter thesis (Kripke 1980).[8]

With regards to Kant's arguments, physicalism applied to the mind has a precise consequence. Kant states that "that which in its connection with the actual is determined in accordance with universal conditions of experience, is (that is, exists as) necessary" (Kant [1787] 2003: 239). But physicalism applied to the mind implicitly (although not intentionally) questions the "universal conditions of experience". If the configuration of the brain changes radically, the conditions of experience change as well; thus, there are no *universal* conditions. Therefore, from a philosophical point of view, if one combines the Kantian perspective with physicalism applied to the mind, the necessity, as defined by Kant, would never be realized. In this tradition, the onus (and its most important philosophical consequences) was placed on the consideration of metaphysics, as when we are speaking of necessity we are speaking of ourselves, not of the world.

On the other hand, according to Kripke there are necessary features of the world that do not depend on our description of the world, but on the nature of things. They cannot be drawn from our conceptual framework. They are *a posteriori*. But Kripke also places doubt on the theories of psychophysical identity, which postulate that if there is a cerebral correlate for each mental state, then each mental state is identical to its correlate. His well known argument—based on the theory of *a posteriori* necessary truths—can be summarized as follows. He maintains that, given a reliable correlation between pain and the stimulation of C fibers, according to identity theory, the equation pain = stimulation of C fibers holds true. The first premise of Kripke's argument lies in the idea that identities such as water = H_2O, the template for psychophysical identities, are, if true, true by necessity, while the second premise arises from the fact that the identity between pain and stimulation of C fibers appears clearly contingent, since it is conceivable that the C fibers can be stimulated without the subject feeling pain, or that the subject can feel pain in a different manner, for example, through the stimulation of other nerve fibers. It follows that the identity pain = stimulation of C fibers cannot be true because it is not necessary.

In summary, Kripke's perspective on necessity implies that physicalism applied to the mental sphere is false; it follows that a rigorous physicalist must have a Kantian vision of necessity as applied to the mental sphere and must thus think that the only necessary truths regarding this sphere are conceptual. One could however argue that the first premise is marred by circular reasoning, as it already assumes physicalism to be false. And if this premise is false, physicalists can continue to argue that necessary *de re* truths apply to the mental sphere.

Kripke's argument against psychophysical identity is difficult to assail. As we have seen, it is based on two premises. The first rests upon the theory of rigid designation, whose confutation seems to imply the adoption of an alternative and equally powerful semantic theory. The second premise may be assailed by questioning the contingent character of the identity between pain and stimulation of C fibers. Once again, this is not an easy task, because arguing that disconnecting the stimulation of C fibers from pain is merely an apparent possibility is highly counterintuitive and must be proven. What could that which we seem to perceive as pain in the absence of C fiber stimulation be if not pain, since pain is nothing but that which we perceive as pain?

Other ways to assert the truth of psychophysical identity are tied to a weakening of necessity, by arguing that the identification of C fiber stimulation with pain holds true for human beings but not for other beings endowed with different neuro-cognitive systems. Although this would support physicalism as applied to the mind of the species *Homo sapiens sapiens*, it would undermine the idea of the post-Kripkean modality and thus make it more difficult to resist the argument proposed here.

Rigorous physicalists who want to follow Kripke in his theory of rigid designators thus find themselves unable to easily assert psychophysical identity without entering into conflict with Kripke's perspective. With regards to the mind, physicalists thus appear to be destined to be "Kantian", in order not to have to admit that the mind is not the same thing as the brain. However, if it is impossible to be rigorous Kripkean physicalists with regards to the mind, a Kantian perspective holds true with regards to the concept of necessity as applied to mental experiments on the mind. It thus seems that we must remain open to the existence incommensurable conceptual schemes. Thus, this conclusion does not seem to be invalidated by confusion between the epistemological and metaphysical levels.

Obviously, one could try to eschew the alternative by questioning Kripke's arguments, as done for instance by Block and Stalnaker (1999), who reject the conceptual analysis. They claim that the irreducibility of phenomenal events to cerebral events cannot be demonstrated. According to them, microphysical events linked to cerebral states of affairs do not imply phenomenal events *a priori*, and the only valid available approach to justify a necessary truth *a posteriori* is the empirical methodological approach. According to Block and Stalnaker, identities do not require any conceptual explanations; they are only facts detected through the empirical method. The experimental data discovered by neuroscientists on the identity between cerebral states and phenomenal states do not require additional conceptual confirmations. This is not the venue for a thorough rebuttal. However, the strongest objection seems to be that which was proposed by Chalmers and Jackson (2001), according to whom the identity proposed by Block and Stalnaker is not explicatory. Indeed, if identities do not need to be explained, then "this seems to conflate ontological and epistemological matters. Identities are ontologically primitive, but they are not epistemically primitive. Identities are typically implied by underlying truths that do not involve identities [. . .]. Once a subject knows all the truths about DNA and its role in reproduction and development, for example, the subject will be in a position to deduce that genes are DNA. So this identity is not epistemically primitive" (Chalmers and Jackson 2001).

Another influential line of argument resorts to the distinction between thin/thick concepts and properties. "Whether a property is thick or thin, then, will be considered here to be a matter of whether it has a hidden essence. For example, water or the property of being water is thick, since whether something is water goes beyond superficial manifestations of it. Examples of thin properties are mathematical properties, at least some functional properties, and phenomenal properties if dualism is true" (Block 2007). Block argues that "phenomenal concepts are both narrow and thick, which is why the phenomenality in the CMoR (cognitive modes of representation) can be physical". Again, it is not possible here to demonstrate why this line of argument does not appear to be fully convincing. However, we can point out that a conceptual independence of real-world items and a subjective phenomenology which is not purely delusive can be the basis for a line of argument that rests upon plausible, commonsense premises.

2.3. An Irrelevant Argument?

From a pragmatic point of view, we can raise another objection to the argument presented here: if we were really to meet someone with a conceptual super-scheme which was incommensurable for us, we would not realize it; we would not be able to realize it in any way. Nevertheless, this objection, in its very premise, admits a sort of conceivableness of the general idea of conceptual super-schemes that are incommensurable for us. By the same token, this objection does not seem to be sufficient to invalidate the argument. Indeed, one could conceive of a situation much like the following.

Owing to the contingency of the super-schemes, which depend on the variable material basis, one can hypothesize a possible world in which the evolutionary tree of hominids had various bifurcations.[9] Consider a system made up of humans like ourselves and other living beings (called *Zoos*) of higher intellectual development, who normally have no relations with us and whose conceptual system is incommensurable from our point of view (as ants are for us), but who are presumably capable to understand our own conceptual system (we know that in the very few cases in which we have been able to enter their territory, they never fail to annihilate us in a matter of seconds, although this is not irrefutable proof that they are able to predict our moves based on some form of mentalism).

Who knows all this? The Zoos do. How do they know it? They understand that, for us, they are like ants. If, however, the Zoos can take this step, one could object that the schemes are translatable. Indeed, they are, but only in one direction. There exists an untranslatable scheme, that of the Zoos for us humans, as beings with material limits; on the other hand, our conceptual scheme is translatable for the Zoos. This is an asymmetric relationship. We can conceive the idea of untranslatable conceptual schemes, even though we cannot "see" them. The Zoos, instead, can "see" them and probably even think them. If we want to avoid drawing excessively strong conclusions from that argument, we could argue that it is an inference to the best explanation, on the basis of the fact that the Zoos physically prevail over us, regardless of our defense strategy, and thus we can presume that they have the chance to mentalize our plans.

The idea of one-way incommensurability can be translated more rigorously, from a philosophical point of view, by going back to the idea of necessity. Leibniz teaches us that what is necessary is that which is true in every possible world that is also accessible for our world (that is, possible in our world). The controversial point thus concerns accessibility conditions: different accessibility conditions answer to different logics. It is plausible to argue—as I will do here—that the accessibility relationship is not transitive. Let us suppose that we find ourselves in World 1 (W1) from which Worlds W2, W3, W4, W5, and W6, taken together, form a horizon of possibility, are accessible in the sense detailed before. From W6, however, Worlds W7, W8, W9, and W10 are also accessible. Those who reject the idea of incommensurable and untranslatable schemes do not seem to consider the problem of possible worlds beyond the first horizon of possibility. Worlds W7, W8, W9, and W10 could instead be inaccessible from W1. That the accessibility relationship is always and necessarily transitive is a strong assumption which, it seems, should be demonstrated by its supporters, while here we attempted to argue against it on the basis of the physicalist premise regarding the mind.

3. PHYSICALISM AND THE NECESSITY OF LOGICAL LAWS

Having postulated that physicalist monism's consideration of the mental leads to the framework previously described, one could maintain that we are in a situation in which traditional thought experiments cannot be as necessary as they claim to be. In fact, within the broader thought meta-experiment, no single experiment can be conceived separately from its own "incommensurable" world, since it is assumed that logical rules are at least partially different (one need only think of quantum logic, which applies to quantum world and could somehow coincide with the logic used by a hypothetical quantum brain), and that the worldview is different as well, the latter intended as the overall integration of sensorial stimuli and conceptual data along with the preceding conceptual categories, which are necessary in order to build this worldview during all following moments of time.

Even within a theoretical-scientific framework that considers the mind/brain as the result of a process of adaptation to a given physical environment—given the stochastic premise of biological evolution—we cannot maintain that there is an element of necessity in the current configuration of synaptic network connections.

Obviously, the scenario of the contingency of our mind/brain does not concern those who follow a Fregean stance, according to which the validity of logical laws does not depend on our brain, since logical laws are not "laws of thought" (which may concern those who follow a Boolean stance on logical laws). In this perspective, should the configuration of our brain be different, we might not be able to understand logical laws, or think that they are different from those we think they are at the moment. But to them, this does not mean that logical laws (or the mathematical laws according to which "2+2 = 4") *would be* different. We *would think* that they are different, but they would always be the same. Those who favour a rigorous application of physicalism to the mind must grapple with the definition of the statute of immutable logical laws, which are independent from the mind/brain but understood by it.[10]

Those who do not want to fully adhere to Platonism, according to which logical laws belong to the non-physical realm of ideas, could thus prefer to limit themselves to questioning the argument that the physicalist perspective on mind leads to a potential threat to the necessary immutability of logical laws, leaving open the question of the latter's ontological status.[11]

A possible reply, which has many supporters and which we can only hint at here, concerns language and the fact that when we use words, we assume certain shared convictions regarding their application. Therefore, the fact that a statement expresses a necessary truth is always at least partly, and often completely, determined by the rules concerning the use of the words the statement contains. A counterargument is that language arises from evolution much like the mind/brain that produces it, as amply illustrated by Chomsky with his innatist theory on generative grammar[12]. Recent studies using functional MRI have found a correlation between the complexity of the hierarchical structure of sentences and the size of the neuron networks involved in their generation, bolstering the argument that grammar is tied to the neurobiological structure of the brain (Pallier, Devauchelle and Dehaene 2011).

One could indeed object that the existence of conceptual schemes—languages—incommensurable with ours does not make truths such as "2+2 = 4" any less absolute, at least to the extent that they remain true in any conceptual scheme in which they can be formulated. According to this line of reasoning, there would not be any conceptual scheme in which a proposition that is true in *our* conceptual scheme would be false: there is no scheme in which "2+2≠4". One could thus argue that there is nothing (no world) that is impossible in our conceptual scheme and that would be possible in another. That which we can consider possible or impossible in our conceptual scheme we cannot even *grasp* (*semanticize*) in another scheme.

This objection, however, rests upon a fully Davidsonian idea of conceptual schemes. The objection could be addressed by stating that, with our current brains, there are no completely untranslatable languages, according to Davidson's argument, but that the incommensurability introduced by a different material configuration of the brain is, so to say, of a different type. We certainly cannot imagine what it would be like to perform arithmetic operation with a brain different from ours, but we know that such a brain could be ideally conceived because ours, which thinks "2+2 = 4", has a structure brought about by randomness and contingency. There is thus no justification for thinking that the apparent absolute truth (in every possible world) of our logical and mathematical postulates cannot be subverted in a manner "obscure" to us by minds/brains with a different physical basis, despite the fact that this very incommensurability would prevent us from fully grasping how this could happen.[13]

Unless, obviously, one rejects this perspective on logic as the law behind thought and appeals to the Fregean third realm, a distinct environment in which different people with different linguistic and cognitive structures can grasp the same thought.

One could still object that our minds/brains do have a contingent structure, but, just like any other biological structure, they must follow the laws of physics and biology. Furthermore, one could maintain that the logical laws in which we believe draw their necessity from the biological and physical laws that govern our physical basis. There are two tentative replies to this objection.

The first one rests upon the fact that—according to physicalists—the brain itself mediates between basic physical laws and the expression of logical laws. The way in which logical laws emerge is not clear, if they do not emerge through the inferences made by individual human beings set into reproducible formulas. And we already know that the brain has a contingent *structure*, even though the functioning of this structure follows basic physical laws and cannot violate them in any way. There remains the possibility that machines, particularly digital computers, will express, without the mediation of the brain, logical laws arising directly from basic physical laws. This is a possibility that cannot be explored here. Nevertheless, there does not yet seem to be proof that there exists non-man-made artefacts that show the capacity to coherently apply known logical laws, unless we consider self-organized physical systems as examples of such laws. I mention this more as a possible argument for critics, rather than as an example I feel is viable.[14]

The second reply has to do with the fact that basic physical laws as a whole are contingent upon the origins of the physical universe, at least according to current (hypothetical) knowledge. It can be hypothesized scientifically that at least some physical parameters could have been different, and thus that the universe's development could have been slightly different from what we can observe today. But this is an empirical question that remains open, as shown by the debate over the so-called anthropic principle.

If, instead, one believes that the rules governing ideal conceivability—those which, for example, forbid us to claim that "2+2 = 5"—cannot in any way be removed under penalty of losing the rationality of philosophical discourse (as Aristotle argued, we cannot abandon the proposition "2+2 = 4" since it is true in any system in which it can be included), it seems that we are left with a disjunction: either the laws of logic are unnecessary (i.e.; not valid in *all* possible worlds, even those where minds/brains are physically different) or we must admit the existence of some type of Fregean Platonism, which is incompatible with strong physicalism.

Indeed, in the Fregean approach, in order to preserve the originality of thoughts one must separate thoughts from the subjective world of consciousness and from the empirical world of experience, in an objective "third realm" of abstract entities. These contain the thoughts that humanity has so far been able to identify, discover, and express through language. In this way, thoughts are not only objective, they can also be grasped by everyone and have effects: the mental act of understanding a thought produces consequences at the social and individual level.

This is because thinking is a subjective psychic act that puts us in contact with something objective, namely the meaning of statements or thoughts. According to Frege, grasping the meaning of a statement or a thought is a "mysterious" act, through which the subject comes into contact with that which is objective. As such, an ontological space not otherwise defined in terms of universal truths, which can be reached in an unfathomable fashion in order to literally discover logical laws and mathematical theorems, is the counterpoint to the radical contingency of material aggregates in evolution.

The thought meta-experiment with a genetically modified brain/mind adopts the reductionist assumption of the mind as a direct "expression" of the material basis constituted by the brain. This is the physical configuration that makes it possible to express the concept of ideal conceivability, which prevents us from stating ~S, when S is a truth that can be mathematically proven. The very idea of possible worlds turns into a generic, nebulous concept because the mind/brain that thinks it is entirely contingent: there could be n real brains/minds who could each think up a different idea of possible worlds.[15]

Materialistic monism, if true, reduces the scope of philosophical practise to compatible interactions with the material world in which we find ourselves. These are microscopic interactions within our brains, but they are macroscopic with regards to our bodies' interactions with the surrounding environment.

In the cited disjunction, accepting as true some sort of Platonism might lead to some form of body-mind dualism. But it does not, in and of itself, explain away the intuition that could lead to the refusal to abandon logical concepts and rules endowed with necessity and unbound to mental contingency. Postulating, from a metaphysical point of view, a substance (or a specific type of properties emerging from the substance investigated by physical sciences) that is at the origin of and supports concepts endowed with necessity is not the only possible way out of this dilemma. Nevertheless, even a sort of Fregean Platonism that places logical thought in an unspecified (and not necessarily physical) location other than the brain would ask physicalists to explain how the material brain can grasp logical laws independent from the laws of thought.[16]

On the other hand, we must also be aware of the fact that highlighting the consequences of physicalism as applied to the mind may raise other problems. It seems indeed that we are entrapped in a paradox: the thought meta-experiment is carried out by a given brain, with a given contingent physical configuration, and thus it could also be "relativized". Indeed, it seems that incommensurable minds/brains are "bubbles" of "good sense", in which the tests of truth for each one remain internally unprejudiced, while propositions of physically radically different minds/brains would not be inter-translatable, and thus, in and of themselves, could not be evaluated as false or impossible from a shared perspective or from a perspective "external" to the individual "bubbles".

From the point of view of physicalist monism, one could maintain that the material basis is responsible for producing the "intuition" or, worse yet, the "impression" that part of what we call thought goes "beyond" its underlying neural configuration.

Nevertheless, if we can talk about possibility, conceivability, and possible worlds in which certain rules or conditions are always valid, then we can consider this to be an inductive element in favour of the second facet of the disjunction, namely that the mind is autonomous to some degree with respect to its contingent material basis in order to access a "realm" of noncontingent thoughts. Obviously, a hypothetical non-physical basis (under our current concept of physics—and this is certainly not a simple task from a philosophical point of view) could be imagined to be equally "relative" as the physical basis. Indeed, it is not clear whether relying on some form of intuition in order to support the second facet of disjunction is justifiable. Actually, supporters of physicalism could accept the minor impasse of the "conceptual super-scheme" and continue to reject Platonism and dualism as wholly implausible from a philosophical and empirical point of view, while Platonists and dualists would have the opportunity to advance a petition of principle: if we can intuitively perceive that absolute necessity and truth can resist any attempt at relativization, it is thanks to a mind component that is not strictly physical, and that must subsequently be identified and establish relations with the material brain (with the possible, well-known problems related to interactions between different substances).[17]

Under such a line of reasoning, it would be difficult to escape from a progressive, and presumably endless, superposition of two (meta-) thoughts. The first is the contradiction between the contingent nature of the material mind/brain, the result of random evolution, and the logical rules and concepts of apparently noncontingent value and necessity. The second (meta-) thought is the reduction of this "intuition" of logical concepts and rules to its empirically investigable material basis, a necessary condition for expressing the first meta-thought as well.

An attempt to exit this vicious circle—and the paradox trap—could lie in the fact that, apparently, all that which we have previously discussed happens only in the minds/brains of humans, not in any other living creatures, nor in any currently available artefacts such as computers. In this case as well, however, the material basis objection applies: Gödel's incompleteness theorem itself could be the result of the particular current set-up of our neural circuits, but it could have been "unreachable" one hundred thousand years ago, and it might become "unreachable" a few thousand years from now, should evolution proceed in an unpredictable manner, as it seems to be doing.

Finally, consider an objection that we could call functionalist: according to this well-known philosophical perspective, the way mental functions are physically implemented is not relevant; rather, computations on symbolic representations are what's relevant. But what can we say about our thought meta-experiment: that the computations continue the way we know, independently from any variation in their material basis? Functionalism seems to assume that the matter with which the circuits that "run the program" are made is not relevant. Wouldn't asserting that the functionalist mind is not influenced by a radical genetic change be an excessive step in the direction of a conception of mentality that completely detaches it from its physical implementation? In other words, if the rules that bind disincorporated computation—such as the ideal conceivability that prevents us from asserting that "2+2 = 5"—were still valid, would this not bring us into the second facet of the disjunction discussed before?

On the other hand, it seems that if we take seriously most contemporary philosophy of mind and the findings of neuroscience, we are led towards the first facet of the disjunction. A monistic and physicalist conception of the mental is at least implicitly accepted by most scholars, even if they do not always completely render explicit the arguments and consequences that derive from them.

4. PLANTINGA'S EVOLUTIONARY ARGUMENT AGAINST NATURALISM

Starting in 1993, Alvin Plantinga developed what has been called the Evolutionary Argument Against Naturalism (Eaan).[18] It argues for the existence of a fundamental, indomitable tension between the theory of biological evolution (as we have referred to it so far in this chapter) and philosophical naturalism, understood by Plantinga as the belief that there are no supernatural entities or processes. According to the author, the fundamental point is that the combination of evolutionism and naturalism as understood by Plantinga cannot exist, because if both were true, the probability that humans could have a reliable cognitive ability would be very low or even indemonstrable.

The root of the argument lies in the "Darwinian doubt", the scepticism that the father of evolutionary theory expressed in an 1881 letter to William Graham on the value of our mental contents, since our minds descend from those of inferior animals. Would anyone trust the mental contents of a monkey, assuming such a mind could have any contents at all? Darwin asked himself. In light of casual phylogenetic evolution, Plantinga argues, naturalism seems to lead to the conclusion that our cognitive faculties cannot be assumed to produce more true beliefs than false ones. For Plantinga, the key point is that evolution does not select our beliefs because they are true, but rather because they are adaptive, meaning useful for our survival in our environment. Thus—in extreme summary and overlooking the author's extensive arguments (which recognize four different categories of mind-body interaction according to which beliefs are more or less efficient)—the likelihood that our minds are reliable in the conjunction of naturalism and evolutionism are low or incalculable. To state that natural evolution is true therefore means to have a low or unknown likelihood of making a statement that is true. From an epistemological point of view, this would considerably weaken the belief that natural evolution is true, and would make the belief that naturalism and evolution are both true internally questionable or inconsistent.[19]

Recently, Plantinga restricted his argument to semantic epiphenomenalism, which holds that from a materialistic point of view, a belief is merely a neuronal event. From this perspective, a belief has two types of properties: neurophysiological properties and the property of having contents. While the former are currently rather well explained, the latter begs a question: how can the contents be associated to the proposition that expresses the belief? Materialists would say: either by reducing the contents to their neurophysiological properties or with the theory of supervenience (or emergentism). But in the second case, which seems plausible to less radical materialists, Plantinga ponders the likelihood—in light of materialism—that the contents that appear are actually true.

This situation cannot be straightened out by arguments that attempt to repair the epistemic damage caused, since any such argument should appeal to the very cognitive mechanisms that have been discarded by evolutionary theory. Plantinga argues that this would lead to pragmatically circular reasoning.

Finally, Plantinga (1993: 226) summarizes roughly in this way: Those who are in the act of accepting N (evolutionary naturalism) and are torn between N and theism should reason as follows: if I were to accept N, I would have a good and unassailable reason to be agnostic about N; this is an argument whose conclusion is irrationality in accepting naturalism, not the falseness of naturalism, but the irrationality of its acceptance. The conclusion to be drawn is thus that the conjunction of naturalism and evolutionism belies itself.The argument proposed in this chapter, which might be called the *Argument of the conceptual super-scheme*, may appear related to the *Evolutionary Argument Against Naturalism*, but it certainly does not arise from it, and it is distinguished from it by its smaller epistemological scope (and by its development and formalization). Nevertheless, it is not inspired by and does not need the supernatural theism that Plantinga puts forth as the context for guaranteeing belief. Neither does it seek to refute physicalism *ipso facto* (in any case, physicalism does not coincide with Plantinga's naturalism). Rather, it aims to highlight certain tensions that arise between philosophical assumptions tied to our cognitive capacities and the materialistic model of the mind as the outcome of causal natural evolution. This same (material) evolution is understood here to be a scientific datum and premise behind our argument, and not as a problem. What seems to be shared is an exploration of the consequences of a full naturalization of the mind in order to ensure the coherence of perspectives that currently do seem fully compatible.

5. CONCLUSION

In this chapter I have attempted to argue that a monistic, physicalist approach to the mind could lead to the validation of the idea of "conceptual super-schemes", arising out of different material bases of hypothetical minds/brains that are incommensurable due to their different brain configurations, the only origin of thought and language. The idea of "conceptual super-schemes" also seems to question the acceptability of thought experiments on the mind, if conceived as endowed with validity and necessity in all possible worlds.

This seems to lead to a disjunction: either one must follow the physicalist conception of the mind and thus admit "conceptual super-schemes" and the non-acceptability of thought experiments on the mind, or one can reject "conceptual super-schemes" and preserve the acceptability of thought experiments and thus must consider some sort of realism or Fregean dualism, which must be made compatible with physicalism.

This is merely a preliminary explanation of the consequences of a rigorous monistic physicalism regarding the mental, an explanation that requires in-depth research and a broader philosophical meditation than has so far been attempted.[20]

NOTES

1. For this thesis, see Williamson (2007: 134). Williamson himself argues that the epistemology of metaphysical modality only requires "a kind of thinking

tightly integrated with our thinking about the spatio-temporal world" (2007: 178). In the strong physicalist hypothesis, this argument seems to depend on the contingent cerebral configuration.
2. It may be possible to specify that they are necessarily valid in our minds/brains' current contingent set-up. Although based on different premises, J.R. Brown (1991) offers a defense from the consequences of physicalism by introducing the Platonic thought experiment—"it is *a priori* in that it is not based on new empirical evidence nor is it merely logically derived from old data"—which is possible due to the existence of natural laws as abstract platonic universals, similar to abstract objects supposed to exist in mathematics and logic.
3. As I stated earlier, Davidson could have questioned such a presentation of the hypothetical scenario, but I am not trying to introduce an argument designed *contra* Davidson; the fact that Davidson's position on the mind-body problem is that which is defined as *Anomalous Monism* (Davidson 1970) is thus irrelevant. The general idea is that any philosophy that is not strictly idealistic must take into account some kind of reality external to the knowing subject.
4. There does not seem to be a circular definition at work here, according to which the different material codification of sensorial data would actually coincide with a surreptitious assumption of a preliminary conceptual scheme. Here we are dealing with a different brain architecture, which would lead to the two different hypothetical brains having different functions. And all arguments against conceptual schemes seem to be based, at least implicitly, on the assumption that all brains are essentially similar in their material basis, or that at the very least we are dealing with rational agents with the usual stock of psychological states. Nevertheless, those who argue that the "third dogma of empiricism" must be surmounted without giving up on physicalist monism may perhaps want to question this line of argument.
5. As an example of the possible alternative descriptions of reality provided by physics, consider D. Bohm's model. He maintains that the universe has an *implicate order*, which we cannot see and is similar to a hologram in which the overall structure can be indentified in that of each of its individual components, and an *explicate order*, which is what we actually see. According to him, the latter is the result of our brains' interpretation of the interference waves (or patterns) that make up the universe. A different brain might be able to grasp the *implicate order* (cf. Bohm 1980).
6. One cannot ignore the naturalization that is taking place in semantics with regards to the most commonly used concepts. These concepts appear to be physically implemented by a specific network of neurons, whose functional architecture has been identified to a reasonably accurate degree. It is thus not unrealistic to think that it could be altered without having to turn to options that are currently far more remote possibilities, such as the one described earlier (cf. Mitchell et al. 2008). Nevertheless, there is a philosophical and psychological research field that has long been concerned with embodied or contextual concepts. According to this approach, concepts are "simulators" of perceptive or motor experiences; there is no conceptual system distinct from perceptive and motor systems; higher cognitive capacities operate through the reactivation and elaboration of information codified as perceptions or patterns of actions (see Barsalou 2005).
7. Conceivable can be understood as imaginable, describable in language and epistemically possible. The third option might be at the same time the most relevant and the most problematic. In the case at hand, the proposition *p* seems epistemically possible, meaning possible "for all we know" (see Szabó Gendler and Hawthorne 2002).
8. In this chapter, the existence of a world external to the knowing subject and independent from our perceptive and conceptual categories is not being

questioned. The fact that our brains have a contingent physical configuration, as described earlier, is the outcome of a shared science, which focuses on at least some of the observable and measurable properties of the reality external to the knowing subject.
9. The very recent discoveries on the recent coexistence of *Homo sapiens* with Neanderthals seem to confirm the actual presence of bifurcations in the past.
10. In this regard, the fact that the current configuration of the human brain, the contingent result of evolution, understands logical laws, and appears to be the only one among living species to have this ability, may suggest the existence of an *anthropic-logical principle*. Much like physicists maintain that a tiny variation in the main parameters of nature would have prevented the establishment of life on Earth, and that the conditions necessary for life are, hypothetically speaking, extremely unlikely to emerge, so it can be argued that a contingent variation in the evolutionary process could have led to *Homo sapiens sapiens* having a brain unable to grasp logical laws. On the other hand, in billions of years of evolutionary history, an immense number of species evolved without a central nervous system or with brains unable to grasp logical laws. In any case, the likelihood of evolving a brain able to grasp logical laws is exceedingly low.
11. Obviously, the Fregean point of view cannot be simplified by referencing Platonism *tout court*, but compared to strong physicalism its strong suits do not appear to be decisive with regards to the present discussion. Consider T. Nagel's words on objectivity and physicalism: "If we find it undeniable, as we should, that the clearest moral and logical reasonings are objectively valid, we are on the first rung of this ladder. It does not commit us to any particular interpretation of the normative, but I suppose it demands something more. We cannot maintain the kind of resistance to any further explanation that is sometimes called quietism. The confidence we feel within our own point of view demands completion by a more comprehensive view of our containment of the world" (Nagel 2012: 31). Therefore, "the existence of conscious minds and their access to the evident truths of ethics and mathematics are among the data that a theory of the world and our place in it has yet to explain" (ibid.).
12. It is interesting to note that T. Nagel does not believe that the existence of language provides an adequate explanation of our ability to grasp factual and practical truths and logical laws, since "the explanation of our ability to acquire and use language in these ways presents problems of the same order, for language is one of the most important normatively governed faculties. To acquire a language is in part to acquire a system of concepts that enables us to understand reality" (Nagel 2012: 73).
13. Although this analogy is rather far-fetched and does not regard analytic philosophy, it can be pointed out that an intuitive conception of completely incommensurable minds has been present for centuries in the Western theological and philosophical tradition: the idea that the mind of God—the perfect, all-powerful, and all-knowing being—is completely inscrutable by human minds, even though human themselves are, in the Christian conception, creatures of God, part of the same ontological "universe", with whom God communicates through the language of his creatures.
14. Studies on engineered biological systems, which can function as logic gates (and, nor, nand, or gates) and signal filters, are very recent (Win and Smolke 2008), but the cells' "logic" seems to be derived and of second order. For a discussion on the issue of primary or derived intentionality see the extensive literature on the "Chinese Room" argument by John Searle.

15. Once again, one could object that this is a *different* but *contradictory* idea, if such a difference is understood to be a classical difference of scheme: in such a situation, no world that is impossible for us could be possible for others, and vice versa. But, as I have tried to argue previously, we are not operating in a context in which different hypothetical languages are supported by the same material basis, but instead we are dealing with different brains, the *primum movens* of the ontological chains, from which conceptual super-schemes arise and depend upon.
16. It should be specified that the non-physical substance postulated here must be part of a *non-spiritual* context: it could for example be a type of special radiation not detected by our instruments. What seems to emerge from the argument presented here is that the "physical basis" as presently known is not sufficient to account for the apparent necessity of the fundamental laws of thought. Accepting some type of dualism between the body and the mind does not, *in and of itself*, make the fundamental laws of thought necessary. It is conceivable that there are as many non-physical bases for our minds as there are material ones. Furthermore, the fact that our minds might have a non-physical basis may be just as random as the fact that they have a certain physical basis. This remains an open question for philosophical and scientific research.
17. Such philosophical "research" can take another look at the various arguments (from primary intentionality to qualia) against physicalism that have been proposed over time. However, this goes beyond the scope of our discussion.
18. Cf. Plantinga 1993: ch.12, "Is Naturalism Irrational?". The argument was taken up again in Plantinga (2000), discussed by the author and his critics in the volume edited by Beilby (2002), and reformulated in Plantinga and Tooley (2008).
19. T. Nagel, without making any reference to Plantinga and excluding theistic references, also seems to approach this line of thinking: "In case of reasoning, if it is basic enough, the only thing to think is that I have grasped the truth directly. I cannot pull back from a logical inference and reconfirm it with the reflection that a reliability of my logical thought processes is consistent with the hypothesis that evolution has selected them for accuracy. That would drastically weaken the logical claim. Furthermore, in the formulation of that explanation (. . .) logical judgments of consistency and inconsistency have to occur without these qualifications, as direct apprehensions of truth. It is not possible to think, 'Reliance on my reason, including my reliance on this very judgment, is reasonable because it is consistent with its having an evolutionary explanation.' Therefore any evolutionary account of the place of reason presupposes reason's validity and cannot confirm it without circularity" (Nagel 2012: 80).
20. An earlier version of this paper was published in Italian, in *Rivista di Estetica*, 2012, 49. I'm grateful to Howard Robinson for relevant comments and suggestions.

4 Materialism, Dualism, and the Conscious Self

David Lund

MATERIALISM

I

I will begin by offering an overview of the materialist view in philosophy of mind, taking note of the broad kinds of positions defended by materialists, with a focus on the constraints imposed upon them by the ontological framework within which they must do their theorizing, severely limiting the resources to which they might justifiably appeal in attempting to defend a thoroughgoing materialist account of human experience. I will follow this with a somewhat detailed summary of a case for a strong dualism, i.e., a substance dualism, focusing on the subject of conscious states.

Though the term 'physicalism' is frequently used instead of 'materialism' in the context of philosophy of mind, I will regard these terms as synonyms. Materialism (or physicalism), then, is a doctrine entailing that all mental entities (if any are deemed to exist) are entirely physical in nature. All substances, events, complex objects, properties, and states are physical in the thoroughgoing ontological materialism I am characterizing. In an entirely material world, every constituent is an objective entity, accessible (at least in principle) to the third-person viewpoint. There can be no irreducible subjectivity, not of consciousness nor of anything else accessible only from a first-person viewpoint, including that viewpoint itself. The experiential center of a person's world can have no place in the centerless material order if it is not reducible to some assembly of material entities.

The difference between mind and body, between the mental (i.e., the *conscious* mental) and the physical, seems undeniable from the perspective of the first person, at least when one takes the introspective turn and focuses upon the conscious states one is then having. Perhaps it is because our conscious states, at least when we reflectively attend to them, do not appear to be material that the great majority of human beings throughout history have explicitly or implicitly rejected the view that a person is nothing more than (i.e., nothing but) a body. In any case, the daunting challenge for the materialist is to present an account of conscious states that accurately portrays their character as we experience them yet also explains how they nevertheless can be totally material in their constitution. The explanations offered may be divided into three broad types: Reductive, Eliminative, and Supervenience Materialism.

II

First, let us look at the Reductive Materialist who acknowledges that the mental does exist but contends that, when properly understood, it will be seen to be reducible to (i.e., nothing other than) the physical. Three kinds of reductive materialism may be distinguished. Logical behaviorism is one of these three kinds. It is the view that the meaning of mental terms can be analyzed into descriptions of behavior and/or dispositions to behave. Such terms do not designate inner states or events, directly accessible to the person having them, but not directly accessible from the third-person viewpoint. For there are no such things, no occurrent conscious states or events. So to say of a person that, for example, she is thinking, or remembering, or in pain is just to say that she is behaving or disposed to behave in a certain way.

This is, of course, highly counterintuitive. It seems undeniable from the first-person perspective that we do experience actual inner states or events whose natures are partially or completely revealed to us as we have or undergo them and thereby revealed to be something beyond behavior and dispositions to behave in certain ways under such and such conditions. An unexpressed pain, for example, is neither a behavior nor an unactualized disposition. Clearly, it is an inner, occurrent phenomenon; something is actually taking place when one is feeling a pain.

The second kind of reductionism, the one with the longest history, is what we would presently call the Identity Theory, according to which mental entities do exist but are identified with physical entities internal to the body. The ancient Greek atomists are early proponents of this view, contending that the mind consists of smaller, smoother atoms located in the chest. A present-day identity theorist would likely maintain that mental states are electrochemical states of neurons in the brain. Though there are two forms of the Identity Theory—the strong thesis of mind-brain *type* identity and the somewhat more defensible weaker mind-brain *token* identity thesis—both are committed to what the weaker thesis asserts, viz., that each *particular* mental state or event is numerically identical to some particular brain state or event. In taking the mental to consist of occurrent inner states, it has an advantage over logical behaviorism.

The central problem for the identity theorist is that an (occurrent) conscious state does not appear, from the first-person perspective, to be anything like some brain state to which it is supposed to be identical. Since the identity theorist's claim is a contingent one whose truth is to be established empirically, the identity theorist usually argues, as Smart originally did, that what is needed is a topic-neutral conception of conscious states or events that would enable us to pick them out in a way that would make it a possibility but not a requirement for them to be nothing but physical states or events with only physical properties (Smart 1959). They would be picked out without ascribing intrinsic properties to them. But such a conception will exclude those properties that make a conscious state seem so unlike a brain state—those accessible only from the first-person perspective and which from that perspective seem essential to what a conscious state *is*. Clearly, those properties would not be topic-neutral. So it seems clear that an occurrent consciousness can have no place in such a view. For the topic-neutral items identified would lack such essential properties as consciousness, and so their turning out to be entirely physical would not warrant any such conclusion about conscious states or events.

That the topic-neutral description of conscious states must fail to capture what is essential to consciousness comes into view again when we see what makes it topic-neutral (at least as Smart depicted it) is its apparent restriction to relational properties (e.g., similarities and causal properties) of the items concerned, a restriction reflecting the belief that relational properties are all that self-consciousness and introspection reveal about such states. That they do reveal more, however, seems undeniable if we are willing to acknowledge that what is accessible from the first-person perspective constitutes fundamental knowledge of conscious states.

So it appears that the topic-neutral approach fails and that the gulf between an experience and the physical entity with which it is supposed to be identical is left as unbridgeable as ever. Because of this and other serious difficulties with the identity theories, they have been largely replaced in contemporary materialist thought by Functionalism, the third form of reductionism.

In the token-identity theory (i.e., token-identity physicalism), each mental entity is held to be identical to some physical entity and thus to have the first-order physical properties of that entity, e.g., its structure and constitution. But in the functionalist view, the focus turns to functional properties, i.e., to second-order properties of physical entities. A mental entity is now defined in terms of its abstract functional or causal role that is constituted by its causal relations to input from the environment, to other internal states, and to behavioral output. What makes a state a mental (or conscious) state is its causal relations, not intrinsic properties. The role is definitive of the type of conscious state, but there is also an occupant—a particular conscious state that occupies the role. The occupant may be conceived either abstractly or as including what is featured in a realization of it. But the latter alternative leads to a token-identity functionalism that is hardly more plausible than a token-identity physicalism. Consequently, the first alternative has become the preferred functionalist view. In this view, the occupant is abstract in the sense that a disposition or readiness is abstract, having no categorical reality. So a conscious state becomes a readiness or disposition to generate internal states along with overt behavior. Physical states embed the disposition but are not identical to it.

It seems clear that functionalism fails to provide anything approaching an adequate account of consciousness. In such an account, consciousness could hardly be more different from the occurrent consciousness whose existence seems undeniable from the first-person perspective. The functional/causal role conception of the mental can lead to nothing more plausible than a behaviorist/dispositionalist treatment of consciousness, a treatment that can have no place for an occurrent consciousness, i.e., the consciousness presently occurring in one's experience of being conscious. Though functionalism fares no better in either its treatment of the qualitative character of the mental or its treatment of intentionality, it is sufficient for my purposes here to limit my remarks to consciousness.

III

In view of the apparently insurmountable difficulties confronting the reductive materialist, one might be inclined to join the eliminative materialist in simply denying that the mental exists in the first place and thus implying that there is nothing to reduce. But such an inclination quickly fades upon seeing how counterintuitive and even paradoxical a thoroughgoing eliminative materialism turns out to be. In its thoroughgoing form, the qualitative aspects of the mental, thinking as well as the other propositional attitudes, and consciousness itself simply do not exist. Though I will not pursue it further here, I will later argue that the eliminationists along with the other materialists must deny that taking the first-person perspective provides us with an epistemic access to a mental reality as it is prior to interpretation.

IV

Some forms of materialism are claimed to be non-reductive and thus invite the question as to whether they constitute a genuine alternative to what the reductive materialist has to offer. For it appears that if, like the reductionist, their proponents are committed to a thoroughgoing, i.e., ontological, materialism, then the sense in which they are non-reductive is not ontological. And this seems to be what we find. Non-reduction is claimed on the basis of such non-ontological dualisms as dualisms of description, explanation, conceiving, and understanding.

A materialist view considered to be non-reductive and requiring some special attention is Supervenience Materialism. It has gained the status of a third alternative for materialists, especially those who have held that all that is needed for a comprehensive materialist view of the mental is to see it as supervening on the physical. But can this be all that is needed, i.e., sufficient, for materialism if the mental were acknowledged to be non-physical? It may be sufficient for what has been called "soft" materialism, but certainly not for *ontological* materialism. Such a materialist view would be a form of dualism and thus clearly not a thoroughgoing (ontological) materialism, however deep and intimate the dependence of the mental on the physical is considered to be. A strong supervenience, according to which the supervenience of the mental on the physical entails that everything mental is physical, would remain faithful to the ontology of materialism but would be reductive. So would any other supervenience materialism subscribing to materialist ontology even if it were claimed to be non-reductive—something it could be only in some non-ontological sense. If, on the other hand, it *is* non-reductive in the ontological sense, something irreducible to the physical (viz., the existent of mental entities) prevents such reduction, in which case it is not a form of ontological materialism.

In view of these (very abbreviated) considerations, it appears that supervenience materialism will not prove to be a third alternative available to materialists. Also, an additional and apparently insurmountable difficulty will come into view later as I lay out my arguments about the nature of the self. Besides, it is very difficult to see what a highly plausible non-reductive position could be, given, of course, that non-reduction in some non-ontological sense will not do. So the options available to the ontological materialist are very likely just two: either reductive or eliminative materialism.

V

Though our examination of the broad kinds of materialist views has been quite brief, it might nevertheless be sufficient to show that none of them can accommodate the occurrent consciousness constitutively involved in all conscious states or events. Yet the existence of such consciousness seems incontestable from the first-person perspective. From that perspective, it seems undeniable that I have a direct access to my own conscious states, an access necessarily *not* available to a third-person perspective and which can function as an epistemic access to these states as they are prior to interpretation.

Though I will later offer a more extensive account of the need to acknowledge that we have an immediate epistemic access to at least some of our own conscious states as they are in their uninterpreted reality, I will conclude this overview of materialism by making two points. First, if one believes that his access to his own consciousness is not immediate but always mediated by some interpretation and infers from this that there is no knowledge of what, if anything, lies beyond our interpretations, it would be easier for him to accept a view that has no place for occurrent consciousness. Indeed, such a belief seems widespread among materialists as many appeal to what is in effect the concept of an interpretation to argue that the deliverances yielded by taking the first-person perspective do not include presentations of an uninterpreted reality but are merely the workings of our conceptual, interpretive powers that have no more epistemic authority than interpretations generally. Frequently the appeal is to the interpretive effect of language preventing our having epistemic access to our consciousness as it is extra-linguistically (if in this view it is anything at all apart from language). Rorty's extraordinary disappearance theory of sensations stems from his view that what we experience is a function of our language (Rorty 1965). And, Davidson, the anomalous monist who argued that "events are mental only as described", is apparently claiming that mental events have no reality apart from language (Davidson 1980).

Even the existence of one's own consciousness to which one seems to have immediate epistemic access might be only a matter of interpretation if P.S. Churchland is correct. She argues that the impression of immediacy is illusory and that even consciousness itself must be understood within a theoretical framework, presumably as a theoretical entity. Since she regards our common sense psychology as a theory that gives 'consciousness' its meaning, if it were to be replaced by a better one, we may then learn that there is no such thing as consciousness (Churchland 1986).

She argues in a similar way that the existence of belief and the other propositional attitudes might be only a matter of interpretation. And Dennett seems to go further yet in equating the having of a belief (or other attitude) with being interpretable as having one (Dennett 1987). As a final example, Putnam has been quite explicit in maintaining that there is no uninterpreted mental reality to access (or, at any rate, no reason to believe that there is). The mental has no existence independently of interpretation (Putnam 1983).

It seems clear that the materialist cannot acknowledge the existence of an uninterpreted mental reality to which we have epistemic access. For then, the admission that our conscious states really are as they introspectively appear to be would be inescapable. Hence there is the need to maintain that the conceptualizing, interpretive powers of the mind provide the interpretations that constitute the limits of our epistemic reach, at least with respect to our conscious states, and thereby rule out any appeal to our having an epistemic access to a given or presentation. This brings me to my second point. There is a problem for the materialist maintaining that interpretations play such a role: they conflict with materialist ontology. How this happens comes into view when we ask what an interpretation can be for a materialist. Since it is a constituent of an entirely material world, it must receive materialist treatment. But there can be no such treatment primarily for the reason that any set of physical elements that the interpretation might be considered to be must itself receive intentional interpretation to be seen as meaningful, that is, seen to have a feature that any *interpretation* must have. For an interpretation has a directedness beyond itself unto that which it interprets, and nothing physical can be seen as directed beyond itself independently of an intentional interpretation imposed upon it. This, however, requires a source of the interpretation that, it would seem, must be a conscious act or state if anything is. But now we must ask of the conscious state that is the source of the interpretation whether it is as it appears to be (and thus fails to succumb to materialist treatment) or it is known only under some interpretation.

Presumably, the materialist will pick the latter alternative, since the former leads to the conclusion that our consciousness *is* sometimes presented to us. But the latter implies that there is now another interpretation which, in a materialist world, must be identified with some set of physical elements—a set that must receive intentional interpretation to be seen as meaningful and thereby implying the existence of a source of the interpretation that apparently must be a conscious state that either is as it appears to be or else is known only under some interpretation. Given that the materialist must reject the first alternative, there is now still another interpretation to be identified with a set of physical items that must receive intentional interpretation ... etc. *ad infinitum*.

This regress stops only if at some point the first alternative is chosen, i.e., the conscious state is as it appears to be; it is or includes a presentation. If that alternative is not available—if every source of interpretation is known only under some interpretation whose source is known only under some further interpretation, etc.—the regress generated can never begin. Thus interpretation, though required in this view of the mental, can never begin and so cannot exist. Neither alternative can be accepted by the materialist.

One might now wonder how a materialist could have come to employ the notion of an interpretation to deny epistemic consciousness of a given or presentation without unreflectively assuming that he is the source of the interpretation imposed upon the phenomena and then failing to see that what is being assumed must also receive materialist treatment. This consideration prompts a word of caution: when one tries to view the world as it would be if materialism were true, one must be careful not to place oneself unwittingly in a privileged position outside of it, while imposing an interpretation upon it. The interpreter, or, at any rate, the source of the interpretation and the interpretation itself, along with the perspective from which the world is viewed or interpreted, must be included in that reality which is to receive materialist treatment. Perhaps materialism would hold far less appeal if this reflection were kept firmly in mind.

DUALISM

I

My primary objective in this part of the chapter is to provide a fairly detailed summary of a set of considerations and arguments which (at least when developed to a length and level of argumentative detail not possible within the space limitations here) may be seen to come together to constitute a powerful, if not compelling, case for a strong dualism—a dualism of particulars. I begin with some remarks about the relevance of physical science to the matter at issue. I then put forward some rather general considerations that motivate a dualist understanding of mental phenomena, pointing out the need to acknowledge the reality of an occurrent, irreducible consciousness and the central importance of the first-person viewpoint as the fundamental epistemic access to it. From that viewpoint, it seems incontestable that (in first-person terms) I have a direct awareness of my own conscious states—an awareness whose fundamental epistemic significance seems as undeniable as the reality of the awareness itself. For it constitutes the grounds of my knowledge of what my conscious states are intrinsically, as well as my knowledge of what I am as the subject having them. Such knowledge must be accorded fundamental importance, since it seems incontestable that something (e.g., a subject of conscious states) is what it is in virtue of its intrinsic properties rather than those that are extrinsic to it, such as its causal/relational properties.

These remarks are followed by the bulk of the essay in which I focus on the subject of conscious states or what I have called the conscious self. I sketch out an argument for the conclusion that the conscious self must be accorded the ontological status of a metaphysically basic particular in the philosophically fundamental account of what exists. The conscious self is the center of consciousness and agency, it has a primitive matter-of-fact unity, and it maintains a "strict" identity through time. It is known, in the first instance, only from the first-person viewpoint, as it is directly known in one's experience of being a conscious subject and conscious agent. Contrary to pure-ego theories, psychological construction (e.g., bundle) theories, and non-entity theories, I contend that one has experiential self-awareness that must be understood as direct knowledge of a subject of conscious states and of its persistence through at least brief periods of time. Such awareness is, in part, an awareness of a real agent of deliberate actions, apparently capable of choosing among genuine alternative courses of action.

II

Given the remarkable advance of physical science in general and brain science in particular, the current and widespread appeal of a thoroughgoing naturalism, and the enormous influence that ontological materialism (in one form or another) has in contemporary philosophy of mind, it seems important to make some remarks about why one might take seriously a dualist ontology in such an intellectual environment. The intensive scientific study of human beings has yielded a wealth of information about the physical dimension of our being in its natural setting and provides support for the conviction that any acceptable account of persons must be consistent with a thoroughgoing naturalism. And though the transition from a science-inspired naturalism to a thoroughgoing materialism seems to be an easy one to make, we should resist it. It leads, I contend, to a view laden with difficulties that are nothing less than insuperable.[1]

Any plausible dualist account of persons must be consistent with our being fully embedded in the natural world and deeply embodied in physical organisms (though I do not mean to rule out the possibility of a plausible phenomenalist account of these organisms). These constraints give rise to serious difficulties for the dualist to meet, but these difficulties do not arise from science as such, that is, from either its method of inquiry or from what, strictly speaking, it finds to be the case. One must carefully distinguish what science itself reveals and what one might be importing by way of philosophical assumption or unexamined presupposition into one's interpretation of the scientific findings.

As we consider the significance of scientific findings to the debate about how the mind-body relation is to be understood, we should remind ourselves that the issues dividing materialists and dualists are not issues that scientific investigation alone can settle. Science shows, for example, that brain states are connected to states of consciousness but not that the connection is one of identity. Nor does it show that experience is subjectless or, conversely, that an experiencing subject is intrinsic to consciousness. It is not the role of science to address such matters. Philosophical examination is what is needed.

III

Possessing the resources needed to accommodate the phenomena is a condition that must be met by any acceptable view of human experience and its place in the natural world. An awareness of the importance of being faithful to the phenomena would help account for the lasting appeal of a mental-physical dualism, in one or another of its forms—an appeal that persists in the face of a full awareness of the challenges the dualist must try to meet, of a contemporary intellectual culture that seems inclined to regard dualism as suspicious at best if not entirely misguided, and of the plethora of recent attacks upon dualist views. For at least some forms of mental-physical dualism have an ontology sufficiently rich to possess such resources. By contrast, the various forms of ontological materialism, whether eliminative or reductive (or allegedly "non-reductive"), might well strike one as so many Procrustean beds, either ignoring, distorting, or denying the phenomena that cannot be made to fit the theory.

Consciousness is at the center of the phenomena that must be saved. Accordingly, the first-person viewpoint must be granted epistemic centrality in this arena at least, as it is the only viewpoint from which consciousness can be accessed directly, that is, from which one has direct access to one's own consciousness in its uninterpreted reality, in virtue of having or being in conscious states. This has ontological implications. What is revealed from this viewpoint is revealed only from it, thus implying that the current attempts to treat it as illusory and eliminable or as reducible to the third-person viewpoint are doomed to fail.

The case for believing that we are immediately aware of, or acquainted with, at least some elements of our own conscious states seems nothing less than conclusive. However, it is difficult to fully appreciate the strength of this case without taking seriously the first-person viewpoint as a unique epistemic access and paying careful attention to what is made available to us from that viewpoint. Perhaps it is a failure at precisely this point that leads so many contemporary thinkers to suggest or imply that there is nothing, even in the realm of thought and experience, let alone in the external world, that is epistemically available to us in its original uninterpreted reality. The cognizing powers of the mind leave their track on everything. At the moment any element of experience or thought (or indeed of our introspective awareness of them or of ourselves as subjects of conscious states) becomes epistemically available to us, it is at least conceptualized, if not propositionalized and cast under the form of language as well. Thus the doctrine that language is primary to thought, and that the mind can be externalized, is spawned along with other associated mistakes (or so I contend).

The notion of an immediate and epistemic awareness, or, in other words, a knowledge by acquaintance, merits further comment. Russell's well-known (and, apparently, widely rejected) distinction between knowledge by acquaintance and knowledge by description is a radical one that has not received the attention it deserves. Following Russell, "We shall say that we have *acquaintance* with anything of which we are directly aware, without the intermediary of any process of inference or any knowledge of truth" (Russell 1912, p. 46). Knowledge by acquaintance is non-propositional (not constituted of "knowledge of truth"), nonlinguistic, and apparently nonconceptual as well. It is logically distinct from (and thus irreducible to) knowledge by description. Though in us (as distinct from lower animals) it may always be entangled with that which is contributed by our linguistic and conceptualizing powers (responsible for our descriptive knowledge), it is what, at least in the first instance, they get to work on. Hesitation to call it knowledge should not prevent us from acknowledging its epistemic significance and its role in shaping the original intuition that there is a mind-body problem. It is also the source of the dualist intuition that conscious states cannot be bodily states. Our acquaintance with our own conscious states enables us (or grounds our ability) to see that they cannot be neural or behavioral/functional states, however intimately connected they may be with those physical states. Also, since what is revealed by way of acquaintance transcends whatever can be captured in even the fullest description, the introspectively grounded conviction that the mind-body problem has a depth or dimension to which our descriptions do not do justice becomes quite understandable.

The acquaintance relation is such that we are acquainted with the items related. In first-person terms, I am acquainted with my own conscious states and *my* being in or having them, as well as with their intentional objects (understood broadly enough to include the qualitative sense contents of which we are directly aware). This constitutes a disclosure of what the relata are intrinsically and is the source of our acquaintance-based concepts of them. Thus our general conception of consciousness is acquaintance grounded, as are our concepts of sense qualities. To illustrate, our acquaintance with an instance of a color quality, say, sky-blue, is needed for us to grasp it *as* an instance of that color or *as that* color quality. This interpretive grasp of it is an outcome of the conceptualizing power of thought, which, in this case, is grounded in acquaintance. Thus the ground of such concepts could hardly be more secure.

That we have such knowledge by acquaintance seems incontestable when we try to conceive of what our epistemic condition would be without it. Without any such knowledge of our own conscious states or of their qualitative contents, we would be unable to grasp any of their intrinsic properties. This should strike us as not boding well, if tolerable at all, when we note that physical science informs us only about the structural and relational properties of objects, not about any intrinsic, qualitative properties. Rather, it is by way of our perceptual consciousness of objects that we learn what they are like *qualitatively*. This is the source of our conception of an object (whether taken to be internal or external) as possessing (intrinsic) qualitative properties. But if we have no direct awareness of these properties or of our consciousness of them—of "what it is like" subjectively to experience them—we would have no epistemic exposure to any empirical properties and thus would be unable to form any of the empirical concepts needed to form a conception of the world as it would be if ontological materialism were true. Such views exclude the concepts needed for their own intelligibility.

The problem for such views arises because their inability to accommodate what is available only to the first-person viewpoint ultimately leads them to a behaviorist/dispositionalist-functionalist theory of the mind. One might try to avoid such a theory by espousing a token-identity physicalism (or materialism), arguing that a mental state just is a brain state but accessed differently. It is the different mode of access that explains why a conscious state appears different from the brain state without really being different. But if physicalism is true, this mode of access is just another physical process and thus accessible from the third-person perspective from which brain states are accessed. Thus this explanation of the apparent difference collapses.

And as we noted earlier, knowledge of brain states would not be sufficient for knowledge of the conscious states associated with them as it would not reveal the "topic-rich" elements accessible only to the first-person viewpoint—a reality incompatible with the truth of physicalism. What it would reveal is knowledge only of their causal/relational properties. But without any knowledge of their intrinsic properties, conscious states would have to be regarded as mere powers or dispositions to produce behavior. Since functioning is nothing other than behaving, we have arrived at a behaviorist/dispositionalist-functionalist view of the mind.

Materialism, Dualism, and the Conscious Self   67

It seems clear that an occurrent consciousness can have no place in a physicalist view, and so one's *consciousness* of an intentional content (or object) would have to succumb to dispositional analysis. And if one can know only the causal/relational properties of what certainly seems to be a directly accessible intentional *content* (whether qualitative or cognitive), then a behaviorist/dispositionalist-functionalist analysis of it too appears unavoidable. At this point, however, the incoherence of any view committed to such a (reductive) analysis of the mind becomes clear: such views require for their own intelligibility a conceptual grasp of a non-dispositional, non-reduced reality that they cannot admit. Not only are they unable to accommodate what is disclosed only from the first-person perspective, but they depend on those disclosures for their own intelligibility.

A sketch of an argument for this conclusion begins with a consideration of perceptual consciousness, that is, a consciousness of a perceptual content.[2] Given the constraints of the materialist framework, what such terms as *awareness* and *consciousness* may seem to pick out must in the end be seen either as a linguistically generated illusion, and thus eliminable, or as reducible to behavioral dispositions, perhaps in conjunction with states of the non-dispositional base (i.e., brain states). Leaving aside the apparently insuperable difficulties standing in the way of accepting such an analysis of consciousness itself, let us simply note that, even if deemed adequate, it would not constitute an analysis of the *content* of perceptual consciousness. Since such content is not plausibly held to be an illusion, and since in the views under consideration we have no direct epistemic access to it by which we could come to grasp its intrinsic properties, our knowledge of it is indirect, restricted to its causal, hence relational, properties. We know of it indirectly by knowing its causes or its effects (or both).

But each route is at best a dead end, if it does not end in incoherence. If a conscious state having a perceptual content can be characterized only as that state that is standardly caused by objects stimulating the appropriate sense organs, a topic-neutral characterization of that state becomes unavoidable, as it has no intrinsic, introspectively discernible properties by which it might be identified. But this route blocks any knowledge, either of the perceptual state or of what causes it. Briefly put, if knowledge of the content and type (and thus the identity) of the experience one is having depends, conceptually, upon knowledge of what standardly causes it, and if, as seems obviously the case, any knowledge we can come to have about the objects giving rise to our experiences must depend at some point on the experience we are having (as we have no other epistemic access to anything), then knowledge of either these objects or our experiences is impossible.

The remaining alternative consists in defending the claim that we come to know (indirectly) the contents of our perceptual states by their effects, more specifically, by way of the behavioral dispositions they bring about in us. The identification of the behavioral dispositions we have when having a perceptual experience is of central importance. For they would have to provide our grasp (at least in the minimal sense of an identification) of the contents of such experience and, presumably, enable us to form the empirical concepts that we undeniably have. But the central reason why such accounts seem doomed to fail is that even a minimal understanding of something as complex as that array of dispositions to linguistic and other relevant behaviors, along with their place in the natural order, requires our possession of a broad range of empirical concepts—concepts that must already be in place for an identification of content to occur. We must already possess the empirical concepts needed for a non-reductive grasp of the world and of our behavior in it; for without such a grasp on reality, we would lack the conceptual background necessary to see ourselves as coming to possess behavioral dispositions in response to perceptual stimuli from external objects.

Since the concept of a disposition necessarily depends upon a concept of its non-dispositional base, our having a concept of a behavioral (i.e., physical) disposition must presuppose our having a conception of a physical world in which bodies move and interact in physical space. Thus our having the concept of a behavioral disposition presupposes that we have an understanding of a physical world in which that disposition is embedded—an understanding that cannot itself be understood, reductively, as a disposition to behavior. But a reductive (or dispositional) account of our understanding of perceptual content implies that we get our understanding of a physical world by way of a reductive understanding of that content. Hence, the reductive account of our understanding of perceptual content implies the absurdity that we gain an understanding of the physical world by a process that presupposes that we already have such an understanding.

Similar, and equally devastating, arguments can be advanced against reductive/dispositional accounts of the content of *thought* or *cognition*. If the content of cognition were reducible to what such accounts require, it could not be that by way of which the world becomes accessible to us in thought. Understood in the ordinary way as that through which we come to have some understanding of reality, thought would be impossible.

Such arguments, though sketchy, seem sufficient to reveal the inevitable failure, if not the outright incoherence, of the attempts to deny that we have a direct, irreducible epistemic awareness of at least some of the intrinsic properties of our own conscious states and their intentional contents. They shed some light on why there cannot be a satisfactory materialist treatment of either the qualitative phenomenality of sensory experience or the intentionality of consciousness. The inability to accommodate the uninterpreted (i.e., nonlinguistic, nonconceptual) reality of an irreducible, occurrent (i.e., non-dispositional) consciousness has devastating consequences. But the apparently undeniable existence of a subject of conscious states constitutes another, equally intractable, problem for the (ontological) materialist.

If (as I have argued at length in another context; see Lund 2005) we must acknowledge the uninterpreted reality of a subject of consciousness, the case for ontological materialism is lost. If the subjectivity of experiences is grounded in a subject of conscious states, then it cannot be assimilated to the privileged epistemic access the subject has to its own experiences. The subjectivity of experiences would be intrinsic to them—a property they have in virtue of being the experiential states of their unique subject. Their subjectivity would consist in more than the special way they are known to their subject—a fact that would effectively block any materialist attempt to provide a reductive analysis in which it is treated as a mere epistemic access to something that is accessible from the third-person viewpoint and which may thereby come to be seen as an item in the objective order.

That the existence of a subject with its intrinsic subjectivity constitutes an intractable (if not insurmountable) problem for the materialist becomes apparent in a somewhat different way upon seeing that the uniqueness of a subject is not that of any object. It becomes clear that the subject has a uniqueness that does not consist in uniquely satisfying an individuating description, and this is a uniqueness for which there can be no place in materialist ontology. In first-person terms, there can be no answer to the question as to what it is for some item in the centerless material order to be *me*.

THE CONSCIOUS SELF

I

In the following sections, I will provide a sketch of an argument for the conclusion that the irreducible reality of a subject of conscious states must be acknowledged, that it is an endurer (as contrasted with a perdurer) maintaining a "strict" identity through time, and that it is an immaterial individual. The first part of the argument is an attempt to establish that a subject of conscious states exists and that the source of our knowledge of it is pre-reflective, a knowledge by acquaintance.

It has been widely known ever since Hume that a careful introspective search for the subject or referent of "I" always seems to come up empty. But such failure is not evidence that there is no subject. Since it is the subject that would be what is doing the observing or having the states that Hume introspectively observed, it could not be what is observed in this way. However, there is a deeper reason why introspective observation must fail: unmediated self-awareness is non-observational. To express the difficulty in first-person terms, I would be unable to recognize any object of introspective observation as myself unless I had a non-observational awareness of myself that enabled me to see that it was I who was doing the observing. Though a self that I could introspectively observe (if this were possible) could be none other than myself, I could have no idea that I am that self unless I possessed an awareness of myself that is independent of anything I could learn about myself through any such observation. I might know that a self is introspectively observed and that any self so observed is observed by itself, but I could not know that that self is *myself* if I lacked that primitive non-observational self-awareness needed for me to have any awareness of myself.

Hume's approach may work for any other item that may become an object of the subject's reflective consciousness, for any other item is not what is doing the grasping. The task for the subject is the apparently impossible one of grasping, as an object of its consciousness, what it is in itself—the subject doing the grasping and thus something that always lies beyond its grasp of objects. The subject, though essentially subjective, must be suitably objectified to be apprehended as an object of its consciousness. But this objectified subject, or object of thought, fails to capture the elusive, uninterpreted reality of the subject—the subject for which it is an object of intentional consciousness. At best it will be only a concept or representation of the subject that could provide nothing more than a mediated awareness of the subject itself.

Such considerations (along with the fact that primitive "I"-awareness is non-observational) might lead one to the view that what might be grasped in this way is a mere appearance or "I"-representation of a subject that fails to be a manifestation of a real subject underlying the appearance and that, consequently, experience is to be analyzed as subjectless. So understood, this appearance gets dismissed as, for example, a linguistically generated illusion, intentionally inexistent, or a logical construction. But such views are untenable. Not only does the notion of a single subjectless experience seem to be unintelligible (much as is the notion of a grin divorced from a concept of a face)—a notion without which all forms of subject-eliminationism must fail—but without the singular viewpoint a unitary subject has of its own conscious states, the subject-eliminationist is deprived of the resources needed to provide an adequate account of the synchronic unity of consciousness. Without a subject directly aware of its experiences, an experience would have to satisfy some (mediating) condition to enter along with others into a synchronic unity. But this renders unavoidable the absurd implication that (in first-person terms) I could initially identify a present experience of which I am non-inferentially aware prior to knowing whether it satisfies the supposed condition and thus without knowing whose it is. The absurdity comes into view upon seeing that I cannot identify such an experience at all unless I identify it as my own.

It is absurd to suppose that I first scrutinize such an experience without knowing whose it is, and then, by noting that it satisfies some condition whose satisfaction is necessary and sufficient for its being one of mine, come to see that it belongs to me. If this supposition were true, I could not be aware of any experience as belonging to me and thus would be unable to become aware of myself at all. For I could become aware of myself only by having an experience, and I could become aware of that experience as one of mine only by seeing that it satisfied the condition supposedly appropriate for establishing that it belongs to me. But I could not know that this condition was satisfied by an experience, no matter what the condition is supposed to be, unless I could see that an experience satisfying it was one of my own. And this I would be unable to see, unless I was already, or independently, aware of it as an experience of mine. For without that awareness, I would be unable to tell that this condition is something whose satisfaction by an experience is appropriate for establishing that the experience is one belonging to me. Absurdly, I would need a prior awareness of an experience as one of my own to see that some condition it supposedly satisfied was one whose satisfaction was suitable to establish it as one of mine, even though, by hypothesis, I would be unable to tell *whose* it is prior to seeing that it satisfies the condition. If I could not be aware of either without a prior awareness of the other, then I could not identify any experience as one belonging to me and thus could not become aware of myself at all.[3]

These arguments are part of a cluster of related considerations that, when brought together, amount to a virtual demonstration that there is a form or level of self-consciousness that is entirely unmediated and that denials of its immediacy lead to absurdity. One of these is that third-person information about oneself (i.e., knowledge of oneself by description) is neither necessary nor sufficient for self-consciousness and therefore cannot mediate one's consciousness of oneself. It is not necessary, for such consciousness would remain even if one lost, as in a case of severe amnesia, all third-person information about oneself. Nor is it sufficient. For (in first-person terms) I would be unable to see that the third-person information is information about *me*, unless I were already aware of myself in a first-person way. Put somewhat differently, if I could be aware of myself only by way of some description that applies to me, then I could not be aware of myself at all. For I would have to be aware of myself independently of whatever information the description provided if I am to see that the description is true of *me*—a conclusion that holds for any suggested description, no matter what it is. Self-awareness cannot be mediated by an awareness of any self-identifying property or description, or, more generally, by an awareness of the satisfaction of any self-identifying criterion or condition whatsoever. Since there is no condition whose satisfaction is either necessary or sufficient for self-awareness, it must be an entirely unmediated phenomenon.

Perhaps the existence of an unmediated pre-reflective self-awareness is not, by itself, sufficient to justify the conclusion that this self-awareness is the self-awareness of a subject of conscious states, i.e., that what is known by acquaintance is a subject. For its existence is compatible with the possibility that a subjectless consciousness is (or becomes) aware of itself and thus is in this sense self-aware. But this conclusion is justified, if not rendered undeniable, when the entire case for believing that consciousness cannot be subjectless is taken into account. Among other things, an adequate account of synchronic unity cannot be provided in the absence of a subject immediately aware of its conscious states. Other accounts of synchronic unity imply the absurdities resulting from denying the reality of such a subject.

II

The next major stage in the overall case for acknowledging the reality of a subject maintaining a "strict" identity through time as an immaterial individual consists of an attempt to show that that very subject of which one has knowledge by acquaintance and whose singular viewpoint is needed for any plausible account of synchronic unity is equally important for providing a plausible account of diachronic unity. Diachronic unity rests upon a diachronic singularity made possible by the persistence of the very same subject that provides synchronic singularity.

This extension of the argument is, of course, highly controversial. There are many who would acknowledge that a singular subject is needed for synchronic unity but would nevertheless maintain that for all we know, or have reason to believe, a subject is an ephemeral thing that quickly gets replaced by a successor. They would agree with Kant, who argued that there could be a switching of subjects that goes on unnoticed—the Unnoticed Subject-Switching (USS) hypothesis.[4] But this hypothesis must, I argue, be rejected. The case I have laid out for this conclusion may be roughly divided into five groups of considerations: (1) those concerned with the phenomenology and analysis of memory, (2) those that focus on the continuity of experience, (3) those that pertain to the character and implications of self-knowledge, (4) those that focus on the metaphysics of a subject of consciousness, and (5) those based upon the apparent failure of all the criterial accounts of diachronic identity. Some of these considerations lead to the conclusion that the notion of an undetected succession of subjects, when carefully examined, is not even intelligible. Others indicate that even if it is intelligible, the hypothesis that undetected subject-switching actually occurs is wildly implausible.

Though the elements in the case I lay out are numerous and detailed, a few remarks about them will have to suffice here. Perhaps the first point to note is that without the assumption that a subject is an unexperienced possessor of an experience, whose presence would make no difference to the phenomenology of experience, the USS hypothesis would have little if any initial plausibility. This hypothesis may retain some plausibility in countering those subject-realist views in which the existence of a subject is to be inferred, perhaps to explain the synchronic unity of consciousness or from the need for a second (though unexperienced) term in an acquaintance relation (e.g., from acquaintance with phenomenal color). But if, as I have argued, the subject of consciousness is known by acquaintance and must be accorded uninterpreted reality, the USS hypothesis becomes wildly implausible if not simply unintelligible. For in this view of subject-realism, the first-person character of experiential memory, the necessary duration of what is experienced now, the especially tight or seamless diachronic unity exhibited by many successions of experiences (such as watching a bird fly by, thinking through an argument, and hearing a clock strike twelve),[5] one's grasp of a succession of experiences *as* a succession, and one's sense of continuous agency can be brought with great force against the USS hypothesis.

Thinking through a complex argument is a continuous mental process that requires a sustained mental effort and control of attention throughout its duration. It is a process in which one's role as an agent seems impossible to doubt—an agent who initiates the process and then continuously wills, directs, controls, and sustains it. The continuity of the process seems entirely dependent upon the continuity of agency, which, in turn, renders irresistible the conclusion that the selfsame agent persists throughout the process. Thus the singularity of an agent willing and sustaining the process seems as incontestable as the singularity of the consciousness that is able to grasp the process as a succession of events through which it has persisted. It seems undeniable that if one is acquainted with a subject at the outset of such mental activity in which one's attention is continuously focused on a task, then that acquaintance continues throughout the activity, providing no occasion for an unnoticed subject-switch. One's memory of the activity bears this out. In first-person terms, I have an immunity to the error of misidentifying the subject of a present experience of which I am directly aware—an immunity that seems to be *preserved* in memory.[6] But it seems clear that the best explanation of this would be that part of what I remember in remembering an experience is the unmediated self-awareness I had in having it. To concede this, however, is to reject the USS hypothesis, at least for the relatively short-term memory needed to remember such activity when it terminates.

Even if we were to put aside all of these considerations, which seem more than sufficient to show that the USS hypothesis must be rejected, we should be led to reject it anyway when we come to acknowledge the failure of all the criterial accounts of diachronic identity. If the USS hypothesis were true and, accordingly, many different subjects were constitutively involved in the temporally extended set of experiences (usually) ascribed to a single person, then there would have to be some condition or criterion whose satisfaction by each of the experiences would be what constitutes their all belonging to one and the same person. The need for a criterion would not arise if a single subject persisted and had them all as its states. Their belonging to it would be unmediated, thus not mediated by the satisfaction of a criterion. But, of course, this route is blocked for the USS theorist. Consequently, if persons persist through time and no criterial analysis of their diachronic identity can be provided, the view that they persist in virtue of the persistence of a single selfsame subject would be inescapable.

III

The attempts to provide a criterial analysis of personal identity (i.e., the diachronic identity of persons) are divisible into two groups: (1) those attempting to show that personal identity is constituted by the diachronic identity of the body (or some part of it, viz., the brain) and employ some version of the bodily continuity criterion, and (2) those attempting to show that personal identity is constituted by psychological factors and thus employ some form of the psychological continuity criterion. I have argued elsewhere that each is open to difficulties that seem fatal to it. I have also argued that beyond the difficulties specific to each, there are others that seem crushing to both, and, indeed, to all criterial accounts—difficulties such as to render these accounts either incoherent or so counterintuitive that they are virtually impossible to embrace (see Lund 1994: 191–221; 2005: 195–246). Here I will focus on the difficulties apparently fatal to all criterial accounts.

One difficulty that seems fatal to any criterial view of personal identity arises from the fact that the identification of any experience of which one is non-inferentially aware, whether past or present, must be an identification of it as one's own, independently of any awareness that it satisfies some criterion. A denial of this fact leads to absurdities, some of which we have noted.

A second difficulty of comparable magnitude is a consequence of the fact that any criterion of personal identity is a relation, or pattern of relations, that can conceivably be duplicated. The possibility of the duplication of these relations implies that two persons existing at time t2 could bear to a single person P1 existing at an earlier time t1 those intrinsic relations that would normally constitute the persistence of P1. But to affirm this is to affirm the possibility that two or more persons existing at t2 should turn out to be *identical* to a single person existing at t1—an affirmation that any plausible view should be able to avoid. To deny that identity over time must be a one-one relation is to deny what would seem to be an unshakable truth of logic. Attempts to avoid such a denial have led, in an apparently inevitable way, to highly revisionist, if not extremely counterintuitive, contentions such as that personal identity may be determined extrinsically, that the multiple occupancy thesis and the four-dimensional metaphysics apparently required by it may be applied to persons, and that there is no *de re* modality for concrete things. Among other difficulties, the conception of a person implicit in these contentions seems unintelligible from the first-person viewpoint.

A third difficulty of apparently equal magnitude arises from the inability of any criterial view to avoid the implication that statements of diachronic identity of persons may be indeterminate in truth-value. Since any criterion admits of degrees of satisfaction, and, consequently, of borderline cases of its being satisfied, the metaphysical possibility of borderline cases of personal identity must be acknowledged—cases in which the criterion leaves undetermined the matter of whether a person P2 is identical to an earlier person P1.

Though one's initial response may be to wonder why an unavoidable commitment to the possibility of borderline cases of personal identity should be deemed problematic, especially if one is thinking of a person as just another complex object, the problem comes into view upon seeing how one's diachronic identity appears from the first-person viewpoint. The view that there could be circumstances in which it may be indeterminate as to whether I exist, or in which there may be no fact of the matter as to whom I am then identical to if I do exist, seems unintelligible when one tries to grasp it from a first-person viewpoint. The experiences occurring in such circumstances would have to be something for me if I am to be involved in them at all, but the suggestion that they would be something for me even though it is indeterminate as to whether I am having them seems simply unintelligible when one takes the first-person viewpoint and reflects upon what it is to have experience. The possibility of there being such circumstances is the possibility of someone being only *partly* me. But to suggest such a possibility is as unacceptable as the suggestion that an experience might be only partly mine, or borderline between being mine and being someone else's.

Though such intuitions may be sufficient to show that there can be no indeterminacy in the diachronic identity of persons, they need not stand by themselves. At least two powerful lines of support are implicit in what we have acknowledged to be true of synchronic identity and experience-memory. The first comes into view when we see that there can be no indeterminacy in one's synchronic identity. Since synchronic unity is a primitive matter of fact unity—the unity of a singular subject—there is no room for any indeterminacy here. Moreover, we might remind ourselves that I cannot identify an experience of which I am non-inferentially aware without identifying it as one of my own. Thus, I cannot identify it as borderline between being mine and being someone else's, nor can there be any indeterminacy in the matter of *who* is identifying it. The suggestion that there might be no fact of the matter as to what subject is identifying it seems transparently absurd.

But the fact that there can be no indeterminacy in one's synchronic identity provides powerful support for the conviction that there can be no indeterminacy in one's diachronic identity either. For it seems very difficult to deny that one's synchronic and one's diachronic identity are to be explained in the same way, more specifically, that one's diachronic identity is just the persistence through time of the (determinate) subject one finds oneself to be at a given time. If one's synchronic identity consists in the existence of a subject that is wholly present at a given time and persists through time in virtue of being present in its entirety at each time at which it exists (i.e., persists by enduring), then the entrance of any indeterminacy into one's diachronic identity would be impossible.

The other line of support results from reflecting on the deliverances of experience-memory. An experience that I remember "from the inside" cannot have been on the borderline between being mine and being someone else's. To suppose otherwise is to deny the truth that my immunity to the error of misidentifying myself is preserved in memory, for I identify the experience in question as one *I* had. Either it was had by me, or it did not occur. Moreover, the truth of subject realism can be shown to imply that the notion of q-experience memory is unintelligible, and thus to imply the unintelligibility of the suggestion that I might be q-remembering the experience of someone who was borderline between being me and being someone else (see Lund 2005: 134–140).

IV

The third step in the argument I am presenting is an attempt to show that a subject (or, more fully, a subject-agent) is an immaterial individual or particular. The argument is of a modal type and proceeds to the conclusion that a subject-agent has modal properties that no physical particular can possess. It attempts to show that (in first-person terms) it is (metaphysically) possible for me to exist, as subject-agent, in the absence of all physical particulars or in isolation from them (e.g., as disembodied), but not possible for any physical particular to exist or to constitute what I would be, under such conditions. If this hypothesis is sound, then it shows that, considered as a subject-agent, I am not a physical particular. But my explication of it here must be exceedingly brief.

I have argued that we can attain a clear and distinct conception of disembodiment, that the conceivability is of the relatively unproblematic positive kind, that clarity of the conception rules out manifest inconsistency, and that distinctness rules out (or at least minimizes the likelihood of) any latent incoherence or inconsistency by assuring that what is clearly conceived is conceived as possessing all of its whatness-specifying properties and thus as self-contained. Any concern that this conception establishes only an epistemic possibility of failing to include some essential property of the mental self or subject, perhaps a necessary connection to the body knowable only a posteriori, is allayed by showing that the content of conscious states is internal and thereby showing the epistemic transparency of the conceivability data available to the internal perspective employed in arriving at the conception.

V

Before closing I will make some brief comments about why there need not be serious concern about the intelligibility of either dualistic causation or the notion of a subject-agent, conceived as a basic, concrete individual, persisting through time as the numerically same individual while undergoing qualitative and relational change. In regard to the latter concern, it can be shown that subjects fare at least as well as objects with respect to both their individuation and their diachronic identity.[7] Perhaps a greater challenge lies in identifying some qualitative characteristic (as distinct from some basic capacity and from its non-dispositional ground) that is intrinsic (i.e., characterizes the subject as it is in itself, independently of its relations to other things) and essential to the subject's existence. This challenge may seem especially serious upon considering the issue of whether the subject continues to exist during periods of apparent unconsciousness, that is, periods characterized by the apparent absence of any *intentional* consciousness. But a variety of plausible responses to this challenge are available to the dualist, not the least of which involves an appeal to the notion of non-intentional conscious states.

Similarly, a commitment to dualistic causation does not lead to intractable difficulties, whether causation is conceived as irreducible or as reducible to noncausal properties. Clearly, how causation itself is to be conceived is a central issue in this context, and so one cannot simply assume that the conditions necessary for physical-physical causation are necessary conditions for all causation. Also, the significance that the experience of intentional causation has for the intelligibility issue should be acknowledged. Even if the impression of exercising causal power in intentional causation should, in fact, turn out to be an illusion, it could nevertheless provide the content for a conception of one's having such power and thus serve to make intelligible the claim that one has.

One might, of course, acknowledge that dualistic causation is intelligible and yet maintain that such causation does not occur in the actual world, perhaps appealing to the view that the physical world is causally closed. But this view is very difficult to defend, especially when the intelligibility of dualistic causation is acknowledged. The phenomenology of reflective consciousness, in particular, renders irresistible the conclusion that one is exercising causal power over one's own thought. It would seem that one's epistemic ground for this conviction could not be more secure, as it consists in one's acquaintance with one's own conscious states. But with respect to the experience of causal power, reflective consciousness is indistinguishable from willing to move one's body. For these reasons, among others, the conclusion that in virtue of one's (nonphysical) conscious states one *does* affect the physical realm seems unavoidable: the physical realm is not causally closed. It is a conclusion grounded in the phenomenology of volitional experience and reflective consciousness. By contrast, the causal closure thesis is highly theoretical and all-inclusive in its scope, asserting that all physical effects, known and unknown, have physical causes sufficient for their occurrence. Given this epistemic difference along with our far from complete knowledge of the workings of the brain, the conclusion that the physical order is not causally closed is the far more justifiable one to draw, at least at the present time.

I now bring to a close my relatively brief explication and defense of the view that a person is (or, at any rate, necessarily includes) a conscious self and that a conscious self is an immaterial center of consciousness and agency. I recognize, of course, that such a view may seem quite difficult to accept, despite an awareness of the extensive and detailed argument (part of which I have presented here) that may be advanced in its defense. If this is true, it may be helpful to remind ourselves of the formidable difficulties that must be confronted in any view purported to provide a philosophically adequate account of persons. For the subject matter at issue may prove to be such that it can never be brought fully within our grasp, in which case all our views of it must fail from a God's-eye standpoint. But if so, we could still evaluate them in relation to one another. And if we do that, we should see my efforts here as part of a more extensive attempt to show that the view summarized in these pages, though clashing head on with so much contemporary thought about consciousness and persons, is, in fact, more defensible than any of the views with which it clashes.

NOTES

1. I have argued at length for this conclusion in my (1994). See also Foster (1991), Madell (1988), and Robinson (1982).
2. I owe many of the insights expressed in the following argument to H. Robinson. See Robinson (1994: 119–150).
3. For an extensive and carefully argued treatment of such considerations, see Madell's (1981) highly impressive work. I owe much to his work on the self.
4. Kant has famously argued for this hypothesis. See Kant (1929: A364n).
5. J. Foster provides a careful treatment of the continuity of experience that, among other things, amounts to an impressive argument against the USS hypothesis. See Foster (1991).
6. S. Shoemaker's argument for this conclusion is, apparently, widely accepted. See Shoemaker (1966).
7. See Lund (2005: 327–340). See also the excellent article by J. Hoffman and G. Rosenkrantz (1991).

Part 2

Dualism and Empirical Research

5 Neuroscience: Dualism in Disguise

Riccardo Manzotti, Paolo Moderato

In this chapter, we have two goals. First, we want to highlight a surprising fact that is often denounced but seldom believed—namely that most of current neuroscientists, contrary to often-heralded physicalist credo, embrace dualism. Second, we want to introduce an original explanation of such a fact—an explanation that casts a disturbing light on many notions of current usage in the field of neuroscience. We will claim that the implicit assumptions adopted by most neuroscientists invariably lead to some sort of dualistic framework.

The observation that neurosciences are based on a dualistic conceptual framework is by no means new (Bennett and Hacker 2003; Hurley and Noë 2003; Rockwell 2005; Uttal 2001, 2004). On the contrary, it keeps resurfacing with the same regularity with which most neuroscientists keep forgetting it.

One of the first to emphasize the intrinsic dualism of neuroscience has been John Dewey who claimed that "the older dualism of soul and body has been replaced by that of the brain and the rest of the body" (Dewey 1916: 336). Similar opinions have been expressed again and again (Gibson 1979; Holt 1914; Varela, Thompson and Rosch 1991; Whitehead 1925). In a strikingly similar note, Bennett and Hacker warn against a mutant form of Cartesianism lurking in neuroscience:

> It was a characteristic feature of Cartesian dualism to ascribe psychological predicates to the mind, and only derivatively to the human being. Sherrington and his pupils Eccles and Penfield cleaved to a form of dualism in their reflections on the relationship between their neurological discoveries and human perceptual and cognitive capacities. Their successors rejected the dualism [. . .] but the predicates which dualists ascribe to the immaterial mind, the third generation of brain neuroscientists applied unreflectively to the brain instead (Bennett and Hacker 2003: 72).

In this regard, the philosopher Ted Honderich prefers to speak of *cranialism* (Honderich 2006a, 2006b). Recently, a very similar notion has been further developed by Teed Rockwell who, in a provocative book, made the claim that

> Modern physicalists have kept the brain-body distinction even though they have thrown away the mind-body distinction, and are thus left with a philosophy of mind that is still in many ways fundamentally Cartesian: Descartes said the soul was in the brain, and identity theorists say the soul is the brain. Descartes' basic concept of mind is not really changed; it is simply demoted to being a concept referring to a particular kind of physical thing (Rockwell 2005: xi).

Hereafter, for coherence, we will make use of Rockwell's choice of words and thus we will refer to Cartesian Materialism to refer to a kind of disguised dualism. In this chapter, we will consider the various causes that determined this curious state of affairs and that lead neuroscience to embrace implicitly what it is, more often than not, publicly rejected. One of the main objectives of this chapter is to show that the standard premises of neuroscience invariably lead to a dualistic framework.

As a proof of the dualism pervading neuroscience, consider these two examples. The first is offered by Christof Koch when summarizing his life of research of the nature of phenomenal experience:

> Subjectivity is too radically different from anything physical for it to be an emergent phenomenon . . . I see no way for the divide between unconscious and conscious creatures to be bridged by more neurons. Experience, the interior perspective of a functioning brain, is something fundamentally different from the material thing causing it and that it can never be fully reduced to physical properties of the brain . . . I believe that consciousness is a fundamental, an elementary, property of living matter. It can't be derived from anything else; it's a simple substance (Koch 2012: 118–119).

So much for the reductionist stance professed in the title! The other example comes from the late Benjamin Libet who remarked "as a neuroscientist investigating these issues for more than thirty years, I can say that these subjective phenomena are unpredictable by knowledge of neuronal function" (Libet 2004: 5).

The structure of the chapter is as follows: First, we will outline the theoretical landscape in which neuroscience is trying to grasp the nature of the mind and that of consciousness. In particular, we will focus on the role of internalism. Then, in the next section, we will show the empirical and conceptual difficulties facing neuroscience when tackling with the issue of consciousness. In the third section, we will outline the main argument—namely that the empirical and theoretical obstacles, plus the internalist assumption, issue ontological promissory notes. In short, since it is impossible to locate consciousness inside neural activity, scholars introduce fictitious entities as foundations of phenomenal experience. This is a preposterous form of dualism in disguise—publicly despised and privately practiced—that hampers any further understanding of the nature of the mind.

1. NEUROSCIENCE IMPLICIT ASSUMPTIONS

Neurosciences are not metaphysically innocent, as they would like to be. Although many scientists claim that their work is free from any undemonstrated ontological premises, this is not (and cannot be) the case. Any empirical data needs to be interpreted from the perspective of some premise. In this case, what are the assumptions on which most of neuroscientific research is based? Let us consider a quick overview of current neuroscientific discussion about the mind.

A first element is the supposed centrality of neuroscience in the study of the mind. It is a fact that a majority of neuroscientists and philosophers alike believe that only the study of neural activity will result in the explanation of the mind. Consider the title of recent book from a well-respected philosopher of the mind like Jessie Prinz: *The Conscious Brain* (Prinz 2012). The title itself reveals the central tenet of Prinz's work—namely that the mind is a property of the brain alone. The widespread consensus in science is that neuroscience is going to be the field that will finally provide a scientific theory of consciousness. The prevailing belief is that "the mind arises from the wetware of the brain" (Modha et al. 2011: 62). Neuroscience is proposing itself as the forthcoming *mindscience* (Manzotti and Moderato 2010).

Christof Koch fleshed out the gist of most neuroscientific approaches: "The goal [of neuroscience] is to discover the minimal set of neuronal events and mechanisms jointly *sufficient* for a specific conscious percept" (Koch 2004: 16, italics in the original). This is a rather precise claim: not only the brain as a whole is expected to produce the mind, but parts of the mind are taken to be the result of the activity going on in parts of the brain (Crick and Koch 1990). Yet, so far, this hypothesis has never been demonstrated empirically. Just to be clear, what is at stake is not whether neural activity has a role in enabling and tuning conscious experience but whether there is a given neural activity that is either sufficient for or identical with a given phenomenal experience.

A second element is that, in reality, neuroscience is mostly a physiological field of enquiry. Its methods are suited to study the activity of the CNS and its cells. In this regard, neuroscience has had incredible success during the last century. As of Golgi and Cajal's time, neurophysiologists unfolded the cellular foundations of our nervous system (Changeux 2001; Gazzaniga, Mangun and Ivry 1998; Kandel, Schwartz and Jessel 1991; Marijuàn 2001). The study of the nervous system has been carried out at all level of analysis and details, from the biochemistry of neurotransmitters up to the computational models of huge cortical networks (Aizawa 2007). Currently, full-fledged models of large portions of the cortex are available, and many research groups are struggling to reproduce a complete working model of the cortex (Ananthanarayanan, Esser, Simon and Modha 2009; Modha et al. 2011; Sporns, Tononi and Kötter 2005; Sporns 2011; The Human Brain Project 2011). However, as amazing as these findings are, this is not exactly the same as studying the mind—an activity for which *neurosciences have not specific skills nor methods.*

A third element consists in a systematic confusion between physicalism and internalism—namely the hypothesis that if the mind is a physical phenomenon, it takes place as a result of neural activity. It is a view that the influential philosopher Jaegwon Kim stated crystal clear: "If you are a physicalist of any stripe, as most of us are, you would likely believe in the local supervenience of qualia—that is, qualia are supervenient on the internal physical/biological states of the subject" (Kim 1995: 160). It is a surprising confusion, since physicalism is the thesis that whatever the mind is it has to correspond to a physical phenomenon. However, this thesis does not entail in any way that the mind has to be *internal to the CNS*. Of course, if internalism would turn out to be true (and it is an empirical question), internalism would be a particular case of physicalism. For instance, behaviorism was definitely a physicalist view, although it was not an internalist one (Watson 1913; Hull 1943). We cannot rule out the possibility that there might be future forms of physicalism rejecting internalism.

It may turn out that internalism is false while physicalism is true. For instance, there are a handful of authors taking into consideration that physical constituents may be physically outside the CNS (Chemero 2009; Manzotti 2006, 2011; Rockwell 2005). It is surprising that so many scholars (Kim is one of the most notable examples) confuse physicalism with internalism.

A fourth element is a kind of historical inertia that neuroscience has accumulated during its development. For many neuroscientists, the final surrender of the mind to neuroscience is neither a philosophical thesis nor an explicit empirical hypothesis. It is just what they take for granted. It is so obvious, that it appears superfluous to state it. Neuroscience is based on a history of successes that originates in medical sciences.

Since the first autopsies at the end of the Middle Ages, medicine has had an enormous success by locating various phenomena inside the patient's body: from infection to blood pressure, from metabolism to movement, and so forth. As a paradigmatic example, consider the discovery of muscular strength inside the myofibrils by Luigi Galvani in the eighteenth century. He was able to make important progress because he was able to locate a function (movement and strength) inside an organ (muscles and myofibrils). The same explanatory template has been applied again and again. Many scholars are quite confident that in order to explain consciousness rather than idle philosophical speculation "a more practical approach is to use the tools of neuroscience that are available now to shed light on the neural structures and activity patterns that underlie consciousness" (Tononi and Koch 2008: 239). As a result, in neuroscience, there are great expectations that the solutions to the problem of consciousness must respect the traditionally successful strategy—namely to single out a proper internal organ (likely the brain).

This successful strategy is still dominant. Like the stomach is the organ for digestion, like the lungs are the organ for respiration, like the heart is the organ for blood circulation, so the brain *has to be* the organ for the mind. At least, this is the prevailing expectation in science nowadays. Yet, it is just an expectation. It may turn out that the mind requires something totally unexpected—either new empirical data or a new conceptual twist. As we will see in the next section, against all expectations, neuroscience is still a far cry from naturalizing the mind.

To recap, the widespread beliefs in neuroscience may be articulated and synthesized in two independent and autonomous premises:

1) The mind is physical [DR, *dualism rejection*].
2) The part of the physical world which is sufficient to the mind is the brain (or some suitable proper part of the CNS) [NC, Neural Chauvinism].

The first premise is tantamount to a denial of dualism. The second premise is akin to what Alva Noë and Evan Thompson dubbed the "thesis of the minimally sufficient neural substrate" that is that "for every conscious state, there is a minimal neural substrate that is nomically sufficient (as a matter of natural law) for its occurrence" (Noë and Thompson 2002: 4). We won't discuss the first premise here. However, we will argue that neurosciences embrace both (and they don't have to) and that, by doing so, they are surprisingly compelled to adopt of form of camouflaged dualism.

As anticipated, these two premises together have the surprising consequence to develop a kind of dualistic picture of the mind in which there is, on one side, the world and, on the other side, the mind. This conceptual outcome is akin to the aforementioned Rockwell's Cartesian Materialism. However, it is not the end of the story. In fact, the same premise also compels neuroscientists to use a terminology that keeps separate the mental domain from the physical domains of neurons.

2. NEUROSCIENCE AND THE REPETITIVE FAILURE TO ADDRESS CONSCIOUSNESS

The previous two premises would not lead necessarily to dualism if it weren't because of neuroscience's failure to locate any phenomenon that may confidently be deemed as being identical with consciousness. In fact, the original formulation inside neurophysiology has been concocted in terms of identity theory (Feigl 1958; Smart 1959). However, identity theory was a failure.

According to Roger Sperry, "from the objective experimental standpoint, it is difficult to see any place in the material brain process for the likes of conscious experience" (Sperry 1969: 532). As result, the repetitive failure to substantiate the identity theory pushed many to withdraw from weaker forms of explanation such as emergence or correlation. Yet, identity theory was the original and natural choice for neurophysiology. It is a fact that any other scientific field of enquiry is based on identity theory. Consider genetic inheritance. Scientists have been looking for the obvious choice: some phenomenon that was the carrier of genetic information. In that case, the identity option was so obvious that it wasn't even discussed. But in the case of neuroscience it is far from obvious, very far.

In this section, we want to stress once again that, so far, neuroscience has been utterly unable to find any convincing physical phenomenon able to play the role of phenomenal experience. This incapability, which is likely the symptom of some wrong premise, has been eventually glorified as a feature of the mind-body problem. From a scientific perspective, there are only three viable options: the first is to admit failure, the second is some form of eliminativism, the third is denial. Apparently, failure is not an option, and eliminativism is no longer fashionable (an exception is, of course, represented by authors like McGinn or Dennett). As we will see, denial is the preferred choice by the scientific community. Denial takes the form of dualism in disguise.

As to consciousness, is the neuroscience situation really so desperate? We are afraid it is. For many years, neuroscience adopted a "don't ask don't tell" strategy with respect to consciousness:

> The already existing fields that study the mind or the brain have ignored consciousness. Psychology, behavioral science, cognitive science and cognitive neuroscience have avoided consciousness or have been reluctant to put subjective experience into the focus of their research programs (Revonsuo 2010: xxi).

Then, as for the '90s—thanks both to the enthusiasm triggered by new techniques for brain visualization and to the interests expressed by famous scientists—neurosciences discovered consciousness (Crick 1994; Edelman 1989; Jennings 2000; Miller 2005; Penrose 1989). The difference between mental processes and their alleged neural underpinnings results in heated discussion as to the causal role of neural activity (Lingnau, Benno and Caramazza 2009). Yet, this enthusiasm was not so successful as many hoped. In 1976, the neurophysiologist E. Roy John maintained that "we do not understand the nature of [. . .] the physical and chemical interactions which produce mental experience (John 1976: 2). In 1989, the psychologist Sutherland was still complaining that "[c]onsciousness is a fascinating but elusive phenomenon; it is impossible to specify what it is, what it does, or why it evolved. Nothing worth reading has been written on it" (Sutherland 1989).

Even Koch in his last book admitted that currently there is no clear model as to how neural activity becomes conscious experience (Koch 2012).

How can this situation endorse the enthusiasm that other authors seems to profess? Consider Prinz's statement that "these twenty-five years of inquiry have borne much fruit. Stepping back from this great mass of research, one can find various strands of evidence that point toward a satisfying and surprisingly complete theory of how consciousness arises in the human brain" (Prinz 2012: 3). Isn't this statement inconsistent with the perduring lack of results as to the physical nature of phenomenal experience?

The answer hides in a common misunderstanding. In fact, to a certain extent, Prinz is right. We know a lot more about the neural processes enabling conscious experience. Thanks to neuroscience, we know a lot more about the neural processes *involved* with arousal, sleep, memory, perception, free will, motor control, and imagery. Unfortunately, we don't know anything about the physical processes that *gives rise* to consciousness or, more poignantly, about the physical processes that *are* consciousness itself. This is a sort of confusion that hampers the discussion about consciousness in neuroscience.

One thing is to show that a neural process plays a role in tuning, enabling, and modifying a moment of consciousness. In this regard, any empirical evidence of this kind is scientifically of high interest, and it may possibly lead to a future breakthrough as to the nature of consciousness. But, *per se*, it does not tell anything about the nature of conscious experience itself. Consider the heating system in Jane's flat. Jane ignores whether it is the result of burning oil, burning gas, or electricity. However, in the basement, Jane discovered a control device that allows her to enable and tune heating. Jane discovers also that there are reliable correlations between the state of the control device switches and the resulting heating. Is the control device actually doing any heating? Of course not. Right now, most of neuroscientific data about consciousness are akin to the relation between Jane's control device and heating. There is a correlation, but scientists do not have a clue as to why such neural activity should result in conscious experience.

As a proof of such a lack of real progress between current neuroscientific data and theories and consciousness, consider this question:

> Is there any neural activity that, at the best of our knowledge, may not happen without any consciousness?

For instance, consider the activity in the fusiform gyrus that we know is strongly correlated with conscious perception of faces (Andrews, Schluppeck, Homfray, Matthews and Blakemore 2002; Kanwisher 2001; O'Craven and Kanwisher 2000). Let's skip the fact that the activity in the fusiform gyrus is not always correlated with conscious experience (Steeves et al. 2006). Even if fusiform activity and conscious perception were perfectly correlated (and they aren't), is there any reason why such a neural activity couldn't occur without any consciousness? We are not aware of any. What would happen if we were able to replicate the same neural activity in a piece of neural tissue in a lab? On this possibility, Ned Block replied that he never heard anyone stating "that if a fusiform face area were kept alive in a bottle, the activation of it would determine face-experience—or any experience at all" (Block 2007: 482).

The same argument holds for all known neural activity. There are no compelling reasons why a neural activity may not occur without any correlated conscious experience. This highlights the big difference with other phenomena, which have been more thoroughly explained. Consider heat. Could we increase the average speed of molecules without increasing heat? No, that would be impossible because heat is the average speed of molecules. Alternatively, could we change the number of hydrogen ions in a liquid without changing its acidity? No, because we know what the relation between hydrogen ions and acidity is. Nevertheless, notwithstanding the impressive amount of collected data, there is no known neural process whose occurrence may not take place in the absence of conscious experience. Maybe there is. The point here is that we don't know of any.

If the mind is not identical with neural activity, there should be some kind of explanation of when, why, and how neural activity brings mental content into existence. So far, neuroscience is not even trying to do this. In the past, it mostly tried to debunk such puzzles by claiming they were ill-posed problems. This scapegoat is no longer acceptable. In order to define the mechanisms that generate a specific conscious experience, we need "to understand the conditions that determine what kind of consciousness a system has" (Tononi 2004: 1). Even if it were possible to identify a neural correlate of consciousness, why should a specific physical process lead to the occurrence of a specific phenomenal experience?

On the basis of which law? Currently, there are no psychophysical laws bridging the gap between physical and mental processes. What we ought to expect from neuroscience is some law of the form

Mental content = F (neural activity)

Where *F* represents a law expressing a correspondence between neural activity and mental content. If anything like *F* were available, it would be straightforward to define a sufficient NCC (neural correlates of consciousness. For instance, the sufficient NCC of my conscious percept of red, C_{red}, would be the neural activity N_{red} occurring in my brain, such that $C_{red} = F(N_{red})$. Up to now, *F* is nowhere to be seen. *F* would endorse an internalist view of consciousness—namely that consciousness is something concocted out of the ongoing neural activity in the brain.

The main reason for the continuous failure of neuroscience to address consciousness is that the chasm between conscious experiences runs as deep as science itself. Modern science originated as a result of a crude oversimplification—namely the separation between phenomenal qualities and quantitative properties (Galilei [1623] 1960). While the former has become hostage of philosophy and psychology, the latter have given rise to the impressive development of science. To recap, modern science expunged the conscious mind from its description of nature, and thus it obtained a simplified but very efficacious picture of physical reality. Yet, sooner or later, the chickens have to come to roost. How is it possible to deal with the mind once the mental aspects of nature have been methodically and, we would add, a priori eschewed from reality? It is like declaring that there are no forces acting at a distance and then trying to explain gravity. Something is not going to work.

Consider Prinz's definition of physicalism (2012: 11) as the "the conjecture that the fundamental laws and elementary parts that we find in things that lack mentality are the only fundamental laws and elementary parts in the universe". It is a surprising definition based on the mental domain admitting as physical entities only those "things that lack mentality". It is questionable for at least two reasons. First, this definition is parasitical on the mental. Second, it rejects a priori that the mental may be part of the physical.

To make a long story short, neuroscience cannot tackle consciousness because the essential properties of the mind have been programmatically and selectively set aside from the physical world. The list of such properties is not exactly the same although there is a consensus on the main ones: quality, unity, duration, intentionality, and first-person perspectives.

At present, neuroscience does not have a clue as to what is the relation between neural activity and consciousness. We learned a great deal on neural mechanisms that influence our conscious experience. Yet, nobody can predict for sure that a certain chemical activity is going to produce a phenomenal experience—not to speak of predicting what kind of phenomenal content. Of course, neuroscientists collected an impressive amount of evidence as to which neural activity is correlated to which phenomenal experience. It is enough to check the available literature either on anesthesia or on perception to see the extent to which we know the details of neural activity correlated with phenomenal experience (Mashour and LaRock 2008; Morimoto, Nogami, Harada, Tsubokawa and Masui 2011; Watkins-Pitchford and Brull 1997). But nothing in the literature explains why a certain neural phenomenon should produce a certain phenomenal experience. The evidence so far collected is just brute data.

Neuroscience faces an impossible mission—namely showing how a physical world which had been a priori defined devoid of those properties that are essential for the mind (unity, intentionality, quality, duration, and causation) may contain/produce those properties. This mission is taken to be somehow possible because inside the brain it is expected that something out of the ordinary may indeed happen. Yet, this would be mostly unexpected and indeed contrary to the starting premises. In this regard, J.J.C. Smart observed that

> There does seem to be, so far as science is concerned, nothing in the world but increasingly complex arrangements of physical constituents. All except for one place: in consciousness . . . So sensations, states of consciousness, do seem to be the one sort of thing left outside the physicalist picture, and for various reasons I just cannot believe that this can be so (Smart 1959: 142).

We do share Smart's concerns. It would be quite surprising, to say the least, to discover that the brain is the only place in the universe where awareness arises.

3. NEUROSCIENCE LEADS TO DUALISM: EPISTEMIC ENTITIES AND ONTOLOGICAL PROMISSORY NOTES

The rejection of dualism and internalism—together with the inability to single out a physical phenomenon identical with consciousness—determines three alternative outcomes: either eliminativism, identity theory, or dualism. The argument is as follows:

1) Neuroscience, for the reasons previously seen, rejects dualism and holds true internalism.
2) As a result, consciousness must be physically located in the brain.
3) So far, in the brain there is no empirical evidence of any phenomenon with the properties of phenomenal experience—namely intentionality, quality, unity, and first person perspective.
4) From a conceptual perspective, since the physical world is devoid of the aforementioned properties and since the brain is part of the physical world, in the brain there cannot be anything with such properties.
5) To conceal 2) and 3) and 4), neuroscience adopts an explanatory strategy that consists in presenting the mind as if it were in the brain. Mental properties are here but not like physical stuff. They are there, and they are not there.
6) That strategy consists in adopting a confuse terminology that makes use of ontological promissory notes such as code-talk, information-talk, computation-talk, and model-talk.
7) That strategy ends up concocting a form of dualism in disguise. They have the logical form of dualism, but they don't want to pay the ontological price for it.

As previously stressed, neither is internalism implied by physicalism nor is it the result of any empirical evidence. It is a hypothesis that got very wide acceptance both into the neuroscientific community and into the philosophical community. Inevitably, this hypothesis entails that something special is going on inside the CNS—something that contradicts the idea that the physical world is devoid of mental properties. In fact, if the world is devoid of them, the brain, which is a part of the world, should be devoid too. Something conflicts.

Frankly speaking, the impression is that internalism's adoption and its inability to find any phenomenon akin to consciousness call back into service the ghost in the machine—albeit in disguise. Yet, this outcome runs afoul of the heralded rejection of dualism. This rather embarrassing situation resulted in entering into debt with ontology by ontological promissory notes that, so it is promised, will be paid back in the future.

In very loose terms, the sleight of hand is the following. The CNS is presented as the place where the mind ought to take place. Unfortunately, the mind does not look like anything material we may find *inside* the CNS. This is often quite embarrassing. Usually the blame is put on consciousness rather than on any potentially wrong premises. Anyway, at this point of the discussion, some other entity—which is not exactly a physical thing but that has some allure of scientific respectability like information, coding, computation, maps, representations, and symbols—is usually introduced in our description of what's going on inside the CNS to fill the gap. Since the hop from neural activity to consciousness appears disheartening, an intermediate stage is introduced. The intermediate entity plays thus the role of an ontological promissory note. It is something that is not really there, at least in material terms, but that nevertheless plays some role. After a suitable amount of discussion, the entity gain sufficient scientific respectability and epistemic prestige to be accepted as the special ingredient that will justify the appearance of the white rabbit of consciousness out of the brain-hat.

Consider information. Is information something more than the physical basis that implements it? This is unlikely, at least for a physicalist. Take my pocket calculator. If it rests on my desk, does it contain information? If it is still in the sealed box from the manufacturer, does it? Isn't it the same from a physical perspective?

Isn't it is just a piece of electronic junk that has a clever causal structure carved in its circuits? This clever causal structure is such that a human being may use the pocket calculator to do math. However, is there anything like information in addition to the causal and physical structure of the pocket calculator? We would rule out such an option because there is no physical mean to measure whether there is anything like information inside it. The pocket calculator may be described adopting an informational stance once a human being uses it to do math. Yet, a human being is able to do so in virtue of having a mind. Moreover, this brings us back to the usual problem of the mind.

Take a mark on a blackboard. Does it contain/bear/connect with a bit of information? How could we know it? We claim that there is no way to do it without knowing whether that mark is used by a human being to represent information. Since we assume that one may use that mark, we attribute to that mark a bit of information. However, information is not there like the mass of the chalk that was used to mark the blackboard. We can check whether that mark, which is a physical object, has mass, charge, length, and so forth. We cannot check whether that mark has information. The same mark may be associated with 1 bit of information or with terabytes of information. It depends on whom and how its physical structure is exploited to connect external causal states of other systems.

In sum, the ontology of information is murky at best. Information is not equivalent with mass, charge, length, and the rest of physical properties. Without any pretense of originality (Floridi 2004; Landauer 1992; Manzotti 2012; Searle 1980), the intuition here is that information is just an epistemic entity. By epistemic entity, we refer to things like a center of mass that does not exist but that are useful concepts. We are not claiming that information is not an important scientific notion. We claim that a theory of information is something different from a theory of electricity. Thus, we stress the ontological lightness of such a notion when it comes to be the basis for further phenomena (consciousness included). Once again, we suggest that information (or computation, modelling, representing, and so forth) is like the notion of the center of mass. In fact, where the center of mass is supposed to be, there may be an empty space. The center of mass is a useful notion, which is the result of our mathematical description of gravity that benefits from assuming that the mass of a body, instead of being spread in a large volume, is concentrated into an ideal point—namely the center of mass. Useful as it is, the center of mass is nothing but an epistemic fiction introduced to simplify computations of gravity forces. The center of mass is particularly convincing because the body dynamics is such that, in many cases, their behavior is as if their mass were concentrated in their center of mass. However, it is only as if. The mass remains spread everywhere the body extends.

When an epistemic entity is used as if it were able to carry on ontological work, it becomes an ontological promissory note. There is nothing wrong in using terms such as centers of mass or information as long as they are taken to be ontologically empty. For instance, suppose that one develops a theory about dark matter such as that dark matter is explained in terms of centers of mass. The theory may be so difficult to verify that the focus on its complexity may distract from the simple fact that it doomed to fail since it is based on ontological promissory notes—that is, on nothing.

Here, we suggest that the hallmark of an epistemic entity is that i) it is something that cannot be ascertained in isolation and that ii) it does not add anything to the causal description of the world. Consider again the center of mass. There is no way to check whether a point in space is a center of mass just by inspecting the proposed location. Furthermore, one could dispense from using the very notion of the center of mass by referring to the actual mass distribution.

Similarly, any attempt to build a theory of consciousness based on vague epistemic entities is condemned to be unsuccessful. Consciousness is a real

Neuroscience: Dualism in Disguise 93

phenomenon. It needs to be grounded on ontologically real entities not just on epistemic entities. Information does not appear to be the right building block.

A nice example of this questionable epistemic strategy is offered by the neuroscientist Ronald Melzack and his neuromatrix theory that "proposes that pain is a multidimensional experience produced by characteristic 'neurosignature' patterns of nerve impulses generated by a widely distributed neural network . . . in the brain" (Melzack 2005: 1378). Once again, we are faced with a vague notion that is neither mental nor completely physical. On top of the mere physical neural activity, we have patterns characterized by neurosignatures. Are these neurosignatures something more than the physical world? Because if they are just physical, they cannot have any mental features (like pain). If they are more than physical, then Melzack is advocating a form of dualism where the pattern/impulse dichotomy substitutes the traditional mental/physical dichotomy. Yet the logical structure remains the same.

A similar dichotomy appears in the work of most neuroscientists (see Table 1). Consider Haggard who is compelled to resort to a curious combination of terms such as "conscious awareness" as if there could by anything like unconscious awareness. Or consider the widespread use of terms like "interpretation", "coding", "mental states", and "mental content" (Haggard 2002; Haynes and Rees 2006; Kay, Naselaris, Prenger and Gallant 2008; Nishimoto et al. 2011), not to speak of other popular tools of trade such as "map" and "computations" (Li 2002; Roe, Pallas, Hahm and Sur 1990; Shagrir 2012; Wandell and Winawer 2011). We have no pretense to exhaust the literature here. Libraries have been written on it.

Consider another favorite example of neuroscientific jargon—modelling. Neural activity models reality. Many neuroscientists find scientifically acceptable the idea that the brain builds a model of the world. For instance, Thomas Metzinger suggested that the mind is the result of a multilayered

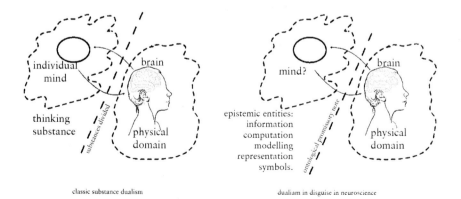

Figure 5.1

structure of models: "The subjective experience of being someone emerges if a conscious information-processing system operates under a transparent self-model . . . you constantly confuse yourself with the content of the self-model currently activated by your brain" (Metzinger 2003: 1). It is a revealing sentence that shows how an intermediate level (ontologically empty) such as that of the "self-model" is used as a foundation for the mind. In order to achieve scientific respectability, the notion is backed up by the whole repertoire of usual scientific-friendly epistemic entities: "information-processing", "emergence", "operation", and "self-model". The notion of "self-model" is proposed as the cornerstone on which the mental manifold develops. However, it is a move that shifts the weight of the mental domain on the intermediate notion of model. It does not solve it.

We are not against the notion of the model. It is a very useful notion like that of information. However, if one speaks of modelling as a generic way to say that, because of certain modifications in the neural structure, a brain is able to deal in a causally efficacious way with certain events, fine. The problem is that one cannot use the word "model" as if it would refer to something real.

One may see a wooden structure of Santa Maria del Fiore in Florence and may conventionally say that it is a model. Likewise, nobody is going to see a model of the world in someone's brain. The use of the word "model" is purely instrumental. The wooden model is a physical entity that is used as a model of a church. There is no physical test to ascertain whether the wooden structure is either a model of a church or a wooden structure that, by chance, resembles some existing, past or future religious building. Furthermore, the fact of being considered as a model does not determine any difference in the causal behavior of the wooden structure. The wooden structure is a physical entity in its own respect. It has a shape, a color, and a mass. It occupies space, and it reflects light. The model is an instrumental role we attribute to a physical structure.

Likewise, in my brain, there is nothing in addition to my neurons whenever they interact causally with the external world. If one uses the term "model" to refer metaphorically to the behaviors of neurons, it is fine. However, if one infers something out of the fact that the neurons model the external world, one may fall into the trap of one more ontological promissory note. The fact is that both with information and with modelling we have contracted ontological debts that we are never going to pay back. We have used terms that are supposed to support the ontological weight of the mind. Such terms are nothing but ontological promissory notes. All ontological payments are postponed in the future.

Ontological promissory notes lift the obligation to address the ontological status of consciousness. However, they do not solve the issue of the nature of consciousness. On the contrary, they entail a dualistic picture of the mind-body problem. In fact, such epistemic entities suggest the existence of an ontologically light domain that is the place of the mind (see Fig. 1). It is a form of dualism because it suggests that only in the brain something special takes place (information processing, modelling, representation, and so forth). Further, it suggests that this special event (which is nothing but an epistemic entity) is the necessary (and perhaps sufficient condition) for the occurrence of the conscious mind.

The resulting dualism is based on the internalist assumption that the mind is the outcome of what is going on inside the CNS. Yet, so far, both empirically and conceptually, there is nothing like the mind inside the CNS because 1) the mind has properties that do not fit with the standard view of the physical world; 2) so far it has been empirically verified that there is nothing like the mind; 3) if neuroscience rejects dualism there cannot be anything but physical stuff. The situation is embarrassing, to say the least. As we mentioned, the three more popular options are eliminativism, emergence, or dualism in disguise. Eliminativism is usually rejected because it appears to throw away the baby with the bathwater. Emergentism begs the question. Once something is emerged, is a new ontology needed? After all, emergentism is not an explanation but rather an admission of ignorance (Kim, 1999). Eventually, neuroscience considers the last option—namely, to resort to some vague entity that may seem to be acceptable from a scientific perspective and yet sufficiently vague both to promise a future explanation and to realize now some epistemic work.

Consider information again. If it were physical, it would add something to the physical system that realizes it. Clearly, it doesn't. As we have seen, since information is not physical, at the end of the day, two options are conceivable. Either information is a pure epistemic concept (i.e. a metaphor to speak of something else)—and thus it may not be used to support any physical phenomenon. Or, we may be serious when we refer to the ontology of information, but in this last case, we would opt for a dualistic picture of reality (Chalmers 1996; Tononi 2004, 2008). The hypothesis is tantamount to assuming the standard physical world *and*, on top of it, a level of information floating above. This is full-fledged dualism, and it brings with itself the usual bunch of issues such as interactionism, ontological prodigality, and truth-conditions. At least, this informational dualism would have the merit of being coherent. On the contrary, in neuroscience, many scholars seem to assume a fuzzy and vague intermediate view—although information is not a physical thing (that would be naïve), it is nevertheless real and thus it may be the basis for further phenomena (guess what? The mind). If this is not an ontological promissory note, we no longer know what it is.

Finally, we would like to spend a few words on the least favorite epistemic entity of choice—namely, the issue of representation. In neuroscience and cognitive science, it is a recurring mantra that a representation of X doesn't need to share the properties of X to represent X. It is a rather obvious consideration as to conventional representations. Consider a traditional praise of the notion of representation:

> We must distinguish features of representings from the features of representeds ... someone can shout "softly, on tiptoe" at the top of his lungs, there are gigantic pictures of microscopic objects, and oil paintings of artists making charcoal sketches ... To suppose otherwise is to confusedly superimpose two different spaces: the representing space and the represented space (Dennett and Kinsbourne 1992: 149).

Every student in cognitive science and philosophy of mind learned that. And yet, when it comes to mental representations, many doubts arise. If

Table 5.1 A comparison between current discussion about the mind in neuroscience and traditional dualism

	Physical domain	Intermediate vague notions	Mental domain
Descartes	Extended substance		Thinking substance
Melzack (Melzack, Israel, Lacroix and Schultz 1997; Melzack 2001)	Neural impulses	Pattern and neurosignatures	Pain
Haynes (Haynes and Rees 2006; Haynes 2009)	Brain activity	Mental activity	Mental states
Haggard (Haggard 2002, 2004)	Neural activity	Coding mechanism Integrated representation	Conscious awareness
Kendrick/Naselaris/ Gallant (Kay, Naselaris, Prenger and Gallant. 2008; Naselaris, Stansbury and Gallant 2012; Nishimoto et al. 2011)	Brain activity	Mental content	Visual experience
Noë (Noë 2009)	Sensori-motor contingencies	Knowledge of sensori-motor contingencies	Qualia
Tononi (Tononi 2004, 2008)	Causation	Information integration	Qualia

your representation does not share any property with what it represents, how can it represent it? The traditional notion of representation seems to work conditioned to the existence of a conscious subject doing the dirty work—namely connecting through the intentionality/semantics/consciousness of the vehicle of representation with the content. The fact is that no one knows how to naturalize representations. Neuroscience did not succeed so far. Nor did anybody else.

4. CONCLUSION

The main reason why neuroscience resorts to various forms of dualism in disguise is twofold: first, the assumption that the physical basis of the conscious mind has to be internal to the CNS; second, the empirical/conceptual failure to find such a basis inside the physical scope encircled by the CNS. It is an empirical failure because so far there is no evidence as to the occurrence of anything with intentionality, unity, quality, first-person perspective, and duration. It is a conceptual failure because the ontological foundations of the received standard physical domain have been defined so to exclude the aforementioned properties.

The result is that many authors consider an intermediate level made of epistemic entities that do not have any ontological weight such as information, computation, modelling, representation, symbol manipulation, and so forth. This level, which is nothing but an ontological promissory note, has the same role once assigned to the mental substance without apparently committing to the same metaphysics. This is an unfortunate strategy since consciousness is a real phenomenon and as such, it must spring out of real phenomena. In the lack of any unexpected empirical breakthrough, the current dualism in disguise does not have the resources to get anywhere. As a result, there are only two available options: either internalism is rejected or dualism is reconsidered in a more explicit ontological framework.

In the end, there are two possible options—either neuroscience rejects internalism and considers an ontologically revised physicalism, or it accepts explicitly its persisting covert dualism and brings into the open its dualistic framework.

6 Quantum Theory of Mind
Henry P. Stapp

1. INTRODUCTION

The great nineteenth century physicist John Tyndall wrote:

> We can trace the development of a nervous system and correlate it with the parallel phenomena of sensation and thought. We see with undoubting certainty that they go hand in hand. But we try to soar in a vacuum the moment we seek to comprehend the connection between them . . . Man as object is separated by an impassible gulf from man as subject. There is no motor energy in intellect to carry it without logical rupture from one to the other (Tyndall 1874: 318).

And Richard Feynman famously said:

> I think I can safely say that nobody understands quantum mechanics! (Feynman 1965: 129).

In the light of these disclaimers, and the raging controversies among quantum physicists about the nature of the reality that lies behind the successful quantum rules, why should any rational person believe, on the basis of uncontroversial scientific evidence alone, that mind is a quantum effect? Quantum mechanics is, after all, about atoms, whereas the brain is a macroscopic object, and macroscopic things are supposed to be described in terms of the concepts of classical mechanics.

My answer to this query begins with the words of Niels Bohr, who, in his 1934 book *Atomic Theory and the Description of Nature*, says:

> In our description of nature the purpose is not to disclose the real essence of phenomena but only to track down as far as possible the relations between the multifold aspects of our experience (Bohr 1934: 18).

The positive part of this message is that quantum theory is ultimately about "our experience". Bohr is telling us, obliquely, that the quantum theory of atomic phenomena is, in the end, about our minds. The theory describes empirically validated connections between the quantum mechanical description of atoms and certain happenings in our streams of conscious experiences. In the more mathematically precise and logically coherent orthodox formulation of quantum mechanics developed by John von Neumann ([1932] 1955) the atoms that are directly relevant to the content of a person's stream of consciousness lie in that person's brain (and perhaps other parts of his nervous system). Thus quantum mechanics becomes, in von Neumann's orthodox formulation, directly and explicitly a theory of the mind-brain connection.

Bohr's statement expounds the original, so-called "Copenhagen Interpretation", of quantum mechanics set forth at the 1927 Solvay conference. That approach to atomic theory emphasizes not only that quantum theory connects our ideas about atoms to the structure of our thoughts. It stresses also that the pragmatic quantum understanding of nature is not based on a *prior* understanding or assumption about the underlying real essences. The aim in Copenhagen quantum mechanics is rather to achieve a practically useful understanding of relations between our experiences, without leaning on any prior presumption about the nature of the underlying "real essences".

There has been between 1927 and 2013 a great lifting of the veil that originally blocked a clear understanding of the connection between the pragmatically successful quantum formalism and conceptions about underlying "real essences". Indeed, the core implication of the highly praised 2012 theorem of Pusey, Barrett, and Rudolph (2012) is that the *empirical validity of certain predictions of quantum mechanics* entails that some supposedly mere practical tools (for the calculation of predictions), namely the actualized quantum mechanical states, can rationally be understood to be real essences. Thus a rationally coherent conception of underlying real essences, and of their connection to the structure of our mental lives, emerged from an adequate understanding of the latter, not vice versa.

That is, indeed, the way of science. Isaac Newton himself proceeded in that way—as he himself emphasized ("I frame no hypotheses")—by deducing from Kepler's understanding of the structure of the astronomical data an idea of the underlying reality. Similarly, John von Neumann deduced, already in 1932, from the Copenhagen understanding of the structure of the (experiential) phenomena a rationally coherent idea of the structure of real essences. That is the scientific method which extracts from an adequate understanding of the empirical data a putative understanding of the real essences, and then tries to move forward on the basis of that putative deeper understanding.

The salient point here is that the prejudice in the minds of both the founders of quantum mechanics, and—even more insistently—of Einstein, that the physical aspects of the pragmatic quantum theory cannot represent real essences, became generally accepted, and that bias threw most physicists and philosophers off course. It caused them to prejudicially dismiss the possibility that a properly formulated quantum mechanics can provide not only a set of practical rules but also a description of what can rationally be considered to be reality itself. If that possibility can be realized, then the properly formulated theory ought to yield—as orthodox quantum theory in fact does—a rationally coherent understanding of the connection between what had seemed, in earlier conceptualizations, to be two aspects of reality that were rationally disconnected, namely our psychologically described minds and our physically described brains.

The prejudices in question, though completely lacking empirical support, are, nevertheless, psychologically potent in the minds of many physicists. They pertain to what Einstein called "spooky action at a distance", and the associated quantum collapses. These "spooky actions" are fundamental features of the quantum mechanical rules. Thus the strong prejudice that reality simply cannot involve such essentially instantaneous transfers of information over large distances enforces the view that the quantum formalism simply cannot describe reality. Yet these spooky actions are also an integral part of the orthodox *relativistic quantum field theory*, which fulfills all of the *empirical* demands of the theory of relativity. Thus the prejudices in question lack any empirical basis, and ought not to, from a scientific point of view, restrict the realm of theoretical possibilities.

This conclusion is strongly supported by the fact that, given the validity of the *predictions* of quantum mechanics, spooky actions at a distance cannot be universally prohibited (Stapp [1977] 2013: Appendix 1). In particular, given a certain experimental setup involving two far-apart experimental regions in each of which a free choice is made between two alternative possible experimental settings of an apparatus located in that region, and given the validity of the predictions of quantum mechanics in each of the four alternative possible cases specified by these choices, it is not possible to require in each of these four alternative possible cases that the outcomes in each region be independent of which free choice is made in the faraway other region: in at least one of the alternative possible cases the outcomes in one region must depend upon which experiment is freely chosen in the faraway region at essentially the same instant of time. This conclusion is based exclusively on empirically verified macroscopic *predictions* of quantum mechanics, and the idea of free choices, which is needed to define the independent variables. There is no reference to, or condition on, anything else.

The predictions of quantum mechanics pertinent to this proof have been validated empirically. Hence we have here an action-at-a-distance property derived from empirical properties of nature herself.

On the other hand, the principles of relativistic classical mechanics ensure that this same action-at-a-distance property cannot hold in classical mechanics. Thus the principles of classical physics forbid an action-at-a-distance property that *empirical properties* of the observed world entail! This undermines the rationality of using the absence of faster-than-light actions in relativistic classical mechanics to impose this condition on nature herself.

2. ORTHODOX QUANTUM MECHANICS

The rationally coherent orthodox formulation of quantum mechanics was given in 1932 by the eminent mathematician and logician John von Neumann. Von Neumann has been called "the last of the great mathematicians" and "the most scintillating intellect of the century". Nobel Laureate Hans Bethe said: "I have sometimes wondered whether a brain like von Neumann's does not indicate a species superior to that of man". Another expression of the same idea was a joking suggestion that von Neumann was actually an outer space alien who had trained himself to perfectly imitate a human being in every way.

Von Neumann's orthodox formulation of quantum mechanics is widely used by mathematical physicists and others who need a mathematically precise and rationally coherent formulation of the theory. This orthodox formulation has the additional virtue of bringing back into the physical theory a mathematically precise and logically coherent putative conception of objective physical reality itself, namely the physically described quantum mechanical state of the universe, evolving according to the rules specified by von Neumann. Those rules link the evolution of the physical reality to certain *psychological* realities, namely to human choices that are "free" in the sense that they are neither determined by, nor even statistically biased by, the totality of the present and past physical realities represented in the theory. In spite of the inclusion of these elements of freedom, the orthodox theory is nevertheless concordant with all of the empirically validated predictions of classical and quantum mechanics, and, moreover, with the capacity of a person's freely chosen mental intentions to influence that person's upcoming bodily behavior in the way that he or she mentally intends.

The main logical problem with the earlier Copenhagen formulation of quantum mechanics was that it introduced, in order to account for our descriptions of our experiences, not only our streams of experiences themselves and the quantum mechanical representation of the physically described aspects of reality. It introduced also a *classical physical description* that is logically incompatible with the quantum description. Thus all sorts of inconsistencies arose. Von Neumann eliminated this classical description, and, along with it, the associated inconsistencies.

The Copenhagen quantum-classical physical description had been introduced in association with a mysterious movable cut, called the Heisenberg cut, which had the incredible property that everything "below" the cut was described in the quantum mechanical language, and every physically described thing "above" the cut was described in the terminology of classical physics. Von Neumann removed the ambiguities and inconsistencies associated with this movable cut by moving it all the way up, so that all physically described elements were placed below the cut, and hence were described quantum mechanically, leaving above the cut only the psychologically described parts of the pragmatic theory. Von Neumann called the psychologically described residue associated with each observer that person's "abstract ego". It comes directly from the pragmatic theory.

This shift places the boundary between the mentally described and quantum mechanically described aspects of nature at the separation between the minds and brains of observing agents, where it naturally belongs, not out at some ill-defined "measuring device", as the Copenhagen interpretation does. It turns quantum theory into a description of the causal connection, via von Neumann's dynamical rules, between our minds and their associated *quantum-physically described* brains. The classical concepts, which are known to be both fundamentally false and incompatible with the precepts of quantum mechanics, are eliminated.

An important virture of the orthodox theory is this: it provides not just a mathematically and logically precise formulation of the pragmatically successful rules. It provides also the principles underlying a rationally coherent and dynamically integrated conception of a psychophysical reality in which we human beings are embedded as *psychophysical agents* that can freely instigate probing actions of our own mental choosing. It allows 'what the theory is describing' to be consistently interpreted as a reality that has both physical and mental aspects, with the mental aspects not determined by the physical ones. The observers are equipped with free choices that are included not "ad hoc", simply because we feel that our choices are somehow free. They are included because they are logically required, in order to break a symmetry and allow our perceptions to have the character that they actually possess, rather than being continuous smears of possible experiences of the kind that actually populate our streams of consciousness. Thus, for example, the pointer on a measuring device will, by virtue of some probing action, and nature's response to it, be either "swung to the right" or "not swung to the right", rather than the mixture of these conflicting possibilities that the purely mechanical part of the law of motion, namely the Schrödinger equation, acting alone would generate.

Stated differently, the central problem in the construction of an adequate quantum theory is to resolve the wave-particle puzzle. This is the fact that the evolution of the physically described quantum mechanical state in accordance with the purely mechanical law of motion—the Schrödinger equation—produces a physically described structure that is a giant smear of systems of the kind that we human observers perceive. If the dynamics were to be governed solely by this purely physical equation of motion, which is the completely natural quantum analog of the classical law of motion, then the dynamics would not be connected to experience in the way that a pragmatic theory should.

Von Neumann solved this core difficulty in essentially the way specified by Copenhagen quantum mechanics, upgraded to achieve mathematical precision and logical coherence. This solution injects free choices made by observing agents into the dynamics. These choices are "free" in the sense that they are not determined by the purely mechanical (Schrödinger) component of the full equation of motion. Each observing ego is empowered to pose probing questions about the facts of the world in which it finds itself. To each posed question Nature either immediately returns a positive answer in the form of a characteristic responding feeling F, or returns no response. If Nature responds, then the system being observed will, *after this answer is returned*, possess the property corresponding to the question. If no response is returned, then the system, after the question is posed, will definitely not possess the property in question.

Von Neumann expressed essentially these ideas in the mathematical framework of quantum mechanics. This probing process allows an observing ego to learn, by trial and error probing, the structure of the world in which it finds itself. This structure will be in the form of relations between its feelings. Thus the brain whose properties are being directly probed is described in the mathematical language of quantum mechanics, whereas the ego's representation of its increasing knowledge is described in terms of its feelings. The connection between these two representations is created by a constructive process governed by von Neumann's rules. This process connects psychological features of the probing ego to physical properties of the brain whose properties it is directly probing.

It is essential here that the physical state *after* the probing question be something depending on the combination of the ego's free choice and nature's statistically controlled response. This newly created state generally differs from the prior state, and hence this pair of choices is influencing the flow of physical events. Thus the observer is not a mere passive witness to a flow of physical events that is proceeding independently of his probing actions.

This profound change in the causal structure is the essential difference between classical and quantum physics. Our understanding of it emerged, only after the fact, from the science-based effort to rationally comprehend puzzling empirical findings that violated classical ideas, not from any preconceived intention to rescue free will.

Although, in von Neumann's formulation, the direct interaction between the probing ego and the physically described aspects of nature is between the ego and its brain; the mathematical structure entails that the entire physically described universe will be instantly reduced to the part of its former self that is compatible with the new state of that brain. These global jumps are the radical new feature of quantum mechanics, and are a cause of consternation in the minds of people who insist on thinking, on the basis of appearances, that nature herself conforms to classical ideas. But these classical appearances are saved in spite of these global jumps, and in fact due to these global jumps, which allow localized free choices to alter global "real essences" without upsetting classical experiences.

I shall later give explanations of these wonderful features. But some physicists, most notably Einstein, hoped to evade this spooky action at a distance. They hoped that because quantum mechanics was a statistical theory about "our knowledge" that is similar in some ways to classical statistical mechanics, that the action-at-a-distance feature could be evaded at the level of real essences by reverting to a quasi-classical theory. That task has been pursued under the title "hidden variable theories" or, euphemistically, "realistic theories", where "realistic" is short for "quasi-classical". Those attempts to recover locality by combining classical concepts with quantum predictions fail. The approach (Stapp [1977] 2013) deduces a non-locality property directly from validated empirical findings and a strong conception of free choices.

3. QUANTUM CONNECTION BETWEEN MIND AND BRAIN

The orthodox quantum theoretical connection between mind and brain is close to the opposite of the classical theoretical idea of that connection. In classical physics our minds are conceived to be puppets controlled by our physical brains. In orthodox quantum mechanics a person's brain is, instead, the instrument by means of which that person's mind/ego, embedded in a physically described world, learns about this physical world in which it finds itself, forms valid expectations about its future experiences, and acts to influence what it will find to be the case.

But how, in more detail, does it all work?

The mind, or "abstract ego", has a battery of efforts E each of which corresponds to an act of putting to Nature a particular question about the world inhabited by that ego. According to the quantum precepts, Nature immediately responds by either returning a feeling F that is tied to the effort, $F = F(E)$, or by failing to return immediately a response. In the first case the *brain being probed* has, immediately after the response is delivered, the physical property that is represented in the mind of the probing agent by the feeling F. In the second case, that brain has the physical property that is the negation of that property. In either case the ego is immediately free to pose another question. If the ego were to "immediately" pose the same question then it invariably would, according to the quantum rules, receive the same answer as before. If this same question were to be posed after a short delay, then, according to the quantum rules, the probability that Nature would deliver the same response is specified by the state of the probed brain, which is evolving in accordance with specified physical laws. This leads, via well defined rules, to predictions about future experiences that turn out to be valid.

The ego of the infant begins in the womb to inquire about the structure of the world in which it finds itself and, by virtue of its intrinsic conceptual capacities, begins, by trial and error, to acquire a conception of that world. This conception is a construction in terms of the validated feelings F that it has experienced as responses to its probing actions.

Now it might seem to a reader honed on the precepts of classical physics that giving these conceptual properties to our minds begs the question. The basic scientific problem, as they might conceive it, is precisely to explain these wonderful powers and properties of our minds exclusively in terms of the physical properties of our brains. But that would mean demanding that a proper science-based understanding of the empirically valid theory conform to the precepts of a different theory that is both inconsistent with it and empirically false.

To achieve both agreement with all empirical data and the rational coherence required of a theory of reality, the orthodox theory backs away from the classical notion that the principles of classical mechanics, that work so well in the astronomical and large-scale terrestrial realms, extend in a direct way to biology and atomic physics. It is the rejection of that extrapolation that is the basic move of quantum mechanics. Yet, in spite this well-known failure of the ideas that work so well in astronomy to extend to the atomic and molecular domains, and in spite of the well-known dependence of brain behavior on atomic and molecular processes, most scientists who seek a deep understanding of the mind-brain connection persist in clinging to the astronomy-based concepts. In conformity with what Sir Karl Popper called "Promissory Materialism", they expect that an understanding of our minds will emerge from dogged adherence to a theory that is known to be invalid, and which, as a matter of basic principle, leaves out the minds that they are trying to understand. They balk at basing their thinking on its empirically valid successor, which is *fundamentally about* exactly what they are trying to find out, namely the connection between the mental and physical aspects of reality, and, more directly, the connection between a person's mind and that person's brain.

Specifically, orthodox quantum mechanics, like Copenhagen quantum mechanics, is a theory of the relations between experiences that belong to various abstract egos (personal minds). It is based on the notion that there exists an evolving physical world that is described in terms of the mathematical principles of quantum mechanics, as described by von Neumann. This notion specifies that the experiences belonging to a person's abstract ego are directly connected to the physical world through that person's physically described brain. The specified connections between a person's mind and brain allow that person, by means of experienced responses to his or her probing actions, to form a conception of the structure of the world in which it is embedded, and, moreover, to influence the future evolution of that world, and thereby its own future experiences.

As regards the powers that the theory ascribes to the minds of the probing agents, let it not be forgotten that the underlying philosophy of quantum mechanics is essentially pragmatic. I have been emphasizing that the intrinsic rational coherence of the mathematical structure described by von Neumann allows that structure to be conceived to be a representation of "reality". But "reality", apart from the thoughts, ideas, and feelings that we directly know, is in the end conjectural. To be useful, the contents and powers that the theory assigns to our minds should match our actual understanding of our minds, in order that we be able to tie the theory to the putative reality. In Bohr's words, "The task of science is both to extend the range of our experience and reduce it to order" (Bohr 1934: 1). In this way of looking at the scientific endeavor, our minds as we know them are the givens. We want to expand them in useful ways built securely on validated empirical findings. Utility is the bottom line, and our theory of reality must encompass it. But to be useful to us the theory needs to inform us about how one's existing mind can, by virtue of its intrinsic powers, form valid expectations about the contents of future experiences and develop ways to influence those future experiences in intended ways. The key to such an understanding is an understanding of the way that a mind is connected to its brain; for that connection is that mind's bridge to the future.

4. UNDERSTANDING INSTANTANEOUS ACTION AT A DISTANCE

But how are the needed instantaneous actions at a distance rationally understood in a world conforming to all of the empirical demands of the special theory of relativity?

When I, by virtue of my understanding of the meaning of my experiences, can conclude that I have seen the pointer swing to the right, I normally find that an immediate re-examination will confirm that prior finding, but that after a while things may change. And if I enquire, I will find that others in the room will have similar experiences.

Inquiring minds, confronted by such findings, have developed a conception of a communal world in which our individual minds are embedded. Efforts by many thinkers, working over many centuries, led to von Neumann's 1932 proposal about the nature of a psychophysical world and the way in which our minds are embedded in it.

A basic need of the theory is to explain *intersubjective agreement* in a rationally evolving world that accommodates our independent, and sometimes seemingly capricious, causal inputs. This problem was solved in von Neumann's theory (following the Copenhagen lead) by collapses of quantum states at certain "instants". These "instants" extend over the entire universe, and the collapses at these instants constitute "instantaneous actions-at-a-distance".

These "instants" were originally considered to be *flat* three-dimensional surfaces that separated the past from the future. By moving forward in time, these instants "now" separated the "open" future of potentialities and possibilities from the "closed" fixed and settled past.

But the notion that these surfaces are "flat" is at odds with the theory of special relativity. In the relativistic quantum field theory proposed independently by Tomonaga (1946) and Schwinger (1951) these instants "now" are taken to be non-flat three-dimensional continuous surfaces in the four-dimensional space-time having the property that every point on such a surface lies outside the (closed) forward light cone of every other point on that surface. This allows one to think that the needed advances into the future are achieved by an ordered sequence of tiny steps in each of which a current "instant" is changed to the next "instant" by a small advance confined to small (say brain-sized) region. The mind-brain connection pertains to what is happening to the mind and the brain in such a localized event. The postulated instantaneous "collapse of the quantum state of the universe" occurs along the new instant "now". That gives a dynamically defined meaning to a point that is both faraway and "now". Although that idea of a physically well-defined faraway "now" is completely contrary to the *ideas* of relativity theory, all of the quantum theoretical predictions about actual observations are absolutely in line with the principles of relativity theory. That is why Einstein was unable to give a convincing argument that faster-than-light actions cannot be real: relativistic quantum field theory has such instantaneous actions at a distance without violating any empirical requirements of special relativity.

5. CONSCIOUS CONTROL OF PHYSICAL BEHAVIOR

> It is to my mind utterly inconceivable that consciousness has nothing to do with a business which it so faithfully attends (James [1890] 1950: 136).

James's feeling may, in the opinion of materialists, be sheer prejudice, unsupported by any solid empirical evidence. But their own contrary opinions might warrant greater credence if they were based on valid physical laws that reduce our conscious experiences to causally inert witnesses. However, the physical theory that had once supported that notion is now known to be fundamentally false. It has been replaced by a theory in which inputs considered to originate, at least partially, in our psychologically described egos have profound effects on the evolution of the physical.

Yet in this new theory the role of the ego in the unfolding of physical events is restricted to the mere posing of questions. So a critical question is how this capacity of an ego merely to pose questions allows its intentions to influence, in the way that it mentally intends, the physical behavior of its brain and body.

The answer rests on a very basic feature of quantum mechanics described by Misra and Sudarshan (1977) and associated by them to one of Zeno's Paradoxes. I call this effect "The Quantum Zeno effect". It must be emphasized, straightaway, that this effect is very different from an effect studied empirically by Wineland's group (Itano, Heinzen, Bollinger and Wineland 1990), and given by them this same name. I use the term to describe the "Zeno" property of quantum mechanics described by Sudarshan and Misra.

This "Zeno" effect is easily understood. The quantum state of a system is often called the state "vector". A vector is a directed line segment in a space: it begins at one point in that space, called the origin of that vector, and ends at another point, that can be called the tip or end point of the vector. The mechanical evolution of the quantum state *under the process controlled by the Schrödinger equation* consists of a motion of the tip of a vector that moves around with both its origin and length fixed. The length is the distance between the origin and the tip.

In the visually accessible case of a three-dimensional space, one can think of a spherical globe, with the origin of the vector fixed at the center of the globe and the tip moving around on the surface. The basic idea of quantum mechanics is that the motion is not always that simple Schrödinger-equation-directed motion. At some instant when the state vector is, say, Vbefore, an observing agent can ask: Will I find the vector that describes my experience to be Vafter? The statistical character of quantum mechanics stems from a single simple rule: the probability that the answer will be "Yes" is the square of the cosine of the angle between Vbefore and Vafter.

The quantum Zeno effect follows directly from a very simple application of this basic rule. Suppose the agent's probing action corresponds to the question: "Will my probing effort yield the response corresponding to my finding the physical state vector to be V0?"

Of course, only someone who understands quantum mechanics will be able to understand the agent's action in this technical way. But it does not matter whether the human agent understands his effort in this way. Realistically interpreted, orthodox quantum mechanics assumes that this is what is really going on and is what the agent has learned to feel and understand in his or her own way. The quantum effect in question is of such great generality that the details of the mapping between the human idiosyncratic experience and the putative underlying reality are not relevant.

Suppose that an agent's felt probing action corresponds to the question: "Will a 'Yes' response to this probing action that I am now initiating signify that the state vector of the system I am probing will, after my probing, be the vector V0?" Suppose that the answer is 'Yes'. And suppose the Schrödinger equation, acting alone, would cause V0 to evolve during one second into some different vector V1, having the same origin and length. The quantum Zeno effect is the fact that, independently of the further details of the physical situation, if the agent were repeatedly to pose the same question at a very rapid rate, during that one second interval, then the answers received will continue, during that interval, to be "Yes", with probability approaching unity as the rapidity of the probing action tends to infinity: in the large N limit the state vector will be frozen at V0.

This result is easy to understand. A little reflection shows that if N is the number of probing actions made during the one second interval, and v is the normal velocity on the constant radius (say r = 1) sphere, then the probability that the vector will still be V0 after one second is the cosine of v/N raised to the power 2N. That number approaches unity (i.e., one) as N tends to infinity: the rapid posing of the same question tends to freeze the state at the value associated with the positive answer to that "freely chosen" probing action.

A simple extension of this result is that if the rapid sequence of probing actions corresponds not to one single vector, V0, but to a sequence of vectors, Vn, that lie along some chosen path on the unit sphere, then the state of the system being probed will tend to be dragged along that path defined by the chosen sequence of probing actions. Thus this quantum process—built directly, and trivially, upon the most elemental quantum rule, the cosine-squared rule—elevates the ego's capacity merely to choose its probing actions to a capacity to cause its brain to behave in a way that will cause its body to behave in the way that the ego mentally intends.

6. LIBET, VOLITION, AND THE ORDERING OF CAUSE AND EFFECT

In von Neumann's orthodox theory, causes logically precede their effects. Our mental volitions are causes, and they logically precede their psychological and physical effects.

Some seminal experiments by Benjamin Libet and his colleagues (Libet, Gleason, Wright, and Pearl 1983) have been interpreted as empirical evidence that nature does not conform to those ideas. But those conclusions stem, according to the orthodox point of view, from a failure to understand what is really happening.

In these experiments the human subject of the experiment performs a physical action that is designed to be a freely chosen action, and that feels to the subject to be a freely chosen action. The plain empirical facts are, first, that this "free choice" appears to precede the physical action, as expected. But several tenths of second before the free choice to perform the action occurs, a characteristic electric disturbance called the readiness potential arises in the brain. The empirical fact that this brain activity precedes the "free choice" to act has been widely interpreted as evidence that the physical brain is in actual control, just as classical mechanics says, and that the mental side effect is merely an after-the-fact mental rationalization that gives credit to the mind for what the physical brain has already done.

In the Libet protocol the subject is instructed to raise a finger sometime in the future, tacitly understood to be within the next 20 or 30 seconds. The subject accepts the instruction, and, according to my understanding of the orthodox theory, his quantum mechanical brain begins to create *potential templates for actions* that conform to the specified instruction. A template for action is a pattern of neurological activity that if actualized, and held stably in place for a sufficient interval, will send out an ordered sequence of physically described signals that will cause the body to behave in a coordinated way.

However, the exact time of the action was not specified by the instruction. Hence the quantum mechanically described brain will create a quantum mechanical *mixture* of various possible templates corresponding to various possible times for the finger-raising action to occur.

But which of the physically equivalent possibilities will be actualized? This is where the radical key idea of the creators of quantum mechanics enters: the *experimenter (here the subject) decides, via a choice that is not determined by the Schrödinger equation*, whether to perform a physical action that is connected in his mind to an expected mental feedback.

But before the chooser can exercise a freedom to meaningfully choose, he must have a conception of the expected, or hoped for, consequences of the choice. The chooser does not choose in a conceptual vacuum. The chooser—in this case the subject that must choose to perform some particular finger-raising action—must have an image of the consequences of that possible action. The readiness potential measured by Libet functions *first* to provide the ego with an image of what he can expect to experience if that template is actualized. This preview must precede the ego's informed choice to act, which must precede the actual physical action.

Many potential templates for action can be considered and rejected by the ego before one is accepted. The rejections leave no direct trace in the mind of the subject, even though each such rejection eliminates from the quantum mechanical brain the strand of potentialities that was rejected.

Von Neumann spends a great deal of effort creating and describing the detailed mathematical machinery that lies behind the surface-level description that I have just given. He pays a great deal of attention to the fact that the different quantum brain states that exist in parallel generally exist not in the form of a *superposition* of possible states, but rather in the form of *mixtures*. This change arises from the fact that the states of the brain of central interest are generally believed to be strongly interacting with their environment in such a way that certain "phase" information becomes irretrievably lost. But that loss of effective information does not alter the fact that the alternative mutually incompatible possibilities continue, according to the orthodox rules, to exist, in the mathematically well-developed form of mixtures.

The upshot is that the observed rise of the readiness potential prior to the actual choice to act is a reflection of the fact that our choices although "free" are not "blind": prior to the choice to act there must be a representation in the brain of the projected consequences of choosing to act, in order for the ego to bring its values to bear on the choice that it makes. Only then can we be rationally responsible for our actions.

The rational basis of this entire way of conceptualizing things rests on a pragmatic view of science. In order to be useful to us the theory must allow us to identify our mental selves as parts of the theoretical construct that have the power to act in ways that tend to produce experiences concordant with our values.

The orthodox interpretation designed by von Neumann meets this requirement and agrees with all reproducible empirical data, but at the expense of demanding that the physically described world be significantly different from what it appears to be.

ACKNOWLEDGEMENTS

I thank Sean O Nuallain for substantive suggestions, and Brian Wachter for editorial suggestions that have contributed importantly to this work.

7 A Dualist Account of Phenomenal Concepts

Martina Fürst

1. INTRODUCTION

Physicalism[1] is confronted with well-known anti-physicalist arguments such as the knowledge argument (Jackson 1982), the explanatory gap argument (Levine 1983), and the conceivability argument (Kripke 1980; Block 1980). These arguments are based on the phenomenal character of consciousness, the distinctive what-it-is-likeness of undergoing experiences such as seeing the blue sky, tasting red wine, or being in pain. In the contemporary debate, the *phenomenal concept strategy* (Stoljar 2005) is considered one of the most powerful responses to these anti-physicalist arguments. The basic idea of this strategy is to rely on special concepts—*phenomenal concepts*—to explain why we draw dualist conclusions from these arguments. Hence, the goal of the phenomenal concept strategy is to give a satisfactory account of dualist intuitions without being committed to ontological dualist conclusions.

For this strategy to work, physicalists have to elaborate the crucial particularities of phenomenal concepts and demonstrate that these features can explain away the anti-physicalist arguments in a satisfactory way. For a first approximation, we can categorize accounts of phenomenal concepts roughly along two lines (see Balog 2009: 303f.). Some accounts take the particular features of phenomenal concepts to be found in their direct reference function and construe phenomenal concepts analogously to demonstrative concepts (e.g. Horgan 1984; Levin 2007). Others focus primarily on the special mode of presentation involved in phenomenal concepts and take phenomenal concepts to be constituted by experiences (Balog 2012; Block 2006; Papineau 2002).

In this chapter, I will analyze the explanatory power of the phenomenal concept strategy with regard to Jackson's knowledge argument. In his paper "Epiphenomenal Qualia" (1982), Jackson asks the reader to imagine the brilliant scientist Mary who has complete physical knowledge of human color vision but was born and raised in an achromatic environment and has never undergone a color-experience in her life. The crucial question is what happens when Mary enjoys her very first color-experience. On the basis of this thought experiment Jackson developed the knowledge argument against physicalism which can be formulated (in a strong version that aims at non-physical *facts*) as following:

> Premise P1: Mary has complete physical knowledge about human color vision before her release.
> Consequence C1: Therefore Mary knows all the physical facts about human color vision before her release
> Premise P2: There is some (kind of) knowledge concerning facts about human color vision that Mary does not have before her release.
> Consequence C2: Therefore (from (P2)): There are some facts about human color vision that Mary does not know before her release.
> Consequence C3: Therefore (from (C1) and (C2)): There are non-physical facts about human color vision (Nida-Rümelin 2010).

In a first step, after briefly considering demonstrative accounts of phenomenal concepts, I will argue that especially constitutional accounts[2] offer a lot for a better understanding of the knowledge argument. In a second step, I will investigate the demands that the physicalist target imposes on a physicalist interpretation of the constitutional account. I will show that the Mary-scenario cannot be explained entirely in terms of physicalist constitutional accounts that draw upon empirical research, for example by holding that phenomenal concepts involve stored sensory templates. These accounts fail to explain how phenomenal concepts can carry introspectively accessible information about the phenomenal character of experiences. In a third step, I will propose a new interpretation of the constitutional account which meets the explanatory constraints best, but involves features that imply non-physical referents. In particular, the self-representing character of the experience involved in the concept turns out to imply non-physical referents. In this respect the defended account of phenomenal concepts differs significantly from those put forward by Papineau (2007), Balog (2012), and Block (2006)—it strengthens the dualist intuitions instead of explaining them away.

2. ANALYSIS OF THE PHENOMENAL CONCEPTS STRATEGY (PCS)

The phenomenal concept strategy (PCS) is put forward by *type B materialists* (Chalmers 1997). Type B materialists grant that there is an epistemic gap[3] involved in anti-physicalist arguments such as the knowledge argument, the explanatory gap, and the conceivability argument, but they doubt the legitimacy of drawing an ontological conclusion from epistemic premises.[4] To explain the epistemic gap, the defenders of the PCS rely on phenomenal concepts. As highlighted in Loar's paper "Phenomenal States" ([1990]1997), the starting point of the PCS is the Fregean idea that one single ontological entity can be known under different modes of presentation. Thus, this reply can be easily formulated on the level of concepts—a move that leads to the notion of phenomenal concepts on the one hand and the notion of physical concepts on the other. Once these two sorts of concepts have been established, defenders of the PCS present, for example, Jackson's Mary-scenario as analogous to standard cases of co-reference. According to the defenders of the PCS, the physically omniscient scientist Mary possesses all physical concepts when being confined to her achromatic environment, but acquires a new phenomenal concept when she enjoys a blue experience for the first time. The key move is the claim that the physical and the phenomenal concept of blue experiences pick out one and the same physical referent.

Since defenders of the PCS aim to explain anti-physicalist arguments, they grant that phenomenal concepts cannot be deduced a priori from physical concepts. In other words, the phenomenal concepts Mary gains from her first color-experiences are *conceptually isolated* (Carruthers and Veillet 2007) from all other concepts she had before. Thus, defenders of the PCS must explain why phenomenal concepts are conceptually isolated from physical ones, despite the fact that they pick out the same alleged physical referents. Those who undertake the PCS point to important particularities of phenomenal concepts to provide such an explanation. Hence, according to those who defend the PCS, no metaphysical entities, such as non-physical properties, have to be invoked to explain Mary's new knowledge. It suffices to highlight the uniqueness of phenomenal concepts. Obviously, the crucial argumentative step of this strategy is to elaborate the decisive particularities of phenomenal concepts.

2.1. What the Knowledge Argument Teaches Us about Phenomenal Concepts

In the following, I confine myself to the knowledge argument because a careful investigation of Jackson's thought experiment helps to illustrate the crucial particularities of phenomenal concepts best. The key issue is the following: What happens when Mary leaves her achromatic environment, enjoys her very first color-experience, and thereby acquires a new concept, providing the foundation of her new knowledge?

In a first step, the knowledge argument illustrates the special acquisition condition of phenomenal concepts. Given the premises of the argument, the physically omniscient scientist possesses all physical concepts but is not able to deduce the relevant phenomenal concepts. Since Mary acquires a phenomenal concept when undergoing her first color-experience, the conceptual isolation of phenomenal concepts can be explained by the special acquisition condition: a person can gain a new phenomenal concept only under the condition of attentively undergoing the relevant experience.[5]

In a second step, the knowledge argument teaches us that Mary makes epistemic progress because of her first color-experience. A wide range of arguments have been developed to explain this epistemic step. Some hold that rather than acquiring new propositional knowledge, Mary only acquires some new abilities, such as the ability to remember, recognize, and imagine color-experiences (Lewis 1988; Nemirow 2007). Others (e.g. Tye 2009) hold that Mary only gains new knowledge by acquaintance, which Tye deems object-knowledge.

In contrast, defenders of the PCS do not rely on different sorts of knowledge but rather focus on the concepts involved. The following examples illustrate the scientist's epistemic progress formulated on the level of concepts: Mary can use her new phenomenal concepts to think new thoughts such as "R (where the term "R" expresses the phenomenal concept of a red experience) is what it is like to look at red tomatoes!" By deploying these new concepts, the scientist can make new introspective judgments such as "Oh, I like R more than the experience I had when looking at the achromatic TV-screen!" Moreover, the subject possessing the concept can use it to recognize or imagine the relevant experience. Accordingly, the second particularity of phenomenal concepts can be stated as follows: phenomenal concepts play a specific cognitive role—they carry information[6] about the phenomenal character of experiences, and they make this information introspectively available to the subject possessing the concept.

To sum up, according to the knowledge argument, Mary's newly acquired phenomenal concepts exhibit two crucial particularities: they possess special acquisition conditions and they play a unique cognitive role. Next, I analyze the question of whether physicalist accounts of phenomenal concepts can explain these two particularities in a satisfactory way.

2.2. Physicalist Accounts of Phenomenal Concepts

In recent literature, sophisticated physicalist accounts of phenomenal concepts have been developed.[7] One of the earliest versions of phenomenal concepts and the locus classicus for the PCS is Loar's *direct recognitional account* ([1990]1997). Loar argues that phenomenal concepts refer directly to phenomenal properties (which are taken to be physical properties), and the very same phenomenal properties constitute the modes of presentation involved in the concepts. Other, subsequently developed accounts focus on one of these two features of phenomenal concepts.[8]

Theories that take phenomenal concepts as involving phenomenal properties are the constitutional accounts (Papineau 2002; Balog 2012b) and accounts that concentrate on the distinct conceptual role of phenomenal concepts (Hill and McLaughlin 1999). These versions often draw on empirical research to explain away dualist intuitions. For example, Papineau (2007) holds that phenomenal concepts involve stored sensory templates analogous to perceptual concepts. Hill and McLaughlin suggest that distinct cognitive faculties are associated with physical and phenomenal concepts and, hence, no distinct reference-fixing properties need be invoked to explain away the anti-physicalist arguments.

Other accounts focus on the *direct reference* of phenomenal concepts to avoid different reference-fixing properties being involved in phenomenal and physical concepts. For example, the causal-recognitional accounts (e.g. Tye 2002)[9] as well as demonstrative accounts (e.g. Horgan 1984; Levin 2007) concentrate on the direct reference function.

I start by briefly recalling why some philosophers think that demonstrative accounts cannot satisfactorily explain away dualist intuitions. Especially, demonstrative accounts that do not rely on a specific mode of presentation involved in the concept are taken to face numerous problems. A general problem of demonstrative accounts is highlighted by Chalmers (2003). He argues that Mary gains a demonstrative concept of the phenomenal character of her experience, but she also acquires what he calls a "pure phenomenal concept" of the same property, which involves a phenomenal mode of presentation. The point is that it is cognitively significant for Mary to find out that these two concepts co-refer. Thus, a pure phenomenal concept cannot be reduced to the demonstrative one. Tye (2009: 51) criticizes demonstrative accounts along another line: according to him, the puzzling question of how a brain state can be identical with a phenomenal state does not seem to be captured by the question of how a brain state can be identical with "*this*". Balog (2009) also criticizes accounts that concentrate on the direct reference function of phenomenal concepts. According to her, these accounts leave too much distance between the concept and the experience, so that the problematic scenario of a basic application of a phenomenal concept in absence of the experience becomes conceivable.

In the next section, I will add to these considerations a new argument for the importance of the special mode of presentation involved in a phenomenal concept to capture the dualist intuitions. I will concentrate on the question of how a phenomenal concept can carry introspectively accessible information about the phenomenal character of experiences. I will argue that this question can neither be answered by pure demonstrative accounts nor by those physicalist constitutional accounts that deny the importance of a specific mode of presentation involved in the concept.

Here are some preliminary remarks to clarify the crucial notions that will be involved in my argumentation:

First, I take phenomenal concepts to be mental representations that can be constituents of thoughts. This means that I am not identifying concepts with modes of presentation. However, I think that a mode of presentation is involved in a phenomenal concept and that this is crucial. Note that this does not mean that I take phenomenal concepts as having modes of presentation in the sense that there could be Fregean cases of two modes of presentation of one single phenomenal concept. Rather I think that phenomenal concepts are mental representations that have modes of presentation as a constituent, i.e. properties that constitute the way the concept presents the referent to the subject. Thus, a specific mode of presentation is necessarily tied to a specific phenomenal concept.

Next, I want to point out that here I confine my analysis to *basic applications* of phenomenal concepts, i.e. phenomenal concepts which are applied from the first person perspective to occurrent experiences. This is because my investigation aims at shedding light on the *referents* of phenomenal concepts and does not aim at giving a full account of phenomenal concepts, including their non-basic applications.[10]

A final note on the notion of "phenomenal character": there is something it is like for a subject to undergo an experience. What it is like to undergo an experience is commonly called its "phenomenal character". Hence, phenomenal characters are properties that are instantiated by experiences. It is plausible to assume that an experience has a specific phenomenal character essentially, i.e. if it had another phenomenal character it would be a different type of experience. I want to emphasize that I am not using the notion of "*phenomenal* characters" to presuppose that these are non-physical properties. At the beginning of my investigation, I leave open the possibility that the phenomenal characters might turn out to be physical properties, although the final outcome of my analysis will be that they are non-physical.

2.3. Physicalist Demands and Problems of the PCS

As noted before, pure demonstrative accounts of phenomenal concepts are taken to face various problems. The next question is: Do physicalist constitutional accounts of phenomenal concepts face problems as well? I will analyze Papineau's account as an exemplar of constitutional accounts that meet the physicalist demands. However, I think that the outcome of my analysis generalizes to all accounts that neglect the importance of the phenomenal mode of presentation involved in a phenomenal concept.

Defenders of the physicalist constitutional account claim that the explanatory particularities of phenomenal concepts can be found in their special nature. For example, Papineau (2002) developed a constitutional account suggesting that phenomenal concepts embed experiences just as quotation marks embed words. According to this view, the structure of the phenomenal concept can be described as follows: *this experience*——, where the blank is supposed to be filled with an actual experience or a copy of an experience.

Recently Papineau (2007) made some changes to his description of phenomenal concepts, abstaining from the demonstrative aspect built into the concept. But he maintains that his current view of phenomenal concepts

> [. . .] retains one crucial feature from my earlier quotational-indexical model, namely, that phenomenal reference to an experience will deploy

> an instance of the experience, and in this sense will *use* that experience in order to mention it. (123)

This view has it that phenomenal concepts *use* experiences. Papineau draws upon an empirical thesis about perceptual concepts to flesh out his version of phenomenal concepts:

> We can think of perceptual concepts as involving stored sensory templates. These templates will be set up on initial encounters with the relevant referents [...]. For the perceptual concept to be deployed, the relevant stored sensory template needs either to be activated by a match with incoming stimuli or to be autonomously activated in imagination. (118)

On this view, phenomenal concepts turn out to be just special cases of perceptual concepts:

> Phenomenal concepts [are] simply a further deployment of the same sensory templates, but in this case used to think about perceptual experiences themselves rather than about the objects of those experiences. (122)

So the idea that a phenomenal concept uses an experience is described in a purely physicalist manner:

> Think about what happens when a phenomenal concept is exercised: Some stored sensory template is activated and is used to think about an experience. (123)

Obviously, Papineau does not concentrate on the mode of presentation involved in the concept anymore. He rather invokes the special vehicle that realizes the concept in order to explain its uniqueness. The use-mention function shall explain why phenomenal concepts are conceptually isolated. Since the phenomenal concept uses an experience, one has to undergo the relevant experience first to acquire the concept. Mary, locked up in her achromatic environment, is not able to store the relevant sensory template and, hence, cannot acquire or deploy the phenomenal concept. This is supposed to be a consequence of the special nature of phenomenal concepts—namely, their use-mention function—rather than an indication of the non-physical nature of the referents.

Let me analyze the explanatory power of this account. Recall that in order to explain the Mary-scenario satisfactorily, I imposed two explanatory constraints. A theory of phenomenal concepts, besides being able to explain their conceptual isolation, must also offer an account of their cognitive role. I think that Papineau is able to explain the conceptual isolation of phenomenal concepts by fleshing out their special acquisition conditions and by pointing at the special vehicles that realize the concepts.

But can this model explain the cognitive role of phenomenal concepts as well? More precisely, can an account of phenomenal concepts that concentrates on their neural vehicles and leaves their mode of presentation aside explain how phenomenal concepts are able to carry the relevant information and make this information introspectively accessible to the subject? My main worry is that every model of phenomenal concepts that leaves the mode of presentation aside fails in explaining the cognitive role of phenomenal concepts. A detailed analysis of Papineau's account will reveal the crucial problem.

First, note that on a physicalist account, the experience that is used in the phenomenal concept has to be understood as a *physical* item. For example, the stored template that is activated in deploying the concept is understood by Papineau as a neural template.

Second, what sort of *usage* of this neural template does Papineau have in mind? I think that the right way is to think of the neural template as a *part* of the concept.[11] This interpretation can easily explain how a phenomenal concept comes to carry the relevant information.[12]

Third, according to Papineau the template constitutes the phenomenology involved in a phenomenal concept, but it does not fix the reference. Rather the reference is fixed by the causal origin of the concept and by the sort of information attached to the concept. Note that a *phenomenal* concept accumulates information about *experiences,* i.e. according to Papineau information about the neural template.

The crucial question is: How can a concept that is partly constituted by a neural template facilitate the specific information about experiences that Mary lacks in her achromatic environment?[13] The demands imposed by physicalism are to cash out the concept in physical terms. This generates a problem for the defender of the physicalist constitutional account. Obviously, the relevant information is not information about a neural template *under a descriptive mode of presentation*, since Mary could know this in her achromatic environment. Nor is it information about a neural template *under a physical mode of presentation*, since Mary could have seen this neural template under a physical mode of presentation in her achromatic environment—for example in another person's brain whilst he is looking at something blue. But this would not help her in figuring out what enjoying a blue experience is like. So the relevant information concerns *what it is like to have that neural template activated.* Thus, the activation of the neural template used by the phenomenal concept has to involve the right *phenomenology* for the concept to carry the relevant information and provide the basis for phenomenal knowledge. To acknowledge the importance of the right phenomenology tied to the phenomenal concept amounts to the claim that the mode of presentation involved in the concept is crucial.

In contrast to my analysis, the physicalist Papineau denies the importance of the phenomenal mode of presentation involved in the concept:

> On my account, phenomenal concepts do indeed refer because of their cognitive function, not because of their phenomenology and therefore other states with a different or no phenomenology [. . .] would refer to

the same experiences for the same reasons. I see nothing wrong with this. (2007: 125)

On my view, there is something wrong with this account of phenomenal concepts. The reason is that—in contrast to other sorts of concepts—a *phenomenal concept* can fulfill its cognitive role only if the experience which partly constitutes the concept involves the right phenomenology.

At this point one might object that Papineau just states that the phenomenology is irrelevant for the *reference* of phenomenal concepts and not for their cognitive role. Papineau thinks that the reference of a phenomenal concept is fixed by its cognitive function rather than by the mode of presentation involved. But he also holds that the cognitive function of a phenomenal concept is to accumulate information about *experiences*. What sort of information about experiences is at stake? The Mary-scenario illustrates that the relevant information is information about *the phenomenal character of experiences,* i.e., according to Papineau, it is information about what it is like to have the neural template activated. Thus, to claim that Mary gains a new phenomenal concept that could be given under another phenomenology (i.e. involving the activation of another neural template), or even under no phenomenology at all, does not do justice to the epistemic situation the knowledge argument illustrates. What is at stake is a phenomenal concept that carries information about a specific phenomenal character of an experience and that makes this information accessible to the subject possessing the concept. Mary might possess concepts like those suggested by Papineau.[14] The important point is that these concepts cannot be the ones we are looking for, namely phenomenal concepts that explain Mary's epistemic development. We are looking for phenomenal concepts that facilitate information about the phenomenal character of experiences and, hence, involve a specific phenomenal mode of presentation.[15]

I want to illustrate the claim that phenomenal concepts have to involve a specific mode of presentation to carry the relevant information and to make this information introspectively accessible by elaborating a reductio ad absurdum: on Papineau's account there is a contingency in the relation of concept and its phenomenology. The phenomenology involved in the concept could vary without the concept varying and vice versa. This model not only leads to implausible scenarios but also to false judgments. Let us imagine for the sake of a reductio ad absurdum a possible world in which Mary possesses a phenomenal concept of blue experiences tied to the phenomenology of an orange experience (but referring to blue experiences). According to Papineau, there is nothing wrong with this scenario. The problem is the following: an account of phenomenal concepts that does not link the phenomenal mode of presentation involved in the concept to its referents cannot explain their cognitive role of delivering the information about a specific phenomenal character of an experience. Imagine that Mary tries to find out if blue experiences belong to unique or to binary hue experiences in her phenomenal color space. If she uses her phenomenal concept of blue experiences, which is tied to the phenomenology of an orange experience, to figure this out, she might end up with the introspective judgment that blue experiences belong to phenomenal binary hues. This seems at least to be an undesirable result.

Further implausible scenarios are close at hand. For example, we can imagine a possible world in which a phenomenal concept of blue experiences is tied to the phenomenology of a tickle. Also in this world, the phenomenal concept is supposed to carry information about the phenomenal character of blue experiences and to make this information introspectively available. Moreover, in cases in which the phenomenal concept involves no phenomenology at all, it remains completely mysterious how one could make *any* introspective judgments about the phenomenal character of the experience at all, using this concept. In this case, Mary would be no better off than she was in her achromatic environment looking at neural activations of another person's brain.

Hence, the claim that Mary might gain a new *phenomenal* concept (which may constitute her new phenomenal knowledge) even if the concept is tied to no phenomenology at all remains mysterious. Thus, we have found strong reasons for the following claim: no account of phenomenal concepts that fails to posit an intimate link between the phenomenal modes of presentation involved in the concepts and their referents can successfully explain the Mary-scenario. Thus, we have to search for an alternative account of phenomenal concepts pointing at specific features that can explain these concepts' cognitive role in a satisfactory way.

Chalmers (2007) reaches a similar conclusion as the outcome of his master argument. He argues that any version of the PCS has to fail because of the following dilemma: either we can conceive of a possible world in which P & ~C holds (= the complete physical truth about the universe holds, but a thesis about phenomenal concepts does not)—then phenomenal concepts are not physically explicable. Or we cannot conceive of a possible world in which P & ~C holds—then phenomenal concepts cannot explain our epistemic situation with regard to phenomenal experiences. Therefore, according to Chalmers, accounts of phenomenal concepts that are physically explicable are too "thin" to explain our epistemic situation, whereas "thick" accounts that meet this explanatory constraint are not explicable in physical terms.

In what follows I will argue for a stronger conclusion. To Chalmers' conclusion, namely, that the explanatory accounts cannot be explained in physical terms and hence do nothing to deflate anti-physicalist arguments, I will add that those phenomenal concepts that have the explanatory power imply non-physical referents. So the difference between Chalmers's argument and the one put forward hereinafter is the following: while in

Chalmers's view, a physicalist could still hold that phenomenal concepts are not themselves physically explicable but that they are nonetheless compatible with physicalism, I argue that an account of phenomenal concepts that explains our epistemic situation satisfactorily is *not* compatible with physicalism.

3. THE ENCAPSULATION ACCOUNT OF PHENOMENAL CONCEPTS

In the previous section, I argued that no account of phenomenal concepts that fails to posit an intimate link between their modes of presentation and their referents can successfully explain the Mary-scenario. Thus, we need a new account of phenomenal concepts. In this section, I will develop the *encapsulation account* that meets both explanatory constraints imposed by the particularities of phenomenal concepts.

A brief reminder of the two explanatory constraints: the first desideratum concerns the special acquisition condition of phenomenal concepts. Phenomenal concepts cannot be deduced a priori from physical concepts and, hence, are conceptually isolated. In accordance with defenders of the PCS, I think that a new phenomenal concept can be acquired only under the condition of attentively undergoing an experience. The second explanatory constraint concerns the cognitive role of phenomenal concepts. When Mary attentively looks at the blue sky and thereby acquires a phenomenal concept of blue experiences,[16] she makes epistemic progress. This epistemic progress is explained by the cognitive role of the phenomenal concept: the phenomenal concept carries information about the phenomenal character of blue experiences and makes this information introspectively available.

In the following, I will present the encapsulation account of phenomenal concepts that does justice to both explanatory constraints. First, I will extend the analysis of the conceptual isolation of phenomenal concepts by offering an explanation as to why phenomenal concepts have this particular acquisition condition. Second, I will argue that the proposed account can also explain the cognitive role of phenomenal concepts in a satisfactory way.

Physicalist defenders of the PCS grant that one has to undergo an experience to acquire a phenomenal concept. This way of formulating the acquisition condition needs to be spelled out in more detail. In order to acquire a new phenomenal concept one has to attend to the experience and discriminate it from all other current experiences. I am assuming that primitive discrimination can be accomplished in a nonconceptual manner.[17] Thus, the act of attentive discrimination is the *basis* of a process that yields a phenomenal concept. The account of phenomenal concepts that I offer is inspired by Lehrer's (2011, 2012) account of conceptualization in what he calls the process of "exemplarization". I take the experience the person attentively discriminates to be conceptualized in a special manner. Following Lehrer,

I hold that in conceptualization, the experience is used to mark a distinction between what is included in the reference class of the phenomenal concept and what is not. The experience can play this role because it exhibits its phenomenal character, i.e. the referents of the phenomenal concept have exactly those features that the experience exhibits. Hence, when acquiring a new phenomenal concept we first are undergoing a nonconceptual experience that, due to attentive awareness, is discriminated from the other current experiences. Next, because the experience exhibits its phenomenal character, we can conceptualize the experience.[18]

This interpretation of the concept acquisition process sheds light on the *nature* of phenomenal concepts. When Mary is attentively aware of her new experience, this process of attentive discrimination combined with the experience's role to mark a distinction between what is included in the reference class and what is not by exhibiting its phenomenal character, leads to a new phenomenal concept that *encapsulates* the experience itself. What I label as *encapsulation* is based on the idea that the experience itself is the core of the phenomenal concept.[19] This constitutional link between experience and concept explains how the reference of the phenomenal concept is fixed: namely, due to the experience's role to directly exhibit the referents of the concept.

Given the constitutional link between experiences and phenomenal concepts the encapsulation account has to provide an answer to the following question: What distinguishes the experience from the concept encapsulating it? To a first approximation we can say that the concept has a structure and cognitive role that outruns the encapsulated experience. The important point is that the concept implies a generalization about the phenomenal character of the experience that enables the subject to distinguish what falls under the concept and what does not.[20] So the generality of the phenomenal concept is what distinguishes it from the non-conceptualized experience. Moreover, the subject possessing the concept can use it to think new thoughts, to make new judgments, etc. For example, she can think "R is my favorite experience!" or "The experience caused by looking at ripe tomatoes is R". In short, the possession of the phenomenal concept enables the subject to attribute a phenomenal property to something. All this cannot be done solely by having an experience—a concept has to be formed which encapsulates the experience and uses it to display its referent.

3.1. Self-Representation: The Key to the Encapsulation Account

In this section, I will start spelling out the decisive feature of the encapsulated *experience* in detail. Subsequently, I will analyze the consequences that the decisive feature of the encapsulated experience has on the *concept*.

My main claim is that experiences, which are encapsulated in a concept and fulfill the role of displaying the referents of the concept by exhibiting their phenomenal character, are *self-representing*.[21] Self-representation is sometimes held to account best for conscious experiences. (See e.g. Kriegel 2004: 3, 153f; Levine 2006: 177f.) A reason for this claim can be stated as follows: conscious experiences are states we are aware of being in. Awareness includes representation. And, according to defenders of self-representational approaches to consciousness, conscious states are not represented via other (higher-order) states but rather are represented by themselves. So we can say that self-representing experiences exhibit two features: first, they represent themselves directly, without any separate mode of presentation involved.[22] Second, the self-representing character of experiences explains our awareness of them.

The first feature explains how an experience can be conceptualized in a way that yields a phenomenal concept as suggested on the encapsulation account: an experience that represents itself can be encapsulated in a phenomenal concept and thereby fix the concept's reference by *directly* exhibiting the referents.

The second feature elucidates why I think that self-representation is the basis for the encapsulation account. The explanatory structure in the concept forming process is the following: self-representation explains our awareness of the experience, and the attentive awareness of the experience is a condition for forming a concept that encapsulates the experience.

Most importantly, the self-representational character of experiences does not only explain how a phenomenal concept can be formed—it also explains how the concept can play its cognitive role. Recall that the cognitive role of a phenomenal concept is to carry information about the phenomenal character of experiences and to make this information introspectively accessible to the subject. First, because the encapsulated experiences are self-representing, they directly display the referents of the concepts. Thus, the encapsulated experience enables the concept to carry the relevant information. Second, the self-representing experience allows us to be aware of it, which explains how the information carried by the concept is introspectively accessible to the subject. Therefore, the self-representing character of experiences can account for the special formation process of phenomenal concepts as well as for their cognitive role.

Next, I will analyze the structure of the *concept* that encapsulates the experience. The self-representing character of the experience has particular consequences for the concept.

First, it guarantees the direct reference of the concept formed on the basis of the experience. Since there is no separate mode of presentation involved, the phenomenal concept picks out its referent directly.

Second, the reference of a phenomenal concept is fixed by the mode of presentation involved in the concept that contains an instance of the concept's referent. Since the reference of phenomenal concepts is fixed by their internal constitution and not by external factors, phenomenal concepts are rigid, viz. they pick out the same referent in all possible worlds. Recall that we were looking for an account that links the mode of presentation involved in a phenomenal concept intimately to its referent. Constitution guarantees such intimate link. Given the internal constitution of phenomenal concepts, the problematic scenarios developed in section two—i.e. Mary employing a phenomenal concept of blue experiences but that is tied to the phenomenology of an orange experience or to no phenomenal experience at all—are ruled out.

Moreover, the encapsulation account evades also a closely related problem that is typically faced by demonstrative versions of phenomenal concepts. As Chalmers (2007) and Balog (2012a) point out, on demonstrative accounts, one can imagine the experience picked out by a phenomenal concept and currently demonstrated as having a different character. I have argued that this scenario is also conceivable on those constitutional accounts that do not concentrate on the mode of presentation involved in the concept (e.g. Papineau's account). Notice that this worrisome scenario is avoided by phenomenal concepts that encapsulate experiences. Such concepts necessarily yield information about specific the phenomenal characters of experiences and pick out the very same referents in whatever context they are exercised.

I argued that phenomenal concepts encapsulate self-representing experiences. This account has strong explanatory power.

It explains the conceptual isolation of phenomenal concepts. Moreover, by offering an account of the concept formation process, it adds an explanation as to why phenomenal concepts have these special acquisition conditions.

Most importantly, the encapsulation account also meets the second explanatory constraint and accounts for the cognitive role of phenomenal concepts. The encapsulation of the experience explains how the concept carries the relevant information. The self-representing character of the encapsulated experience explains why the relevant information is introspectively accessible. Once the cognitive role is explained by an account of phenomenal concepts, an explanation of the epistemic progress one makes because of the new concept acquisition is close at hand. The encapsulation of a self-representing experience in the phenomenal concept explains, for example, how Mary can think new thoughts such as "I like Yves-Klein-blue experiences more than light-blue experiences!" Since the experience itself is a constitutional part of the phenomenal concept, she can compare the two experiences by deploying the relevant concepts.[23]

Finally, the encapsulation account does justice to the intuition that, for example, a phenomenal concept of a red experience necessarily facilitates information about the *phenomenal character of red experiences*. The encapsulation provides what we were looking for, namely an intimate link between the mode of presentation involved in phenomenal concepts and their referents. Thus, the worrisome scenarios discussed in section two are ruled out.

I conclude that the encapsulation account provides the best account of the uniqueness of phenomenal concepts—their conceptual isolation as well as their cognitive role.

3.2. The Dualist Consequences of the Encapsulation Account

In the previous section I presented an account of phenomenal concepts featuring the encapsulation of self-representing experiences, and I argued that this account has strong explanatory power.[24] Next, I will investigate the ontological consequences of the encapsulation account of phenomenal concepts.

One may think that the proposed account of phenomenal concepts encapsulating experiences is similar to the physicalist constitutional account, which also has it that phenomenal concepts are constituted by experiences. It isn't. There are several differences between these accounts, and these differences have important ontological consequences regarding the referents of phenomenal concepts. Most importantly, physicalist constitutional accounts aim at a *physicalist* explanation of anti-physicalist puzzles. Hence, they have to explain the conceptual isolation and the cognitive role of phenomenal concepts in a way that does not introduce non-physical entities.

In section two we noticed that Papineau meets the physicalist requirement in a first step, when he introduces neural templates as the vehicles of phenomenal concepts. The second step in a successful physicalist account of phenomenal concepts consists in giving a *physicalist* account of how a neural template can be part of a phenomenal concept and how it can yield introspectively accessible information about the phenomenal character of experiences. This attempt fails because the physicalist move to point at neural templates involved in phenomenal concepts does not suffice to explain how the concepts can facilitate the relevant information. To facilitate the relevant information, the phenomenal concept has to involve the right phenomenal mode of presentation. Thus, the outcome of my analysis was the following: accounts of phenomenal concepts that deny a constitutional link between the phenomenal mode of presentation involved in the concept and its referent—i.e. pure demonstrative accounts as well as Papineau's account—cannot reach the explanatory target of the PCS.

Contrary to Papineau's model, there exist physicalist constitutional accounts that acknowledge the importance of the phenomenal modes of presentation involved in phenomenal concepts. For example, Loar's [1990]1997) direct recognitional account, Hill and McLaughlin's conceptual role account (1999), as well as Block's (2006) constitutional account all utilize the phenomenal mode of presentation to explain the uniqueness of phenomenal concepts. The outcome of my analysis so far is that this is exactly the right path to an account of phenomenal concepts that has strong explanatory power. But, I will argue, the physicalist cannot take this path.

Let me explain. The appeal to the mode of presentation involved in a phenomenal concept has to be spelled out in detail to explain the concept's cognitive role. The self-representing character of the experience provides such an explanation. But granting the self-representing character of the encapsulated experience turns out to be problematic for the physicalist. In order to see this, we need to notice that defenders of the PCS grant that experiences involved in the concepts do not seem physical.[25] From this, I will

A Dualist Account of Phenomenal Concepts 127

first infer that experiences seem non-physical, and then argue that experiences *are* non-physical.

I start by considering an objection that targets my claim that experiences that do not seem physical, do seem non-physical. One might point out, following Armstrong's (1968) argumentation illustrated by the "headless woman illusion", that "the experience does not seem physical" doesn't entail that "the experience seems non-physical". I do not think that this objection applies to self-representing experiences.

Let me start by pointing out a disanalogy between Armstrong's original example and the case of experiences. Note how Armstrong states his argument:

> What the example shows is that [. . .] it is very natural for human beings to pass from something that is true: "I do not perceive that X is Y", to something that may be false "I perceive that X is not Y". (Armstrong 1968: 48)

On the first interpretation, the example is intended to show that there may be Xs that are Y but which are not perceived as being Y. In other words: one might falsely pass from a statement about how X *seems* to a statement about the *nature* of X. Thus, the fact that the example is put in terms of "perceiving"—a success word—is crucial. Note that in our case we are concerned with how an experience *seems*. "Seeming" is not a success word, and we do not intend to infer something about the ontological nature of experiences; i.e. we do not infer that experiences *are* not physical. Hence, there is no room for a scenario that parallels the headless woman illusion.[26] In contrast to the headless woman illusion, the entailment in the experience-case remains at the level of seemings and does not pass to the ontological nature of the thing. So the inference from "an experience does not seem physical" to "an experience does *seem* non-physical" cannot be in the same sense fallacious as the original Armstrong case.

Next, one might admit the disanalogy, but object that the Armstrong example is open to a second interpretation that does not focus on "perceiving" as a success word. Rather it concentrates on the illegitimate shift of the scope of negation. This second interpretation also applies at the level of seemings and amounts to the following claim: an experience can fail to seem physical, because it seems something else, say Z, and from that one cannot conclude that it seems non-physical. I admit that this is a possible scenario for many cases of representations. However, I think that experiences are a special case. There are two possible ways to argue for the conclusion that the experience seems non-physical.

First, when we reflect on the ontological status of an occurrent experience by explicitly considering two possibilities—physicality or non-physicality— the experience does not seem physical. Therefore, from the statement "X does not *seem* physical" and the additional consideration whether X seems physical or non-physical, we can conclude that "X *seems* non-physical".

Second, even if we do not consider the physicality of the experience explicitly, we can see that the experience seems non-physical. The reason is that the experience does not seem physical because it seems Z, where seeming Z is such that it entails *seeming non-physical*. (Let me emphasize that we are not looking for a seeming that entails that something *is* non-physical. The question is rather if there is a seeming that entails that something *seems* non-physical.) Note that such Z would add also a further explanation as to why experiences do not seem physical.

I think that there is such a decisive seeming that is part of every experience. It is the subjective character of an experience (Nagel 1974). Experiences are necessarily experienced from the first person perspective. Thus, every experience, regardless if it is a blue experience, pain experience, or tasting red wine experience, is constituted by appearing as a subjective one. I take the fact that the subjective character of an experience seems inseparable from how an experience seems to us, to generate the widely accepted intuition of distinctness.[27] States that are accessed from a first person perspective and hence subjective *seem* fundamentally distinct from those that are accessible from a third person perspective and hence objective. Physical states are taken to belong to the latter class, which *seems* fundamentally distinct from the former, subjective class. The upshot is when a state seems subjective, it *seems* non-physical.[28] Hence, the first outcome of my analysis is that the experience which is encapsulated in a phenomenal concept and constitutes its mode of presentation seems non-physical.

The further conclusion that the experience *is* non-physical is independently supported, namely by the self-representing nature of the experience. Self-representation is a mark of entities which do not give rise to a distinction between the representing and the represented item. In this case, we do not have to search for the represented item; it is right there, in the representation. Note that an X, that represents itself, can do this in various ways. It can do this via one of its properties, say Z, and nonetheless fail to display another of its (maybe essential) properties, say Y.

This is the main line that the defenders of the physicalist constitutional account advocate: the self-representing experience simply does not represent itself in terms of its fundamental nature—it has a hidden physical nature that is not part of the representation.[29] I grant that an experience can represent itself in different terms than those of its fundamental nature (Y), say via Z, and fail to display Y. However, an experience cannot represent itself in terms of a property that *contradicts* its fundamental nature, i.e., the experience cannot represent itself as being non-Y, while its hidden nature is Y. In the case of self-representation this would amount to the claim that an experience is both Y and non-Y. Therefore, a self-representing experience that represents itself as being non-physical can have a lot of other properties that are not part of the representation, but physicality cannot be among those hidden properties. My conclusion is that a self-representing experience that seems non-physical cannot be physical.

This dualist outcome can be put also in another way, by utilizing Block's (2006) distinction between the cognitive mode of presentation and the metaphysical mode of presentation. The former is seen as a property of the representation and the latter is seen as a property of the referent. Block argues that different cognitive modes of presentation do not require different metaphysical modes of presentation and, hence, no property dualism follows from the fact that an experience can be cognitively presented in different ways.

According to my analysis, in the case of phenomenal concepts, an instance of the referent is part of the concept and constitutes the concept's mode of presentation. Therefore, the property of the cognitive mode of presentation does not only fix the reference, it also *is* a property of the referent. This property is not represented as a physical one. On the additional assumption that we either consider the physicality of the property explicitly or we focus on the subjective character of the property, we can conclude that it is represented as a non-physical one. It might be the case that the referent has *further, hidden,* properties that are not part of the cognitive mode of presentation. But the cognitive mode of presentation cannot exhibit a property that *contradicts* the metaphysical mode of presentation. Therefore, physicality cannot be part of the metaphysical mode of presentation of the referent of a phenomenal concept. In short: experiences cannot be physical.

The upshot is that the structure of phenomenal concepts is not neutral with respect to the ontological nature of their referents. The explanatory feature of the experience involved in the concept—its self-representing character—gives the encapsulation account an ontological bite. Therefore, the physicalist faces a dilemma:

If she denies the importance of the mode of presentation involved in the concept, as demonstrative accounts as well as Papineau's (2007) account do, she cannot explain the cognitive role of phenomenal concepts satisfactorily.

But if she explains the cognitive role by defending a constitutional account that involves the phenomenal mode of presentation (as e.g. Block (2006) does), then, according to my argumentation, she also has to accept that *self-representing* experiences constitute phenomenal concepts. Once granted that there is no separate mode of presentation involved, the experience cannot be seen as just a mode of presenting a physical referent. In particular, it cannot be seen as a mode of presenting a physical referent in terms *other* than it really is. Thus, the physicalist will end up with non-physical entities being the direct referents of phenomenal concepts. Obviously, in the latter case the physicalist target of the PCS can no longer be reached.

4. CONCLUSION

The physicalist attempt to reduce consciousness is challenged by anti-physicalist arguments based on the phenomenal character of mental states. The PCS is often seen as a powerful contemporary response to these arguments. My analysis targets new insights on phenomenal concepts and their consequences for the problem of consciousness.

I demonstrated that, in accordance with the PCS, the new concepts involved in the Mary-scenario differ in several significant respects from any other concept-type. Jackson's knowledge argument teaches us that phenomenal concepts are conceptually isolated and have very special acquisition conditions. I combined this with another outcome of the Mary-scenario, namely that phenomenal concepts play the cognitive role of carrying introspectively accessible information about the phenomenal character of experiences. These two insights from the knowledge argument capture the particularities of phenomenal concepts best, and they require an explanation.

First, I argued that the existing physicalist accounts cannot meet both explanatory requirements. Second, I presented an account of phenomenal concepts that can explain both particularities of phenomenal concepts in a satisfactory way. To establish this account, I argued that phenomenal concepts are structured in a very particular way—they encapsulate self-representing experiences. In a third step, I demonstrated that the self-representing experiences best explain the cognitive role of phenomenal concepts. In a last step, I argued that in the case of self-representation, the representation cannot display properties that contradict properties of the represented item. Since self-representing experiences seem non-physical, we can conclude that the referents of phenomenal concepts are non-physical.

Hence, the encapsulation account of phenomenal concepts not only has strong explanatory power. Because the reference of a phenomenal concept is determined by its inner constitution involving self-representing experiences, it also implies dualist consequences. To conclude, the account of phenomenal concepts that explains their uniqueness satisfactorily cannot be used to explain away our dualist intuitions. Rather, it reinforces dualism.

ACKNOWLEDGMENTS

I am grateful to Marian David, Johann C. Marek, Nenad Miščević, Howard Robinson, Leopold Stubenberg, and particularly Keith Lehrer for very helpful discussions and detailed comments on earlier drafts of this paper. Special thanks go to Guido Melchior for insightful comments and suggestions. I presented earlier versions of this paper at the CEU Budapest, the University of Rijeka, the University of Innsbruck, and at the workshop "Perception and Knowledge" in Graz. I want to thank the audiences for fruitful discussions and comments. The research was funded by the Austrian Science Fund (FWF): T-507-G15.

NOTES

1. Physicalism can be roughly defined as the thesis that the world is entirely physical. Physicalism can be stated in terms of *facts*, which would amount to

the following claim: all facts about the world are physical, or necessitated by or supervenient on physical facts. Anti-physicalism denies this claim and often points at phenomenal facts as a paradigm case of non-physical facts.
2. In the following, I subsume the quotational and the constitutional accounts under the label "constitutional account", since both accounts share the idea that a phenomenal concept is constituted by an experience—but this does not entail that the constitution needs to be understood as analogous to a quotation-relation. For example, one could count Lehrer's (2012) account of exemplar concepts as a version of the constitutional account, but Lehrer explicitly rejects the idea of quotation in exemplarization.
3. For example, Mary's epistemic gap is illustrated by the fact that she cannot deduce a priori a phenomenal truth from all the physical truths.
4. There are various ways of cashing out the idea that Mary gains new knowledge while holding that this does not entail an ontological dualist conclusion. If physicalism is construed as a thesis about *facts*, one might think that Mary gains knowledge of a new (fine-grained) proposition that is made true by some "old" fact she already knew. If one states physicalism in terms of *truths* (i.e. all truths about the world are necessitated by the complete physical truth), then one might choose another way. For example, assuming coarse-grained propositions (e.g. sets of possible worlds or Russellian propositions), one might hold that Mary gains only a new mental representation of an "old" truth. All of these responses question the inference from the epistemic premise (Mary lacks some kind of knowledge) to the ontological consequence of the knowledge argument.
5. It is subject to discussion whether this acquisition condition should be formulated as a necessary condition. One might, for example, think that Mary can gain a phenomenal concept of orange-experiences by combining her phenomenal concept of red-experiences and her phenomenal concept of yellow-experiences and, hence, without necessarily undergoing an orange-experience. A possible rejoinder is the following: in the case that this imaginative combination of *phenomenal* concepts should turn out as successful, Mary would create an instance of an orange-experience and this would provide the basis for her new phenomenal concept. Unfortunately, for the lack of space, I cannot pursue this issue in detail here. So I just want to point out that this consideration has no impact on the knowledge argument, since Mary had no color-experiences at all in her achromatic room.

Also Dennett (2007a) formulated an argument against the view that undergoing an experience is a necessary condition for gaining a phenomenal concept by invoking Swamp-Mary's possession of phenomenal concepts. If one agrees with Dennett, no epistemic progress has to be explained in the Mary-scenario—it could be the case that Mary already possesses phenomenal concepts in her achromatic environment. This paper is not aimed at responding to this consideration. Thus, I confine myself to note that defenders of the PCS grant that the scientist makes epistemic progress by attentively enjoying her very first color-experience and that she can acquire the corresponding concept only on the basis of this experience. This is what Balog labels the "Experience Thesis" (Balog 2009: 299), and defenders of the PCS commit themselves to this special acquisition condition.
6. Philosophers like David Lewis (1988) may argue that in claiming that the phenomenal concept carries information, I have already given the game away to the anti-physicalist. Hence, I want to point out that I am using the notion of "information" here in a very weak sense. At this stage of my argument, I leave it open whether this notion implies that Mary gains new information or simply gains "old" information carried in a new way.

7. For an anti-physicalist approach to phenomenal concepts see Chalmers (2003, 2007) and his notion of "direct pure phenomenal concepts".
8. Unfortunately, for the lack of space, I can only give a rough categorization of the extensive literature on phenomenal concepts and have to leave several details and accounts aside. More detailed characterizations of the numerous sophisticated accounts of the PCS can be found, e.g. in Balog (2009).
9. For Tye's current position on phenomenal concepts, namely, that there are no phenomenal concepts which meet the physicalist requirements, see Tye (2009).
10. When we think about experiences of other persons (or, as some philosophers hold, also in the case of thinking about our own future or past experiences), phenomenal concepts are applied in a non-basic (or "derivative") way. There are different ways of fleshing out the relation between basic and non-basic applications of phenomenal concepts. On a weak interpretation, non-basic applications depend on previous experiences; on a stronger interpretation non-basic applications depend on previous basic applications of phenomenal concepts.
11. I see two options to interpret the claim that a concept uses a neural template. On the first interpretation, this claim is intended to capture just a *simultaneous occurrence* of concept and neural template. Thus, the template is not part of the phenomenal concept, and hence it is not the *concept* that carries the relevant information. What carries the information is the template which is only contingently connected to the concept. Moreover, on this reading it is unclear how a neural template can make the relevant information accessible to the subject possessing the concept. The second way to go is to think of the neural template as a *part* of the concept. This interpretation evades the problem of explaining how the concept comes to carry the relevant information.
12. For example on Dretske's (1981) account, a regular co-occurrence might suffice to account for information. Contrary to this, I will argue that a more intimate link between concept and experience is needed to explain the concept's cognitive role of carrying the relevant information and making it accessible to a subject. Moreover, I will argue that scenarios in which a basic phenomenal concept is applied in the absence of its referent should be ruled out by an adequate account of phenomenal concepts—but this seems to be conceivable if there is no constitutional link between the phenomenal concept and the experience.
13. Levine (2007) argues as well (but in a different way than I will propose hereinafter) that the physical presence of the represented experience within the concept does not explain its cognitive presence.
14. For example, perceptual concepts can be like that. What it is like to have a specific neural template activated might not be reference-fixing in the case of concepts that refer to external objects. But phenomenal concepts refer to *experiences*. Experiences have their phenomenal character essentially. Thus, the mode of presentation involved in a *phenomenal* concept is crucial for the referent, i.e., if a phenomenal concept uses the phenomenal character of blue experiences to present its referent, then the referents are blue experiences.
15. A motivation for the view that a specific phenomenology involved in a phenomenal concept is irrelevant for its reference can be the commitment to the *transparency thesis*. Papineau (2007: 124) explicitly points out that his theory can account for the transparency thesis, since on his account deploying a perceptual concept referring to a bird and deploying a phenomenal concept referring to a bird-experience will involve the same phenomenology. The reference of these concepts is determined by what sort of information is attached to the experience that is used—if it is bird-appropriate information, then it will turn out as a perceptual concept; if it is information about

bird-*experiences*, then it will turn out as a phenomenal concept. Accordingly, defenders of the transparency thesis (e.g. Harman 1990; Tye 2002; Crane 2003) might hold that Mary's new experience represents properties of external objects. Hence, on this account the phenomenology is not necessarily tied to the referent of a phenomenal concept, since it is not seen as a property of an experience anymore.

It is beyond the scope of this paper to analyze the merit of the transparency thesis. I think that experiences *can* represent the external world, but they also can represent themselves. Here I am concerned with the latter case. The following scenarios illustrate that the phenomenal character is a property instantiated by an experience. Imagine Mary who is exposed to a flash of red light that fills her whole visual field. Or consider that a neurologist evokes a red experience in her, by manipulating her brain. Also well-known examples that point to blurry vision, where the experience itself, not the objects of experience, is experienced as blurry, challenge the transparency thesis. I think that these cases illustrate that Mary acquires a new phenomenal concept that refers to the *phenomenal character of her experience*. Since experiences have their phenomenal character essentially, an account of phenomenal concepts that do not involve specific phenomenal modes of presentation, fails in explaining their cognitive role.

16. Here I am describing what happens to Jackson's Mary. As Lehrer (2012) suggests, one could imagine Mary having undergone a stroke and, hence, still being able to have experiences though lacking all her conceptual capacities. Therefore, undergoing an experience might not be a sufficient condition for gaining a phenomenal concept. In this paper, I leave it open if having an experience is a sufficient condition for acquiring a phenomenal concept; the important point here is that having an experience is a *necessary* condition.
17. Note that I do not claim that occurrent experiences are always discriminated in a nonconceptual manner. I just think that primitive discrimination does not depend on possessing a concept and *can* be accomplished nonconceptually.
18. I want to highlight that using Lehrer's account of *conceptualization* on the basis of experiences for spelling out the encapsulation account does not mean that I buy wholesale into his account of exemplarization. Importantly, I think that only self-representing experiences can constitute a phenomenal concept. In contrast, Lehrer holds that exemplarization is not restricted to experiences. In Fürst (2012), I argue in detail that Lehrer's notion of exemplarization faces serious problems when it is not confined to self-representing experiences.
19. Balog (2012b), Block (2007), and Chalmers (2003) defend accounts of phenomenal concepts that share the structure of the here advocated encapsulation. Where Balog and Block think that such an account is compatible with physicalism, Chalmers holds that the content of "direct phenomenal concepts" is not conceptually reducible to the physical or functional. In the following, I will argue that if the encapsulation account is spelled out in detail, it has more explanatory power than the physicalist accounts and it will turn out to be *incompatible* with physicalism.
20. Lehrer (2011, 2012) argues that the experience in the concept can be used to mark a distinction between the entities that fall under this concept and those that do not. This way of fleshing out what makes the phenomenal concept encapsulating an experience to a *concept* is borrowed from Lehrer.
21. For a historical discussion of the notion of self-representation see Brentano (1874) and Meinong (1899). For a contemporary discussion of self-representation see, for example, Kriegel and Williford (2006) and Lehrer (2004, 2006, 2012).

22. Of course, besides this, they can also represent properties of objects of the external world.
23. The encapsulation account also offers some elucidation regarding phenomena like the following: someone vehemently refusing to talk about a painful experience undergone in the past, or someone eager to talk about her feelings towards a new love. Because the employed phenomenal concepts encapsulate relevant experiences, one will be eager to discuss pleasant experiences and disinclined to relate painful memories.
24. The following objection might be raised against a constitutional account of phenomenal concepts: If the experience is a constitutional part of the phenomenal concept, how can proponents of this thesis account for Mary's true thought involving a phenomenal concept that she is currently not having a red experience? Note that my considerations aim at basic applications of phenomenal concepts, viz. applications of phenomenal concepts to occurrent experiences. I find it highly plausible to hold that on a *basic application of a phenomenal concept,* Mary cannot truly think she is currently not having a red experience. But I am open to different accounts of what sort of concept of red experiences she can employ to truly think this thought. For example, some philosophers (Balog 2009; Papineau 2007) answer this question by pointing at *derivative* applications of phenomenal concepts that do not imply an occurring experience and are used in the true thought mentioned before.
25. Some representationalists (for example, Hill (forthcoming)) react to the fact that experiences seem non-physical in the following way: they claim that, besides our intuition to the contrary, we need to introduce a distinction between the appearance and the reality of experiences. Their main claim is that representations explain the appearances of experiences. Hence, the non-physicality is taken to concern only the seeming (representation) and not the reality of experiences. It is easy to see why this explanatory move does not succeed in the case of the encapsulation account: on the encapsulation account, the representing item represents in terms of the represented one. If the non-physicality concerns the representation and the representation is constituted by the represented item, the non-physicality also applies to the represented item.
26. One might try to construe the "seeming" case as *structurally* analogous to the original Armstrong case. To do this, a seeming/reality distinction has to be introduced also on the level of seemings. I think that this is problematic, for it does not make sense to say that there are experiences that fail to seem Y, but their real *seeming-nature* is Y. Experiences might have a hidden ontological nature, but it is implausible to hold that they have a hidden *seeming* that goes beyond the way that they seem to us. (Some philosophers doubt this. For example, on Lycan's higher-order theory (1997: 758): "[. . .] a second-order monitor could break down and make a first-order state seem to seem to me in a way that the state does not in fact seem to me".)
27. Papineau (2007: 135) states the intuition of distinctness as follows: "It seems undeniable that most people have a strong intuition of mind-brain-distinctness—an intuition that pains are something extra to brain states, say. This intuition (. . .) persists even among those (like me) who are persuaded (. . .) that dualism must be false". Note that he explicitly holds that "[the intuition of distinctness] is not an intuition of apparently contingent truth (. . .) but simply a *direct intuition of falsity*" (2007: 134, my emphasis). Papineau thinks that the direct intuition of falsity of physicalism can be explained by the joined exercise of a phenomenal and a physical concept. I argued that his account fails in its attempt to explain away dualist intuitions. But I think there is another, more natural, explanation for the "direct intuition

of falsity of physicalism" at hand, namely, that experiences seem subjective and, hence, non-physical.
28. One might object, following Loar (1997: 610), that "there is no incoherence in the thought that the 'subjectivity' of a phenomenal quality is identical with an objective physical-functional aspect of that property". I want to emphasize again that I am not claiming that the subjective character implies non-physicality. I just hold that seeming subjective implies *seeming* non-physical.
29. One example of this explanatory move is found in Hill (forthcoming):"It is necessary to explain how it is possible to grasp X experientially without appreciating its identity with Y. It is normally possible to provide such an explanation by invoking some sort of appearance/reality distinction. Thus, we might distinguish between X itself and a property that serves as the mode of presentation for X. Or, if there is no other property that serves as the mode of presentation for X, [. . .] then we might distinguish between X-as-it-is-in-itself and X-as-it-is-represented by an experiential representation".

Part 3
Cartesian (Substance) Dualism

8 What Makes Me Me? A Defense of Substance Dualism

Richard Swinburne

I argue in this chapter that although there are many different ways of describing the world or some segment thereof, any way which fails to entail a logically separable body and soul as the two constituents of each known human being (the body being a contingent part and the soul the essential part of the human) will fail to give a full description of the world.

1. DEFINITIONS

I begin with some stipulative definitions. I understand by a property a monadic or relational universal, and by an event the instantiation of a property in a substance or substances (or in properties or events) at times. Any definition of a substance tends to beg philosophical questions, but I'll operate with a definition which does not, I think, beg the questions at issue in this paper. A substance is a thing (other than an event) which can (it is logically possible) exist independently of all other things of that metaphysical category (viz. all other substances) other than its parts.[1] Thus tables, planets, atoms, and humans are substances. Being square, weighing 10 kilos, or being-taller-than are properties (the former two being monadic properties, the latter being a relational property which relates two substances). Events include my table being square now, or John being taller than James on March 30, 2001 at 10:00 a.m.

There are different ways of making the mental/physical distinction, but I propose to make it in terms of the privilegedly accessible/public.[2] A mental property is one to whose instantiation the substance in whom it is instantiated necessarily has privileged access on all occasions of its instantiation, and a physical property is one to whose instantiation in it, a substance necessarily has no privileged access on any occasion of its instantiation. Someone has privileged access to whether a property P is instantiated in him in the sense that—given that he knows what it is for something to have P (that is, has the concept of P)[3]—whatever ways others have of finding this out, it is logically possible that he can use, but he has a further way (by experiencing it) which it is not logically possible that others can use. A pure mental property may then be defined as one whose instantiation does not entail the instantiation of a physical property. A mental event is one to whose instantiation in a substance, that substance has privileged access; and a physical event is one to whose instantiation in a substance that substance does not have privileged access. A pure mental event is one which does not entail the occurrence of a physical event. (Most but not all mental events involve the instantiations of mental properties.) A mental substance is one to whose existence that substance necessarily has privileged access, and a physical substance is a substance to whose existence that substance necessarily has no privileged access, that is a public substance. Since having privileged access to anything is itself a mental property, and someone who has any other mental property has that one, mental substances are just those for which some mental properties are essential. A pure mental substance is one whose existence does not entail that of a physical substance.

Now the history of the world is the history of one thing and then another thing happening, in a sense of "thing happening" which includes both things remaining the same and things changing. I suggest that the things that happen are events in my sense. It is this substance existing for a period of time (which can be analysed as it having its essential properties), coming to have this property or relation to another substance at this or that time, continuing to have it and then ceasing to have it. And I suggest, there are no other things that happen except events in my sense. Some have cited flashes and bangs as examples of things which happen but are not events in my sense. But they can easily be analysed as the instantiation of properties in regions of space, or (if you do not think that regions of space are substances in my sense) as themselves substances which exist for a very short time. To know the history of the world you need a canonical description of these events in terms of the properties, substances, and times involved in them; and these latter have to be picked out not by descriptions of them but by words which say what they are—rigid designators, but not just any rigid designators. For some rigid designators don't tell you much about what you are talking about—'water' as used in the eighteenth century or 'Hesperus' in very ancient Greece for example. We need what I shall call 'informative designators'. For a rigid designator of a thing to be an informative designator, it must be the case that someone who knows what the word means (that is, has the linguistic knowledge of how to use it) knows a certain set of conditions necessary and sufficient (in any possible world) for a thing to be that thing (whether or not he can state those conditions in words, or can in practice ever discover that those conditions are satisfied). To know these conditions for the application of a designator is to be able (when favourably positioned, with faculties in working order, and not subject to illusion) to recognize where the designator (or, if it is defined in words, the words by which it is defined) applies and where it doesn't and to be able to make simple inferences to and from its application. Thus "red" is an informative designator of a property, of which "the actual colour of my first book" is a mere uninformative rigid designator. I can know what "red" means in the sense of being able to identify things as red and make simple inferences using the word without knowing which things in our world are red. The ability to use the word "red" can exist without the knowledge of which things are actually red. But knowing how to use the expression "having the actual colour of my first book" does not give me the ability to recognize things other than my first book as having the colour of my first book. When I can designate a property (or whatever) by an informative designator, then I possess the concept of that property; I know fully what I am saying about an object when I say that it has that property. Even if, when subject to illusion, I misidentify an object as red when it is not, I know what I am saying when I say that it is red. I am saying that it has the colour which would look this way if the circumstances were normal. Hence if we designate a property (or whatever) by an informative designator, we know the essence of what is involved.

There are many different criteria for event, property, or substance identity advocated in the philosophical literature, and we need a metacriterion for choosing between them. Our present interest being to give a full description of the world, I suggest as a metacriterion that we individuate properties, substances, and times in such a way that if someone knows which (informatively designated) properties were instantiated in which (informatively designated) substances when, they know everything that has happened. A canonical description of an event will say which properties, substances, and times it involves, by picking them out by informative designators—and conjointly the properties, times, and substances involved will form an informative designator of that event. Then it will be the case that someone who knows all the events that have happened under their canonical descriptions knows everything that has happened (and someone who knows all the events that have happened under their canonical descriptions in some spatiotemporal region knows all that as happened in that region).

To give some person the knowledge of everything that has happened, it will suffice (given that that person has sufficient logical competence) to list any of many different subsets of all the events. For the occurrence of some events entails the occurrence of other events. There is one event of my walking from A to B from 9:30 to 9:45 a.m., another event of my walking slowly from 9:30 to 9:45, and a third event of my walking slowly from A to B from 9:30 to 9:45. But the third event is "nothing over and above" the first two events. To generalize, there is no more to the history of the world (or the world in a region) than any subset of events whose canonical descriptions entail those of all the events, and no less than any least subset which will do this. This suggests that we should count as the same event not merely two events which involve the instantiation of the same properties in the same substances at the same time, but also two events whose canonical descriptions (their informative designators) entail each other.[4] For if you know that the one has occurred, that puts you in a position (if you have sufficient logical competence) to know that the other has occurred, and conversely. The occurrence of one event is then nothing in the history of the world 'over and above' the occurrence of the other event. But the canonical descriptions of two events may entail each other without the properties, substances, and times involved all being (in any obvious sense) the same. One case of this is where a substance having some property entails and is entailed by some part of that substance having that property. For example, a table is flat if and only if that table's top is flat; but the former is not an occurrence in the history of the world additional to the latter, nor is the latter an occurrence additional to the former.

But now what are the identity criteria for properties and substances? (Alas, I shall not have time to consider the interesting issue of what are the identity conditions for times—e.g. whether (if it is July 25, 2005 today) P being instantiated in S today is the same event as P being instantiated in S on July 25, 2005.)

2. PROPERTIES

To begin with properties—to satisfy my metacriterion it is necessary and sufficient that each property named by informative designators which are not logically equivalent counts as a different property; though, since some entail others, we shall not need to mention them all in order to give a full account of the world. It is important to distinguish a description of a property P in terms of some property which it possesses, from an (informative or uninformative) rigid designator of P. "Green" is an informative designator of the property of being green; it applies to it in all possible worlds, and someone who knows what "green" means knows what an object has to be like to be green. "Amanda's favourite colour" or "the colour of spring grass" may function as descriptions of the property green in terms of its properties, possibly (in our world) uniquely identifying descriptions. These words may be used to describe the property of being green by informatively designating a different property—the property of being Amanda's favourite colour or the property of being of the same colour as spring grass—which properties the property of being green possesses. "Green is Amanda's favourite colour" is then a subject-predicate sentence where "Amanda's favourite colour" informatively designates the property of being Amanda's favourite colour and thereby (in our world) describes the property green. It says that the property "green" has itself the property of being Amanda's favourite colour. If it were (unusually) being asserted as a statement of identity between two informatively designated properties, it would be false. But any property name can be turned into an uninformative rigid designator of another property which has the first property. "Amanda's favourite colour" can be used to rigidly designate that colour which in the actual world is Amanda's favourite colour. In that case "Green is Amanda's favourite colour" will be a (true) identity statement. The device of rigidification allows us to turn any uniquely identifying description of something, including a property, into a rigid designator of that thing. But it does not make it into an informative designator of that thing. For—to take a different example—someone who knows what the rigidified predicate "the colour of spring grass" means need have no ability to identify any colour property (other than that of spring grass) as being that colour property—for they may never have seen spring grass.

To revert to the main theme—it follows from properties being the same if and only if they have logically equivalent informative designators, that such mental properties as 'being in pain' and 'looking red' are not the same properties as any brain properties, and from events being the same events if and only if their canonical descriptions involve the same properties, substances, and times or mutually entail each other, that mental events such as me being in pain are not the same as brain events such as my C-fibres firing. And in my view the same goes for intentional events such as me having such and such beliefs, desires, and purposes. More generally since mental events are ones to which the substance involved has privileged access, and physical events are ones to which the substance does not have privileged access, no physical event can be the same as any mental event nor can it entail it. Some mental events entail the occurrence of physical events (e.g. 'My intentionally moving my arm' entails 'my arm moving'). But some do not—"my thinking about philosophy" is a pure mental event. And the pure mental events clearly cannot be omitted from a full description of the world. If using some other criterion of property or event identity than ones similar to mine we were to conclude that mental events are the same as physical events, we would not be able to tell the whole history of the world by listing all the events under their canonical descriptions. We would have to say one event sometimes had different 'aspects' or 'features'—mental and physical. Some form of dualism of characteristics is inevitable in a full description of the world, and—in order to describe it by means of as few metaphysical categories as possible—it had better be a property dualism generating an event dualism; then we don't need to involve 'aspects' and other such things in our world description.

3. SUBSTANCES: GENERAL CONSIDERATIONS

I turn now to substances. For a substance at one time t_2 to be the same substance as a substance at an earlier time t_1, two kinds of criteria have to be satisfied. First, the two substances have to have the essential properties of the same species of substance to which they belong. Fairly clearly there are different ways of cutting up the world into species of substance, any of which would enable us to give a true and full description of the world. Suppose I have a car which I turn into a boat. I can think of cars as essentially cars. In that case one substance (a car) has ceased to exist and has become instead another substance (a boat). Or I can think of the car as essentially a motor vehicle, in which case it has continued to exist but with different (nonessential) properties. All three substances exist—the car which is essentially a car, the boat which is essentially a boat, and the motor vehicle which is essentially a motor vehicle. Yet I can tell the whole story of the world either by telling the story of the motor vehicle, or by telling the story of the car and the boat.

The second requirement for a substance at one time to be the same as a substance at another time is that the two substances should consist of largely the same parts, the extent to which this has to hold varying with the genus of substance. At least five kinds of thing have been called "substances"—simples, organisms, artefacts, mereological compounds, and gerrymandered objects (such as the right top drawer of my desk together with the planet Venus). Despite the view of some[5] that only some of these are really substances, my metacriterion gives no justification for such an arbitrary restriction. For each of these genera of substance there is its own kind of identity criterion, varying with the extent of replacement or rearrangement of parts which is compatible with the continued existence of the substance (e.g. for a mereological compound, no replacement is possible; for artefacts such as a car, boat, or motor vehicle, a small amount of replacement is possible). A full history of the world will need to mention only certain genera of substances—e.g. if it tells us the history of all the fundamental particles (considered as mereological compounds) that might suffice (if we forget for a few paragraphs about obvious problems arising from substances having mental properties). There is no more to any substance than its parts, and the history of the substance is the history of its parts. It might sometimes be explanatorily more simple if one took larger substances, e.g. organisms, rather than their parts as the substances in terms of which to trace the history of the world; but the causal properties of large substances including organisms are just the causal properties of their parts, even if the latter have causal properties such that when combined with other parts, they behave in ways different from the ways in which they behave separately. Alternatively, instead of telling merely the history of fundamental particles, we could include in our history of the world organisms and artefacts, saying when they gained or lost parts, or their internal parts were rearranged. We might then need to describe the history of the fundamental particles only in so far as they did not form unchanging parts of the organisms or artefacts. And certainly we could do without describing the behaviour of gerrymandered objects.

Being the same part may itself be a matter of having all the same subparts, and so on forever; or some replacement of subparts may be allowable, but in the end—if we are to operate with a sharp criterion of identity which allows a full description of the world—we must reach a level at which no replacement is possible if the subpart is to be the same subpart, a level of what I shall call ultimate parts. Being the same ultimate part will involve, as with any substance, having the essential properties characteristic of the kind—being this hydrogen atom will involve having a certain atomic mass,

What Makes Me Me? A Defense of Substance Dualism 145

number, etc. It will involve also something else, for it to be the same token of that kind—a principle of individuation.

What that principle is depends crucially on what sorts of things substances are. One view is that substances are simply bundles of co-instantiated properties. The alternative view is that some substances have thisness.[6] A substance has thisness, iff there could exist instead of it (or as well as it) a different substance which has all the same properties as it, including past and future related properties such as spatiotemporal continuity with a substance having such and such monadic properties.

If no substances have thisness, then the history of the world will consist of bundles of co-instantiated properties having further properties, including spatiotemporal relations to earlier bundles, coming into existence and ceasing to exist, and causing the subsequent existence and properties of other bundles. There are many different ways (equally well justified by our initial metacriterion for a system of metaphysical categories) to cut up the world into substances at a time, according to the size of the bundle and which members of the bundle are regarded as essential to the substance which they form. And, according to which members of the bundle are regarded as essential, so there will be different ways of tracing substance continuity over time. Ultimate parts will also be individuated by properties. The obvious such property for individuating parts which occupy space is spatiotemporal continuity with a substance having the same essential properties of the species, conjoined perhaps with causal continuity (that is, the earlier substance causing the existence of the later substance); for nonspatial substances, temporal plus causal continuity would seem to be the obvious requirement. We need some uniqueness requirement, to ensure that at most one substance later than a given substance which satisfies both of these requirements is the original substance. But there are again alternative ways in which these requirements could be spelled out, any of which would allow us to tell the whole story of the world. If we make spatiotemporal continuity necessary for the identity of substances over time, then we shall have to say that if an electron disappears from one orbit and causes an electron to appear in another orbit without there being spatiotemporal continuity between them, they are different electrons. Yet if we insist only on causal continuity, then they will be the same electron. But we can tell the whole story of the world either way, and both stories will be true; electrons of both sorts will exist.

If, however, some substances have thisness, a full history of the world will have to describe the continuities not merely of bundles of co-instantiated properties, but of the thisness which underlies certain bundles (that is, of what it is which makes the difference between two bundles of the same properties with qualitatively the same history). So it must be a necessary condition of ultimate parts of substances being the same that they have the same thisness.[7] For those physical substances which are material objects, thisness is being made of the same matter. We have then the hylemorphic theory that sameness of a material object requires sameness of essential properties of the species and sameness of underlying matter. In that case if (and only if) the electron in the new orbit is made of the same matter as the old electron, it is the old electron. Spatiotemporal continuity is now no longer an independent requirement for a physical substance continuing to exist, but probably (fallible) evidence that the same matter has continued to exist and so (given that the other arbitrarily chosen essential properties of the species are preserved) that the same material object exists. Spatiotemporal continuity is evidence of sameness of matter in so far as the best (i.e. most probable) physical theory of how matter behaves has the consequence that it moves along spatially continuous paths.

We do not know whether the inanimate material objects of our world have thisness, and in this respect we do not know what would constitute a full description of our world.[8] If they do, then not any account of the world which describes the patterns of property distribution in the world will be a correct one. We need one which individuates the ultimate parts of inanimate material objects (picked out as such in some clear way) as being the same substances only if they have the same matter. Then mereological compounds will have to have the same matter throughout their existence, while organisms may gradually replace matter.

Now, to give the full history of the world, I have claimed, involves listing all the events of some subset which entails all the events that have happened under their canonical descriptions. We saw in the case of properties that that involves picking out the properties involved by informative designators. And surely we need to informatively designate the substances too—merely giving a description of them, even a rigidified description, won't tell us what was green, square, or in pain. Informatively designating a property involves knowing a certain set of necessary and sufficient conditions for something to be that property. Similar considerations must apply to substances. But here we have to note that while we do know informative designators for many properties, we do not know informative designators for many substances. We often do not know the conditions necessary and sufficient for a substance to be that substance; for often we do not know what would make a later substance or a substance in another world that substance. A major reason for our inability to informatively designate substances is that we do not know with respect to some kinds of substances and in particular inanimate material objects, whether or not they have thisness (and so, for example, are to be individuated partly by their underlying matter) or whether they are to be individuated solely by properties, including (spatiotemporal and/or other) properties of continuity.

4. MENTAL SUBSTANCES

Now suppose that no substances have thisness, and so the bundle view of all substances is correct. Mental substances are those substances which have

What Makes Me Me? A Defense of Substance Dualism

mental properties essentially. Then whether there are mental substances depends on how one bundles together bundles of properties into substances. Mental properties with physical parts (such as the property of intentionally raising one's arm) are naturally thought of as belonging to the substance to which the physical part belongs. But one may put pure mental properties (such as the property of trying to raise one's arm) either in the same bundle as the physical property to which it is most closely related causally—the one which causes it to be instantiated or whose instantiation is caused by it[9]—or, following Hume,[10] one can put the pure mental properties into a bundle with other pure mental properties to whose instantiation it is related causally (and perhaps also related by relations of similarity and apparent memory). In the Humean model clearly there will be mental substances, for some bundles of properties would be individuated by their mental properties. It might seem however that in the non-Humean model one could individuate substances solely by their physical properties and regard mental properties as merely contingent members of bundles, and then the only substances would be physical substances. Alternatively, one could individuate substances at least partly in terms of mental properties, and then there would be mental substances. Either way of describing the world would yield a full description. It then becomes an arbitrary matter whether we say that there are mental substances.

Contrary to this model however, it is not possible to have a full description of the world in which all substances are individuated only by physical properties. For it is an evident datum of experience that conscious mental events of different kinds (visual sensations, auditory sensations, etc.) are co-experienced, that is belong to the same substance. Any description of the world which had the consequence that co-experienced events did not belong to the same substance would be a false one. There must therefore be substances whose identity is constituted in part by being the substances to which some set of co-experienced mental events belong. If these substances are also substances to which the physical events belong, which are causally most directly connected to those mental events—let's call them the physical correlates of the mental events—then their spatial boundaries at a time and over time can be no narrower than those of the physical correlates of the co-experienced events. The identity of the substance is thus constituted by a mental property, that its boundaries are no narrower than the boundaries of the physical correlates of what I co-experience. We cannot cut up the world in an arbitrary way and individuate substances solely by physical properties, and suppose that the mental properties are merely contingent properties of these substances. For even if (as seems not to be the case empirically) the brain basis of, for example, my visual sensations and my auditory sensations were the same, that would still not entail the datum of experience that they were both had by the same person. We can only include that datum in a full description of the world if we suppose that the identity of substances which have conscious mental properties is determined by whether the mental properties which they have at the same time are co-experienced.

It is also an evident datum of experience that certain mental events are had consecutively by the same person. Experiences take time—if only a second or two; and every experience which I have, I experience as consisting of two smaller parts. I am the common subject of the experience of hearing the first half of your sentence and the experience of hearing the second half of your sentence. And yet the mere fact that these experiences are caused by events in the same part of the physical substance which is my brain does not entail that. It follows for both of these reasons that we cannot describe the world fully except in terms of mental substances which—if they have physical properties—are the substances they are both at a time and over time, whose boundaries are no narrower than those of the physical correlates of what a subject co-experiences.

It will be evident that it will make no difference to the fact that there are mental substances if the bundle theory of all physical substances is false, and inanimate material objects including brain-molecules have thisness (and so being the same substance is not solely a function of properties, but of the matter in which those properties are instantiated). For still nothing would follow from that for which mental properties were co-experienced. We can describe the facts of co-experience only if we allow the existence of mental substances.

This conclusion is reinforced when we consider some well-known neurophysiological data and thought experiments. The crucial issue when a patient's corpus callosum is severed is whether (on the assumption that experiences are produced by both half-brains) the experiences produced by his left brain are co-experienced with the experiences produced by his right brain. It is not merely that some ways of dividing up the brain or defining when it began or ceased to exist would provide simpler explanations of how the brain or body behaves than do others, but that some ways would entail the nonoccurrence of a datum of experience, whose occurrence would be evident to its subject or subjects—that a subject had both sets of experiences, or that he had only one set. Whether there is one person or two is not entailed by which experiences are connected with which half-brains, or anything else physical. To describe what is going on we need to individuate persons in part by the experiences they have, and not by the extent of the unity of a brain. Merely to describe, not to explain, experience, we need mental substances individuated at least in part in this way.

This conclusion is further reinforced when we consider the thought experiment of half-brain transplants. S's brain is taken out of his skull, divided into two halves, and these halves are put into two different skulls from which brains have been removed. A few additional bits are added from a clone of S; the bits are connected to the nervous system, and we then have two functioning persons with mental lives. But if we know only the history of all the physical bits, described in terms of their properties (and, if required, their underlying matter), and which mental properties are instantiated in all the persons involved, there seems to be something crucial of which we are ignorant—which (if either) of the subsequent persons is S. Whether S has survived such a traumatic operation seems an evidently factual issue, and yet one underdetermined by the physical and mental properties associated with physical substances. Only if S is a mental substance (to whom the co-experienced experiences occur), can there be an unknown truth about whether or not S has survived this operation—which surely sometimes there will be. And even if (as some philosophers have supposed[11]) in such cases each of the later persons would be partly me, that cannot be a necessary truth because the history of all the physical bits and all the mental properties associated with them is compatible with neither person being fully me, or with just one of them being fully me. We would still be ignorant about which (if any) of the subsequent persons would be fully me.

It follows that mental substances are not identical with and their existence is not entailed by that of physical substances, since there can be worlds in which the physical substances (brains and the extent of their continuity) are the same but there are different mental substances (two in one world, only one in another).

5. PURE MENTAL SUBSTANCES

My final claim is that human beings, you and I, are pure mental substances. Many thought experiments in the spirit of Descartes seem to describe conceivable situations and, so, to be strong evidence of the logical possibility of me existing without a body, or continuing to exist when my body is destroyed. Let us take Descartes's original thought experiment:

> I saw that while I could conceive that I had no body, I could not conceive that I was not. On the other hand, if I had only ceased from thinking ... I should have no reason for thinking that I had existed. From this I knew that I was a substance the whole nature or essence of which is to think and that for its existence there is no need of any place, nor does it depend on any material thing (Descartes 1972: 101).

We can make sense of this and many similar suppositions (disembodied life after death, and others); they do not appear to contain any contradiction—and that is strong evidence that what we appear to conceive is logically possible. But, says the objector, and this objection is relevant also to earlier thought experiments which I've mentioned, the issue is whether such suppositions are "metaphysically possible". A logical possibility is simply one whose negation does not involve a contradiction. But 'Hesperus is not Phosphorus' or 'water is not H_2O' ('Hesperus', 'Phosphorus', and 'water' being used in ancient senses) involve no contradiction, but what they claim is absolutely impossible, "metaphysically impossible". The metaphysically impossible is wider than the logically impossible. But this divergence between the logically impossible and the metaphysically impossible only arises when substances or properties are picked out by uninformative designators. If we don't know fully what Hesperus is, then we won't know fully what it can be. However 'I' (or 'Richard Swinburne' as used by me) is an informative designator.

For I do know the conditions necessary and sufficient for a substance to be that substance. I can recognize (with faculties in working order, favourably positioned, and not subject to illusion) when it applies and when it doesn't, and I can make simple inferences from its application. For I can always be maximally favourably positioned and totally free from illusion when I pick out myself as the subject of experience and action—infallibly. In this I am in Shoemaker's phrase, "immune to error through misidentification" (Shoemaker 1994: 82). I cannot recognize that a present conscious experience is taking place and yet misidentify it as yours when it is really mine, or conversely. I can misidentify myself if I pick out myself by means of a body—for example, believing falsely that the person seen in the mirror is me—but that will be a case of illusion.[12] Hence I know the essence of what I am talking about when I talk about me.

Of course I can still misremember what I did in the past, and indeed misremember how I used the word "I" in the past. But this kind of problem arises with every claim whatsoever about the past. "Green" is an informative designator of a property, but I may still misremember which things were green and even what I meant by "green" in the past. The difference between informative and uninformative designators is that (when my faculties are in working order, I am favourably positioned and not subject to illusion) I can recognize which objects are correctly picked out at the present time by informative designators, but not generally when they are picked out by uninformative designators (in the absence of further information). And so I know what a claim about the past or future amounts to when it is made by informative designators, but not when it is made by uninformative designators. I know what would constitute a future or past experience being mine, what it is for some future or past person to be me. This is not so with Hesperus or water. I don't know (in the sense defined) what would constitute a past or a future substance being water or Hesperus if I am merely in the position of the "water" user in the eighteenth century, or the "Hesperus" user in the early ancient world or even today—if I don't know whether a planet has to have a certain thisness in order to be Hesperus.

I conclude that, in the absence of some hidden logical (and I mean "logical") contradiction in Descartes's description of his thought experiment—to suppose which would be immensely implausible—the experiment shows what it purports to show: Descartes is a pure mental substance. He could exist without anything physical existing, and so pure mental substances exist logically independently of physical substances. Each of us can do the same experiment about ourselves and so show that we are pure mental substances. And each of us can consider the earlier thought experiment as done to themselves; and then this objection about the logically possible not always being metaphysically possible will not have any force.

There are however two kinds of pure mental substances—those which do not have a body as a contingent part, and those which do. Ghosts do not have bodies, for example, whereas human beings living on Earth do have bodies. But since the body which is currently mine could continue to exist as a living body without having any causal connection with any mental substance, or could become instead the body of a different mental substance, and since I could under such circumstances go on existing and have a mental life without a body, I now consist of two disjoint parts—my body (the contingent part of me) and the rest of me which we can call my soul (the essential part of me).

Whether or not material objects have thisness, my soul has its own thisness, independently of any thisness possessed by any brain to which it is connected. For clearly my soul could have had a different mental life from the one it had, and it seems conceivable (and so is probably logically possible) that two different non-embodied souls could always have had the same mental life at the same time—the same succession of mental properties could be instantiated in each. Hence the mental substance is not the substance that is in virtue merely of the properties which it has. So a Humean view of personal identity as constituted by the causal (and other relational) connections between our actual instantiated mental properties must be rejected. The same point is brought out by the apparent conceivability of a world W_2 in which for each substance in W_1 there is a substance which has the same properties as it and conversely (and any physical matter underlying the properties is the same in both worlds), but where a person S who exists in W_1 does not exist in W_2. The person who lives in W_2 the life (physical and mental) which S lives in W_1 is not S. And surely this world could be different solely in the respect that the person who lived my life was not me. For it is not entailed by the full description of the world in its physical aspects and in respect of which bundles of mental properties are instantiated in the same substance that I, picked out as the actual subject of certain mental properties, have the particular physical or mental properties which I do and am connected with the body with which I am connected. I am essentially my soul, whose identity is irreducible to anything else.[13]

NOTES

1. "The notion of a substance is just this—that it can exist by itself without the aid of any other substance" (Descartes 1984–1991: vol. 2, 159).
2. There are in the literature other ways of understanding the mental/physical contrast; the most common of which are the intentional/non-intentional and the non-physical science/physical science contrasts. I expound these solely in terms of events. On the former account a mental event is one which involves an attitude towards something under a description—it is fearing, thinking, or

believing so-and-so; when the subject does not necessarily fear, think, or believe something identical to so-and-so, a physical event is any event other than a mental event. On the latter account the physical is what can be explained by an extended physics, and the mental is what cannot be so explained. The former account has the unfortunate consequence that pains and colour qualia are not mental events; yet these are the paradigmatic troublemakers for "mind-brain" identity and must count as mental if we are to deal in any way with the traditional mind/body problem. The latter account is hopelessly vague, for it is totally unclear what would constitute a science incorporating present-day physics as still being a physics. Hence my preference for my way of defining "mental" and "physical" properties, events, and—analogously—substances.

3. I am grateful to David Armstrong for pointing out to me that my original definition of 'privileged access' without the clause beginning 'given that' had the consequence that as animals or babies could not find out whether 'having a red image' and so on were instantiated in them because they did not have the concepts required for gaining knowledge by introspection, they could not have privileged access to these properties; and from that, it followed that there could not be mental properties in my sense. The additional clause makes the mental character of a property a matter of whether someone who does have the concept of that property has a way of learning about it which is not available to others.

4. And so by the transitivity of identity, if E1 is the same event as E2 by one criterion, and E2 is the same event as E3 by the other criterion, then E1 is the same event as E3.

5. See van Inwagen (1990: sec. 13) and Merricks (2001). Van Inwagen considers that mereological compounds, artefacts, and gerrymandered objects do not exist, and so of course they cannot be substances.

6. For a more detailed account of thisness and of what would be evidence that material objects do or do not have thisness, see Swinburne (1995). This article has been subject to some detailed criticisms by O'Leary-Hawthorne and Cover (1997). One quite unjustified criticism which they make is that my "principle concerns intra-world duplication solo numero" and that "it is surprising that Swinburne does not explicitly address inter-world versions of his principle" (O'Leary-Hawthorne and Cover 1997: 104). However, I did make it explicitly clear (Swinburne 1995: 130) that all the principles which I discussed (including, therefore, that principle in terms of which I defined thisness) "concern not merely the identity of individuals in a given world, but across possible worlds".

7. If ultimate parts have the same thisness, then the substance composed of these will have a thisness constituted by these and conversely. I thus reject a view which Gallois calls "strong haecceitism", the view that two objects (O in world w, and O* in world w*) could yet be different, even if they have all the same properties and are composed of identical constituents. See Gallois (1998: 250–251).

8. See Swinburne (1995) on how physics may provide evidence on whether material objects do have thisness.

9. As proposed by, for example, Shaffer (1961).

10. "The true idea of the human mind, is to consider it as a system of different perceptions or different existences, which are link'd together by the relation of cause and effect, and mutually produce, destroy, influence, and modify each other" (Hume [1739] 1888: 1.4.6.).

11. I give very brief arguments in favour of the necessary indivisibility of the soul, by arguing against the possibility of fission of persons in Swinburne

(1997: 149–150), and against the possibility of fusion of persons in my contribution to Shoemaker and Swinburne (1984: 44–45).
12. The need for some sort of qualification on Shoemaker's phrase is the subject of recent discussion. See Coliva (2003).
13. This paper is a shorter and revised version of Swinburne (2007). The ideas developed in this paper are explored at a greater length in Swinburne (2013).

9 Naturalism and the Unavoidability of the Cartesian Perspective

Howard Robinson

1. WHY THE PERSPECTIVE IS UNAVOIDABLE

Dennett recounts the following story from Nozick:

> Suppose . . . some beings of vastly superior intelligence—from Mars, let us say—were to descend upon us, and suppose that we were to them as simple thermostats are to clever engineers. Suppose, that is, that they did not *need* the intentional stance [i.e., our ordinary 'folk psychology'] . . . to predict our behavior in all its detail. They can be supposed to be Laplacean super-physicists, capable of comprehending the behavior on Wall Street, for instance, at the microphysical level . . . They can predict the individual behaviors of all the various moving bodies they observe without treating any of them as intentional systems. Would we then be right to say that from *their* point of view we were not believers at all (any more than a simple thermostat is)? (Dennett 1997: 68)

The apparent consequence of Novick's tale is that, if physicalism (together with closure under physics—the absence of emergent laws) is true, then normal psychological explanations are mere heuristics which can be legitimately ignored if the heuristic is not needed. Although the story is told with respect only to the intentional stance, the implications of the Martian's microphysically based method might reasonably be taken to be more general: higher order ontologies—the subject matters of the special sciences, including not only psychology but chemistry, biology, and the rest—are similarly not needed by the Martian. We have indeed here a case of what Kim calls the exclusion principle. We will return to this generalized point later, for it helps to undermine Dennett's response.

That response is as follows:

> Our imagined Martians might be able to predict the future of the human race by Laplacean methods, but if they did not also see us as intentional systems they would be missing something perfectly objective: the

patterns in human behavior that are describable from the intentional stance, and only from that stance, and that support generalizations and predictions. (69)

Dennett illustrates the value of the intentional stance with a further story.

> Suppose . . . that one of the Martians were to engage in a predicting contest with an Earthling. The Earthling and the Martian observe (and observe each other observing) a particular bit of local physical transaction. From the Earthling's point of view, this is what is observed. The telephone rings in Mrs Gardner's kitchen. She answers, and this is what she says: "Oh, hello dear. You're coming home early? Within the hour? And bringing the boss to dinner? Pick up a bottle of wine on the way home then, and drive carefully." On the basis of this observation, our Earthling predicts that a large metallic vehicle with rubber tires will come to a stop on the drive within one hour, disgorging two human beings, one of whom will be holding a paper bag containing a bottle containing alcoholic fluid . . . The Martian makes the same prediction, but has to avail himself of much more information about an extraordinary number of interactions of which, so far as he can tell, the Earthling is entirely ignorant. For instance, the deceleration of the vehicle at intersection *A*, five miles from the house, without which there would have been a collision with another vehicle—whose collision course had been laboriously calculated over some hundreds of meters by the Martian. The Earthling's performance would look like magic! How did the Earthling know that the being who got out of the car and got the bottle in the shop would get back in? The coming true of all the Earthling's predictions, after all the vagaries, intersections and branches in the paths charted by the Martian, would seem to anyone bereft of the intentional strategy [to be] marvelous and inexplicable . . . (69–70)

Dennett then draws our attention to a serious flaw in this latter story, namely that

> The Martian is presumed to treat his Earthling opponent as an intelligent being like himself . . . against whom one can compete . . . a being with beliefs . . . and desires. So if the Martian sees the pattern in one Earthling, how can he fail to see it in others? (70)

Dennett concludes

> . . . the moral to be drawn: namely, *the unavoidability of the intentional stance with regard to oneself and one's fellow intelligent beings.* (70)

He explains this as follows

> This unavoidability is itself interest relative; it is perfectly possible to adopt a physical stance, for instance, with regard to an intelligent being, oneself included, but not to the exclusion of maintaining at the same time an intentional stance with regard to oneself at a minimum, and one's fellows *if* one intends, for instance, to learn what they know . . . We can perhaps suppose our super-intelligent Martians fail to recognize *us* as intentional systems, but we cannot suppose them to lack the requisite concepts. If they observe, theorize, predict, communicate, they view *themselves* as intentional systems. Where there are intelligent beings, the patterns must be there to be described, whether or not we care to see them. (70–71)

So, though one could avoid treating others as intentional systems, Dennett, by contrast, believes in the inevitability of taking oneself to be a thinking being, or, as I shall put, is *taking the Cartesian perspective* on oneself, for one cannot avoid the thought "*cogito*, I think, I am a thinking thing". The topic of this paper is whether the necessity of this perspective is consistent with physicalism or any form of naturalism, or whether the apparent implication of Nozick's story is correct. I shall be arguing that the Cartesian perspective and physicalism or naturalism are not compatible. Put slightly differently, the question concerns whether something which is constituted solely as an organized mass of particles can be a subject with a Cartesian perspective on the world and, therefore, on itself as such a subject. What kind of property of an organized physical system could this be? The seeming implication of the Martian story is that, if that is all we were, we could not be subjects at all.

2. PHYSICALIST ATTEMPTS TO EXPLAIN THE UNAVOIDABILITY: (I) BEHAVIORAL PATTERNS

Dennett refers to

> . . . something perfectly objective: the *patterns* in human behavior that are describable from the intentional stance, and only from that stance . . . (Dennett 1997: 69)

The claim that the patterns are 'objective' suggests that they are there in their own right as patterns irrespective of anything dependent on the subject. But Dennett concedes, in the quotation I have just given, that it is only from the intentional stance that these things are discriminable as patterns, so the idea that these are simply physical patterns—more or less similar physical shapes or movements—which we are picking up on is already abandoned. This is obviously the case. Dennett cites the following as a case of a pattern:

Take a particular instance in which the Martians observe a stockbroker deciding to place an order for 500 shares of General Motors. They predict the exact motions of his fingers as he dials the phone and the exact vibrations of his vocal cords as he intones his order. But if the Martians do not see that indefinitely many different patterns of finger motions and vocal cord vibrations . . . could have substituted for the actual particulars without perturbing the subsequent operations of the market, then they have failed to see a real pattern in the world they are observing. (69)

The reference to finger movements leaves open the possibility that we are talking about straightforward physical similarities, but in fact quite different movements could constitute buying these shares. Activities on a computer, where the movements would have no physical similarity to bidding actions in an auction room, could achieve the same objective. So the sense of 'patterns' cannot be taken in a literal physical sense. Of course, the foundations of these judgments of similarity—the movements of bodies through space—are entirely real, but their reification as patterns—as seen as unities of a certain sort—involves the action of mind. So the invocation of patterns as mind-independent physical realities, in the kinds of cases Dennett has in mind, is mistaken.

In fact this is true of the term 'pattern' in general, even where there is genuine physical similarity. If there are a collection of dots arranged in what we would see as a circle, a visually more sophisticated mind might see it as a polygon with the appropriate number of sides. Patterns are reified by the action of the mind. Otherwise—in the case of the dots—there are just dots in certain physical places. In the case of share-dealing behaviors, there are just bodily movements. The Cartesian perspective makes sense of these—in the sense that there must be a subject to whom standard folk-psychological characteristics are attributed and who appreciates them—but this requires that the Cartesian perspective be retained as a primitive component in our idea of what there is.

3. PHYSICALIST ATTEMPTS TO EXPLAIN THE UNAVOIDABILITY: (II) REALISM ABOUT MACROSCOPIC PROPERTIES

It might seem that it is enough that certain things or types of behavior fall under psychological concepts for the deployment of those concepts to reveal truths not available in their absence. But concepts presuppose concept users, and it is the ontological status of these that is in dispute. If this strategy is to be deployed, one must be a realist about psychological *properties* and not merely affirm the applicability of psychological concepts.

Is there a problem for the naturalist in being a realist about psychological properties without being a property dualist (which, for the moment I am taking to be inconsistent with naturalism)? This can be regarded, from a physicalist perspective, as a sub-problem of the issue of the ontological status of the properties of non-fundamental entities. To resist the Martian, one can affirm the reality of properties at all levels, not just the microphysical: if these are real, then there is something that the Martian is missing, and if these include psychological properties, then he is missing out on those. Of course, to achieve this there would first have to be a physicalistically acceptable account of mental properties, but that this is on the cards must be assumed at this point in the argument.

The Martian story points to what one might call the second crisis of physicalism. The first crisis is the problem of consciousness: if closure under physical science is to be maintained and epiphenomenalism avoided, one must have a physicalist account of consciousness. Most of twentieth century philosophy of mind has been concerned with preserving the unity and monopoly of physical science whilst also preserving the efficacy of mental states. Showing these states could be physical seemed to be the way of doing this. But mental properties certainly do not feature in microphysics, so if the properties found in the special sciences are non-efficacious, then so are mental states and properties, even if they are physical. If this is the outcome, the whole purpose of a physicalist theory of the mind, namely to preserve the mind's efficacy in a physically closed world, would be lost.

Kim (1998, 2005) propounds a principle which can be deployed to suggest that the ontologies of the special sciences have no independent efficacy, and this at least prepares the way for denying that they have an independent real existence. This principle is the *causal exclusion principle*, which is as follows:

> If an event e has a sufficient cause c at t, no event at t distinct from c can be a cause of e (unless this is a case of genuine causal overdetermination). (Kim 2005: 17)

Kim initially uses this to argue that a weak definition of physicalism in terms of supervenience and which tries to avoid reduction, cannot avoid epiphenomenalism, but he then considers the *generalization argument,* which extends the exclusion principle, given closure under physics, to the special sciences. Kim rejects this argument, in effect because he does not think that different ontological levels are in competition with each other. This position might be defended as follows. The truth makers for higher-level explanations are just as real as those for physics. If bricks are real, then so is a house made of bricks. And if bricks have causal powers, so does the house, in virtue of the bricks' powers. So if atoms have real force, combinations of atoms can constitute a real object which has real causal efficacy compounded from the real forces of the atoms of which it is made. This seems to be common sense. Kim states the commonsensical nature of this position emphatically:

> The errant baseball didn't after all break the window, and the earthquake did not cause the buildings to collapse! This strikes us as intolerable. (1998: 81)

A very firm version of this view is taken by Jerry Fodor. In Fodor (1974), he argued that physicalism does not require reductionism. An important part of this claim is that non-reductionism does not in any way cast doubts on the reality of those physical entities that cannot be reduced: they are not in any way 'secondary quality-like', in being dependent for their reification on human categorization or response. He even calls the properties found in the special sciences 'natural kinds'. This is a very different sense from that deployed following Putnam, according to which natural kinds are those kinds of stuff categorized by reference to the sameness of their hidden real essence. They are the opposite of multiply realizable properties, which are the ones in which Fodor is interested in psychology, and the reason why he rejects reductionism. For Fodor, 'natural kinds' in the special sciences are simply properties found in nature—not, in some way, dependent on us. To emphasize their naturalness, he even seems to go to the extreme of denying that they supervene necessarily on their base. Taking psychology as a case of a special science, he says:

> Only God gets to decide whether there is anything, and likewise only God gets to decide whether there are laws about pains; or whether, if there are, the pains that the laws are about are MR ['Metaphysically Real']. (Fodor 1974)

Fodor here seems to be denying the standard physicalist maxim that once God had created all the facts of physics, he had nothing more to do, and this does place him in a bizarre situation. In challenging Fodor's extreme realism, Barry Loewer distinguishes between what he calls *Non-Reductive Physicalism, Metaphysical (NRPM)* and *Non-Reductive Physicalism, Light (NRPL)*. The former is Fodor's position, and the latter is Loewer's alternative.

> *NRPM* and *NRPL* agree that the special sciences are conceptually, epistemologically, and methodologically autonomous/irreducible to physics but disagree about what autonomy/irreducibility consists in and how it is to be explained. *NRPM* says that the autonomy/irreducibility is metaphysical and seeks to explain the conceptual and epistemological autonomy in terms of the existence of metaphysically basic special science kinds and laws. (Loewer 2009: 222)

Loewer then raises the question of what the difference would be between a world, W1, in which *NRPL* held and one, W2, in which *NRPM* obtained. Given closure under physics, everything would behave in exactly the same way, so the addition of the further entities and their concomitant laws appears to be vacuous.

One might argue that Fodor does not need to go over the top in this way. The realist, about the special sciences, might simply deny that W1 is possible, on the grounds that, once the microphysical reality has been created, the higher order entities and concomitant laws are *eo ipso* present too. It is a case of what has been called an 'ontological free lunch'. So God need only create the world of physics, but it does not follow from this that the more macroscopic objects and properties of the special sciences do not exist in their own right.

Nevertheless, the phrase 'ontological free lunch' might still leave one puzzled over what the difference between the 'light' and the 'metaphysical' consists in. Asserting that it means that a further set of entities exist, without any consequences, makes the assertion look suspiciously empty. The expression 'ontological free lunch' itself suggests something very dubious, namely that there both is, and is not, something more. Only the 'human perspective' account of the non-basic can provide us with a coherent explanation of the ontology of the special sciences. Let us look more closely at the 'light' *(L)* and the 'metaphysical' *(M)* versions of non-reductive physicalism.

Loewer says of *L* that it

> attempts to account for the conceptual/methodological irreducibility of the special sciences in terms of facts and laws of microphysics and our epistemological situation in the world. (Loewer 2009)

This seems to involve the human perspective—'our epistemological situation'—in the constitution of the *L* view, but there are different possible interpretations of this. One might think that the difference can be stated as follows:

(A) M says that the ontologies of the special sciences are *basic* and L says that they are *derivative*.

But this is ambiguous because

(B) M says they are basic, but L says they are derivative *but perfectly real in their own right,* that is, no reference to human activity or perspective is involved in what it is for them to exist.

On this interpretation, the role of 'our epistemological situation' is to decide what we pick out of what is there in any way. This contrasts with

(C) M says that the ontologies of the special sciences are basic, in the sense that they exist independently of our sensibilities, and others, but L denies this, giving our perspectives or concerns a role in their reification.[1]

One might characterize (B) as the *Selective Realist* conception of the special science ontologies, and (C), recalling what was said earlier about the reification of patterns, as the *Gestalt Constructivist* conception.

If we look at Loewer (2007), we can see that the conception of a 'genuine property' (G-property) is neutral as between (B) and (C):

> In addition to the fundamental properties [of physics] any property that corresponds to a kind term in any science is a G-property. Kind terms are predicates or concepts involved in the appropriate way in laws. By "law" I mean a simple true generalization or equation that is counterfactual supporting and projectable. This includes fundamental laws of physics and also *ceteris paribus* laws of the special sciences. (Loewer 2007: 245)

This account simply deems anything to be a property that has a certain role in science and does not make a distinction between (B) and (C). I do not think that Loewer in any of his (2007), (2008), or (2009) works distinguishes between these options. I think that the dialectic between him and Fodor, however, shows that he should come down in favor of (C), for the following reason.

In Loewer's words, Fodor

> finds it "*molto mysterioso*" that the motions of particles to-ing and fro-ing in accordance with F = ma . . . lawfully end up converging on special science laws. . . . How do particles that constitute an economy "know" that their trajectory is required (*ceteris paribus*) to enforce Gresham's Law? [i.e. the law that 'bad money drives out good money'.] [Fodor] grants that every special science system is microphysically constituted and that the dynamical laws of physics are complete but he claims that the laws of physics are *explanatorily* and *modally* incomplete. He adds that there are explanations and counterfactuals expressible in the language of the special sciences that are not necessitated by the laws and facts of fundamental physics. In his view special science counterfactuals and explanations require for their truth irreducible special science laws. So while a regularity expressed by a special science law is not independent of physics (i.e. it is implied by microphysics' laws and facts) its status as a law is independent of physics (Loewer 2007).

Loewer believes that his argument, cited before, that W2 adds nothing to W1 shows this to be false, but whether this is so depends on what one means by 'its status as a law'. The physical facts determine that events will follow the pattern that make the special science laws applicable, but unless one brings the special science laws to bear, one will not have the explanations that those laws make possible. You could not say "if such and such had not happened then *reproduction would not have taken place*" or " . . . *bad money would not have driven out good*". So without the laws you cannot provide certain kinds of explanation, but explanation—as opposed to making it the case that matter is where and how it is—is a human activity. What is missing without the special sciences is essentially anthropocentric. We are back to the problem of the Martian: the Cartesian perspective is simply assumed.

Kim's intuition about the baseball and the window seemed initially convincing, but it failed to establish the ontological status of the entities in question, and it fails to assist the opponent of the generalized exclusion principle. What is at stake is whether the human perspective has an essential role in reifying as objects in their own right, things which are really just clouds of microscopic entities. There is a sense in which any mereological combination of atoms could be treated as an entity and so could the combined sum of their forces. Which are chosen are a matter of human interest and perspective—not arbitrary, of course, but well-groundedness of conceptual practice does not entail a strict realism. What is at stake is whether the human perspective is essential for certain parts of the world, which are in fact microcomplexes, to appear to us to be natural wholes. We cannot directly perceive microstructures as such. We perceive them 'blurred', so to speak, into homogenous wholes. If we can see the independent constituents of an entity, we are less likely to think of that entity as basic. We can see the elements in a crowd, in a swarm of bees, or in a weather system and so are less likely to think of these things as fundamental, even if they seem to have a dynamic of their own. We are generally inclined then to think of such entities as no more than a collection of their parts.

When it comes to most organisms, however, we see them only whole, for such parts as we do see are essentially parts of the thing—branches, leaves, limbs, teeth, etc.—not independent parts. If we saw a plant as a swirling mass of particles passing in and out of an organizational vortex, like a rioting crowd, or as Aristotle saw the weather, then, once we came to believe that the organization was a product of the interaction of the particles following only the laws of physics and not an extraneous imposition, we would probably find it natural to make a conceptualist interpretation of plants. As it is, the nature of our perception seems to endow them with a greater degree of natural integrity than they would seem to possess from a more microscopic viewpoint.

Can the macro-realist appeal to our senses to justify our acceptance of macro objects as real in their own right? Doubly not! First, for the reason just given, namely that it is an accident of our perceptual abilities that they ever present themselves as autonomously real. Second, this very way of viewing our senses presupposes the perspective of the subject. For the Martian, the inflow of particles or waves through points at the surface of the 'human' particle cloud is just that. That they should come together to constitute experiences at all, and ones of a certain grain or resolution, is quite beyond the physicist's account. This way of taking the senses already adopts the perspective and assumes the ineliminable reality of the conscious human subject.

Davidson (1993) rejects Kim's exclusion principle, but, rather ironically, we can draw on a legitimate point of Davidson's in its support. Davidson claims, very plausibly, that it is only at the fundamental level that there are what he calls *strict laws*. Laws at other levels involve *ceteris paribus* clauses and a certain degree of approximation. This strongly suggests that, though they are useful explanatory tools, formulated on the basis of more exact processes that underlie them, the laws of the special sciences are not entities in their own right. It would be natural to argue the same way for the entities to which those laws attach. Davidson's reason for rejecting the exclusion principle rests on some very controversial features of his position. He claims that causal relations are entirely extensional and so events are not efficacious *in virtue of* any of the properties involved in them, so you cannot claim that some of them are active and others idle. The motive behind this is some kind of nominalism, which wishes to treat properties as simply 'descriptions' under which events fall, and, as such, not agents in the world. At the same time he wants to treat the mental as 'purely conceptual' and the basic physical as, in some sense, more real.[2] So Kim's 'common sense' acceptance of the ball, the window, and their interaction does not show that these are autonomous realities. On the contrary they illustrate the vital role of the Cartesian perspective in reifying our manifest world.

4. NATURALISM WITHOUT PHYSICALISM? (I) MCDOWELL

We have so far been investigating ways in which more or less standard forms of physicalism might try to accommodate the Cartesian perspective, and we have seen that they fail. But there are philosophers who describe themselves as being naturalists whilst denying that they are, in the normal sense, physicalists. They are, so to speak, one step more 'liberal' than non-reductive physicalists. We must investigate whether this approach is any more successful in accommodating the Cartesian perspective without falling into dualism. There is a great variety of philosophers making such a claim, and it is not clear that they all have any one thing in common, beyond their affirmation that they are 'naturalists but not physicalists'. In the following two sections, I shall concentrate on philosophers who find their inspiration for this position in the later Wittgenstein. Prominent amongst these is John McDowell.

McDowell's version of 'naturalism without physicalism' rests on his doctrine of *second nature*. This is a tantalizing notion and peculiarly hard to engage with. It can be regarded as a theory, in the sense that it is an attempt to come to grips with and solve a problem, namely the relation between our physical nature and our psychological nature. (Or, maybe, between physical nature as a whole and psychosocial reality.) But this understanding naturally gives rise to a demand for an explanation, in something like detail, about how the relation between these two 'realms' works. McDowell firmly rejects the demand for such an explanation. In regretting his use of the term 'foothold' to suggest some kind of articulable link between the two, McDowell says:

> I should have restricted myself to the obvious claim that the second-nature is no less natural than the first-nature. There was no need to offer to make a connection between them beyond their both being natural. (2008: 221)

Whilst, on the one hand, this is in a sense a natural response from one who believes in 'Wittgensteinian quietism', it is not obvious that it is acceptable. One can feel a somewhat *de haut en bas* implication that if you cannot just see that there is no problem here, you are a lost case, forever caught in the maze of language. But physics and chemistry are both parts of nature, and it is obviously necessary that there be some account of how the two fit together, even if this falls short of a classic reductionism. Why is this not so for the physical sciences in general and the psychosocial? The 'human animal' is, after all, for a naturalist like McDowell, one, albeit complex, thing.

McDowell does, however, seem to have a kind of transcendental argument in hand. In discussing his use of labels such as 'Aristotelian naturalism', 'Greek naturalism', 'naturalism of second nature', 'relaxed naturalism', and 'liberal naturalism' he says the following:

> Now my use of these labels . . . comes in contexts in which I am considering the plausibility of theses to the effect that some region of human life exemplifies free responsiveness to reasons, with such theses understood to imply that the characteristic phenomena of those parts of human life are beyond the reach of natural-scientific understanding. And the point of these labels is captured by this thought: by dint of exploiting, in an utterly intuitive way, ideas like that of the patterns characteristic of the life of animals of a certain kind, we can insist that such phenomena, even though they are beyond the reach of natural-scientific understanding, are perfectly real, without thereby relegating them to the sphere of the occult or supernatural. (217–218)

He goes on to say that he is not denying that some things may be genuinely supernatural:

> But for my purposes it is enough to consider a position that, without necessarily ruling out supernatural phenomena altogether, holds that

Naturalism and the Unavoidability of the Cartesian Perspective   165

they had better not be taken to include phenomena that are biological, in the sense that they are characteristic of the lives of animals of our species. The point of my call for a relaxation is this: the fact that such phenomena are natural, in the sense of not being supernatural, provides no grounds for supposing that the conceptual apparatus that captures free responsiveness as such must be naturalizable, in any sense congenial to scientific naturalism. (218)

I call this a transcendental argument because it is roughly of this form:

(1) We know that human beings are just natural biological entities.
(2) We also know that we are free rational beings.
(3) And we know that rationality and freedom cannot be reduced, in any sense, to natural scientific processes.
(4) It follows from this that we, as living, rational human animals, possess a nature in addition to the nature that physical science explores.

This is presented as being 'utterly intuitive', but it entirely begs the question against the dualist. It is not intuitively obvious that the human capacity for abstract thought, and for aesthetic and spiritual inspiration, are 'phenomena that are biological', especially when it is being specifically denied that they can be accommodated within the natural science of biology.

Again the suggestion is that it is some sort of howler to think that there is any sort of conflict in supposing these two natures to be in the same creature in a wholly 'naturalistic' way. But this ignores the fact that the intuition that there are features of human nature that cannot be put down to our nature as animals is very common through human history.

McDowell says of the 'sphere of the occult and supernatural' that it is

a region whose extent has shrunk for us with the advent of a modern scientific outlook, in the most extreme version of the outlook to nothing at all. (217)

This seems to be an attempt to have one's cake and eat it. On the one hand the 'modern scientific outlook' has led us to believe that there is nothing about the human being that is not, in some naturalistic sense, 'biological'; on the other hand biological science cannot accommodate the most typically human phenomena.

Perhaps it is not clear what McDowell would mean by 'naturalistic', nor by the contrasting categories of 'occult' and 'supernatural'—words seemingly used more for their emotive force, rather than with any exact sense. Does naturalism allow for what others would call 'property dualism', or even substance dualism, so long as there is no question of the 'immaterial' component being able to survive the body? Is it compatible with belief in the closure under physics of the behavior of all physical elements? I think he believes that it is not compatible with the latter, and he might simply regard the former as unhelpfully ideological and theoretical characterizations of the situation.

McDowell's refusal to explain himself and his reliance on 'persuasive definition' mean that he throws little light on how the Cartesian perspective can be part of nature in the secular sense.

5. NATURALISM WITHOUT PHYSICALISM? (II) PRICE AND RORTY

There are others coming from a similar orientation to McDowell, who are not so reticent about developing their position. They are explicitly pragmatist, and therefore closer to the scientific paradigm, and even want to attribute such a view to the later Wittgenstein. Rorty (2010), Horwich (2006), and Price (2004) are examples of this.

Price distinguishes between two kinds of naturalism, which he calls *object naturalism* and *subject naturalism*. The former is the standard naturalist view that all there is is the world as studied by science, and all knowledge is scientific knowledge. It is represented by, for example, the naturalism of Armstrong, Lewis, and Jackson. Subject naturalism is less familiar.

> According to this second view, philosophy needs to begin with what science tells us *about ourselves*. Science tells us that we humans are natural creatures, and if the claims and ambitions of philosophy conflict with this view, then philosophy needs to give way. This is naturalism in the sense of Hume, then, and, arguably Nietzsche. (Price 2004: 73)

Price endorses the *priority thesis*:

> Subject naturalism is theoretically prior to object naturalism, because the latter depends on validation from a subject naturalist perspective. (74)

According to Price, the problem for object naturalism is to find a way of coping with various recalcitrant phenomena within the framework of 'the world-as-studied-by-science'. He twice gives a list of such problems, which may seem to differ only by a natural abbreviation. They are as follows:

> ... common candidates [for "hard problems" for the object naturalist] include meaning, value, mathematical truth, causation and physical modality, and various aspects of mentality ... (73)

This is invoked later:

> ... how are we to place moral facts, mathematical facts, meaning facts, and so on? (74)

Naturalism and the Unavoidability of the Cartesian Perspective 167

Price's solution is radical. It is a mistake to think that when we worry about these things, we are worrying about *things* of a certain sort which we know from experience are there. This is the *material conception* of the problems. The alternative is the *linguistic conception*, according to which the issue concerns coming to understand how we use the term 'X' in the language, not where some object, X, fits into our ontology. So we concentrate on how the 'natural subject' deals with these topics of discourse, not where their supposed subject matter fits into a scientific ontology.

This is where Price's abbreviation of his list becomes salient, for what has gone missing is 'various aspects of mentality'. Perhaps some aspects of mentality—intentionality, for example—are as plausible as candidates for the linguistic treatment as the other things he mentions (which does not mean very plausible). But to claim that the 'hard problem' of sensations and consciousness can be treated by means of the 'linguistic conception' has no plausibility whatsoever. Perhaps it is no coincidence that none of 'consciousness', 'sensation', or 'hard problem' occurs in the index of Price's *Naturalism without Mirrors* (2011). A form of quasi-realism might stand a chance for modality or morals, but it is hard to see how it can work for consciousness.

Rorty, in his defense of 'quietism', is more direct than Price and has no reservations. For the subject naturalist, the import of Price's dictum that "we are natural creatures in a natural environment" is that we should be wary of drawing lines between kinds of organisms in non-behavioral and nonphysiological terms. This means that we should not use terms such as "intentionality", "consciousness", or "representation" unless we can specify, at least roughly, what sort of behavior suffices to show the presence of the reference of these terms.

> For example, if we want to say . . . that there is something it is like to be a bat but nothing it is like to be an earthworm . . . we should be prepared to explain how we can tell—to specify what behavioral or physiological facts are relevant to the claim [otherwise] we are inventing spooks to make jobs for ghost-busters. (Rorty 2010: 61–62)

Facing the suggestion that this 'emphasis on behavioral criteria is reminiscent of the positivists verificationism', Rorty says that it is not a product of a general theory of meaning but an insistence that

> . . . rather the traditional philosophical distinctions complicate narratives of biological evolution to no good purpose. (62)

If quietists of this type have abandoned the metaphysical imperialism of scientism, they have adopted instead a cultural imperialism for science. But the linguistic conception cannot dissolve the Cartesian perspective for a further reason, namely that it presupposes it. To regard something as a language rather than as just a series of sounds and marks already sets it into a human context. Calling it 'linguistic *behavior*' does not somehow reconcile the fact that the words are just physical noises with their meaningfulness.

Rorty, of course, was one of the original eliminativists about sensations, claiming that he did not want to fight again battles that Wittgenstein had already won. If acceptance of the anti-private language argument is the price that one must pay for quietism in the philosophy of mind, then I would happily let others pay it!

One can, I think, be confident that McDowell does not want to go down the same road as Price and Rorty—even if he is sympathetic to the anti-private language argument—for that is, indeed, to try to explain how the two natures are reconciled; but without some such effort I can see no reason to think that 'quietism' offers any enlightenment about the unavoidability of the Cartesian perspective.

6. THE ROOT OF THE PROBLEM

The fundamental question we have been asking is: Assuming that materialism is true *and* that the world is closed under physics, what ontological status, or causal clout, is left to the human level—or to objects of the special sciences?

We have seen that neither Dennett's reconciliation, nor Kim's pluralism, nor certain variations on quietism, work. Let us look at the history of the problem of how to integrate the ontologies of the 'lived world' and the special sciences with that of basic physics.

Translation reduction. The original positivists believed that all true statements (at least about concrete reality) could be translated into the language of physics. If this were possible it would seem to solve the problem of reconciliation, for physics could, in principle, tell you everything and all other discourses could, in principle, be abandoned. It has, however, at least two fatal problems. First, such translations are not even in principle possible. Furthermore, the translations Carnap and co. had in mind were not to basic physics, but to such things as neurology and behavior, which are relatively macro phenomena, and 'brains and behavior' have an intuitive link to mentality—especially behavior. Translations into forms of development of the quantum field just miss the point of the discourse. Second, even if the translation could be carried out, it would still presuppose the Cartesian perspective. Translation reduction is a relation between meaningful theoretical statements, and theories are only accessible to a thinking subject. What it is to recognize the meaning equivalence of the basic and non-basic modes of discourse would have to be expressed in terms of basic physics, but this would entirely lose the topic and point of the discourse.

Nomological reduction. This is the classic view of Nagel (1974), and it replaces translation with the existence of bridge laws from psychological

Naturalism and the Unavoidability of the Cartesian Perspective 169

state types to physical state types, facilitating identity. (If they signified merely correlations, they would not be of much help to the physicalist.) Like the first theory, it seems that the basic task cannot be carried out. Simple mental states, like sensations, might be susceptible to type identity, but complex propositional attitudes, for example, are much more likely to be multiply realized. Even so, the second objection deployed previously also applies. The perspective remains that of the theorizing, thinking subject, which remains fundamental.

Quine's pragmatism with scientific realism. Quine is at the beginning of the postwar mainstream on this issue. The human perspective—which for him seems to mean propositional attitude states—are pragmatically necessary but not part of our ontology, which is restricted to more exact phenomena, which means the ontologies of physics and formal first order logic. The pragmatic necessity is not *pro tem*, until we get a more complete science, but will, I think, always be required.

Why, if their ontologies are strictly not correct, should the non-fundamental perspectives be essential?

One response to this question is:

Eliminativism. These problems might lead a physicalist simply to scrap the human perspective—and the special sciences altogether. Or, rather, to say that they are only needed until we have a more complete fundamental theory. But this is hopeless. It means that I have never actually worried about the validity of the ontological argument or the problem of free will, or wondered whether I was about to get flu. And still, the theory of physics remains a theory held by a thinking subject. Perhaps all physicalists are forced to eliminativism, but that would only show how self-refuting physicalism is. Quine is not strictly eliminativist, I think, because he believes that the way the human senses and faculties operate condemns us to reacting at a certain level of approximation, so we cannot help but spontaneously operate at levels that lack scientific accuracy. He does not make Churchland's mistake of thinking that what we perceive is a function simply of what theory we use to report our experiences, rather than of the actual sensitivity of our senses. So we can never abandon our strictly inaccurate theories. An analogy might be the following: our colour perception does not map objective differences in objects, but no amount of learning the difference between reflected and illuminated red will enable us to see them as different.

Quine does not talk much about these issues—the mind-body problem seems hardly to figure explicitly in his writings. It is Dennett who develops the pragmatic angle of Quine's thought on the subject. But we have already seen that this does not work. Even to see our ordinary concepts as the product of our senses involves taking the subject's perspective as fundamental.

Nevertheless, even McDowell's theory is located with respect to Quine's. This should be less surprising if one sees Davidson as the bridge. One can see McDowell as saying that, if the human level is unavoidable, then it must be part of nature and leave it at that. One might even risk the following seemingly bizarre thought, namely that, putting aside the question of closure under physics, McDowell and Quine more or less agree. They both hold that the human perspective is an essential feature of our existence as biological creatures, that it cannot be reduced to 'hard' science, and that this has no 'supernatural' consequences and can be accepted without qualms. The difference is more or less entirely one of tone—whether one talks 'scientistically' or not. Price and Rorty, though not 'object naturalists', are more blatantly scientistic than McDowell.

7. CONCLUSION

The Cartesian perspective is unavoidable and neither standard physicalism nor looser kinds of naturalism have a plausible account of how they can accommodate it. Descartes is, therefore, right. The reality of the *cogito* establishes conscious, thinking things as essentially different—ontologically as well as behaviorally—from the rest of nature.

NOTES

1. Loewer kindly leant me a draft of his paper which I quoted in Robinson (2012b), in which he said that L was to be accounted for "in terms of facts and laws of microphysics and *our conceptual scheme* and epistemological situation in the world" [italics added]. When I quoted this, I did not realize that the italicized phrase was later excised. This suggests that Loewer was torn between (B) and (C), for if our conceptualization is needed for their existence, then what is real is merely the grounding for our practices.
2. For further discussion of Davidson's confusions, see Robinson (2001).

10 On What We Must Think

Ralph C. S. Walker

The thesis of the first part of this chapter is that mind is irreducibly different from matter because it has the capacity to be influenced by reason, which takes the form of imperatives that are objective in the sense of being independent of what we think or feel about them. The influence of reason is different from the cause-effect relationship and analogous functional relationships that characterise matter. There are other differences between mind and matter, which may equally be used to establish that the mental properties of a person are different in kind from the physical properties, and not in principle reducible to them. I shall only be considering the influence of reason. This first part of the paper is based on Kant.

The thesis of the second part is that the mind and the body are distinct substances. Substance dualism is not in fashion, though it still has its supporters. It does not require that mind and body should actually exist apart, but only that they be capable of existing apart, and this is a perfectly coherent idea. This second part of the paper is based on Descartes, whose arguments on this question (as on so many others) have been repeatedly battered down since his own day, only to rise up again repeatedly too.

I

In a much discussed passage, Kant says:

> I maintain that to every rational being possessed of a will we must also lend the Idea of freedom as the only one under which he can act. For in such a being we conceive a reason which is practical—that is, which exercises causality in regard to its objects. But we cannot possibly conceive of a reason as being consciously directed from outside in regard to its judgements; for in that case the subject would attribute the determination of his power of judgement, not to his reason, but to an impulsion. Reason must look upon itself as the author of its own principles independently of alien influences. (Kant 1900-: vol. IV, 448)[1]

What matters for our purposes is not Kant's idea of free will, but his claim that we must think of ourselves as directly influenced by practical reason. He takes the moral law to be a demand of practical reason, and holds that an action can have moral worth only if it is done out of a sense of duty, which involves a direct response to practical reason itself. But practical reason can make other demands on us besides moral ones, and theoretical reason can make demands on us too. As he says, in judging we must think of ourselves as responding to those demands, not as being programmed to respond in a mechanical way. To be rational is not just to come up with responses that *conform* to what reason requires, as the programmed response might: to be rational is to come up with responses that one sees reason requires and *because* reason requires them.

This distinction causes Kant a serious problem, because he thinks he has proved that the spatiotemporal world is governed by deterministic causal laws, rendering our thoughts and actions wholly predictable on the basis of such causes. But morality, and rationality more generally, requires that we should act on the basis of reason and think on the basis of reason. Reason does not belong to the spatiotemporal world, and does not fit the cause-effect model. This leads him to think that although every thought and action in the spatiotemporal world is fully determined, we can somehow make free choices in an underlying intelligible reality. Fortunately we can set aside the difficulties of that position, for unlike Kant, we—or most of us—are not committed to causal determinism. Kant's own attempt to establish it failed, and it remains at best a scientistic conjecture, one that physics has long passed by.

What matters for us is the idea that rational beings must at least think of themselves as capable of being moved by reason itself, and not as always reacting to causal forces. That we must *think* of ourselves in this way is all Kant is claiming, at this point anyway. But if we *are* capable of being moved by reason itself, there must be more to us than what is material, or accountable in material terms. For I take it to be characteristic of matter that its behaviour can be explained (where it can be explained at all) by causal and statistical laws, and if we can be affected by reason itself, the affecting cannot be understood either in terms of causal laws or in terms of statistical relationships.

Reason does not make us do particular things, nor does it make us think particular things. It affects us by presenting us with "oughts", imperatives. Kant is particularly concerned with the moral "ought", which he sees as an imperative of pure practical reason; I should like to defend him on this, but it would take too much space here, so I shall set the moral "ought" aside. There are other and less controversial "oughts" that rational beings must think themselves obliged by: other imperatives, both theoretical and practical. The theoretical ones include the principles of logic, the principle of induction, and the principle that enjoins us to seek for simple explanations. A practical principle on which we regularly depend is the one that says we should always adopt the best available means to our ends. The imperatives of reason present themselves as objective, in the sense that they must hold independently of anything we may think or feel about them: it is by trusting them that we achieve objective truth about the world, and success in action.[2]

Such principles cannot affect us like ordinary causes. They do not regularly produce the same effect in us, as the striking of matches regularly makes them light. If they can indeed affect us, it is by making us aware of something we ought to do or think. Our response is to the *content* of what reason tells us, and typically (though of course not invariably) it consists in our doing, or seeking to do, whatever reason requires of us in the context. If we fail to get things right the first time, responding to reason will involve rethinking and correcting the mistake. We must try to accommodate ourselves to what reason requires. This ability to respond to an "ought", as we conceive it, is distinctive and does not lend itself to analysis in terms of cause and effect. If we do have this ability, it is not the only property we have that is distinctively non-physical; the same can be said of consciousness and of intentionality, but it is our responsiveness to imperatives that I want to concentrate on here.

No doubt we do think and act i*n accordance with* these principles a good deal of the time. But computers can do that, at least to a considerable extent; they can make accurate calculations and generate logical and mathematical proofs. What may be doubted is whether we are actually moved by the rational principles themselves, thinking and acting *because of* our awareness of what they require. Can we establish that we really are able to think and to act *in response to* our awareness of rational principles, and not just in conformity with them?

Kant begins by claiming that we *must think* of ourselves as having this ability. Obviously we *do* think of ourselves that way. But must we? We have plenty of thoughts about ourselves which are misleading or illusory. The lines of Kant's own argument are not entirely clear, but there seems to be room for an argument which is broadly in Kant's spirit: first that we *must* think of ourselves in that way—we have no live alternative—and then that this gives us the best possible reason for accepting that we really are like that. Section IA will seek to show that we must indeed think of ourselves in this way. Section IB will argue that this is sufficient to establish that we are indeed capable of thinking and acting in response to our awareness of rational principles, and that therefore there is something importantly non-physical about our minds.

IA

First, then: *Must* we think of ourselves as able to respond to rational principles? And just what is meant by "must" here? The first question subdivides, and answering it will make it clearer what is meant by "must". It might be argued we do not *have* to think of ourselves as rational at all, even to the extent of *conforming* to these principles; (1) and (2) following are concerned with that suggestion: first in respect of theoretical principles, then in respect of practical ones. It might also be argued that it would be enough to think of ourselves as conforming to them, without having to think of ourselves as able to respond to them. That is discussed in (3).

(1) It may be said that the whole idea of objective principles of theoretical reasoning is mistaken, along with Kant's conception of reason as *a priori*. That might be thought to be implied by Quine's refusal to give any special status even to the basic principles of logic. He held that our statements about the world, including even the most elementary logical ones, "face the tribunal of sense experience not individually but only as a corporate body" (Quine 1963: 41). But that cannot be right: they could not face any tribunal unless facing it had some consequence: which would require at least assuming that the principle of noncontradiction holds, and *modus tollens* also. When Aristotle raised the question of justifying the principle of noncontradiction, he said that if anyone rejected it he could not conduct an argument with him (Aristotle [ca. 340 BC] 1984: Γ, 4). Kant calls the principle of noncontradiction "the ultimate logical ground of all that can be thought", and says that without it "all possibility vanishes, and there is nothing left to think" (Kant 1900-: vol. II, 82).

One might ask, is there really nothing left to think? Nothing left to think *without contradiction*, perhaps, and no chance of a conversation with Aristotle. But perhaps Kant and Aristotle are just expressing an *attitude* that they, and no doubt most of us, have towards contradiction: they do not think it objectively wrong, but disapprove of it.

This suggestion is interesting because no argument can destroy it (which was Aristotle's point). It cannot be shown to be wrong, but it is untenable—an important distinction. Anyone who made it would have to rely on noncontradiction to make the claim and to reject its negation as false. More generally, anyone who suggests that the basic principles of logic, or of inductive and abductive reasoning, are merely attitudes that people often have, instead of being objectively right, thereby undermines his own claims to knowledge of an objective world. Our claims to knowledge of an objective world rest firmly on these principles, for familiar reasons of a broadly Kantian kind. It is only by taking the principles as guides to how things are that we can regard the conclusions they give us as true of an objective reality.

(2) It may be said, quite separately, that there are no a priori principles of practical reasoning. Setting aside Kant's Moral Law, I claimed that status for the principle that we should always adopt the best available means to our ends. People sometimes suggest that there is no place for a principle of practical reason here, because someone who failed to take the best available means would show that she did not have that end after all. Unless of course she did not know what that best means was, either not knowing the relevant facts, or having gone wrong in working things out; but a failure in working things out would be a failure in theoretical reasoning, not practical

reasoning. Some have even claimed Kant thought this himself, because he introduces the principle as "analytic: for in my willing of an object as an effect there is already conceived the causality of myself as an acting cause—that is, the use of means" (Kant 1900-: IV, 417).[3] But what makes it analytic is that Kant uses the word "willing" (*Wollen*) not for "wanting" but for "rational wanting". The *will*, he has said a little earlier, is "nothing but practical reason" (Kant 1900-: IV, 412). So the rational thing for the agent is to take the necessary means to her objective; but she may not.

Kant must be right about this. There is room for a failure of practical reason. She might have known perfectly well what the appropriate means were, and just failed to act. The temptation to think this is impossible is similar to the temptation to think that akrasia is impossible. We like to think of ourselves as more rational than we are, and consciously failing to take the appropriate means is irrational. But we can be irrational. Someone who stays in bed despite an all-things-considered desire to get to work on time may stay in bed because he wants to, and in that case we call him akratic. Equally, though, he may have no particular want to stay in bed but just lazily does, despite his all-things-considered desire. Again, I may set out on a task, and know what I have to do, but let my mind wander and fail to do it. Mark Platts uses the example of someone of sitting in a room full of smoke, wanting to clear the smoke, knowing he can do it by opening the window, yet just sitting there doing nothing. Such behaviour is not impossible, just irrational (Platts 1991: 20).

We could not achieve much unless we accepted the practical norm that requires adopting the appropriate means for our ends, and acted accordingly. So to reject it, and not to act in accordance with it, is again not a live option for us. Meeting at least some of our objectives is necessary for us if we are to keep going.

I am claiming that we *must* think of ourselves as capable of responding to objective imperatives, and not just as conforming to what they would require. The discussion of (1) and (2) has at least to some extent clarified what is meant—and what Kant must have meant—by saying "we must think that *p*". It is not that everyone will be prepared to assent to *p*, as something they believe; there are always people who will dispute any particular proposition. What is meant is that unless we tacitly relied on the truth of *p*, we could not think or act coherently. (1) and (2) have, I hope, shown that we could not think or act coherently if we did not accept the relevant rational principles as being *right*. They have not shown that we must do more than that, and think of ourselves (in the sense just indicated) as aware of them and capable of acting in response to that awareness. Must we?

(3) The third suggestion is that we do not have to. We could manage perfectly well so long as we thought of ourselves as thinking and acting *in accordance with* reason, without thinking we are influenced by objective imperatives themselves. Some people regard our reasoning capacities as habits of thought that are natural to us, and nothing more.

These habits, they would say, allow us to reject arguments and theories that are contrary to the standards of theoretical rationality, and to criticise the irrationality of the person who does nothing to get rid of the smoke. If these habits lead us to do just what the rational imperatives would demand of us, then surely we must be *right* in doing these things—right by the standards of rationality, even though we are not influenced by those standards directly.

We should be right. But if we thought of ourselves as guided *only* by habits, we could have no basis for believing we were right or for thinking of our successes as more than accidental. There is nothing wrong with thinking that our propensities to be rational are habits of thought that are natural to us: they are. But habits of thought can mislead us, and we need some grounds for thinking that these are the ones to rely on. Some people hold that we can rely on them because they have been implanted in us by evolution: it was their tendency to get things right that enabled the survival of those who thought in accordance with them, while those who thought along different lines failed to reproduce successfully. But that will not do by itself. The theory of evolution could at best tell us that certain ways of thinking had worked in the past, those that were required for our ancestors' survival and reproduction. The theory gives us no assurance that these principles will also be reliable when applied to cases of a complexity on which our ancestors' success did not depend, in molecular biochemistry and atomic physics. Nor does it give us any reason to think they will apply at all in the twenty-first century. To get that, we should have to rely on a quite general form of the principle of induction, which the theory of evolution could not possibly guarantee.

Certainly evolution must be largely responsible for our capacity to access rational principles. The simpler forms of life do not have it. It is quite consistent to hold that we acquired this capacity through evolution, and also to hold that it enables us to detect an objective reality independent of us, a reality of rational requirements. And that is what we do hold. For we hold that these principles are objectively right, and only if they are objectively right can they give us reliable access to truths about an objective reality. It is uncontroversial that our perceptual abilities were formed in us through evolution, but that is no reason for questioning that we can perceive what is objectively there. The same applies with our rational capacities. We hold them to give us an objectively sound basis for discovering truths about the present and achieving successes in the future, instead of being merely habits of thought inherited from an earlier age and different circumstances.

Some in the tradition of Hume would reject this line of argument. It depends on the idea that getting things right is not enough: we need a justification for thinking that our successes are not merely accidental. But Hume, and Quine also, seek to do away with the idea of epistemological justification, though neither of them is entirely consistent about it.[4] It is hard to be consistent in taking this position, because the position itself prevents you from showing anyone else that their views are unjustified. All you can do is express your own disapproval of their position, or say that they are arguing in a way that does not fit with some system (like classical logic) that you take to be widely approved amongst your friends. Someone who really thought that the principles governing our thinking were nothing more than habits could have no real grip on the idea of objectivity—of things being thus and so independently of their own thinking. They could distinguish what was consonant with the habits they approved of, and what was not. But that would be all.

So we are committed to thinking of ourselves as able to be guided by objective imperatives; only so can we think coherently about ourselves. In this sense, it is something we "must think". Only so can we think of ourselves as being reliable about reality, able to distinguish truth from falsity, and capable of distinguishing coherent from incoherent thought. We could not discard the idea that we can think and act *in response to* the requirements of rationality, without losing our basic conception of objective reality.

It remains possible that we might be wrong: that actually we *are* incapable of responding to these imperatives, so that much that we think is ungrounded or incoherent. I shall argue however that this is not a possibility that we can take seriously. It is analogous to the possibility that we are brains in vats or deceived by a malignant demon.

IB

Since we are committed to thinking of ourselves as able to respond to the demands of reason, the possibility that we are not is the possibility that we are trapped in an unavoidable illusion. The suggestion that we are material systems, operating like complex automata, is at least logically possible. But so is the *malin génie* hypothesis. There are limits beyond which argument cannot go, and anyone who calls in question those things upon which argument depends inevitably cannot be silenced by argument. But their position cannot be taken seriously. Often philosophical arguments have to end, not when one side has been reduced to contradiction, but when it becomes clear that a possibility is one that nobody could seriously hold, once its implications were properly understood. This is the strategy used by Descartes. It is also the strategy used by Kant. Given the projects they were pursuing, there was no alternative, and I believe there is no alternative in the present case: and no need of an alternative either.

Descartes recognized that nothing can absolutely refute the most radical scepticism. Any argument against it might itself be merely the deception of a malignant god or demon, who could "bring it about that I go wrong even in those matters which I think I see utterly clearly with my mind's eye" (Descartes 1641 [*Meditations on First Philosophy*]: VII, 6).[5] That includes "I think therefore I am". The point about the *cogito* is that it is not possible for us to doubt it, and we cannot get further than that. He puts the point most clearly in the *Second Replies*. When we have a "conviction so firm that it is impossible for us ever to have any reason for doubting" it,

> then there are no further questions for us to ask: we have everything that we could reasonably want. What is it to us that someone may make out that the perception whose truth we are so firmly convinced of may appear false to God or an angel, so that it is, absolutely speaking, false? Why should this absolute falsity bother us, since we neither believe in it nor have the smallest suspicion of it? For the supposition which we are making here is of a conviction so firm that it is quite incapable of being destroyed; and such a conviction is clearly the same as the most perfect certainty. (Descartes 1641: VII, 144f.)

This is clearly right: if there are things that we cannot doubt, and which cannot be shaken by any sound reason, then we have all that we can reasonably ask for. And this does—must—leave open a sort of possibility that we are entirely astray, and that God or an angel who knows the real truth can see that it is otherwise. But Descartes rightly dismisses that. It is not something we can take seriously.

Why could we not say: the very existence of that possibility constitutes a sound reason for doubting the firmest convictions? Well, most at least of these convictions—all those we are concerned with here—are indispensable, in the way that the law of noncontradiction was for Aristotle.[6] They include "I think" and the basic principles of thought. Nothing could count as a reason for doubting these things, since the very consideration of them would presuppose the things being questioned. In the *Third Meditation* Descartes does seek extra security, by ruling out the possibility of a deceiving god. But this is unnecessary. If there is a deceiving god, none of our arguments can be relied upon, so it is a suggestion we can do nothing with.

His point is not that we have a psychological inability to doubt these things. It is that there can never be good reason to doubt them: and a reason we cannot take seriously is not a good reason. In Meditation I he raises the doubt that he is mad, but refuses to take it seriously, and we can now see why: the idea that he is mad is the idea that all his basic ways of thinking and argument are confused and askew from reality. He is committed to them, and there is no way of dealing with the possibility that they might be wrong. Argument can take him—and us—no further than that. By recognising this, even if not completely clearly, Descartes makes a major contribution towards understanding at what point sceptical doubts must cease to be of interest.

Kant too, in the first Critique, seeks to show that there are certain beliefs, certain principles of thought, and certain fundamental concepts like the concepts of cause and object, without which experience would not be possible for creatures like us. We are therefore committed to them: we "must think" in accordance with them. The only justification that can be given for these beliefs, principles, and concepts is that they are indispensable; but it is a satisfactory justification; nothing more is needed. Kant might be asked: Why assume that there is such a thing as experience at all? And why assume (as he does) that our experience is of a spatiotemporal kind? He does not answer this explicitly, but the answer would be the same as Descartes's response to the idea that he might be mad. There is no absolute way of ruling out the possibility; but it is not a possibility anyone can take seriously. Somebody who seeks further assurance on this kind of thing is of as little interest as somebody who demands an absolute proof that he is not a brain in a vat.

Kant does seem to countenance further possibilities in a way Descartes does not. He envisages an underlying reality of things in themselves, unknowable but perhaps very different from the world we know. But this is *not* like Descartes's idea that our beliefs might be seen to be false by God or an angel. For Kant is emphatic that our ordinary beliefs are not made false by the underlying reality: they are not about the underlying reality. They are about the spatiotemporal world that we can know, and our indispensable beliefs, principles, and concepts apply to the spatiotemporal world, and yield us truth about it. Truth about the world is truth about this world. Things in themselves are postulated by Kant because of the needs of his theory, but we cannot know about them, and nothing about them could threaten the security of our knowledge of the spatiotemporal world in which we live.

In a similar way, someone who denies that we ever act in response to the demands of reason, or think in response to those demands, cannot be taken seriously because she herself must rely on these principles to think, act, or argue coherently. She can raise the possibility that we are actually incapable of responding to reason, but only in the way that one can raise against Descartes the possibility that the *malin génie* hypothesis is true, or raise against Kant the possibility that the concept of an object is incoherent. We cannot take any of these possibilities seriously, and we do not need to. We are committed to relying on these principles and on taking them to be reliable. So is she.

But what if she came up with a well-argued scientific case for the conclusion that every human thought and every human action is the product of ordinary physical causality, leaving no room for reason to influence us in the way I have been arguing it must? If her case were really well-argued by all our ordinary standards and well-supported by all our ordinary standards, it might seem strange to say we could not take it seriously. But she is still committed to the idea that reason does influence her, for she uses it to support her case; so she is in a paradoxical position. By relying on rational principles, she has reached the conclusion that reliance on rational principles is impossible. What is to be said about that?

The rational principles govern everything that is rationally thinkable, or discoverable by using induction, abduction, and those other principles by which we must think. By and large they are self-correcting; if they seem to lead us into contradictory positions, they provide ways to resolve that.

So the proper response to her would be to show some inadequacy in her argument, emphasizing the unavoidability of relying on rational principles. But we must recognize that there is always a possibility, of a sort, that these principles on which we inevitably rely do ultimately lead to contradiction or self-refutation. That would show that they were not reliable after all; it would show that the objective rightness that I have been claiming for them was only a delusion. Against the possibility that there is some radical incoherence internal to reason, and therefore to human thought, we have no guard. We have no guard against it just in the same way that we have no guard against the *malin génie* hypothesis. These are possibilities that we cannot take seriously, for if they were true there is nothing we could do about it, nothing we could usefully even begin to think about it.

This concludes Section I. It has sought to show that we are influenced by reason itself, which evokes from us a response different in kind from the sort of effect that a physical cause could produce in a physical thing. This shows that the mind is not simply physical; it does not yet show that it is a non-physical substance. The next section will argue that it is.

II

The basic idea of a substance is that of a thing that has properties. Since it seems very plausible to say that our minds have a number of properties that are not physical, and that our bodies have a number of properties that are not mental, it seems odd that so many people are reluctant to countenance the idea that a mind and a body are distinct substances. First, though, we must fill out the concept of substance a little.

Descartes defines a substance as "a thing which exists in such a way as to depend on no other thing for its existence" (Descartes 1644 [*Principles of Philosophy*]: VIIIA. 24). Strictly this makes God the only substance, but he says that created things can be called substances if they depend for their existence on no other created thing. Various other features were associated with the idea of substance in his day, but he rejects some of them—for example, the idea that substances must be active—as remnants of scholasticism. His corporeal substances are not active. But substances were generally taken to persist through time, and he agrees with that: they depend only on God for their existence, and it is in their nature to go on existing until God chooses to destroy them.

His conception of a substance is thus fairly close to our conception of an individual particular thing. His claim that his mind is a distinct substance from his body is the claim that his mind and his body are two individual particular things. They are closely linked, of course; there is a "very intimate union" between them. He has three arguments for their distinctness, but two of them are unsatisfactory—the argument that he can doubt that he has a body but cannot doubt that he has a mind, and the argument that bodies are divisible and minds are not (though this raises interesting questions about what "dividing a mind" could mean). The third one, his main argument, is much more interesting.

> I know that everything which I clearly and distinctly understand is capable of being created by God so as to correspond exactly with my understanding of it. Hence the fact that I can clearly and distinctly understand one thing apart from another is enough to make me certain that the two things are distinct, since they are capable of being separated, at least by God. . . . Thus, simply by knowing that I exist and seeing at the same time that absolutely nothing else belongs to my nature or essence except that I am a thinking thing, I can infer correctly that my essence consists solely in the fact that I am a thinking thing. It is true that I [have] . . . a body that is very closely joined to me. But nevertheless, on the one hand I have a clear and distinct idea of myself, in so far as I am simply a thinking, non-extended thing; and on the other hand I have a distinct idea of body, in so far as this is simply an extended, non-thinking thing. And accordingly, it is certain that I am really distinct from my body, and can exist without it. (Descartes 1641: VII, 78)

The last few words are important. Descartes is not trying to prove that the mind ever *does* exist independently of the body, only that it is possible that it should. The writers of the *Second Objections* complained to him "you say not one word about the immortality of the human mind"; he replied that he had not intended to (Descartes 1641: VII, 78).

He brings in God because he believes God guarantees that whatever he conceives clearly and distinctly is at least a genuine possibility. Without God, however, his procedure is one that is still sound enough, in that conceivability remains ultimately our best, indeed our only, guide to what is metaphysically necessary or metaphysically possible. Care is needed here, though. In order to show that something is properly conceivable, it is not enough just to show that conceptual analysis reveals no contradictions in it. There may be a latent incoherence. If it belongs to the essence of gold that it has the atomic number 79, then there is a latent incoherence in the suggestion that there could be pieces of gold with a different atomic number. So this is not really conceivable, although it is not built into the meaning of the word "gold" that it has this essence, or not overtly. Our use of the word "gold" is nowadays *deferential* to what science shows about an indicated kind, and science considers identifying elements by atomic number to be appropriate. The reason people think of this as determining the essence is that we (or many people anyway) *can't conceive* of the ultimate natures of physical things as being any different from the way physics and chemistry take them to be. Conceivability is the ultimate test.

Descartes claims that thinking belongs to the essence of his mind. That seems about as plausible as such claims can readily be, particularly given the wide range of mental activities that he counts as "thinking".

He also claims that his essence "consists solely" in thinking, and that is more readily disputable. Arnauld pointed out that one can be clearly and distinctly aware that a triangle has been so constructed as to be, of necessity, right-angled, without also knowing that the square on its hypotenuse is equal to the sum of the squares on the other two sides, though this is equally necessary to the triangle. So Descartes's mind may be essentially bodily for all he knows (Descartes 1641: VII, 221f.). Similar points were made against him by Hobbes and Gassendi, and by many others since.

Descartes's reply is that a triangle is not a substance, and it seems a good reply as far as it goes (Descartes 1641: VII, 127f, 153). Substances are things which exist in such a way as to depend for no other thing for their existence; triangles are not—many necessary relationships must hold if something is to be a triangle. Descartes is claiming that he can clearly and distinctly, in other words coherently, conceive of a mind existing without a body. It seems easy enough to *imagine* this; but is it a genuine metaphysical possibility?

Many people would say it is not, agreeing with Descartes's objectors that it belongs to the essence of a mind to be embodied. This is because they think there is a latent incoherence in the conception of a mind existing without a body. There are two important arguments for thinking that. One, which worried Descartes himself, is that a mental substance and a physical substance could not interact. The other is that a purely mental substance would have no satisfactory identity conditions and could neither perceive nor act, so that if there were any such thing, it could not be much like what we think of as a mind.

The argument about interaction made good sense in the seventeenth century, when it was thought that there had to be some relation between cause and effect that reason could discover. Since Hume, that has not seemed plausible. Cause and effect are "distinct existences", the relation between them discoverable only empirically. When we see the input to some complex system generating some determinate output, we naturally look for an intervening mechanism that shows how it works, but clearly we must eventually come to a basic level beyond which no further mechanism is to be found. Once it was thought that that was when one atom hit another and moved it in accordance with a basic law describing such interactions; nowadays physics can take us further, but it must always come to rest in fundamental laws which simply describe relationships that regularly obtain. That there should be such relationships between mental states and physical states poses no difficulty of principle, though there is plenty of work to be done in ascertaining what they are—just as there is in the case of relationships between physical states.

If it is possible for a mental substance to cause effects in the body, and to have effects caused in it by the body, it is hard to see why a mental substance which lacked a body might not both perceive the material world and act on it too. Its causal relationships with the physical world would be direct, not mediated by a brain. Telekinesis may be a subject for frauds and charlatans, but there is no reason to think it conceptually incoherent for a mind to produce physical effects at some distance without the help of a body or a brain. Equally the reports of out-of-body experiences may provide no actual evidence for thinking that minds can leave their bodies and perceive them from outside, but there is no apparent incoherence in the idea. It might be thought that disembodied minds would perceive the world differently, since they would lack our perceptual mechanisms, but this would be pure speculation; there is no particular reason why they should.

Perception presupposes that a disembodied mind could have a place, a point of view from which it could perceive things. It could not *occupy* a place, because it would not be impenetrable: impenetrability is a characteristic of matter. Because it could not occupy a place, it could not prevent another disembodied mind from occupying the same place. An infinity of them could fit on the head of a pin.

So, what would distinguish them? People commonly think that if two things are numerically different, they must differ in some property, if only in spatiotemporal location. It would be possible for disembodied minds to be distinguished by their positions (points of view), for although there *could* be two of them in the same place, it might be that there never were. Or they might be distinguished in some other way. Even if they shared the same point of view on the world throughout their existences, they would be bound to have different memories and different attitudes; their different memories and thoughts could differentiate them. John Foster, defending dualism, develops a highly sophisticated conception of co-consciousness for this purpose (Foster 1991: ch. 6). Michael Inwood discusses Plato's Myth of Er, in which souls are repeatedly reborn in new bodies a thousand years after the deaths of their old bodies, and suggests that in their disembodied state souls could recall something of their previous lives to justify claims of continuing identity: "My earthly lives will be related to my periods in the underworld rather in the way that my dreams are related to my waking experiences in this life" (Inwood 2009: 34).

Actually there is little serious argument against the possibility of two things sharing *all* the same properties, even spatial and temporal ones. Leibniz conceded that this was possible, but argued that it would never happen, because God would have no reason for making two absolute duplicates (Leibniz and Clarke 1717; Leibniz's 5th Letter: §§ 25–26): not an entirely compelling argument. Probably the main consideration that moves people nowadays is that if two things shared all their properties, including their spatiotemporal properties, we should not be able to know that there were two. But there are many things that we are not able to know.

In any case, there are conceivable situations in which we should have good grounds for recognizing two things as having exactly the same properties. We can imagine two pens that differ only in spatial position, except that one has a slight mark on it. They are then moved closer and closer together until they merge into what looks and feels like one pen. After a while this divides into two separate pens again, one with the mark and one without. That might happen frequently and predictably, and it might happen with pairs of pens neither of which was marked. Then, it might be natural to think that there were periods when two pens occupied exactly the same place, and had all their other properties in common—except (so far) their temporal properties: they have different pasts and futures. Of course that does not happen with pens, though something like it may happen at the subatomic level. If it did happen, it would seem not unreasonable (and certainly not incoherent) to conjecture that there were cases in which two pens shared exactly the same place and exactly the same properties throughout the whole time of their existence; indeed, it might even be that the simplest laws we could find to explain things required us to conclude that this was so.

It is standardly said that there must be *criteria* for numerical identity. This view gains apparent plausibility from an ambiguity in the word "criterion". Its basic meaning is "means for judging or trying, standard, test" (Liddell and Scott 1940), but in philosophical usage it often means "what is constitutive of the nature of a thing". Personal identity clearly has criteria in the first sense; we have various ways of judging whether a person today is, or is not, the same as a person we met some time ago. Similarity of appearance, character, and apparent memories are relevant, as is bodily continuity. But that is not to say that any of these, or any package of them, is determinant of personal identity. If minds (or persons) have an intrinsic identity that persists through time, it does not need to have criteria in the second sense—criteria determinant of what that identity consists in. There may be nothing that their identity consists in, except itself.

In practice we need criteria in the first sense, for our own convenience in distinguishing and re-identifying things. But so far as material things are concerned, we have no particular interest in real, intrinsic identity through time, if that can be ascribed to material things at all. So, as Hobbes and Locke recognized, we develop criteria for judging, but then make them determinant of a kind of factitious cross-time identity: we create sortal concepts, for which these criteria are deemed to fix what is to count as the same F over time (Hobbes [1655] 1981: ch. 2; Locke [1706] 1975: III, ch. 3). Although these sortal concepts are designed to suit our own purposes, there is nothing unsatisfactory about that, so long as we recognize that it is we who have decided to cut up reality in this way. It would be inconvenient *not* to be able to call something the same mountain that we saw yesterday, just because some rocks had fallen and some earth had been carted away from it. It would be equally inconvenient not to be able to call something the same rock, or the same desk, because small parts had been broken off, or because it was made of different atoms. In general it is convenience that determines what we say about the continuing identity of material things.[7] What we say about the pens will thus also be a matter of what it is most convenient to say. There could be circumstances in which it was convenient and appropriate to say there were two different pens with all their properties in common.

Our purposes in considering minds, and one's own mind in particular—or persons, and one's self in particular—do not allow us to be altogether satisfied with re-identifying them under such made-up sortals. We do of course make up sortals in this case too, and for many purposes (particularly bureaucratic ones) physical continuity of body will do perfectly well. This is what determines sameness of *man*, according to Locke, though he is evidently tightening up ordinary language here. As he recognizes, there are other purposes for which an alternative sortal may be more appropriate, and he proposes sameness of *person*, determined by continuity of consciousness. There may be others again. But as Locke also recognizes, there is also room for a different question, a question about *real* continuing identity: one that is not to be answered in terms of our convenience. This is the question about sameness of *spiritual substance* (Locke [1706] 1975: II, ch. 27).

He is often thought to have rejected the idea of spiritual substance, because he points out that there is no decisive way of answering questions about the identity of spiritual substance. For all we know, the soul of Socrates may be in the mayor of Queenborough. Certainly he thinks it more useful to be able to identify people under our made-up sortals. In contrast "same spiritual substance" is of no practical use to us. But that is not to say there is no right answer to questions about sameness of spiritual substance, only that we have no way of answering them. The same is to be said for sameness of substance generally, whatever kind of substance is involved. Locke does not deny that there *are* substances, with their intrinsic identities; he only denies that we can know about them (Locke [1706] 1975: IV, ch. 4).

There is no incoherence in holding that minds have an intrinsic identity that persists through time and that is not dependent on any criteria we may find convenient for identifying them. This view has been defended by others than Locke, including Richard Swinburne (Shoemaker and Swinburne 1984; Swinburne 1986: ch. 9). It would be hard to produce a decisive argument in a matter like this. But if we think that the identity of a person, or a mind, *consists in* anything other than identity itself, it will always be possible that at some point the person, or mind, should divide, leaving two persons, or minds, both equally qualified, under the criterion concerned, to count as the same original person or mind. Derek Parfit has made out a persuasive case for thinking that this should lead us to replace talk of *identity* with talk of *survival*, survival being a matter of degree (Parfit 1984: part III). Immediately after the split, neither of the new persons would be identical with the former single person, but the former single person would survive in both of them to quite a high degree. Actually, of course, such splits do not occur, but that is a contingent matter. Clearly we undergo great changes during life, and that may make it seem relatively natural to say that a child of three survives to some degree in me now, but in a much smaller degree than a man of fifty does.

This seems to leave out something important about ourselves and the way we think about ourselves. People who lose their memories in old age, and whose character changes, still seem to be ineluctably the same people; at least it seems hard to deny that there is a *right answer* to the question whether they are or not, a question not answered by information about bodily continuity or continuities of any other kind. It is easy to anticipate being in such a condition oneself—meaning by "oneself" *oneself*. It is also perfectly possible to imagine being reincarnated, and reincarnated without retaining one's present character or any memory of one's present life. Some philosophers have declared that to be unintelligible, but it is odd to claim that the beliefs of half the world are unintelligible.

Moreover, it is a condition of self-consciousness that we should at least *think* of ourselves as subjects that continue through time, at least to a short extent. This is the requirement of what Kant called the transcendental unity of apperception. When I try to articulate a thought or an argument, I must think that the same "I" is responsible for the premise of an argument as is responsible for the conclusion, and that the same "I" is responsible for the beginning of a word as for the end of it. Otherwise there could not be an argument or a thought at all; there would only be, at most, what Hume would call "particular perceptions", each of them "distinct existences". Hume himself had to "plead the privilege of a sceptic" and admit that his theory was not able "to explain the principles, that unite our successive perceptions in our thought or consciousness" (Hume [1739] 1888: 366). There must be *something* that unites them, and we cannot but *think of* that something as the subject self.

Can we not then conclude that there must *be* a subject self, persisting through time—at least through enough time for us to frame thoughts and arguments? For this is something to which we are inevitably committed. And, as we saw in the previous section, when we are inevitably committed to something in this way, the idea that we might be wrong need not concern us: it cannot be taken seriously.

What I *must think* is that the same self is responsible for one part of a thought as is responsible for another. So I am committed to a thought about the identity of the self, a thought which makes the identity claim without going on any bodily criteria. Peter Strawson agrees that our self-ascription of mental states is not based on any criteria, but he insists that "reference to the empirically identifiable subject [is] not in practice lost in criterionless self-ascription" (Strawson 1966: 165). This is because he thinks that what *determines* whether I am in a particular mental state must be something capable of public manifestation. This verificationism seems quite unfounded. If the capacity to manifest mental states is thought to be important, disembodied minds might be able to manifest them to one another telepathically. But it is a familiar feature of everyday life that we are often in mental states that we cannot properly manifest to others, and the difficulties we have in trying give rise to much great literature.

Do we have to think of ourselves as lasting for more than the very short duration needed for having a thought, or putting together an argument?

Certainly when I think about what happened to me yesterday, or ten years ago, I do not feel I have any option in ascribing these memories to my continuing self. But it is not so clear that I am committed to them in the way I am committed to thinking of myself as open to objective rational principles, or as a subject existing through the short period of my present thoughts. I rely on these things as preconditions of my being able to think and argue at all. That is why I cannot take seriously the idea that I am not open to reason, or am only a bundle of perceptions. I certainly do rely on my longer-term memories for many things that are important to me. I rely on them to engage in long-term projects, and indeed to engage in the long-term project of living a life. So it is true that if someone were to suggest that my memories of yesterday were erroneous, I could not take it *very* seriously. But I do know that memories can deceive, and I am not *committed* to my memories of yesterday being right in the unavoidable way that I am committed to being able to think and act in response to reason.

Still, because I am committed to being able to think and act in response to reason, I am committed to thinking of myself as more than just physical. I am committed to thinking of myself as a subject that thinks, and that persists through at least a short period of time, and quite possibly more. This subject has mental properties, including important ones I have barely mentioned here, particularly consciousness. I can clearly and distinctly conceive that it could exist without my body. That is not to say I have any reason to think that it ever does exist without my body. But it is to say that it is a mental substance.

NOTES

1. References to Kant's works are to the Academy edition, Kant (1900-). The translations used are Kant (1948) and Kant (1992), which have the Academy pagination in their margins.
2. For a much fuller defense of this, see Walker (1993), cf. also Walker (1998).
3. On Kant's use of *Wollen* and *Wille* see Walker (1978: ch. XI) and Walker (1998: ch. 3).
4. Quine (1969). His position is criticized very effectively in Stroud (1984: ch. 6).
5. References to Descartes are given by the date of original publication, to indicate the work, but the translation used is Descartes (1984–1991), and the pagination is that of Descartes (1964–1976), commonly given in the margins of editions and translations.
6. Descartes himself makes the point about indispensability, though not very clearly Descartes (1641: VII, 38f).
7. It may seem less obvious that this applies to organisms, and I do not claim that it does with animals that have minds. It seems to apply to plants, though; if two separate trees grow together and join, it is a matter of convenience whether we say there are still two trees or only one. I recognize, of course, that there is much more to be said on this general issue.

Part 4
Non-Cartesian Dualism

11 The Promise and Sensibility of Integrative Dualism

Charles Taliaferro

This chapter has three aims. First, I argue for what may be called the primacy of the mental. Much contemporary philosophy of mind proceeds on the grounds that we have a problem-free concept of what is nonmental, or mind-independent, or taking up the so-called third-person point of view. I argue that the very notion of a third-person point of view rests on the intelligibility of an antecedent subjective, first-person point of view. To appreciate the natura and cogency of mind-body "dualism" historically and today, one needs to recognize the importance of methodology and of securing a commonsense, initial starting point of inquiry that takes the first-person, subjective experience seriously. Second, I advance a case for what may be called *integrative dualism*. Too often, critics of dualism fail to recognize that one may embrace the metaphysical distinction of person and body, or the mental and physical, and yet claim that in a fully functioning, healthy embodiment, the embodied person functions as a unified subject. The second part of this chapter, then, seeks to redress the charge that dualism employs an implausible bifurcation between the observable, material body and the invisible, incorporeal mind. Third, I argue that the objection to mind-body interaction in a dualist framework is overrated. Contemporary critics of dualism such as Paul Churchland assume that we have a problem-free account of physical causation, but we are (or we should be) baffled about how to square "thoroughly" and "unambiguously" physical causation with mental causation. I argue for the reverse: we should not be baffled or suspect of mental causation, lest we undermine the very intelligibility and practice of the physical sciences.

I have defended elsewhere a modal argument for mind-body dualism.[1] This chapter will not directly contribute to that argument, which I find persuasive, but it will address three challenges facing dualism in terms of method, integration, and causal interaction. If successful, this chapter will indirectly contribute to the modal argument insofar as its concluding portrait of personal embodiment seems both coherent and promising.

The primacy of the mental: Some physicalists assume that we are first and foremost in possession of a sound understanding of what it is to be physical. This is sometimes articulated in terms of the problem of causal interaction in dualism. Consider three claims. Here is Jaegwon Kim:

It simply does not seem credible that an immaterial substance with no material characteristics and totally outside physical space, could causally influence and be influenced by, the motions of material bodies that are strictly governed by physical law. Just try to imagine how something that isn't anywhere in physical space could alter in the slightest degree the trajectory of even a single material particle in motion. (Kim 1996: 4)

Here is a similar claim by Eliot Sober:

If the mind is immaterial, then it does not take up space. But if it lacks spatial location, how can it be causally connected to the body? When two events are causally connected, we normally expect there to be a physical signal that passes from one to the other. How can a physical signal emerge from or lead to the mind if the mind is no place at all? (Sober 2000: 24)

And here is Daniel Dennett:

There is only one sort of stuff, namely *matter*—the physical stuff of physics, chemistry and physiology—and the mind is somehow nothing but a physical phenomenon. In short, the mind is the brain ... we can (in principle!) account for every mental phenomenon using the same physical principles, laws, and raw materials that suffice to explain radioactivity, continental drift, photosynthesis, reproduction, nutrition, and growth. (Dennett 1991: 33)

There are a number of matters to challenge in these claims. First, there is the presupposition that we have a sound, problem-free understanding of what it is to be material. Evidently, for Kim and Sober, something is material if it is spatial. This is not a unique or minority report. Peter van Inwagen writes, "A thing is a material object if it occupies space and endures through time and can move about in space" (van Inwagen 1990: 17). But this seems highly problematic. Many philosophers have believed that the mind or soul is spatial and yet not physical (the Cambridge Platonists), and philosophers like G. E. Moore and H. H. Price have contended that visual sensations (not limited to but including dream images and after-images) and sense or sense-data are spatial but not physical (see Taliaferro 1994: ch. 2). If any of these positions are plausible, we have reason to doubt the thesis that space is unified (every spatial object is some spatial distance from every other spatial object). Related to this is the fact that we only know of spatial objects and their relationships through our experience. Our appreciation and understanding of space requires the adequacy and reliability of our perceptual experience, our understanding, and consciousness. Indeed, when philosophers articulate what it is to be spatial (e.g. space is intersubjective; two persons can have experiences of the same object), they seem to grant that subjectivity is a key, conceptual, even prior category. Without an understanding of subjectivity, how can I understand intersubjectivity? We only have views about physical signals on the grounds of experience and understanding.

Some of the terms used by Kim and Sober also seem open to question. Why is the mental (on a dualist view) described as "totally outside physical space"? On any standard dualist account, the physical and mental are interwoven: we smell material objects, see them, hear them, taste them, and so on, where this seeing, hearing, tasting, and smelling involves more than the physical. Do physical signals smell, are they colored, or do they feel hot or cold? If so, it is not clear that "physical signals" are purely and exclusively physical sorts of things: perhaps they are objects that appear to us in certain ways, and this appearing is not thoroughly physical. Also, without a good grasp of what counts as physical, how do we know that "material bodies are strictly governed by physical law"? When I smell a rose, perhaps this is a matter of *psycho-physical causation*, and this is not a narrowly physicalistic affair. Also, van Inwagen's view of material objects seems to rule out immobile material objects that are not enduring temporally—a phenomenon that does not seem impossible.

Dennett's account of what he terms "the contemporary orthodoxy" of the current climate leads to the question of the primacy of the physical or mental in terms of our thinking itself. In "Who's On First," Dennett (2007b) claims that the only proper way of understanding what is going on subjectively in persons is by making inferences based on what we externally observe others reporting from what Dennett calls the third-person point of view. This outlook presupposes that I can be more certain of what others say than I can be about my own thinking, hearing, reasoning, feeling, interpreting, and so on. Here is an extensive passage in which Dennett advances his position as obvious and uncontroversial, but I suggest it is anything but obvious and uncontroversial:

> This third-person method, dubbed heterophenomenology (phenomenology of another not oneself) is, I have claimed, the sound way to take the first-person point of view as seriously as it can be taken . . . Most of the method is so obvious and uncontroversial that some scientists are baffled that I would even call it a method: basically, you have to take the vocal sounds emanating from the subjects' mouths (and your own mouth) and *interpret* them! Well of course. What else could you do? Those sounds aren't just belches and moans; they're speech acts, reporting, questioning, correcting, requesting, and so forth. Using such standard speech acts, other events such as button-presses can be set up to be interpreted as speech acts as well, with highly specific meanings and fine temporal resolution. What this interpersonal communication enables you, the investigator, to do is to compose a catalogue of what the subject believes to be true about his or her conscious experience. (Dennett 2007b: 81–82)

In reply, I suggest that it is baffling to think you could be more sure of what vocal sounds emanate from a subject than you can be sure of your subjective experience of hearing, seeing, thinking, and interpreting. Taken to an extreme, Dennett would be committed to thinking that the best, scientific way of my having self-awareness would be by listening to what others infer, based on their investigation, from the vocal noises emanating from my mouth. Or, as Dennett implies, I might listen to myself say "I feel tired" and then, upon investigation, interpret this noise as a speech act I probably undertook because I subjectively feel tired. Again, how might I be so sure I heard myself say *anything* unless I trust my first-person experience of listening, thinking, feeling, and interpreting? As an aside, Dennett's initial way of describing speech as "vocal sounds emanating from the subject's mouth" seems bizarrely detached from any commonsense, ordinary way of describing or interpreting what it is to speak or to be in conversation. Speaking is an activity, not a matter of noises that simply emanates or that we find wheeling up within us. Fortunately Dennett recognizes that speech is different from belches and moans, but it is telling that he has to point this out to his readers. Why would one need to make this point explicitly unless his initial portrait of speech and self-awareness comes dangerously close to confusing speaking with belching? Using Dennett's terminology, a conversation between two persons could be (preposterously) described as two organisms whose mouths are a conduit of various noises at different times which an observer and the two persons themselves may interpret as something called a discussion about philosophy of mind.

I propose that a more reasonable place to begin thinking about human nature and the world than that which was proposed by Kim, Sober, and Dennett is with what we know is incontrovertible, namely that we have subjective experiences and we are thinking and acting persons. We write books and go to conferences; we eat, sleep, run, make love, and so on. These I believe to be obvious. Dennett seems to have boundless confidence in "the physical stuff of physics, chemistry, and physiology" and treats "the mind" and "mental phenomenon" as second class citizens, but physics, chemistry and physiology are not possible without mental phenomena: experience, observation, and concepts. Arguably, the *concepts* of radioactivity, continental drift, and so on, are better known and need to be grasped in order to investigate the less well-known phenomena at hand. While I am not an anti-realist, I sympathize with Hilary Putnam's lament about mind-independent, transcendent objects:

> I am not inclined to scoff at the idea of a noumenal ground behind the dualities of experience, even if all attempts to talk about it led to antinomies. Analytic philosophers have always tried to dismiss the transcendental as nonsense, but it does have an eerie way of reappearing. (. . . [A]lmost everyone regards the statement that there is *no* mind-independent reality, that there are *just* the 'versions', or there is just

'discourse', or whatever, as itself intensely paradoxical.) Because one cannot talk about the transcendent, or even deny its existence without paradox, one's attitude to it must, perhaps, be the concern or religion, rather that of rational philosophy. (Putnam 1995: 241)

I do not follow Putnam all the way in these remarks, but it does bring out the primacy of our concepts, our versions, or discourse vis-à-vis (to use Dennett's example) photosynthesis. While I am more concerned with the primacy of the mental than the primacy of value, I view with approval Putnam's further point about the primacy of value over and against what in the old days we called facts (or scientific facts).

> ... and Quine's critique of the logical positivists' picture of what they called the language of science as neatly divided into a "factual" part and an "analytic" part, the whole argument for the classical fact/value dichotomy was in ruins, and that, as far as logical empiricism could tell, science might presuppose values as well as experiences and conventions. Indeed once we stop thinking of "value" as synonymous with "ethics," it is quite clear that it does presuppose values—it presupposes epistemic values. (Putnam 2003)

Back to the mental: In affirming the primacy of the mental, one is not ipso facto assuming dualism, idealism, or physicalism. The way some philosophers today characterize dualism is that dualists ask us to imagine two categories: the material and the immaterial. Perhaps following Descartes and philosophers like van Inwagen, they construe the first as spatially extended and the latter as not. But historically this is not how Descartes proceeded, and it is not how so-called "dualists" in the past or present usually develop their position. Even Descartes first establishes that he exists and only then does he consider what he is. Is he his body? He comes to conclude that he is not, because he believes it is possible that he can exist without his body, but it is not a matter of beginning with two well defined categories (the material and immaterial) and then wondering whether he is in one category or the other. I think it would be less misleading historically if Plato, Augustine, Descartes, Leibniz and other so-called "dualists" were considered non-monists or "pluralists" (these figures did not themselves use the term "dualism" to identify their position). They are best seen as affirming the reality of the mental (or the self) and then doubting that the mental (or the self) is metaphysically identical with what materialists from Democritus to Hobbes to Dennett claim. They are therefore most charitably (and reasonably) seen not as affirming something like two-ism, but as affirming that the mental is more than the body and the bodily, especially as this is articulated by those in the tradition of materialism/physicalism.

One way to argue further for the non-identity of the mental and the physical (such as neurological events) would be to articulate and defend a modal argument that seeks to bring to light the contingent relationship of the mental and physical and their possible separability (metaphysically possible, not just epistemically possible to believe). As noted earlier, this chapter is a little less ambitious, with the focus on matters surrounding (and not directly on) the modal argument, and so I conclude this first of three sections stressing, once again, the primacy and our greater grasp of the mental as distinct from having a problem-free grasp of what it is to be physical and nonmental.

The primacy and ineradicability of the mental became apparent in considering the implausibility of eliminating the mental. For a recent case, consider Alex Rosenberg:

> A single still photograph doesn't convey movement the way a motion picture does. Watching a sequence of slightly different photos one photo per hour, or per minute, or even one every 6 seconds won't do it either. But looking at the right sequence of still pictures the rate enhances the illusion, though beyond a certain rate the illusion gets no better for creatures like us. But it's still an illusion. There is nothing to it but succession of still pictures. That's how movies perpetrate their illusion. The large set of still pictures is organized together in a way that produces in creatures like us the illusion that the images are moving. In creatures with different brains and eyes, ones that work faster, the trick might not work. In ones that work slower, changing the still picture at the rate of one every hour (as in time-lapse photography) could work. But there is no movement of any of the images in any of the pictures, nor does anything move from one photo onto the next. Of course, the projector is moving, and the photons are moving, and the actors were moving. But all the movement that the movie watcher detects is in the eye of the beholder. That is why the movement is illusory.
>
> The notion that thoughts are about stuff is illusory in roughly the same way. Think of each input/output neural circuit as a single still photo. Now, put together a huge number of input/output circuits in the right way. None of them is about anything; each is just an input/output circuit firing or not. But when they act together, they "project" the illusion that there are thoughts about stuff. They do that through the behavior and conscious experience (if any) that they produce. (Rosenberg 2011: 191)

There are two problems. First, Rosenberg's position seems to be self-refuting. If he is right, his own thesis has no meaning. There is the problem, then, that if thoughts are not about things, neither are Rosenberg's. There is the further problem Anthony Kenny points out in his *Times Literary Supplement* review of Rosenberg's book:

> In *The Atheist's Guide to Reality*, Alex Rosenberg asserts repeatedly that physics is the whole truth about reality: the physical facts fix all the

facts. But that there are no facts other than physical facts is not itself a physical fact. If it is a fact at all, then there is at least one fact that is not a physical fact. If it is not a fact, but a falsehood, then there are facts other than physical facts. The self-trap snaps shut. (Kenny 2012)

Second, in watching a film, the experience of seeing a person running is not an illusion. The images do move—as images—depicting or representing or perhaps even disclosing (in a case of non-animation or digital reproduction) a person running. I should also add that for familiar Cartesian reasons, I think Rosenberg's thesis is self-referentially absurd.

In wrapping up this first section, what of the pervasive objection to dualism that it confuses epistemology and metaphysics? Perhaps there is not really a primacy of the mental but only a primacy of our concept of the mental over our concept of what is physical. Why cannot there be a conceptual dualism between the mental and physical (what we conceive of as pain is distinct from what we conceive of as brain processes) and yet no actual (metaphysical or ontological) distinction? I suggest that behind this proposal rests a fundamental misunderstanding: when it comes to the mental, the *appearing* is ontologically significant. Arguably, it is a fact that there are appearances, whether or not they are threatened by a scientific worldview that ultimately denies the reality of appearances. As Raymond Tallis writes:

> We seem, therefore, to have a *disappearance of appearance* as we move from subjective experience towards the scientific, quantitative and ultimately mathematical account of the world as matter. This loss of appearance is strikingly illustrated by those great equations that encompass the sum total of appearances, such as, "$e = mc^2$". But it is also present at a more homely level when we try to envisage material objects as they are in themselves. Think of a rock. I can look at the rock from the front or from the back, from above or below, from near or far, in bright light or dim. In each of an (innumerable) range of possible circumstances, it will have a slightly or radically different appearance. *In itself*, it has not definite appearance; it simply offers the possibility of an appearance to a potential observer (although those possibilities are constrained—the rock cannot look like a sonnet). So we can see that, as we get closer to the material world "in-itself," as a piece of matter, so we lose appearances: colour, nearness or farness, perspective. (The history of science, which is that of progress towards greater generalization is a gradual shedding of perspective—a journey towards Nagel's "view from nowhere.") (Tallis 2011: 142)

I turn now to what may be called *integrative dualism* to correct a common misunderstanding of dualism.

Integrative dualism: Some critics (Antony Flew, Gilbert Ryle, Anthony Kenny, Peter Hacker, Daniel Dennett, and Trenton Merricks) today depict dualists as supposing that there is a radical bifurcation between the person (soul, mind) and body (see Goetz and Taliaferro 2011). Dualists are said to believe the mind is a ghost in the machine, or a tiny person in the head (a homunculus), or they think that, if dualism is true, then you never see other persons, only their bodies or their containers. In one of the more interesting arguments in philosophy of mind, Trenton Merricks argues that if dualism is true, his wife is a soul. You can't kiss a soul (an immaterial, nonphysical being). He kisses his wife. Hence dualism is false (see Taliaferro and Goetz 2008).

Now, some dualists write in a way that lends some support to a picture of bifurcation. Consider Richard Swinburne's characterization of what it is to have a body, from the standpoint of his dualist perspective.

> We humans have bodies. A body is a physical object through which we can make a difference to the world and learn about the world; and ordinary humans are tied down to acting and acquiring information through their bodies. I can only make a difference to the world by doing something with some part of my body—by using my arm to move something, or my mouth to tell you something. And I can only learn about the world by stimuli landing on my sense organs (light rays landing on my eyes or sound waves landing on my ears, for example). (Swinburne 2008: 6–7)[2]

I do not doubt that the above is true, but without significant qualification it creates the impression that "I" am not so much embodied, located in and as my embodied self, but that "I" seem remote from my body or virtually detached except by virtue of my ability to control it and learn things about the world through it. Swinburne's picture of embodiment is better than Dennett's initial account: at least, in Swinburne's view, I am said to tell you things by moving my mouth whereas Dennett does not begin with a subject speaking but with vocal sounds emanating from the subject's mouth. Under difficult, perhaps damaged circumstances, a person might feel merely tied to their body or feel that their body is like some communicative, learning device. But dualists can offer a completely integrated understanding of embodiment in which the embodied person functions as a unity.

When we are functioning in a healthy way the embodied person is a functional unity: to see me talking is not seeing an immaterial soul manipulating a chunk of matter. To hit my body is to hit me, and so on. When I kiss someone, I do so as an embodied, feeling being. To use a line inspired by G. E. M. Anscombe, just as legs do not walk, people walk (a pedant might add, people walk by moving their legs), so lips do not kiss, people kiss (and again a pedant might add that they do so with their lips). At the risk of bringing analytic philosophy into the bedroom, assuming integrative dualism, for a kiss to be a kiss there must be a combination of intentional movement, embodiment, and expression. You do not really kiss someone if you stumble toward them and press your lips on their cheek or even if you press your lips on your beloved's lips and she or he seems to respond, unless there is an integration of the person and body, a functional unity. Even if metaphysically a person and mental states are nonspatial, we inhabit and act as spatial, embodied persons who are capable of kissing and embracing or injuring and killing each other. But tragic, damaged conditions can arrive in which the caricatures set up by Ryle and others seem accurate. Brain damage accompanied by profound psychological disorders could make me seem like a ghost in a machine. If I lost all motor control over my body except through tapping out Morse code with one hand, I might be like a little homunculi inside my head and not fully embodied. Partial disorders may limit embodiment—visual agnosia may limit my agency—and moral decay can get in the way of kissing. I may believe I am kissing my beloved, but he or she is the moral equivalent of a zombie, merely going through the motions in order to gain wealth. What the critics of dualism confuse is the portrait of a damaged person with the portrait of a healthy integrated, embodied person. I would also suggest, returning to the material in the first section of this chapter, that if I found myself in the position that Dennett commends—I have to rely on myself and others to interpret the vocal noises coming out of my mouth in order to know what I am feeling—I would have an impaired embodiment. It would be the philosophical equivalent of losing proprioception, the inner ability to know of one's bodily location without having to resort to visual observation.

In an effort to combat the prevalent view (especially among theologians) that mind-body dualism foists on us a denigrated treatment of the body, I have sought to recover the notion that embodiment involves the coordination and function of several, interrelated nonmoral goods. By a nonmoral good, I mean a good that is not a matter of the virtues or duties. In "The Virtues of Embodiment" (Taliaferro 2001) I argue that being able to have sensations is not only part of a characterization of being embodied, but it is a good power. Similarly, the power to act is not merely a power, but a good power. To fully support this position here would be difficult, given the space available, but I commend this value-oriented account of embodiment as more in common with our ordinary conception of being an embodied person. If it was reported to you that after I finished writing this chapter, I lost all powers to act or feel, and you were unsure whether this was good or bad, most of us would conclude you did not really believe the report or some other extenuating conditions were in play. Our ordinary concept of embodiment is the concept of a good integration of the body and the conscious, sensing, cognitive, and agentive powers of persons.

On causal interaction: once we adopt the primacy of the mental, the framework for stating the challenge of causal interaction between the mental and physical shifts from its current format. Paul Churchland's articulation of the problem of interaction for dualism is representative. In what follows, Churchland puts the problem of interaction in terms of a neuroscientist trying to find how to fit the mental into her study of the brain.

Put yourself in the shoes of a neuroscientist who is concerned to trace the origins of behavior back up the motor nerves to the active cells in the motor cortex of the cerebrum, and to trace in turn their activity into inputs from other parts of the brain, and from the various sensory nerves. She finds a thoroughly physical system of awesome structure and delicacy, and much intricate activity, all of it unambiguously chemical or electrical in nature, and she finds no hint at all of any nonphysical inputs of the kind that substance dualism proposes. What is she to think? From the standpoint of her researches, human behavior is exhaustively a function of the activity of the physical brain. And this opinion is further supported by her confidence that the brain has the behavior-controlling features it does exactly because those features have been ruthlessly selected for during the brain's long evolutionary history. In sum, the seat of human behavior appears entirely physical in its constitution, in its origins, and in its internal activities. (Churchland 1984)

I suggest that matters should be reversed.

The neuroscientist should first and foremost believe that she is a person who has concerns; she is tracing parts of the brain; she is feeling awe about the structure and delicacy of what she is studying; she is thinking about human behavior and evolution; she is seeking to explain human behavior. These suppositions cannot be suspect without undermining her practice of neuroscience (which requires thinking, observing, explaining, and so on). It is obviously a reasonable question to ask about the role of the brain and one's overall anatomy when we are thinking in general or doing neuroscience in particular, but any account of the brain-mental activity in causal terms must not begin with greater certainty about how the brain functions than the certainty that one is engaged in thinking about and practicing neuroscience. The task, in other words, should not lie with trying to fit the mental into the physical, but how to understand the physical in relationship to the mental. Arguably, the neuroscientist does not just have hints that she is thinking, feeling awe, and is engaged in neuroscience; she should be certain of this, and if she does not observe the thinking, feeling awe, and the active practice of neuroscience in the observable, "unambiguously chemical or electrical" brain events or any other "thoroughly physical" phenomena, that is good reason for her to believe that thinking, feeling awe, and so on are not identical with such physical events and phenomena.

Once one appreciates the primacy of both the mental in general and the certainty we have (and need to have to practice science or philosophy) the abilities to think, feel, draw inferences, and so on, a position like Colin Blakemore's seems (in my view) to carry an enormous burden of proof.

> The human brain is a machine which alone accounts for all our actions, our most private thoughts, our beliefs . . . All our actions are products

of our brain. It makes no sense (in scientific terms) to try to distinguish sharply between acts that result from conscious attention and those that result from our reflexes or are caused by disease or damage to the brain. (Blakemore 1988: 257)

Blakemore's claim that it makes no sense to distinguish conscious attention and brain process is curious, when you take into account that his writing these passages must surely be explained in terms of his own conscious attention. Perhaps Blakemore thinks that brain processes *are* conscious states? But how can this even be articulated without either eliminating conscious states or preserving a non-identity in which conscious states (the hurtful feelings of pain) still exist and yet are correlated with brain states or in casual interactions but not metaphysically identical with brain states? Surely, eliminating conscious attention as playing a causal role in why Blakemore is speaking, thinking, moving, and so on, is too high a price to pay no matter what, for if we do eliminate conscious attention it seems we would not have anything like what we normally assume when people speak, think, and move. It would mean that Blakemore does not ever say that his position is correct because he thinks his position is correct, if thinking turns out not to play a primary causal role such that he would not say his position is correct unless he thought it was. As it has been argued by Kenneth Einor Himma in "What Is a Problem for All Is a Problem for None: Substance Dualism, Physicalism, and the Mind-Body Problem":

> Eliminating the ontological distance between mental states and brain states by reducing the former to the latter solves the conceptual puzzle of how the mental and physical can interact because there is no conceptual mystery about how one physical state can cause another. But it solves this puzzle only by ruling out, as a conceptual or nomological matter (depending on the character of the reduction), any causal role for the hurtfulness of pain. (Himma 2005)

The reason why (I believe) Blakemore faces such an enormous burden of proof is because mental causation (causal relations involving experience) is so pervasive and unmistakable—from withdrawing one's hand from flames to giving a paper at a conference, both involving conscious, intentional activity by a subject.

Back to Sober's claim about causal integration having to involve physical signals: we have the challenge (as noted earlier) of identifying the boundaries of the physical, but if we stipulate that all and only material objects are spatial, and all and only nonspatial objects (things, events, states) are mental, why think that causation only occurs through spatial contact or between spatial objects? This simply seems question begging; there are multiple theories of causation that are not question begging such as counterfactual theories and nomological theories. Either could well accommodate the nonphysical/physical interaction as itself (at the most basic level), as direct, and as not requiring an intermediary causal mechanism.

What of the pairing problem posed by Kim and Sosa? Both Kim and Sosa have argued that a dualist is unable to explain why in a case of qualitatively identical sons, a blow to one body may cause one soul pain, but not another. They argue that in physical causal interaction, this problem does not arise.

Consider three replies. First, as Audi has argued, the pairing problem can arise in physical-to-physical causal relations. He asks us to imagine a universe of two qualitatively indistinguishable spheres with a power P that has the same probability of producing a L-particle equidistant to each other. Imagine that L-particle appears and yet the spatial relations do not tell us which sphere causally brought about L nor whether the occurrence of L is over determined. As Paul Audi maintains: "Space, then, does less to confer structure on physical events than defenders of the pairing argument are inclined to think . . . It is not impossible for two things to have exactly the same pure spatial relations to all other particulars, let alone all those with which they causally interact" (Audi 2011). If Audi is correct, and I believe he is, then the pairing problem arises with physical-to-physical interaction, and so if the problem is fatal to dualism, it seems equally fatal for accounts of exclusively physical causal interaction.

Second, if the mental (or some subset of what is mental) is spatial, then there is no advantage to being spatial when it comes to being physical. The spatiality of the mental (as held by the Cambridge Platonists and G. E. Moore) is not in the same space as "unambiguously" physical phenomena, but it is still "unambiguously" spatial.

Third, there may be nomological laws to the effect that particular souls are embodied by way of primitive, and not further explainable, powers. The causal relation is on no worse grounds than the supposed identity relation posited by physcalism: Why is it that certain brain states are identical to phenomenal states? My own view—sometimes called singularism—is that there can be primitive or basic, not further analyzable, causal relations. In physical-to-physical interaction there must be (I propose) such relations, and to deny this would incur a vicious infinite regress. The identity relation seems nothing like the familiar identity relations some physicalists employ. We see that water is H_2O! In that case we have an evident compositional relation, but this is not evident in the case of the physical and mental.

I close with a question about dualism and scientific explanations: Does dualism (or, as I prefer, integrative dualism) involve any impediment to the brain sciences or to a scientific inquiry into human nature? Dennett charges that "to be a dualist is, by definition, to be a mystery-monger, a despiser of science." Might that be true?

A full reply to this charge may take a book, and fortunately other authors address this matter (Robinson 2008). But I cannot resist adding my own counterclaim. I doubt there is any force to Dennett's charge. I do not see why the brain sciences cannot continue with its study of psycho-physical interaction. The failure to identify metaphysically consciousness with brain states does not for a nanosecond impede the study of correlation. Moreover one may be a dualist and treat consciousness and brain states, the person and body, as functional units without supposing that there is only one kind of thing metaphysically that is in play. Mind-body (or, as I prefer to call it, integrative) dualism is a thesis in metaphysics, as is the identity theory, functionalism, anomalous monism, and so on. Like many positions and questions in metaphysics (are there abstract objects?), integrative dualism is not a scientific hypothesis that competes with any scientific claims. A neurologist who seeks to explain prosopagnosia (a subject is unable to recognize familiar objects) and presupposes physicalism (the underlying cause of right brain damage) will be no different scientifically from a neurologist who adopts integrative dualism and presupposes that the subject's experiential states and cognitive powers are causally intertwined with neurological (and other) events without identifying the two.

In all, while I have not re-worked or re-presented my principle reason for accepting dualism (the modal argument), I have addressed three areas where dualism has been denigrated philosophically, challenging the primacy of the physical and the third-person point of view, the idea that dualism involves an implausible bifurcation, and the charge that dualist causal interaction should be ruled out.[3]

NOTES

1. I have defended the modal argument in Taliaferro (1994) and more recently in Taliaferro and Evans (2010).
2. Despite my pointing out that Swinburne does not offer what I think is a properly integral understanding of the person-body relationship, I thoroughly endorse much of his defense of dualism in *The Evolution of the Soul* and elsewhere.
3. I am very grateful to Allison Rodriguez for comments on earlier drafts of this chapter and editorial assistance.

12 The Dialectic of Soul and Body

William Hasker

Philosophical discussions of substance dualism almost invariably begin with Descartes, and with the challenges and difficulties that arise from his version of mind-body dualism. In many ways this procedure is justified; Descartes was arguably the first to discern clearly the challenges to our understanding of the human person posed by the rise of mechanistic natural science, and his view has set the stage for many of the subsequent debates on the topic. However, there is another, older tradition of substance dualism, one that still today has numerous adherents, and that can be seen as offering correctives to some of Descartes's more questionable claims and emphases. I speak, of course, of Thomas Aquinas's version of dualism, one which follows Aristotle in designating the human soul as the "form of the human body". The present discussion will be directed at this version of dualism, and will also consider some other views that show some promise of overcoming objections to Aquinas's position.

The Thomistic doctrine of the soul as the form of the body has all the right intentions. It aims to promote a close integration of soul and body, and more broadly of the human person with the overall world of nature. Yet it does this without denying or minimizing the distinctive attributes of human beings as rational, moral, and religious creatures. And while emphasizing that the normal and the best state for human beings is as embodied persons, it makes room for their disembodied persistence after biological death and their eventual re-embodiment in the resurrection.

It is all the more regrettable, then, that the view as usually understood cannot accomplish these goals in a way that makes it a good candidate for our acceptance. So, at any rate, I shall argue. I will then go on to consider a modification of the view that remedies the flaws noted in the standard version, but in the process becomes vulnerable to new and equally formidable objections. Finally, I shall present two additional options, options that are perhaps slightly more distant from the Thomistic doctrine, but that share enough of its assumptions and motivations to qualify as worthy successors.

1. AQUINAS ACCORDING TO STUMP

I begin with a brief survey of Aquinas's view of the soul, following the exposition of that view by Eleonore Stump (2003).[1] The place to begin is with Aquinas's notion of form, specifically with his notion of *substantial form*. (There are also accidental forms: when Socrates, who was formerly standing, sits down, he acquires the accidental form, *being seated*. For the most part accidental forms will not concern us here.) According to Stump, "A substantial form is the form in virtue of which a material composite is a member of the species to which it belongs, and it configures prime matter" (194). (Prime matter, of course, is the ultimate, featureless "stuff" of which everything material is composed. Prime matter never exists in its pure state; it always comes configured by a substantial form of some kind.) All material things are composed of matter and form, and "The complete form (the substantial and accidental forms taken together) of a nonhuman material object is the arrangement or organization of the matter of that object in such a way that it constitutes that object rather than some other one and gives that object its causal powers" (194). There are several points here that deserve notice. First, the "form" of a material thing is not limited to its external shape; it includes also what we may term the item's *functional organization*, the internal structure and operations which "make it tick" and which are essential to its being the thing it is. The external shape of my tablet computer is pretty uninteresting: it is a fairly thin, rigid rectangle with some minor complications around the edges. But its form, properly speaking, includes its astonishingly complex internal organization and functioning—an organization and functioning that I am very far from comprehending in detail, though fortunately there are people at Microsoft who do understand it! And the form of a typical living creature is far more complex even than that.

Another important point is expressed by the final clause: the form "gives to the object its causal powers". As we shall see, the causal powers given to living creatures, in particular to animals, by their forms are quite impressive. Also worthy of note is the specification to *nonhuman* material objects. Humans are indeed material objects, but the substantial form of a human being is of a different sort than the forms of other such objects. This contrast holds in particular between humans on the one hand and plants and animals on the other. Plants and animals have souls (the "vegetative soul" and the "sensitive soul"), but "Unlike human souls, the souls of plants and nonhuman animals are nonetheless material forms, and even a material form that is a soul goes out of existence when the material composite it configures goes out of existence" (201). Such a form is characterized by Stump as a "configurational state" of the matter which it informs.

Human souls, however, are another sort of thing. In addition to material forms, there are "subsistent forms". These are immaterial rather than material; an angel, for example, is a subsistent immaterial form. Such subsistent forms can exist without there being any matter which they configure: according to Aquinas, "if there is a subsistent form, it is immediately an entity and one" (quoted in Stump 2003: 198); that is, it is a real thing in itself, not needing matter to enable it to exist. He also says, "nothing keeps a form from subsisting without matter, even though matter cannot exist without a form" (199). Now, it might occur to us at this point that, in employing the same term to designate both these immaterial subsisting entities and the configurational states of material composites, Aquinas is simply equivocating on the word 'form'. I am inclined to think there is something in this complaint,[2] but Stump explains the commonality of meaning by saying that "for Aquinas, to be is to be configured or to have a form; and everything, material or immaterial, is what it is in virtue of a form" (200). Since this is so, "although Aquinas is perfectly content to deny matter of God, he refuses to deny form of God: being, even divine being, is configured" (200).

The human soul, however, is different from other subsistent immaterial forms, in that the human soul, unlike an angel, does configure matter. Aquinas puts it like this:

> the human soul has subsistent being, insofar as its being does not depend on the body but is rather elevated above corporeal matter. Nevertheless, the body receives a share in its being, in such a way that there is one being of soul and body, and this is the being of a human. (quoted in Stump 2003: 201)

Stump sums up the situation by saying, "So, for Aquinas, the human soul is the noblest and highest of the forms that configure matter, but it is the lowest in the rank of intellectual subsistent forms, because it is mixed with matter, as the intellectual subsistent forms that are angels are not" (201).

It remains to say something about the way in which the material composite which is a human being begins and ends its earthly existence. "Aquinas thinks that a human being is generated when the human soul replaces the merely animal soul of the fetus in the womb and that a human being is corrupted or decomposed when the human soul leaves the body and is replaced by whatever other substantial form is in the dead corpse" (203). Note that it is not a *pre-existing* human soul that replaces the soul of the fetus; rather, the soul is created and infused in the same instant; the soul is created as the soul of this particular body. (According to Aquinas, this occurs some 40 days after conception for a male, and 80 days for a female. An interesting consequence of this is that an early-stage fetus not only is not a human being, but *will never become a human being*. When one substantial form replaces another, the commonality between the two consists merely in the "prime matter" which is the same in both (Brower, forthcoming). What we can say of the fetus, then, is that it consists in part of the prime matter that, if all goes well, will in time come to be the prime matter of a human being.[3])

There is much more in Aquinas's view that invites discussion, but the bare bones as set forth here should be sufficient to enable us to see how the view meets the desiderata outlined at the beginning of this essay. By making the soul the form of the body, which structures the body and enables its distinctive powers and activities, the view points us to a closer and more profound integration of the two than is apparent either in the Platonic dualism which Aquinas rejected, or in modern Cartesian dualism. At the same time, the distinctive nature of the human soul, as contrasted with the souls of animals, makes it plain that humans are not *merely* animals; rather, they are "rational animals", with all that implies. The fact that souls are subsistent, immaterial forms means that they are fully capable of continuing to exist after physical death, albeit in an imperfect state which looks forward to fulfillment in the resurrection. One might well ask, what is there in all this not to like?

Unfortunately, the answer to that question is, "Quite a bit". The problems I shall indicate become evident if the view is scrutinized in the light of certain more recent developments in both science and philosophy—developments, obviously, which Aquinas could not have taken into account. I will now argue that (1) this Thomistic view fails to convincingly integrate human beings with the rest of nature, (2) the work actually done by the human soul, following Aquinas's theory, is surprisingly limited, and (3) the case for including such souls in our system, as opposed to thinking of human beings as composed of matter and nothing else (or nothing but materials forms), is comparatively weak. Here is the argument.

I begin by pointing out that, by making the human soul so fundamentally different from the souls of animals, the view already postulates a pretty wide gap between human beings and the rest of the animate creation—a gap which is papered over but not narrowed by the claim that each has a soul which is the "form of its body".[4] Beyond this, however, I have claimed that the work actually done by the human soul is surprisingly limited. In fact, I shall argue that this work amounts practically just to the difference made in human life by the fact that humans are rational creatures. That is no small matter, to be sure. But it falls considerably short of the wide-ranging influence on human biology one would expect, given that the soul is said to be the substantial form of the body. To see why I say this, consider that, by the time the soul is infused into the fetus (which may be a relatively late-stage fetus, if we follow Aquinas), most of the essential biological structures are already in place, albeit in early stages of development. Consider, also, that very similar structures exist in the fetal development of an animal—say, a gorilla or a chimpanzee—at a comparable stage. Now, the chimpanzee fetus, quite unaided by any "subsisting immaterial form", will naturally develop into the magnificent animal we have recently learned so much about. This animal will function biologically in ways that are essentially similar to the functioning of a human being, and will exhibit a rich and complex mental, emotional, and social existence which, while lacking in some of the distinctive features of human life, nevertheless compels our admiration and wonder. Must we not suppose that the human fetus, if it were not infused with an immaterial soul, would be capable of the same sort of development?[5]

To this it will be replied that the "sensitive soul", which is said to guide the development of the animal organism, does not continue in the human fetus but is rather replaced by the subsisting human soul. And on account of this, it is indeed the immaterial human soul that guides, and accounts for, the development of the biological structures and functions of the mature organism. To which I reply: that is what the theory says, but this metaphysical fact, if it is a fact, seems to make no biological difference at all. According to the theory, the human being, which has an immaterial soul as its substantial form, is a *new substance,* different from the purely material substance which previously existed; nothing carries over from the early fetus to the human being but prime matter. But a physician observing a fetus at the moment of infusion will not see its characteristic structures and processes suddenly disappear, in order to reappear an instant later under the supervision of the subsistent soul. Biologically, everything carries on just as before. The only difference, even granting the theory, is that certain distinctively rational capacities will gradually become apparent, capacities which by hypothesis would not be present in the absence of an infused soul. It is very difficult to avoid the impression that the configurational state of the organism remains (whether or not it is still called the "sensitive soul"), and that it retains the causal efficacy which it had before the soul's infusion. And this, of course, leaves quite a lot less work to be done by the immaterial soul. That is what I meant by saying that, practically speaking, the difference made by the soul is limited to human rationality.

The other criticism is that the case for the existence of subsistent souls is weak. The main philosophical reason given for their existence is that the activity of reason has no material organ. Unfortunately, this is one point at which it is very difficult for us to agree, in the light of contemporary brain science. Stump, for one, simply admits that the traditional view was mistaken about this.[6] We should not, however, overlook the point that this is very nearly the *only* philosophical argument which is available for the immateriality of the soul.[7] (There will of course be the theological argument from an afterlife. But we would greatly prefer not to have a vitally important metaphysical position rest solely on such a theological argument.)

But why must this be so? Are there not other arguments which can be used, and which are in fact used, by dualists and others opposed to materialism? Indeed there are. There is the notorious "hard problem" of consciousness—the problem, as some have put it, of how soggy grey brain-stuff gives rise to technicolor phenomenology. There is the problem of intentionality: How is it that a state of a physical system can represent, can "mean", something entirely different from itself, perhaps something that does not exist at all? There is the problem of teleology: How can mere matter behave in a way that is genuinely purposive, as opposed to merely giving the impression of purpose due to a clever design (say, like a thermostat)? In particular, how can the course of our inquiries be oriented to the desire for truth, rather than being guided merely by the mechanistic processes of our bodies and nervous systems? There is—one of my own favorites—the unity-of-consciousness argument: How can a mere collection of physical parts exhibit a unified consciousness, given that a complex conscious state cannot exist "parceled out" among the many pieces of a complex physical system?

There are, then, all of these arguments, though of course there are also answers to them by materialists, and so the controversy rages on. But for the Thomistic dualist, there is a more fundamental problem, namely this: *the Thomistic dualist cannot use any of these arguments, because she has already conceded all of the points in dispute.* She holds that animals, who by hypothesis have no subsistent souls but only the appropriate configuration of the material organism, exhibit all of the phenomena in question: sensory experience, pleasure and pain, intentionality (who that has loved, and been loved by, a dog can doubt that the dog has ideas of particular individuals?), purposefulness, and unified states of consciousness. For her, none of these phenomena gives any purchase for an argument to the existence of an immaterial soul. And other arguments that will serve that purpose for her may be hard to come by.[8]

2. MORELAND'S "THOMISTIC DUALISM"

Next we examine a version of dualism developed by J. P. Moreland (Moreland and Rea 2000).[9] Actually Moreland's dualism comes in two versions, corresponding to the two traditional Christian ideas about the origin of the soul: "creationism" and "traducianism". Creationism, by far the majority Christian view, holds that each human soul is directly and individually created by God; whereas traducianism holds that human souls are in some way derived from the parents through the natural process of reproduction. We consider here Moreland's creationist version.

Moreland terms his view "Thomistic substance dualism", though he acknowledges that he deviates at some points from Aquinas's view. For our purposes three of these deviations are especially important, since they provide the key to alleviating the difficulties noted earlier for the original version.[10] They are as follows:

1. The possession of immaterial subsistent souls is not limited to human beings, but rather is common to all animals, indeed to all living things.[11]
2. The infusion of souls occurs, not at a later stage in the development of the organism (as it does for Aquinas), but rather at the very beginning; for humans, at the time of conception.

3. The infused soul is unambiguously involved in, and necessary for, both the development of the essential biological organs and their successful functioning.

It is this third point that I take to be most central,[12] because it enables Moreland to make good on the full integration of soul and body that was aimed at, but not convincingly achieved, in Aquinas's original version. Here are some quotations which illustrate the nature, and the intimacy, of this relation as Moreland conceives of it:

> The soul is a substance with an essence or inner nature . . . [which] contains, as a primitive unity, a complicated, structural arrangement of capacities and dispositions for developing a body. Taken collectively, this entire ordered structure can be called the substance's *principle of activity* and will be that which governs the precise, ordered sequence of changes that the substance will go through in the process of growth and development. (204, emphasis in original)
>
> The various physical and chemical parts and processes (including DNA) are tools—instrumental causes employed by higher-order biological activities in order to sustain the various functions grounded in the soul. Thus the soul is the first efficient cause of the body's development as well as the final cause of its functions and structure internally related to the soul's essence. The functional demands of the soul's essence determine the character of the tools, but they, in turn, constrain and direct the various chemical and physical processes that take place in the body. (205)

Moreland sums up his view of the human organism in a series of points:

> The organism as a whole (the soul) is ontologically prior to its parts.
>
> The parts of the organism's body stand in internal relations to other parts and to the soul's essence; they are literally functional entities (the heart functions literally to pump blood).
>
> The operational functions of the body are rooted in the internal structure of the soul.
>
> The body is developed and grows in a teleological way as a series of developmental events that occur in a lawlike way, rooted in the internal essence of the human soul.
>
> The efficient cause of the characteristics of the human body is the soul; the various body parts, including DNA and genes, are important instrumental causes the soul uses to produce the traits that arise. (206)

This material elaborates the third of the points noted earlier in which Moreland deviates from Aquinas's original version of Thomistic dualism. The other two points, it will be seen, are natural complements of the third. If it is the soul that guides and directs the development of the organism throughout, then it is appropriate and perhaps inevitable that this will begin to occur coinciding with the beginning of the organism's existence, rather than at some later time. The similarity in the biological growth and development between humans and other animals and plants argues strongly for a similarity in their basic causes, thus the attribution of immaterial, subsistent souls to plants and animals as well as to humans. This does not mean, of course, that animal souls, let alone those of plants, are similar in all respects to those of humans. We can gain some grasp of the differences by observing the differences in the capacities typically exercised by well-developed adult members of the various species. Nevertheless, the souls of animals and plants belong to the same metaphysical category as the souls of human beings. This seems to be inherently plausible, and it also does much to bridge the ontological gulf between humans and other living creatures that, in spite of all good intentions, still remains for Aquinas's version of dualism.

Even this brief summary, I believe, is sufficient to indicate that Moreland's view of the soul-body relationship is well-developed and deeply considered; it is a view that demands in turn our serious consideration. The view clearly overcomes all three of the objections urged against the original version of Thomistic dualism. In light of the quotations cited before, the close integration of soul and body requires no further comment. But the view also makes it possible, as Aquinas's own view does not, for its advocate to utilize the full battery of arguments critical of materialism and in favor of dualism. This is because Moreland, unlike Aquinas, does not at the outset concede to the materialist the phenomena that are the basis for those arguments. Since the active involvement of the soul is said to be essential from the very beginning of the organism's life and development, and for animals as well as for human beings, Moreland has no need (and no inclination) to concede that such phenomena as qualia, intentionality, purpose, and unified consciousness can be adequately explained by structures and processes that are wholly material. Admittedly, arguments based on these phenomena can and will be resisted by materialists, and this debate shows no signs of ending in the foreseeable future. But a dualist who has access to such arguments has available formidable dialectical resources for advocating and defending her view, something which (as we have seen) is not the case for the traditional Thomistic dualist.

There are, however, at least two major areas in which Moreland's version of dualism encounters new problems of its own, problems that were not an issue for Aquinas's view.[13] First of all, it is abundantly clear from the material quoted earlier that the view is committed to *vitalism*, which holds "first, that in every living organism there is an entity that is not exhaustively composed of inanimate parts and, second, that the activities characteristic of living organisms are due, in some sense, to the activities of this entity".[14] Now it is an undisputed fact that vitalism has had an extended history in the biological sciences, and has been advocated by many prominent biologists. It is also a fact, however, that the view has lost credibility for almost all biologists for about a century; it is now universally regarded as a failed research program that has been abandoned for good reason.[15] The association of Moreland's version of dualism with this failed research program is not, to put it gently, a point in its favor.

Moreland is aware of this complaint, and devotes some effort to defending his view against it. In brief, his answer is that the cruder forms of vitalism were rightly rejected because they made unjustified assumptions concerning the "individuated essence", assumptions which his view has no need to accept. He goes on to say that

> A more adequate vitalism—if we wish to use this term of the Thomistic substance view (and we prefer the term *organicism*)—grounds the doctrine of substance in factors like the irreducible organic, holistic relation among parts to parts and parts to whole, the species-specific immanent law of organization and development, and the internal structural form and normative functioning found in living things. (217)

The features to which Moreland appeals here can be grouped under the general label of *antireductionism,* and he clearly believes that biological research gives some support to such claims, even though (as I trust he would admit) the specific claim about the "entity that is not exhaustively composed of inanimate parts" whose activities are responsible for "the activities characteristic of living organisms" is generally rejected by biologists. Perhaps he hopes that this more specific claim will eventually be supported by a vitalist research program that is better conceived than those that have been abandoned. Or, he may consider that the more specific claim is not one that can be expected to have observable biological consequences, and thus is outside the scope of a legitimate biological research program. Either way, he seeks to insulate his view from the failure that such endeavors have met with in the past. Whether this is a promising and attractive line to take must be left to the reader to decide.

The other major difficulty for Moreland's version of Thomistic dualism is found in the theory of biological evolution. It is quite difficult to see how his theory can be reconciled with any plausible version of evolutionary theory. The options are narrowed considerably when Moreland states, "For the Thomist, a genus and a species in the category of substance are not degreed properties. That is, either they are fully predicable of an entity or they are absent. . . . An entity either is or is not a human person or some other type of person" (224n). This is admirably clear and definite, and it rules out immediately the widely held notion that, in a broad evolutionary perspective, biological classifications such as genus and species are blurred and mutable. To be sure, it need not be the case that "species" in Moreland's metaphysical sense map directly onto the biological concept of species, a concept which is itself very much in dispute. But in view of the detailed way in which the soul directs and energizes the development of the organism, the kinds of souls must themselves be very numerous; kinds of organisms that are different in any major or substantive way will need to have different kinds of souls overseeing their growth and functioning. These "species" of souls, furthermore, are immutable and immutably distinct. Nor is it at all plausible, in the light of this view, that God first waits until a suitably advanced organism has evolved, and then supplies a new soul with enhanced capabilities to animate it. For one thing, this would contradict the fundamental assumption that "the organism as a whole (the soul) is ontologically prior to its parts"—parts such as DNA, for example. Nor would such a view make sense biologically; absent the right sort of soul, the DNA that codes for the evolutionary advance would be nonfunctional and would not be preserved by evolutionary selection.

So far as I can see, the only variety of evolution compatible with Moreland's view would be one in which God simultaneously brings about the desired changes in the mechanism of heredity (DNA and so on) and also provides a new kind of soul with the capability to develop and energize the functions of the new, "higher" organism. But this, of course, would not by any means be evolution *as a natural process*, and we can confidently predict that it would be rejected by evolutionary biologists, theists and non-theists alike. The more likely position, for one who accepts this variety of dualism, is the theory of "progressive creation", according to which God from time to time creates *ex nihilo* new kinds of organisms as the surrounding environment has become ready to accept and support them. Moreland himself probably would not see this as a defect of his view, since he may already be inclined for other reasons to accept both progressive creationism and the "intelligent design" theory which provides support for creationism.[16] For those of us, on the other hand, who regard such approaches as unpromising, the evolutionary objection forms a formidable barrier to an acceptance of his creationist version of dualism.

At this point I must acknowledge that the objections I have raised against both Aquinas's original version of dualism and Moreland's adaptation of it are not likely to prove compelling to everyone. I hope, however, that I have done enough to motivate us to consider some additional views on the soul-body relationship, views that have enough in common with the Thomistic doctrine that they can be recognized as kindred attempts to reach some of the same objectives. To these alternatives we now turn.

3. EMERGENT DUALISM: TWO VARIETIES

The final pair of views to be considered can be viewed as standing in a certain dialectical relationship to the views already surveyed. The original Thomistic view establishes a kind of balance between the capabilities attributable to matter—material stuff plus the material forms, including the vegetative and sensitive souls—and those attributed to immaterial, divinely created souls. Matter and the material forms suffice for all subhuman life-forms and for the earlier stages of human development, whereas immaterial, subsistent souls are required for human rationality and everything that goes with it. I have argued that this balance tends to be unstable, and that the Thomist has few resources with which to oppose the counter-claim that the inherent powers of matter and the material forms suffice for human life as well. Moreland's creationist version of Thomistic dualism, on the other hand, tilts the balance decisively in favor of the divinely created souls. Both for animals and for plants, such souls are essential for both the development and the functioning of the organism, at all stages of its life. The genetic and other materials present at the beginning of life have the status merely of tools—"instrumental causes employed by higher-order biological activities in order to sustain the various functions grounded in the soul"—but are incapable of creating and sustaining life on their own, absent the active powers of the soul. Arguably such a view is more coherent internally than the original Thomistic version, but as we have seen it runs afoul of conclusions which are widely held to have been established by the biological sciences.

The view now to be considered, namely the "traducian" version of Moreland's view, tilts the balance in the opposite direction, in favor of powers held to be inherent in the nature of matter itself.[17] It amounts, then, to embracing the alternative that was seen to be threatening the original Thomistic doctrine, the view that the powers inherent in matter are sufficient for human life in all of its aspects. Here is Moreland's statement of the traducian version of his view:

> In addition to physical and chemical properties and parts, egg and sperm have soulish potentialities that, on the occasion of fertilization, become actualized. Here the union of sperm and egg amount to a form of substantial change in which the two different entities come together, and this gives rise to the emergence of a new substantial whole—a whole that informs the zygote body and begins to direct the process of morphogenesis. This traducian view has much in common with the Thomistic creationist position . . . The main difference between them is whether the soul is created upon the occasion when [the physical conditions involved in reproduction] obtain or whether those conditions are sufficient for the soulish potentialities within sperm and egg to give rise to a new soul" (Moreland and Rea 2000: 221).

Here "soulish potentialities" of the egg and sperm are what produces the soul, so these potentialities are indirectly responsible for everything that occurs subsequently, as the soul guides the development of the organism to maturity. As was stated before, the balance has been shifted decisively towards the physical basis of the organism, which is now responsible for the emergence of the soul and thus, indirectly, for everything that follows from that. In view of this, it seems appropriate to characterize this traducian view as a kind of "emergent dualism".

This view was not, of course, developed for the purpose of answering the two objections, noted earlier, to Moreland's creationist Thomistic dualism. We may, nevertheless, ask whether the view has the potential to meet those objections. Here, it seems to me, the answer must be equivocal. On the one hand, by placing the full potentialities for later development in the physical conditions of reproduction, it avoids the notion of the soul as an entity added from outside to supervise the organism's functioning and development. Still, the role of the soul, once generated, remains primary; and it still seems to be the case that, as stated in the definition of vitalism, "in every living organism there is an entity that is not exhaustively composed of inanimate parts and . . . that the activities characteristic of living organisms are due, in some sense, to the activities of this entity" (Beckner, 1967: vol. 8, p. 254). Indeed, consideration of this point reveals what may seem to be an anomaly or incongruity in this traducian view: the very earliest stage in the development of the organism, namely the "physical conditions involved in reproduction", is capable of generating a complete, fully developed soul, already endowed with all the potentialities of the mature organism.[18] And yet, those "physical conditions" immediately thereafter revert to the status of mere tools, instrumental causes employed by the soul as it goes about the work of developing and energizing the organism. It would seem that the extremely powerful capacities attributed to the physical conditions at this early, undeveloped stage match poorly with the later role of the physical features of the organism merely as "tools" to be used by the soul.

What about the evolutionary objection to Moreland's Thomistic view? Here again, the answer must be equivocal. The decisive barrier to a solution is Moreland's insistence on immutable, and immutably distinct, "natural kinds" of living creatures. Given this insistence, the apparent "intermediate forms" between well-established kinds of creatures cannot really be that; rather, they must be seen as defective versions of one or the other of the established natural kinds. An evolutionary perspective, in contrast, will recognize that the "kinds" in question really are in a state of flux, with the sometimes long-enduring species and genera representing "islands of stability" in the flow of change. However, this insistence on unchanging natural kinds seems to be logically independent of other aspects of Moreland's view, and if he were willing to modify that insistence, the view could be well fitted into a broader evolutionary narrative.

The final view to be considered is the *emergent dualism* that has been proposed and developed by me in a book and a series of articles.[19] This view shares with Moreland's traducian view the assertion that the mind/soul is something that emerges naturally from the structure and functioning of the organism, but it differs in certain other respects. For one thing, the emergent soul is not assigned responsibility for the organism's biological functioning as such; rather, its role is seen in relation specifically to conscious awareness and the processes that go with it. This means that it is not essential to posit an emergent mind/soul for all living creatures, but only in those cases where we find evidence for some degree of awareness, however limited. (There will of course be the inevitable uncertainty about this as we consider simpler and simpler living creatures.) Nor is it essential to posit a fully developed soul, armed with all the potentialities of the mature adult organism, at the very beginning of the organism's life. While the existence of some sort of awareness, and thus of a soul, may be all-or-nothing, the capacities of the soul emerge only gradually, in parallel with the developing sophistication of the organism (especially, we think, the brain and nervous system) on which the soul depends for its existence and functioning.[20] Evidently this view addresses successfully the two difficulties noted earlier for Moreland's creationist Thomistic dualism, difficulties which were not clearly resolved by the traducian version of his view. There is not here an immaterial entity that is responsible for organic function as such, so the view is not one of vitalism. And since the view does not posit immutable natural kinds of living creatures, it can readily be incorporated into an evolutionary narrative.

Perhaps the most important questions that need to be addressed revolve around the worry that if we adopt this view we shall be conceding too much to the materialists, and will be unable to maintain the distinctive character and dignity of human persons, to say nothing of their destiny in an afterlife. I do not believe this worry is justified. It is true that emergent dualism attributes some rather remarkable powers to ordinary matter—though not a great deal more than is the case with Stump's version of Aquinas, and arguably less than Moreland's traducian variation. (Actually I believe that the ascription of these powers to the physical stuff of the world is the most important metaphysical cost of the emergent dualist proposal. But then, this "dust" of which we are made is itself the creation of an all-wise God.) But as was mentioned previously, there are a number of arguments available to us that show the inadequacy of the currently popular forms of materialism.[21] There are compelling arguments in favor of the view that mental properties are neither eliminable nor reducible to the sorts of properties that feature in the physical sciences. There are, to be sure, the "non-reductive materialist" views that do recognize the existence of ineliminable mental properties. Such views, however, typically insist that the mental properties are wholly determined by the physical properties of the organism, and those physical properties in turn evolve in a way that is governed exclusively by the fundamental laws of physics; this is the "causal closure of the physical domain". Such views amount in effect to epiphenomenalism, the view that mental properties are causally inert, which is already massively implausible.[22] And the "argument from reason", as it is coming to be called, argues forcefully that views such as this are unable to account for human rationality: it is simply essential that the process of rational inference should be governed by (for example) the logical relationship between premises and conclusion in an argument, and not by the mechanistic laws of physics and chemistry.[23] These arguments, I believe, establish the necessity for mental properties which are not only distinct from, but are not in their operation determined by, the physical properties of body and brain. But do we also need a mental *substance?* Yes we do, and the key to establishing this is found in the previously mentioned unity-of-consciousness argument.[24] Here the key question is, when we are aware of a complex state of consciousness, *what is it that experiences this awareness?* It is out of the question that a complex state of awareness should in its totality be experienced by, say, a single neuron—let alone by a single atom, or a single elementary particle. But here is the key insight: *a complex state of consciousness cannot exist divided among the parts of a complex physical object.* Even if each bit of the conscious state were encoded in a single neuron, that would still leave unanswered the question, *What is it that is aware of the conscious state as a whole?* And the answer to this, we maintain, must be found in the emergent soul. As Leibniz said long ago, "it is in the simple substance, and not in the composite or in the machine, that one must look for perception" (1991: par. 19). I have said a bit more about this argument than the others, since it is likely to be less familiar. It should be evident, however, that a full appreciation of the force of any of these arguments requires a much fuller treatment than is possible here.

Finally, what of the life to come? If the mind or soul is a distinct substance, and not merely an aspect of the physical organism, then it is at least logically possible for it to exist apart from the organism after the latter has decayed in death. To be sure, the soul is initially generated from that very same organism, and is in its ordinary functioning sustained by it. But it is open to us to suppose either that, once generated, the soul acquires the capability to exist on its own after the death of the body, or if not that, then that it can be sustained in existence by God in the absence of its ordinary bodily support. Actually some such supposition is needed by any view that extends the possession of souls to animals in general, assuming that we do not wish to hold that all animals are naturally immortal.[25]

By way of summary: the hypothesis of emergent dualism accomplishes all of the desiderata for a mind-body theory set out at the beginning of this essay. It portrays a close integration between soul and body, and between the human person and the rest of nature; it also enables us to honor the distinctive excellences of human beings, and to affirm their existence in an afterlife after biological death. Arguably it is more successful in the task of integration than is the original Thomistic dualism. Since it does not postulate a soul which is immediately created by God, it has no need to defend such a view, unlike the original Thomistic view. However, it is well placed to use any or all of a battery of arguments directed against the currently fashionable varieties of materialism. Unlike Moreland's version of Thomistic dualism, it is not committed to any form of vitalism, nor is it obliged to defend the absolute fixity of species, whether they be species of biological organisms or of souls. Without doubt, there is much more that can be said both for and against such a view. But since the space available for this essay is gone, I must leave those discussions for another occasion.[26]

NOTES

1. Page references in this section are to this book.
2. David Braine, who is in general a defender of Aquinas, nevertheless suggests that Aquinas "may have been deceived by confusing two different uses of the word 'form' of quite different origins: on the one hand, we have the use of the word form to refer to "natures" or "predicates" . . . and, on the other hand, we have this notion of 'form' as a correlate of matter originating with the idea of shapes" (Braine 1992 499n).
3. I recognize, of course, that Aquinas's basic metaphysical position is consistent with the possibility that the subsistent soul is present at the very beginning of life; contemporary Thomists will undoubtedly want to avail themselves of this possibility. For discussion see Haldane (2013).
4. Haldane understands me to be saying that "for Aquinas the human soul is quite unlike the souls of non-rational animals and hence there is no significant biological overlap". My point, rather, is that *in view of* the extensive biological overlap we should not posit the sort of metaphysical gap involved in assigning subsistent immaterial souls to humans but not to animals.
5. It may be that this is impossible, because it is inconsistent with divine goodness. If so, however, the impossibility would be moral and not metaphysical, so I think it is legitimate to consider the possibility by way of a thought-experiment.
6. "Aquinas mistakenly supposes that the intellect is tied to no particular body organ" (Stump 2003: 213).
7. Stump mentions another argument relevant to this point used by Aquinas, but admits that "Aquinas's argument . . . rests on premises more likely to be persuasive in his time than ours" (205).
8. But perhaps not impossible. Professor Haldane refers us to his "Atheism and Theism" and "Further Reflections" in Smart and Haldane (2003).
9. See especially chapter 6, "Substance Dualism and the Body: Heredity, DNA, and the Soul". (Page references in this section are to this book.) While the book as a whole is co-authored, Moreland is responsible for the material on the metaphysics of the soul-body relation. My thanks to Professor Moreland for providing further explanations and clarifications of his view through both e-mail correspondence and oral discussion.
10. There is an additional difference from Aquinas that should perhaps be noted here: Moreland does not identify the substance which is the human being with the body-soul composite, as Aquinas does. Instead, "the one substance is the soul, and the body is an ensouled biological and physical structure that depends on the soul for its existence" (201).
11. For the most part the discussion in *Body and Soul* focuses on animals and does not mention plants as such. But on p. 213 Moreland states, "If by *soul* we mean individual nature, then every living organism is identical to its soul".
12. I want to emphasize that the analysis of the significance of these points is my own; I make no claim to reproduce the process by which Moreland developed his hypothesis.
13. In addition to these two areas, Moreland also devotes his attention to problems which arise concerning the origin of the soul in "abnormal cases" such

The Dialectic of Soul and Body 219

as twinning, cloning, frozen embryos, reproduction through fission (in animals), and the like. See pp. 218–224.
14. The definition is from Beckner (1967: 254).
15. According to Beckner, "vitalism showed a curious tendency to come out on the losing side of biological controversy: after Darwin, it was anti-Darwinian, and it supported the view that organic syntheses could be effected only in a living organism. It also supported the useless and misleading conception of a primordial living substance, the protoplasm, a term and idea that unfortunately still survive" (255).
16. See in this connection Moreland's contributions to Moreland (1994). Moreland comes out clearly in support of intelligent design theory, but he does not express support for a single view concerning the progression of life on earth. He has, however, affirmed in discussion his support for progressive creationism.
17. In *Body and Soul* Moreland does not express a preference as between the creationist and traducian versions of his view. He has, however, affirmed in discussion that he is a traducianist.
18. Timothy O'Connor and Jonathan Jacobs have written, "one is apparently asked to contemplate a composite physical system's giving rise, all in one go, to a whole, self-contained, organized system of properties bound up with a distinct individual. Applied to human beings, the view will imply that at an early stage of physical development, a self emerges, having all the capacities of an adult human self, most of which, however, lie dormant owing to immaturity in the physical system from which it emerges" (O'Connor and Jacobs 2003: 549). This comment may not have been directed initially at Moreland's traducian view, but it does seem to apply to that view.
19. See Hasker (1999); articles include *inter alia* Hasker (2011, 2012).
20. One might say, Moreland's view pulls a much bigger rabbit out of a much smaller hat!
21. An important resource here is Koons and Bealer (2010), which contains a veritable arsenal of arguments against materialism, and an impressive variety of anti-materialist positions.
22. In my judgment neither "supervenient causation" nor "token-identity" theories suffice to meet this objection, but the point cannot be argued here.
23. Different versions of this argument are widely available; see for instance Reppert (2003); also Hasker (1999: ch. 3).
24. For this argument see Hasker (1999: 122–144), also "The Emergence of Persons" and "Persons and the Unity of Consciousness" in Koons and Bealer (2010: 175–190). An interesting variant form of the argument is found in Barnett (2010).
25. Moreland considers briefly the possibility of an afterlife for animals; he concludes that "It seems best to be skeptical about animal survival after death, but the case cannot be considered a closed one" (Moreland and Rea 2000: 216).
26. A shorter version of this essay was published under the same name in *American Catholic Philosophical Quarterly* 87:3 (Summer 2013). My thanks to the journal and to the Philosophy Documentation Center for permission to reuse this material. The present version has benefited from "Response to William Hasker's 'The Dialectic of Soul and Body'" by John Haldane, which appeared in the same issue.

13 Dualism, Dual-Aspectism, and the Mind

David Skrbina

1. INTRODUCTION

For some four thousand years, humanity has been systematically studying the nature of mind and body. And yet after all this time, the questions continue to confound us. Even in the present day, when we have made such progress in our understanding of physics and physiology, in science and analysis, we are still unable to resolve the central questions that face us. Consciousness is still largely a mystery; mental causation is as puzzling as ever; the emergence of mind is an unexplained miracle; and basic metaphysical issues remain open to dispute. We have many theories but little consensus.

Perhaps we could benefit from a slightly different approach. Over the past century, philosophy of mind has been dominated by analytic methodologies, and by scientific, positivist approaches—to the point where we often debate minutiae without reflecting upon the larger vision. In the dogged pursuit of technical rigor, we seem to have been led astray. I submit that we have lost sight of the metaphysical forest for the analytical trees. I propose here a rather different tack. Let us take a step back, reorient ourselves, and approach the situation with fresh eyes.

My plan is as follows. I will return to the beginnings of our reflections on mind-body dualism, to remind ourselves of whence we have come. I then attempt to clarify the terminological landscape. After this, I spend some time recapping the relevant historical views; this is particularly important in an era when our functional philosophical memory is fading. For many of us, our event horizon seems to extend no further back than the 1980s. This is unfortunate. Our forebears were every bit as clever as we, and in many cases a good bit more creative. We ought to take their insights to heart. I close the chapter with a proposal for a solution to the mind-body problem that takes the mind seriously, one based in a panpsychic, dual-aspect metaphysic. Let me start, then, at the beginning.

2. ORIGINS OF THE MIND-BODY QUESTION

Dualism has held a grip on human consciousness since the beginning of recorded history. The oldest known writings are the pyramid texts of ancient

Egypt, dating to roughly 2350 BC. Among the many hieroglyphic passages we find this: "Akh, to the sky! Corpse, to the earth!"[1] The Akh was the nonmaterial aspect of a human being, capable of eternal life. The body decayed, but the Akh—the combination of a person's soul and his life energy—could survive bodily death to dwell in the divine realm of the cosmos. More generally, we know that Egyptian mythology is full of tales of the afterlife, and of the soul's eternal existence. In fact the pyramids themselves were not simply tombs, but rather carefully designed structures to facilitate the transition of the soul to the world beyond.

At the same time, however, the Egyptians were also inclined toward thoughts of theological, and even metaphysical, monism. Amidst their flamboyant polytheism, a divine hierarchy existed, and at various times and in various regions of the country, certain gods held the uppermost status. A highest god would have greater power than the others, and perhaps would have created them; they would be virtual manifestations of him. Re, Horus, Isis, Atum, Amun, and Ptah were each, at times, declared to be a kind of unifying divine power. But it was not until the reign of Akhenaten (circa 1353–1336 BC) that a true monotheism emerged, one which quickly evolved into a metaphysical monism—the first in recorded history. For Akhenaten, the one god was the Aten, the sun, who was manifest in the solar light. Assmann (1997: 188) writes that, under this view, "everything could be explained as workings, 'emanations', or 'becomings' of the sun". Therefore, "the concept of 'One' has not a theological but a physical [read: metaphysical] meaning: the One is the source of cosmic existence". In this way, Akhenaten devised his own "religion of light", to use Hornung's (1995) evocative phrase. But it was also the first truly metaphysical monism—a "monism of light", we might say.

This tension between dualism and monism carried over to the Greeks. Several of the earliest philosophers, as we know, were monists.[2] But dualism was there as well—in Empedocles, for example, with his duality of matter (the four elements) and force (Love and Strife). Mind-body dualism was central to Pythagoras's outlook; it found sympathy with Socrates; and it led Plato to write detailed passages on the nature of the afterlife.[3] Platonic ideas influenced later Christian theologians like Augustine and Aquinas, both of whom argued, unsurprisingly, for a dualistic conception of soul and body.

Today, by contrast, many of us have a strong intuition that the world is fundamentally one. We live, by all appearances, in one universe. Though rife with a diversity of structures, the cosmos seems to function on a uniform basis, and according to a common set of principles. Even under the weird multi-universe or many-worlds thesis of quantum physics, reality is still "one"; the other universes are not envisioned as operating under different principles than ours, nor are they composed of different substances. Furthermore, a monistic world is parsimonious. It yields to Occam's Razor; one ought not multiply metaphysical entities needlessly. A dualistic or pluralistic metaphysic cries out for explanation. But for all this, we are left with a nagging sense—and sometimes more than this—that conventional materialistic monisms offer an unsatisfactory picture of the world.[4]

So we are torn: we have intuitive pressure toward both monism and dualism, both within and across cultures and eras. How can we make sense of this? How can we do justice to both intuitions? *Should* we do justice to both? I think we must. Mind is an indubitable reality. Mind, or experience, is, after all, that thing of which we are most certain. Descartes was surely correct—we think, and we are. This is the first fact of existence. In the words of Galen Strawson (2009: 36), "nothing in life is more certain". Everything proceeds from the fact of our functioning mental life, and of our immediate experience of the world around us. But only slightly less certain are we of the nonmental component of reality, the world of physical things. Barring a Berkeleyan idealism, we also have to accept the existence of a material reality—or at least a material dimension to it.

Let us, then, accept uncontroversially the reality of both mental and physical[5] aspects of the world. Of the two, we must grant epistemological priority to the former. But of course this does not entail an ontological priority, i.e. some form of idealism—though it cannot be ruled out. But I won't argue that point here. Rather, I simply note at the outset that there is mental reality, and there is physical reality. How can we reconcile these two realities, while doing justice to our monistic intuitions?

It's an old question—as old, at least, as Parmenides. On his view, we have two primordial facts: there is thinking, and there is being. Rejecting the dualistic option, he embraced a strong monism and proclaimed that "it is the same thing to think and to be" (*to gar auto noein estin te kai einai*).[6] Felix Cleve (1969: 536) describes this as the idea that "inextensive, uncorporeal thinking . . . is present whole and undivided in each and every part of the seeming space". Tony Long (1996: 132) calls this the "mind/being identity" reading of Parmenides; roughly speaking, it is the view that "mind is being and being is mind". This interpretation is confirmed by a later fragment, in which Parmenides wrote, "Thinking and that which prompts thought are the same. For in what has been said, you will not find thinking separate from being".[7] And it is clear that he did not mean anything like classical idealism. For one, the notion that existence was ultimately nothing but mind was unknown to the pre-Socratics. But we furthermore have testimony from Theophrastus, who argued that, for Parmenides, "absolutely all being possesses some cognition" (*holos de pan to on echein tina gnosin*).[8] Thinking is thus one property, or one aspect, of being. It is intrinsic to all existence.

3. TAKING THE MIND SERIOUSLY

There are a few key problems that seem to be primarily responsible for misleading us. One of these, ironically, is that most philosophers of mind *do not take the mind seriously*. By this I mean that the vast majority hold to some version of physicalism—defined here as a monism in which physical stuff or physical properties are the ultimate reality.[9] In this case, mind necessarily takes a back seat. It is dependent upon, or arises from, or supervenes on, the physical. Mind is seen as a derivative and secondary reality which must then be shoehorned into our worldview. But this, I claim, cannot be correct. The starting point for our metaphysical investigations must be that the mind holds at least equal metaphysical standing with the physical. This is a core datum that derives from the simple fact—noted before—that nothing happens, philosophically or otherwise, without the action of the mind. If we take the mind seriously, standard physicalism cannot be true. Granting this, new alternatives open up to us.

For most of philosophical history, we did in fact take the mind seriously. Mind held an equal, if not superior, status to the physical. This was an unquestioned truth; it could hardly be denied that mind was of preeminent importance. But by the early years of the twentieth century, things changed. Progress in the physical sciences, along with advances in technology, combined to give the widespread impression that material reality was the dominant, or even sole, reality.[10] Mind was seen as secondary to matter, and as emergent from it—under the appropriate (and rare) conditions. To claim an equal or superior role for mind was dismissed as unwarranted metaphysical speculation. And indeed, men like Rudolf Carnap called for the outright "rejection of metaphysics" as little better than mere poetry.[11] The physicalists and logical positivists had sole access to the truth, and philosophers who wished to be "scientifically legitimate" had to join along.

With few exceptions, this is still true today. One hundred years later, analytic philosophy is dominant at our major universities. Metaphysics has returned, only to become co-opted by the movement;[12] traditional "speculative" metaphysical approaches remain banished to the fringes. Philosophy of mind is almost exclusively of the physicalist persuasion—typically in reductive or functionalist guise, and occasionally bordering on outright eliminativism. Some take issue with reducing consciousness or intentionality to a physical basis; but rather than questioning the physicalism, they opt for non-reductive versions. The only other traditional option, substance dualism, is generally left to the theologians.

At present, then, mind takes a decided backseat to physical reality—despite its epistemological priority. Physicalists are confident. Consider this assessment by Zimmerman:

> [A] majority has managed to hammer out a common credo—a kind of minimal physicalism . . . [T]hey are confident of one thing: that serious science will never need to posit fundamental properties that divide things up based upon patently psychological or mental similarities and differences. Ultimately, reality will prove to be nothing but 'atoms in the void' or some equally non-mental phenomenon. Whatever the terms of the most fundamental causal transactions, they will not be minds or

include mental states. And everything else will supervene upon, and be determined by, the facts describable in terms of this fundamental, future physics. (2010: 123)

This, I submit, is a mistake, and is one reason why key problems regarding the nature of mind remain unresolved. Reductive physicalists cannot explain how qualia or intentionality are possible, or indeed, how or why certain privileged physical states qualify as "mental". Non-reductive physicalists cannot explain brute emergence of the mental from the physical, and they must accept either epiphenomenalism or surrender causal closure of the physical. Identity theorists cannot explain why only certain, select neural configurations give rise to consciousness and others do not; and they have ongoing problems with the multiple realizability objection.[13] And to repeat once more, all these views give ontological priority to the physical.

4. PROPERTY DUALISM AS NON-REDUCTIVE PHYSICALISM

The presumed priority of the physical, however, is not always apparent. The failure to find a coherent reductive theory of consciousness or intentionality has led many to adopt non-reductive forms of physicalism—resulting in what is commonly called property dualism. Strictly speaking, this is simply the recognition that both physical and mental properties exist as distinct entities, with the latter being non-reducible. But as a form of physicalism, it insists that the mental properties are ontologically subordinate to the physical ones; they "arise" or "emerge" from the physical basis, without reducing to it.

Property dualism finds varying expression in the literature. Dardis (2002: 70) offers this straightforward definition: "each mental property is distinct from every physical property". Zimmerman (2010: 120) sees it as "the thesis that the mental properties of persons are significantly independent of, or in some other way distinct from, the physical properties of persons"—clearly a highly anthropocentric interpretation. Schneider (2012: 61) defines it succinctly as the view that "both mental and physical properties are sui generis". For Searle (2002), property dualism is as follows:

> There are two mutually exclusive metaphysical categories that constitute all of empirical reality: they are physical phenomena and mental phenomena . . . [M]ental states are not reducible to neurobiological states, [and] are something *distinct from* and *over and above* neurobiological states . . . [Therefore, any conscious being] will have two sorts of properties, mental properties and physical properties. (58–59)

Others examine it in detail without offering any concise definition, as if it were more or less self-explanatory.[14]

In broad outlines, and read as a version of physicalism, the theory is widely held. Zimmerman remarks that "not so long ago, almost every philosopher was a property dualist"; and even today, "property dualism remains popular" (2010: 120). It is easy to see why. If one accepts that there are physical properties of things, and that there are non-reductive mental properties of (at least some) things, *and if these are not identical*, then one may be counted as a property dualist. For the identity theorist, mental properties 'just are' physical properties, and thus have no independent existence. In this sense, identity theorists are not much different than eliminativists, who are prepared to deny outright the existence of mental states or properties. But apart from these two positions, all others seem to accept the existence of mental properties, and thus qualify, at least in a loose sense, as property dualists.

Its popularity notwithstanding, property dualism—conceived as a form of materialist monism—is unsatisfactory, for a number of reasons. First, the very name suggests a metaphysical dualism, including perhaps a substance dualism. Writers will even refer to it simply as dualism, with no qualification. Among the specialists this is not an issue, but it risks interdisciplinary confusion. And it is an unnecessary confusion, given that the most common (and default) usage refers to a monist ontology.

Second, because of its broad conception, it is sometimes used merely to designate non-identity theories. So-called type identity theories (or type physicalism) claim that properties of mental types are identical with the physical properties of neural types. There is ultimately only one property type—physical (neural)—and this is identical to the mental type property. From this perspective, any theory that treats the mental as non-identical must thereby take it as a second property type—hence, property dualism. Every theory which is not "property identism" is, by default, "property dualism". Gozzano and Hill (2012: 4–11) seem to employ this usage.[15] They also refer to it simply as dualism, thus raising the first issue noted before.

Third, the very concept of mental properties emerging from a physical substrate, without reducing to it, is arguably incoherent. By definition, the physical basis is nonmental; that is, it is utterly and completely devoid of mental properties, experientiality, and so on. The emergence of *physical* properties from a physical base is no mystery at all, but the emergence of *mental* properties from a nonmental physical base borders on miraculous.[16] Or at least, no one has yet offered a coherent and rational explanation for how such a thing is possible.

But there is a further concern, one based in Hume's bundle theory of substance. Orthodox property dualism implicitly accepts a realist notion of a material substance as something in which the dual properties inhere. But we have a notoriously difficult time conceiving of a substance as something existing apart from its properties. Historical attempts to do so have produced such vague concepts as Descartes's "extended, flexible, changeable thing", Locke's "something, I know not what", and Kant's unknowable *Ding an sich selbst*, hence the bundle theory, which claims that a thing is nothing more than its properties. In this case, however, a "property dualist monism" is incoherent. If in fact there were a substance with two mutually exclusive sets of properties—to wit, experiential and non-experiential—it would in fact be two substances, not one. The variety of physical properties, such as mass, charge, spatiality, and so on, are mutually compatible, and thus can exist quite happily together under the "physical" heading. But when the physical is defined as being non-experiential, then experientiality has no home. Where it is present, there must be a separate substance. But then we are back to dualism.

An illustrative discussion was offered by John Searle (2002), in his piece "Why I Am Not a Property Dualist". Evidently the debate began back in 1996, when Chalmers referred to him as such: "The non-reductive materialism advocated by Searle turns out to have internal problems and collapses into one of the other views (most likely property dualism)" (1996: 164). And again later: "Searle (1992) admits the logical possibility of zombies, and in fact holds that there is merely a causal connection between the microphysical and conscious experience, so he is perhaps best seen as a property dualist" (1996: 376). Velmans (2000: 39) follows suit.[17]

Searle responds with a number of relevant comments. He first distinguishes property dualism from its putative siblings: "I will say nothing about neutral monism, panpsychism, and the various forms of dual aspect theories" (2002: 58)—correctly viewing those as distinct alternatives. He then runs aground of my first concern, cited before, by declaring property dualism to be a form of dualism (ibid.).

Upon recapitulating the property dualist position (explained before), Searle argues that the causal role of consciousness, on this view, is deeply flawed. If physical causal closure holds, then consciousness is epiphenomenal—an unacceptable conclusion for him. If not, then it contributes to causal overdeterminism, because both neural action and consciousness have overlapping causal roles—on moving a limb, for example.

By way of contrast, Searle then explains his own view. We live in "one world" (59), a world "consisting entirely of material phenomena such as physical particles in fields of force" (62)—evidently making him a materialist monist. Consciousness is a "biological phenomena" not unlike digestion or photosynthesis (60). It is causally but not ontologically reducible to brain processes—thus making him a non-reductive materialist.[18] Consciousness is not "a distinct, separate phenomenon", but rather "a state that the neurobiological system can be in", in the same way that liquidity or solidity are states that water can be in. Thus, consciousness is ultimately a *physical feature* of the brain. Being physical, consciousness plays a normal causal role in the body, and hence there is no problem of epiphenomenalism or over-determination.

The confusion about property dualism, he says, stems from three underlying problems. One is the historical tendency to define the physical as non-experiential, thus disallowing a physical standing for consciousness. Second is the mistaken belief that causal reduction implies ontological reduction—even though this implication holds in all cases *except* consciousness. Oddly enough, this consciousness exception "does not give it any mysterious metaphysical status" (62). Consciousness is simply a poorly-understood physical phenomenon, he claims. The third problem is precisely the issue I cited before, namely that property dualism strongly urges one toward substance dualism, and thus is, strictly speaking, incoherent as a monism.

At this point we can also see that there are issues with Searle's own theory of biological naturalism. His non-reductive materialism is itself arguably incoherent because it demands an inexplicable emergence of consciousness. Furthermore, his 'special exception' for consciousness cries out for elaboration. How can it be just another physical feature, and yet be so uniquely resistant to explanation? It seems that it *must* have some special ontological standing.

The basic problem with property dualism is this: ordinary property dualists want to respect the autonomy of mental experience, but they are bound by the larger physicalist framework. This results in an imbalanced duality; mental properties exist, and they are distinct from the physical properties, yet both sets of properties emerge from a physical base. The mental properties are thus at a decided disadvantage, and occupy an untenable metaphysical position. Either it is a case of miraculous emergence from a nonmental basis, or it is one of virtual substance dualism—a terrible dilemma.

We have alternatives. We can return the mind to a position of equal standing. Let me propose that we once again take the mind seriously. Let us not identify it with physical states, nor demand that it be reducible to the physical, nor insist that it miraculously emerge from the physical. But let us still respect our monist intuitions. We can hold both views at once. This is a venerable approach to the mind, and it promises to be fruitful once again.

5. NEUTRAL MONISM AND DUAL-ASPECTISM

If the mental and the physical have equal status, and if we wish to retain our monist metaphysics, we have two options. The first is *neutral monism*: the mental and the physical are both, equally, reducible to some undefined third entity. This is certainly a conceptual possibility, but it raises significant problems. As normally conceived, the monist basis is in itself neither mental nor physical, yet gives rise to both. But if it is neither mental nor physical, then we have a case of dual strong emergence.[19] Ordinary strong emergence—as explained in the previous section—is itself deeply problematic;[20] dual emergence only magnifies the difficulties. Arguably one can define the monistic basis in such a way as to minimize the emergence problem. Whitehead's process approach attempts to do this, with its "event" or "actual occasion" embodying both mental and physical poles.[21] But it is not clear that this qualifies as a true neutral monism. In fact it is disputable that we have even a single well-articulated theory of neutral monism.

These problems, along with the many issues surrounding conventional property dualism, can be circumvented if we shift our focus to an alternative conception—namely, *dual-aspectism*. This has a number of intrinsic advantages. First, it is unquestionably a form of monism.[22] The monist reality is described simply in terms of its two distinct aspects, the mental and the physical. Second, by maintaining the fundamental significance of the two aspects, it respects our dualist inclinations without disadvantaging the mental—and in such a way that the mind need not emerge at all. So conceived, this places the mental on an equivalent standing with the physical, thus taking the mind seriously. Additionally, by avoiding talk of properties, we sidestep the bundle theory debate. And finally, dual-aspectism is less likely to back us into conceptual corners regarding limitations on how widespread mentality is distributed. I believe it to be our most promising path forward.

There are a number of important milestones in the history of dual-aspectism that deserve examination. But before reviewing this history, I need to make a few additional terminological clarifications. The first is trivial: dual-aspect theories are sometimes labeled "double aspect", or "two aspect". On the former, Chalmers (e.g. 1996, 2010) is a recent case in point, but we find it as far back as Josiah Royce in the late nineteenth century.[23] The latter appears, for example, in O'Sullivan (2008). I will treat all these as synonymous.

More problematically, dual-aspectism is sometimes viewed as equivalent to property dualism. This is a significant issue. Consider a few examples. Nagel (1986: 31) writes: "dual aspect theory [is] the view that one thing can have two sets of mutually irreducible and essential *properties*, mental and physical". And in the discussion that follows, he continually mixes reference to properties and aspects, using the terms interchangeably. Nagel, incidentally, takes a highly ambiguous stance on dual-aspectism. On the one hand he says, "Because of the apparent intimacy of the relation between the mental and its physical conditions . . . I am drawn to some kind of dual aspect theory" (30). On the other, this is merely due to his self-professed "lack of imagination". The view itself is "probably nothing more than pre-Socratic flailing about", and thus is "largely hand waving". He also notes, in passing, that "it isn't always clear what should count as a dual aspect theory" (ibid., n1)—citing Peter Strawson (1959), Hampshire (1971: 210–231), Davidson ([1970] 1980), and O'Shaughnessy (1980) as potential examples.

Similarly unnecessary confusion creeps in to Block's (2006) discussion. The focus of his essay is the "Property Dualism Argument", but he inserts periodic reference to dual-aspectism, evidently equating the two. He even defines the dual-aspect theory as one "in which mental events are held to be identical with physical events, even though those mental events are alleged to have irreducible mental *properties*" (4–5, italics added).[24] Later Block remarks, "again, 'aspect' means property, a property of the state" (18). Near the end of his piece, he further complicates the picture by stating that properties themselves can have aspects (52–54). Overall, Block seems to equate property dualism and dual-aspectism, much as Nagel has done.

O'Sullivan (2008) addresses what he calls the "two aspect" argument for property dualism, again connecting the two concepts. As an example, he considers the property of being in pain. In the two-aspect view, pain, itself a *property*, has both internal (subjective) and external (objective) *aspects*. Notably, he adds that "there is something (nearly) overwhelmingly natural about this [dual aspect] picture when we consider phenomenal properties . . ." (543). Yet he declines to endorse the view.

These issues and complexities are largely avoided if we stay with the dual-aspect notation. There is no confusion with ontological dualism. Dual-aspectism is a monism—a monism not with mental properties and physical properties, but rather a single metaphysical ground that displays itself in the two ways. The one stuff of the world has a mental (experiential, intentional) reality to it, even as it has a physical (non-experiential, non-intentional) reality—doing justice to our dualistic intuitions. And we avoid the property/substance dilemma by downplaying talk of properties.

Let me summarize things so far, and be clear about where my concerns lay. The vast majority of philosophers today are physicalists, which means that for them, mind is a derivative or secondary reality. From my perspective, this is not taking the mind seriously. Most of these individuals are property dualists, because they take mental properties as real but do not identify them with physical properties. But this is arguably an incoherent position, and, if we accept the bundle theory of substance, it implies a kind of substance dualism. Furthermore, virtually all current philosophers see the mind, or mental properties, as highly restricted in scope; it is limited to humans and a few select (but always unidentified) higher animals. Virtually all discussion centers on human beings and human neurophysiological states, and thus the question of emergence rarely arises. And mental causality is an unresolved and problematic issue, frequently terminating in either epiphenomenalism or a rejection of physical causal closure.

Dual-aspectism, to repeat, is necessarily a monism. The monistic base presents itself to us in the two ways (mental and physical), but in itself is not presumed to be something physical. So conceived, dual-aspectism takes the mind seriously; both aspects hold a kind of equal metaphysical standing. It furthermore is not biased towards a limited extension of mentality—and indeed, it strongly suggests something approaching universal extent. Additionally, if mentality is a fundamental aspect of the monistic base, it does not emerge; hence, no emergence miracles. And even the vexing problem of causation may yield to a kind of solution. Perhaps these advantages are becoming more apparent; Zimmerman (2010: 120) remarks that "the dual-aspect theory seems to be enjoying something of a comeback".

All these points deserve elaboration. And the best place to start is with a reexamination of the historical background, in order to draw on and benefit from the wisdom of some of our more insightful predecessors.

6. HISTORICAL PERSPECTIVES ON DUAL-ASPECTISM

I have proposed that dual-aspectism is the preferred terminology, and our most promising conceptual framework. Variations on this theme are prominent throughout history; they provide a guide for future development. Differences in dual-aspect theories seem to center on the nature of the metaphysical base. Some philosophers name a specific entity, while others only examine the two aspects and leave the "ground" undefined. This latter position, incidentally, is not neutral monism; the aspects do not emerge from, or reduce to, this basis. They are simply two views, or two perspectives, on the monistic reality.

Dual-aspectism begins, arguably, with Giordano Bruno. On his view, the sole reality is matter, a substance that embodies two aspects. As Calcagno (1998: 146) explains it, "[for Bruno,] matter is one, yet it can be considered in two modes: *Potenza* and *Soggetto*". *Potenza*, or power, represents a potency or capacity for action. Matter is causally efficacious in the physical realm. The other aspect, *Soggetto*, is subjectivity. Matter has a subjective dimension, expressible in conative terms. "Bruno views matter as being motivated by desire. That which draws and attracts matter together is desire" (148). Matter is both physical and intentional, "both corporeal and incorporeal" (150).

Spinoza evidently followed a similar line of thinking. He was, as we know, a pantheist monist. The one substance, God or Nature, possesses infinitely many attributes (aspects), of which the human mind can grasp but two: thought and extension.[25] Individual objects are modes of extension, and individual mental states are modes of thought. This duality of mind and matter posed a special problem for Spinoza. Because of the underlying monistic unity to all things, there must be a direct correlation between the modes of extension and those of thought. In other words, each object must possess a corresponding mental mode, or "idea"; this is his thesis of psychophysical parallelism.

As an object undergoes change in the physical realm, so too does its corresponding idea. As he says, "The order and connection of ideas is the same as the order and connection of things" (*Ethics*, IIP7).[26] This is so because, in the end, there is still only one monistic reality: "the thinking substance and the extended substance are one and the same substance, which is now comprehended under this attribute, now under that" (IIIP7S). There is no causal link between the two; they are simply two aspects of a single series of events. Neither reduces to the other. And they both have equal standing with respect to the underlying monism.

Leibniz implicitly articulated a dual-aspect view in his monadology. The monads possess a physical aspect given by a handful of qualities—agency, mass, simplicity, shapelessness. And they have a mental aspect consisting of two components, *perception* and *appetite*.[27] This is significant, and underappreciated: in perception we find the germ of experience (qualia), and in appetite (desire) the germ of intentionality. In his parallelistic schema, each aspect exists in its own "kingdom", without causal interaction: "bodies act as if there were no souls (though this is impossible); and souls act as if there were no bodies; and both act as if each influence the other" (Leibniz 1991: sec. 81). Hence we are easily deceived about the true nature of mental causation.

Some 40 years later, Boscovich proposed that the ultimate nature of matter lie in the forces present in it; this theory came to be known as dynamism.[28] Joseph Priestley adopted this approach and extended it to account for the mind. By resolving matter into pure force, he believed that he could overcome the Cartesian opposition of mind and matter. Both could be seen as manifestations or "modifications" of force. In his treatise of 1777, "Disquisitions Relating to Mind and Spirit", he wrote:

> [S]ince it has never yet been asserted, that the power of *sensation* and *thought* are incompatible with these [forces of repulsion and attraction], I therefore maintain, that we have no reason to suppose that there are in man two substances so distinct from each other as have been represented ([1777] 1972: 219).

It was roughly at this time that French vitalistic materialism emerged. Seeking a strictly naturalistic solution to the mind-body problem, Julien de La Mettrie proposed that reality was simply the embodiment of both physical and mental aspects or properties. The physical properties included spatiality and motion, which were complemented by an experiential aspect, feeling. Maupertuis extended this approach, adding gravitational attraction to the physical side, and reworking the experiential in terms of "intelligence"—which was further resolved into "desire, aversion, and memory". Diderot defined the physical aspect in terms of force, extension, and impenetrability, and the mental simply as "sensitiveness".[29]

Johann Herder put forth another dynamist theory based on a monistic reality called *Kraft* (force). In describing the material and mental aspects of it, Herder adopts a perspectival terminology of "inner" and "outer". The material aspect was the external manifestation of *Kraft*, and the mental or spiritual was the internal: "All active forces of Nature are, each in its own way, alive; in their interior there must be something that corresponds to their effects without. . .".[30] A further version of dynamism is found in Schiller (1891).

One of the most influential dual-aspectists was Schopenhauer. The world, he said, can be comprehended in two ways: as will (*Wille*) and as idea (*Vorstellung*). When we perceive things from without, we observe only sensory impressions—as per classical idealism. But unlike Berkeley, Schopenhauer believed that there must be an inner or intrinsic nature to things. This nature he found in himself, or more precisely, in his will. Knowing that he was not of different metaphysical construction than other objects in the world, he inferred that all things, intrinsically, must also be will. As with Spinoza, there is only one reality, but it possesses the two distinct attributes. "For as the world is in one aspect entirely idea, so in another it is entirely will" (Schopenhauer [1819] 1995: 5). This yields a metaphysics in which mind and matter are two sides of the same coin:

> Now if you suppose the existence of a mind in the human head, as a *deus ex machina*, then, as already remarked, you are bound to concede a mind to every stone ... All ostensible mind can be attributed to matter, but all matter can likewise be attributed to mind ... ([1851] 1974: 213; for the original source, see *Parerga and Paralipomena*, vol. 2, sec. 74)

Schopenhauer's dual-aspect approach is clear and unambiguous, because there is no third entity which displays itself as will and idea. There is only the will, and all nominally material objects are nothing less than the will "objectified". Externally, the will displays itself in its material aspect, as force (mechanistically) and as sensory impressions (ideas). Drawing—we may speculate—from Herder, and implicitly, Leibniz, Schopenhauer's "inner" and "outer" aspects of reality are, in the end, aspects of the will. It is true that the internal aspect is conceived of as the fundamental reality, but the external aspect is of equal standing, metaphysically speaking.

Others followed in Schopenhauer's footprints. Among these was Herman Lotze, who argued that "[matter] has a double life, appearing outwardly as matter, and as such manifesting ... mechanical [properties, while] internally, on the other hand, moved mentally" ([1856–1864] 1971: 150). Friedrich Paulsen ([1892] 1895) adopted this approach, as did, in modified form, Friedrich Nietzsche. Nietzsche wrote that "the victorious [and external] concept of 'force' ... still needs to be completed: an inner will must be ascribed to it, which I designate as 'will to power'" ([1906] 1967: 332–333). In *Beyond Good and Evil*, he claims "the right to define all efficient force unequivocally as: *will to power*. The world seen from within ... would be will to power and nothing else" ([1886] 1973: 67). Or more succinctly, "the innermost essence of being is will to power" ([1906] 1967: 369).

In his early writing, Ernst Haeckel was an implicit dual-aspectist. His book *History of Creation* ([1868] 1876) lobbied against both mind-body dualism and matter-energy (or force) dualism. There is no duality, he said, only a two-sided unity: "body and mind can, in fact, never be considered as distinct, but rather that both sides of nature are inseparably connected..." ([1868] 1876: 487). Later he echoed the French materialists, claiming that matter possessed the property of feeling. By the time of his most famous work, *The Riddle of the Universe* (1899), Haeckel modified his view once again; now it was "substance" (*Substanz*) that was the monist reality, presenting itself as mass (body) and energy (spirit).

Ernst Mach argued for a pure dual-aspect ontology based on the concept of "sensations"—roughly, sensory perceptions as they exist "objectively", that is, apart from the perceiving subject. Much like Schopenhauer, sensations are perceived as mental qualities from the first person standpoint, and as physical qualities from the third person. As he says, "the elements given in experience . . . are always the same, and are of only one nature, though they appear, according to the nature of the connection, at one moment as physical and at another as psychical elements" ([1886] 1959: 61). There being only sensations, Mach has no need to postulate a neutral basis:

> [T]he view advocated here is different from Fechner's conception of the physical and psychical as two different aspects of one and the same reality. [O]ur view has no metaphysical background, but corresponds only to the generalized expression of experiences. . . . [W]e refuse to distinguish two different aspects of an unknown *tertium quid* . . . (ibid.)

The upshot is a system in which there exists a *"complete parallelism of the psychical and the physical"*—in other words, "a physical entity corresponds to every psychical entity, and vice versa" (60).

Mach had no "metaphysical background" for his dual-aspect theory, but other philosophers took clues for this background from advances in science. For Henri Bergson, the emerging concept of *energy* served this purpose. Bergson frequently spoke in dual-aspect terms, describing a kind of reciprocal duality between mind and matter, with both arising from an underlying energetic source—a kind of "consciousness/time" that he variously called "images" or *durée*: "We may surmise that these two realities, matter and consciousness, are derived from a common source. If . . . matter is the inverse of consciousness . . . then neither matter nor consciousness can be explained apart from one another" ([1911] 1920: 23).

In his thesis of "objective idealism",[31] Charles Peirce rejected conventional mind/matter dualism, opting instead for the notion of *hylopathy*—the view that matter is able to feel. In his important 1892 essay "Man's Glassy Essence" he was clear and direct:

> [A]ll mind is directly or indirectly connected with all matter, and acts in a more or less regular way; so that all mind more or less partakes of the nature of matter. Hence, it would be a mistake to conceive of the psychical and the physical aspects of matter as two aspects absolutely distinct. Viewing a thing from the outside, considering its relations of action and reaction with other things, it appears as matter. Viewing it from the inside, looking at its immediate character as feeling, it appears as consciousness. ([1892] 1992: 349)

Much like Peirce, Royce adopted an absolute idealism that was described in dual-aspect terms. He also wrote of the distinction between "inner" and "outer" perspectives: "it is not ours to speculate what appreciative inner life is hidden behind the describable but seemingly lifeless things of the world" ([1892] 1955: 427). Later Royce was even more emphatic:

> In consequence we have no sort of right to speak in any way as if the inner experience behind any fact of nature were of a grade lower than ours, or less conscious, or less rational, or more atomic. . . . No evidence, then, can indicate nature's inner reality without also indicating that this reality is, like that of our own experience, conscious, organic, full of clear contrasts, rational, definite. We ought not to speak of dead nature. ([1898] 1915: 230)

Into the 1940s, Julian Huxley proposed a neutral dual-aspect theory. Progress in science and in evolution theory, he argued, banished conventional dualism, leaving us with an unassailable monism. "There exists one world stuff", he wrote, "which reveals material or mental properties according to the point of view" (1942: 140). Material reality is the world "from the outside", and it is mental "from within".

The physicist David Bohm also employed a dual-aspect terminology: "The mental and the material are two sides of one overall process. . . . There is one energy that is the basis of all reality. . ." (1986: 129). At other times Bohm took a new entity, the *implicate order*, as the one reality. In 1980 he stated that "consciousness and matter in general are basically the same order (i.e. the implicate order as a whole)" (Bohm 1980: 208). He elaborated in a 1982 interview, explaining that the implicate order "contains both matter and mind", and thus must "in some sense . . . be aware" (1982: 37).

On yet other occasions, Bohm put forth *information* as the sole basis for reality—an idea first presented a decade earlier by Gregory Bateson. As Bateson saw it, information was "difference that makes a difference" (1972: 459), and was the key element of the feedback ("cybernetic") system of the mind: "The elementary cybernetic system with its messages in circuit is, in fact, the simplest unit of mind" (1972: 465). Information thus plays both a physical and a mental role in the world. In similar fashion, Bohm argued that "the notion of information [is] something that need not belong only to human consciousness, but that may indeed be present, in some sense, even in inanimate systems of atoms and electrons" (1986: 124–125). As a consequence, "it is implied that . . . a rudimentary consciousness is present even at the level of particle physics" (131).

Another form of dual-aspectism refers to quantum phenomena as the ground of reality. J. B. S. Haldane was the first to propose this, in his 1934 essay "Quantum Mechanics as a Basis for Philosophy". Here he associates mind with the wave-like aspect of atomic particles, and ordinary matter with their particle-like aspect. This idea was elaborated in 1971 by the physicist Andrew Cochran, who suggested that "the quantum mechanical wave properties of matter are actually the conscious properties of matter", and that therefore atomic particles "have a rudimentary degree of consciousness, volition, or self-activity" (1971: 236). Noted physicist Freeman Dyson put forth the same view in *Disturbing the Universe* (1979: 249), as did Danah Zohar (1990: 80). Lately we have the work of Stuart Hameroff, whose concept of "objective reduction" associates the collapse of quantum micro-states with moments of experience—see his writings (1998, 2009).

Among recent developments are three notable proposals. Following the lead of Bateson and Bohm, Chalmers (1996) put forth a tentative dual-aspect ("naturalistic dualism") theory in which information is the metaphysical basis. Regarding the dualistic interpretation, he remarks:

> I should also note that although I call the view a variety of dualism, it is possible that it could turn out to be a kind of monism. Perhaps the physical and the phenomenal will turn out to be two different aspects of a single encompassing kind, in something like the way that matter and energy turn out to be two aspects of a single kind. (129)

It's a valid point: we treat mass-energy as a single kind that displays itself in one of the two manifestations. Thus it is certainly conceivable that, by analogy, "matter-mind" is a single metaphysical kind, with its own two aspects. Chalmers then conjectures that information may serve as the proper designation for this single kind: "We might put this by suggesting as a basic principle that information . . . has two aspects, a physical and a phenomenal aspect" (286). It is a promising approach, but his later works (e.g. 2010) make no attempt to further develop the theory.

Secondly, Max Velmans (2009) advocates a view he calls "reflexive monism". This schema "suggests a seamless, psychophysical universe, of which we are an integral part, which can be known in two fundamentally different ways . . . [T]hese physical and experiential aspects of mind arise from what can best be described as a 'psychophysical ground'". (327–328). Velmans's theory lies firmly in the established dual-aspect tradition. Mind and matter, he says, are complementary aspects of a single reality, roughly analogous to the wave-particle duality of quantum physics.

A third approach comes from Galen Strawson. Articulated over a series of writings (see Strawson 1994, 2006, 2009), he proposes the thesis of (variously) "mental and physical monism" or "equal status, fundamental duality (ESFD) monism". He summarizes his view this way:

> Reality is irreducibly both experiential and nonexperiential (both mental and nonmental), while being substantially single in some way W that we do not fully understand . . . [Way W] does not involve any sort of asymmetry between the status of the [two] claims . . . [Furthermore,] it is not correct to say that the experiential is based in or realized by or otherwise dependent on the nonexperiential, or vice versa. (2010: 73)

Strawson (2006: 241–246) gives a more extended discussion, wherein his ESFD monism is argued to be the most realistic approach to the mind-body problem. His description is again succinct:

> Reality is substantially single. All reality is experiential and all reality is non-experiential. Experiential and non-experiential being exist in such a way that neither can be said to be based in, or realized by, or in any way asymmetrically dependent on the other.

It is the position he advocates, and believes "it may very well be a truth beyond our understanding" (246). It meets his entirely reasonable demand that we retain some form of underlying monism ("There is, I feel sure, a fundamental sense in which monism is true, a fundamental sense in which there is only one kind of stuff in the universe"—p. 274), while at the same time doing justice to the duality of the mental and the physical ("it is extremely natural to think that we cannot in the end do without some such duality"—p. 256).

To close this section, I note that Thomas Nagel is another who seems to have taken this lesson to heart. As early as 1979, he proposed that the material constituents of the physical world might have "proto-mental properties" to them.[32] Earlier I cited his *View from Nowhere* in which he admits that he is "drawn to some kind of dual aspect theory". In 2002 he again flirted with the topic, rejecting both substance and property dualism, and leaning toward a kind of non-reductive dual-aspect neutral monism. He proposed that all of matter might possess "inert mental potentialities", but declined to elaborate. In his most recent book, *Mind and Cosmos* (2012), he again tackles the issue, coming across as ever-so-slightly more sympathetic. "I believe the weight of evidence favors some form of neutral monism over the traditional alternatives of materialism, idealism, and dualism" (4–5). Mind is built into the structure of reality, and he clearly favors that theory "that makes mind central, rather than a side effect of physical law" (15). To his credit, Nagel takes the mind seriously. The irreducibility of consciousness "suggests that the explanation may have to be something more than physical all the way down" (53)—that is, some mental property or aspect. Speaking cautiously, and using classical dual-aspect terminology, he notes: "We ourselves are large-scale complex instances of something both objectively physical from the outside and subjectively mental from the inside. Perhaps the basis for this identity pervades the world" (2). But for all this discussion, Nagel offers no concrete proposal for a dual-aspect theory.

Overall the historical lesson is quite clear: once we have abandoned classical substance dualism and followed intuitive and conceptual pressure toward monism, *and if we take the mind seriously*, then some form of a dual-aspect theory is worthy of serious consideration.

7. EMERGENCE OR PANPSYCHISM

As I have said, any form of physicalism and most versions of property dualism necessarily give ontological priority to physical reality. The mind must then somehow be smuggled into the physicalist worldview. That we are unable to do this satisfactorily is evidence that the assumption was erroneous in the first place.

Hidden in the previous discussion is a second major concern, regarding the extent of mentality. With only a handful of exceptions, every philosopher of mind today holds a highly restrictive view of mind. The mental aspects, or properties, or the reductive base, is explicitly or implicitly taken to be the human brain, or the human body, or, at most, the bodies of the so-called higher animals. The possibility of the applicability of mental attributes to other life forms, or to other entities generally, is virtually never considered.

The guiding assumption here is that the mind emerges from the physical: mental qualities come to exist only in certain highly specific, highly complex physical structures. Less complex structures exhibit not less, but zero mentality. Thus the emergentist assumes that there is a concrete but unspecified level of complexity necessary for the existence of mind. This assumption is almost never questioned, nor is it defended. I contend that it is mistaken.

The only alternative is to hold that mind does *not* emerge at some critical threshold of complexity, and that therefore it must exist, if only in primitive form, as an elemental quality of material reality. This is panpsychism—the view that mental qualities are universal in extent. There is apparently no middle ground here: one is either an emergentist or a panpsychist.

To call emergentism the dominant view is an understatement. Unfortunately it suffers from severe problems, not the least of which is the very coherence of a stance in which mental reality emerges from an utterly non-mental material substrate. This is the problem of strong or brute emergence. A compelling statement against the intelligibility of strong emergence is given by Strawson (2006, 2009). In brief, all coherent forms of emergence do not demand the appearance of radically new metaphysical qualities. Liquidity, Bénard convection cells, even life (to use Strawson's examples) are all forms of conventional ('soft') emergence, and are wholly explicable given what we understand about the nature of physical reality, likewise with the coming-to-be of stars, planets, individual species, football teams, computers—in fact, virtually all physical structures of the world around us. These things all emerge quite naturally and explicably from elementary physical particles and the relevant laws of physics. Emergence can and does happen all the time. The cosmos is indeed a creative and transcendent realm. We require only that certain physical properties, like mass, charge, spin, quantum state, etc., are taken as brute realities of the physical world—at least until such time as we are able to reductively explain them in terms of simpler and fewer entities.

Strong emergence, however, is a completely different story. It is inconceivable that spatiality, for example, emerges from an entirely nonspatial substrate. This is not to say that such a thing is *impossible*, only that, at present, we have no conceivable understanding of how it could be true—and therefore, as rational beings, we must hold it to be false. The same is true for mentality (experientiality, intentionality). We lack any conception of how mental states or properties could emerge from something wholly and completely nonmental. And since emergence of mind is inconceivable, panpsychism obtains. Strawson argues that any "real" physicalist must accept this fact:[33]

> [R]eal physicalism . . . entails panpsychism, given the impossibility of 'radical' emergence. All physical stuff is energy . . . and all energy, I trow, is an experience-involving phenomenon. This sounded crazy to me for a long time, but I am quite used to it now that I know that there is no alternative short of 'substance dualism,' a view for which there has never been any good argument. Real physicalism . . . entails panpsychism, and whatever problems are raised by this fact are problems a real physicalist must face. (2009: 53)

Apart from the incoherence of strong emergence, the traditional view has at least three very specific problem areas to contend with. First is what I call the historic question of emergence: When in evolutionary history did mind first appear? And why? Was it in some protohuman, like *Australopithecus*? Or perhaps even earlier, in some prehistoric mammalian species? Second, there is the phylogenic question: Which species on Earth today have mental phenomena? Is it restricted to humans and the (always unspecified) higher animals? Where is the dividing line, and why is it "just there"? The third question is ontogenic, by which I refer to the developing human organism. When in the life of a fetus does it suddenly acquire a mental life? On the emergentist view, it has none as a single cell, and yet the fully developed organism must certainly have a rich mental existence. So, when in the course of those nine months does mind appear, and why just there? Emergentist philosophers have no answers to these questions, precisely because, I believe, the presumed emergence is a fiction. And if it is a fiction, these questions can have no answers.

Furthermore, and independently speaking, panpsychism is not so 'crazy' as it might appear. The view has a long and noble tradition in western philosophy, one that is largely unknown.[34] Note well: with perhaps the lone exception of Nagel, *every philosopher that I examined in the previous section is a panpsychist*, or at least strongly sympathetic to it. Dual-aspectism, by its very nature, tends to promote a panpsychist view of the mind. This is not a reductio, but a virtue. Indeed, it may be our best hope for resolving of some of our most long-standing philosophical problems. This seems to be Chalmers's view:

Overall, type-F [panpsychist] monism promises a deeply integrated and elegant view of nature. No one has yet developed any sort of detailed theory in this class, and it is not yet clear whether such a theory can be developed. At the same time, however, there appear to be no strong reasons to reject the view. As such, type-F monism is likely to provide fertile grounds for further investigation, and it may ultimately provide the best integration of the physical and the phenomenal within the natural world. (2010: 137)

Chalmers is optimistic; we ought to share his view.

8. TOWARDS A VIABLE DUAL-ASPECT THEORY

What lessons can we draw, then, from this lengthy discussion? Let me propose the following, based on the notion, mentioned before, of "matter-mind" as the monistic reality. My term for this view is *hylonoism*: material reality ('hyle') as coexisting at all levels with a mental ('noetic') dimension.[35] The following brief comments will have to suffice as an outline of a theory.

Reality is a dual-aspect monism, one that respects equally the physical and mental dimensions of existence; in this sense I take the mind seriously. Each aspect may be attributed to all of reality; no part of it lacks either one. Every real and concrete entity is both, and at once, mental and physical.

Each of the two central aspects may be further resolved into individual discrete manifestations, with their own identifiable properties. 'Physical' resolves into mass, charge, spin, quantum state, and the other brute physical properties. 'Mental' resolves into the two fundamental components of *experience* (the foundation of qualia, consciousness, and phenomenality) and *intentionality* (the foundation of desire, belief, and cognition). Leibniz, I believe, was right: the physical ultimates possess something like perception and appetition as the two base components of their mental existence, in addition to their purely physical properties.

In order to fully respect the equal status of the mental and physical aspects, we must have a one-to-one matching of all physical states and all mental states. Mach's intuition was correct—to every physical particular there is a psychical particular, and vice versa. Every physical state is a composition of ultimate particles and their brute physical properties. Corresponding to every such state is a unique mental state, existing as a composition of the brute mental properties of experience and intention.[36]

The picture thus described is one of a true psychophysical parallelism. Again, the views of Mach, Leibniz, and Spinoza are substantially correct. I am tempted to describe it as a kind of mirror-image scenario, where each physical entity has its mental counterpart 'in the mirror'. But this analogy is deficient, because the mirror image is inevitably seen as less real than the object itself. A hylonoetic parallelism is rather one in which there are *two images*, so to speak, each reflecting the other, neither one more or less real than the other. Clearly there is an epistemic imbalance, as we see outwardly only the physical aspect, and inwardly only the mental aspect. But we ought not let this bias us in favor of the physical. And yet, if such a parallelism holds, all entities must experience such a dual outlook on the world—precisely as Schopenhauer claimed.

Such an outlook furthermore offers some interesting conclusions about mental causation. Parallelism respects causal closure, *of both sides*. The physical world is indeed causally closed, and the physical aspect is sufficient to explain—to the degree that causality is explainable—the interactions of things in the physical world. However, parallel to this must exist a sequence of mental events, equally causal in their own right, and matching exactly the causal sequence in the physical realm. Spinoza had it right: "the order and connection of ideas is the same as the order and connection of things" (*Ethics*, IIP7).

Thus the physical realm is causally closed, *and the mental realm is causally closed*. This is not epiphenomenalism. There is simply a symmetric acausal relation between the mental and the physical. Mental events have wholly mental causes, just as physical events have wholly physical causes. As my brain/body complex changes physical state, so too does that complete mental state that corresponds to my bodily existence. My body does not causally interact with my mind in any way.

What about mental unity? Why do we have such a strong sensation of being a unified consciousness? Hylonoism demands that mental unity parallel physical unity. Our bodies are relatively well-defined, and exist as relatively distinct objects. Therefore, also our minds exist as relatively well-defined and distinct mental objects. The more concrete and definable the physical object is, the more concrete and definable the mind of that object is. Of course, at the atomic level we know that our bodies diffuse out into space, to an arbitrarily large degree. Thus, strictly speaking, our minds also extend to encompass reality outside of our physical bodies.[37] Just as mass/energy is best understood as a *field*, so too mind is best conceived as field-like in nature.

Furthermore, objects with less well-defined boundaries have correspondingly less well-defined mental unities. 'Fuzzy' objects like clouds, rivers, and forests, will possess correspondingly fuzzy mental lives. I prefer to think of it in terms of mental *intensity*. A fuzzy physical object will possess a low-intensity mental unity—that is, it will tend to blur into the background mental reality that parallels the physical realm. In many cases, such objects are fuzzy because they are *collectives* of smaller discrete objects—as a forest is a collectivity of trees, other plants, animals, etc. Yet consistency demands that all such collectivities possess a corresponding mental unity, of lesser or greater intensity, paralleling the degree of integration of the physical entity.

And what about the mental realm itself? On the hylonoetic view, there must exist a vast, complex and rich mental realm as a counterpart to the vast, rich, and complex physical realm—"two kingdoms", as Leibniz said.

Just as physical space embodies a variety of physical structures and states, so too must "mind space" embody a variety of mental structures and states. A question, then, is how to depict it in objective, third-person terms. Progress has been made in recent years, beginning with Edwin Land's 1977 notion of a 'color qualia cube'. P. M. Churchland (1986) expands upon this idea, arguing that any sensory modality can be modeled in a comparable qualia state space. Such a space is one of very high dimensionality, and allows for extreme discrimination of qualia states and pattern recognition. It may helpful, he suggests, to think about qualia and experience "geometrically", in terms of structures and shapes in just such a high-dimensional mental space: "it seems possible that we will also find cognitive significance in *surfaces*, and *hypersurfaces*, and *intersections* of hypersurfaces, and so forth. What we have opening before us is a 'geometrical', as opposed to a narrowly syntactic, conception of cognitive activity" (304). I myself have argued in a similar vein, employing concepts from chaos theory and nonlinear dynamics; see Skrbina (2009).

A closely related conception was recently put forth by Guilio Tononi, in his thesis of consciousness as "integrated information". He explicitly postulates the existence of a qualia space (Q) in which the set of informational relationships generated by a complex system constitutes an n-dimensional "shape" that wholly defines a given experience. Any physical system with any degree of integrative activity possesses a corresponding qualitative Q-space. In this view, "consciousness exists . . . as a fundamental quantity—as fundamental as mass, charge, or energy" (2008: 233). Tononi's theory is thus very much in line with the one presented here, and gives us yet one more way of articulating a parallel mental space.[38]

In each of these cases, mind space is viewed as a true *state space*, with various locations in it corresponding to different qualitative states or qualia. But this addresses only the experiential dimension of mind; intentionality seems harder to conceptualize. Here is one speculative possibility: since intentionality is a directedness or aboutness, it may be that it is established through higher-order patterns or structures in mind space—perhaps even in the joint space of two or more objects. Given that the mind 'moves' through qualia space in a complex manner, we may be able to conceive of intentionality in terms of patterns, shapes, or trajectories in this mental space.

What about a concrete linkage between the two realms, the mental and the physical? It is clear that both have one dimension in common: time. This provides the connection. Just as space is best understood as space-time, so too the qualitative or mental space is best understood as something analogous, perhaps "qualia-time". On this reading, the sum total of reality must be a conjunction of these two spaces, resulting in something that we may call the *space-time-qualia complex*. This would encompass the whole psychophysical parallelism within a single concept—a single monist reality.

The picture, I think, is clear and elegant. It resolves or avoids most of the problems facing conventional theories. And it casts light on a number of other standing issues, of which I can only make a few passing comments:

- To reiterate, there is neither supervenience nor reduction of mental to the physical, or vice versa. Each aspect is whole, complete, and self-standing.
- Regarding free will: Due to causal closure and the parallelist metaphysics, determinism exists in the physical realm, and a corresponding determinism exists in the mental realm. Classical free will does not exist. However, as a reflection of the underlying creativity of the universe, we each embody the principles of spontaneity, order, and transcendence that allow new forms to come into existence. In this sense, then, we can be said to possess a higher-order creative freedom.
- We can see the motivation for identity theories: the one-to-one parallelism can certainly seem to be an identification process. But conventional identity theory is a one-sided physicalism. This fails to take the mind seriously.
- Many current proposals are overly complex, and rely upon fairly arcane terminological distinctions. A parallelist hylonoism is not only elegant, it has the virtue of theoretic simplicity. As always, we should seek the simplest solution that satisfies our conceptual requirements.
- There is no need to search for psychophysical laws. The mental realm is not simply grafted onto the physicalist tree, thus calling out for special terms of relationship. It is as complete and extensive as the physical realm, and perfectly aligned with it. The only 'law' would be this very parallelistic structure, which is a brute condition of reality.
- Zombie arguments are purely theoretical, and thus inconsequential. Within this scheme, any atom-for-atom duplicate would have an identical mental state. Zombies are neither logically nor metaphysically conceivable; they offer no defense for dualism, as is alleged.

Finally, due to the thorough-going parallelism, *hylonoism may rightly be counted as a form of dualism*. There are indeed "two kingdoms", but they are conjoined at every point and thus constitute a single monistic system. Dualism within monism: justice is done to both our central intuitions.

NOTES

1. Pyramid of Unis, "Spells for Leaving the Akhet". Cited in Allen (2005: 57).
2. Thales, Anaximenes, Anaximander, and Heraclitus are the obvious examples.
3. For Socrates, see for example *Apology*, where he explicitly accepts the possibility that death may be "a change and a relocating for the soul from here to another place" (40c). Plato's well-known "Myth of Er" (*Republic*, 614–621) is one discussion of the afterlife. *Phaedo* and *Phaedrus* provide further elaboration.
4. The present volume is a testament to this, as are the recent anthologies from Skrbina (2009), Koons and Bealer (2010), Lange et al. (2011), and Göcke (2012).
5. By 'physical' I mean simply that which is wholly nonmental, or non-experiential.

Dualism, Dual-Aspectism, and the Mind 243

6. Fragment 3, Freeman translation.
7. Fragment 8, cited in Long (1996: 136).
8. *De sensibus*, 3; cited by Long (1996: 147).
9. For present purposes, I will treat materialism and physicalism as synonymous terms.
10. There were of course earlier materialists, but I set aside here the ideas of such diverse thinkers as Epicurus, Hobbes, Kant, and Marx.
11. See his *Philosophy and Logical Syntax* (1935), for example.
12. For the most part, metaphysics today has been reduced to "formal ontology".
13. See Gozzano and Hill (2012) for a recent discussion of the relevant issues.
14. For example: Robb (1997), White (2007), O'Sullivan (2008), Mackie (2011), and Lycan (2013).
15. If they do not mean this usage, then they are ignoring a vast range of competing theories.
16. I examine this problem in more detail later.
17. "Given their insistence that mental properties do not reduce to the physical properties of neurons . . . both Sperry and Searle are property dualists".
18. If true, then clearly not all non-reductive materialists are property dualists.
19. It does no good to refer to the neutral foundation as proto-mental or proto-physical. If proto-mental is experiential to any degree, it must count as mental—in which case the basis is no longer neutral. If it is completely non-experiential, then the emergence problem remains. And similarly for proto-physical.
20. See Strawson (2009: 41–49) for a cogent explanation of the difficulty with strong, or brute, emergence. For a counter view, see Vision (2012).
21. First elaborated in Whitehead (1926: 114). For a fuller discussion see Skrbina (2010).
22. I have yet to hear of any argument for a "dual-aspect dualism".
23. "The theory of the 'double aspect,' applied to the facts of the inorganic world, suggests at once that they, too, in so far as they are real, must possess their own inner and appreciable aspect. . ." ([1892] 1955: 419).
24. This would seem to be an incoherent definition. It is not clear that one can hold identity and irreducibility at the same time.
25. Following the lead of Descartes, undoubtedly.
26. Curley translation—see Spinoza ([1677] 1994).
27. See "Monadology", sections 14, 15, 19 or *Principles of Nature and Grace Based on Reason*, sections 2, 4 (Leibniz 1991).
28. First articulated in his book *Theoria philosophiae naturalis* (Boscovich 1758).
29. For details see Skrbina (2005: 101–108).
30. From his *Ideas for the Philosophy of the History of Humanity* (1784–1791), as cited in Clark (1955: 311).
31. Captured in the striking phrase "matter is effete mind" ([1891] 1992: 293).
32. Actually he gives us a clue even earlier, in his famous "What Is It Like to Be a Bat?" article of 1974. The final footnote includes this comment: "It seems to me more likely, however, that mental-physical relations will eventually be expressed in a theory whose fundamental terms cannot be placed clearly in either category" (1974: 450).
33. To be clear: Strawson's 'real physicalism' is much more like a true dual-aspectism than a conventional physicalism.
34. Though less so in recent years. The primary overview is my 2005 work *Panpsychism in the West*, but other sources include Griffin (1997), de Quincey (2002), and Clarke (2003).
35. Elsewhere I have taken inspiration from Skolimowski's (1994) participatory philosophy, and referred to the metaphysical ground as a particeptikon, a participatory matrix.

36. Ideally we should find a one-to-one matching of the fundamental properties on each side; it seems that we do not yet understand the situation well enough to do so.
37. This is known as the extended mind. For a good overview see Manzotti (2009).
38. Tononi's approach, and the corresponding panpsychist implications, have also been embraced by Christof Koch; see his (2012: 124–134).

14 Why My Body Is Not Me: The Unity Argument for Emergentist Self-Body Dualism

E. J. Lowe

Philosophers have long pondered the nature of the *self*, their judgements concerning its existence and identity ranging from outright nihilism—its dismissal as a sheer illusion—to affirmations of its absolute centrality to the whole of reality and our knowledge of it. This enormous variety of opinions makes one wonder if all these philosophers can really have meant the same in speaking of 'selves'—a term which is, in any case, hardly in widespread everyday use. And yet all such talk is centred ultimately upon a linguistic phenomenon that is ubiquitous: the first-person pronoun, 'I'—a term which always seems to have a perfectly definite and indisputably real reference whenever it is employed, referring as it does to *whomsoever* or *whatsoever* is uttering it on any occasion of its use. But for all its ubiquity and seeming familiarity, this pronoun occasions some of the most puzzling problems in metaphysics and philosophical psychology that we ever encounter. The most challenging of these problems is the topic of the present chapter.

1. THE QUESTION: 'WHAT AM I?'—AND WHY IT IS PUZZLING

Very arguably the most important question in the metaphysics of mind, which needs to be answered before all others, is the question that Descartes raises early in the *Meditations*: 'What *am* I?'—or, in its plural form, 'What *are* we?'.[1] The plural form of the question presents some difficulties, however, which don't seem to attach to the singular form: in particular, the difficulty of deciding what or whom to include under the term 'we'. It seems that I need to decide in advance what *kind* of thing I fundamentally am in order to decide which is the relevant plurality to regard as the referent of 'we' in the plural form of the question—for whoever says 'we' intends to include *him or herself* within that plurality, together with certain others relevantly *like* him or herself. It is clear, anyway, that Descartes's question *is* just the question of what kind of thing I fundamentally am, where 'kind' here, I suggest, should be understood to mean *ontological category*. This latter notion needs to be spelled out, of course, but it should be clear that we are not talking now about merely superficial classifications—so that 'philosopher', for example, would *not* be a good answer to Descartes's question, whereas 'animal' might be, as, perhaps, 'material object' might also be.[2]

Descartes's question can seem to be an odd one, for this reason: he raises it only *after* having satisfied himself that he certainly *exists*. Thus, he represents himself as knowing with certainty *that* he is, without yet knowing *what* he is. In short, he claims to know of his own *existence* before knowing, or at least knowing clearly, his *essence*—for to know a thing's essence is precisely to know *what it is*, in Descartes's sense of this phrase, which goes back ultimately to Aristotle's. The oddity lies in the fact that one would normally suppose that one cannot know that a certain thing, *X*, *exists* unless one has at least some grasp of what it is that one takes *X* to *be*. If I were just to assert 'Gronash exists', but professed to have no idea whatever *what* Gronash is, I would rightly be accused of complete vacuity. My assertion would amount to nothing more than the claim that *something*, I know not what, exists. Perhaps I do indeed know this, because I know that something rather than nothing exists. But then I shouldn't try to make this claim by saying 'Gronash exists', because that misleadingly suggests that I know, regarding some specific thing, that *it* exists.

2. THE BEGINNINGS OF AN ANSWER IN THE CONCEPT OF THE SELF

Part of the solution to this conundrum is that we *don't* know absolutely *nothing* about the referent of 'I', prior to asking the question 'What am I?'. I know, for example, that I am the thing asking this question about myself, and hence that I am the sort of thing that *can* ask intelligible questions—so I know, as Descartes points out, that I am at least a thing that *thinks*, and indeed that thinks about *itself*. In short, I am at least a self-reflecting subject of thought—a 'self' or 'person', to use those technical philosophical terms. A self or person—at least as I propose to use those terms—is just, by definition, a *self-reflective subject of thought*, to which I would add that it is thereby also a subject of *perception* and an agent of *actions*, on the grounds that only a perceiving agent can be capable of thought. Demonstrating this latter point is no simple matter, however, so I shall just leave the claim as an undefended assertion for present purposes.[3]

But then why isn't it sufficient to answer Descartes's question—'What am I?'—with the perfectly simple response, 'I am a *self* or *person*'? Well, that *would* be an adequate answer, I think, if we could establish that 'person' denotes a fundamental ontological category, comparable with 'animal' or 'material object'. But the trouble is that this is not just obviously so. And Descartes himself rightly acknowledges this. It may seem, rather, that 'self' or 'person' is just a *status* that can be conferred upon something of some fundamental kind *if* it satisfies certain conditions—or, to use terminology that is currently popular in this sort of context, if it occupies a certain 'functional role'—specifically, if it does everything that is necessary to qualify as a self-reflective subject of thought. Then our attention will be directed to the question of what *kind* or *kinds* of things can satisfy this condition. Can an animal, for instance, or a material object? (Of course, it may be said that animals are themselves just a kind of material object—in which case, consider instead the category *inanimate material object*, which presumably includes such things as mechanical or electronic *robots*.) If it should turn out that things of fundamentally *different* kinds can qualify as selves or persons, then this will imply that 'self' does *not* denote a fundamental kind and that *my* answer to Descartes's question need not be the same as that of every other self or person. By the same token, it will then turn out that by 'we' I should mean things of the same fundamental kind as *me*, not necessarily things of *other* kinds which also qualify as selves or persons. That need not have the alarming implication that I should have no moral concern for such 'alien' persons, because it may be that it is still *personhood* that qualifies something for warranting moral concern, not what *kind* of thing it is.

3. HOW CAN WE DETERMINE THE ONTOLOGICAL STATUS OF THE SELF?

So, how do we *decide* whether or not 'self' or 'person' denotes a fundamental ontological category? Well, one obvious way of proceeding is to see whether or not we can rule out all alternative possibilities. So let us begin by examining whether we can at all plausibly regard the term 'self' as picking out a certain 'functional role' which things of various *different* kinds could potentially occupy—rather as very differently shaped and composed material objects can occupy the functional role of the *bishop* in a game of chess. Now, we can see well enough how an arbitrarily shaped piece of wood or metal could occupy the bishop's role in a chess game, since its occupying that role is simply a matter of its being moved around the chessboard in accordance with the rules governing the movement of a bishop. So the idea would be that if something, of whatever fundamental kind, could be *a subject of thoughts about itself*, then it could thereby qualify as *being* a self or person, in virtue of occupying the 'self' role. If an *animal*—a living organism—could do that, then *it* could be a person, and if an animal's *brain* could do that, then *it* could be a person's brain, and so forth.

But, it may be asked, what about *my own actual case*? Our question now seems to reduce to something like this: What is it that does *my* thinking? Whatever it is, that thing is *me*, and *what* I am is the kind of thing that *it* is. Thus, if it is a *living organism* that does my thinking, then I am that organism and *what* I am is a living organism. Similarly, if it is a *brain* that does my thinking, then I am that brain and *what* I am is a brain. Similarly again, if it is an *immaterial spirit* that does my thinking, then I am that spirit and *what* I am is a spirit. And if *any* such answer is correct, then it will follow that 'self' or 'person' certainly does *not* denote a fundamental ontological category.

4. AN UNACCEPTABLE ANSWER TO THE QUESTION: NIHILISM

What, however, if we find that *no* such answer is forthcoming? Suppose I find that, plausibly, there is *no* entity that belongs to an independently acknowledged ontological category that can plausibly be identified with *me*. One imaginable response would be the *nihilist* one of deciding that, after all, I *don't exist*—there is no such thing as 'me'. But any such answer teeters on the edge of at least pragmatic inconsistency and seems at best a desperate last resort. Descartes's confidence in his own *existence* does not seem to be misplaced. Part of the reason for this is that it seems incoherent to suppose that there could be thoughts without a *subject* of those thoughts, so that to deny one's existence is to deny also the existence of one's thoughts—and yet the very raising of the question 'What am I?' seems to presuppose the reality of my thoughts, since it actually expresses one such thought.

But, it may be asked, why *must* thoughts have a subject? Ultimately, I think they must because thoughts can only be *individuated* by their subjects—and unless they can be individuated, little sense can be attached to the idea that numerically distinct thoughts really exist at all. By 'individuated' here I don't just mean, of course, *singled out in thought*, but *singled out in reality*.[4] Something in reality must make one individual thought distinct from another—and the mere content of a thought, even taken together with its time and place of occurrence (if indeed thoughts can be said to be spatially located), does not serve do this. Distinct thoughts, with the *same* contents, occurring at the *same* space-time locations, can very plausibly exist, at least in principle.

No one disputes, I suppose, that distinct thoughts with the same contents can occur at the same *time*, since you and I might now be having thoughts with the same content. Now, if one could uncontentiously identify a thought with, say, a *neural event*, and argue that no two neural events realizing the same thought content could occur in the same place and the same time, then one could argue that thoughts are individuated by their contents and space-time locations. But that is a very big 'if'. Quite apart from the difficulty of establishing that a thought is identifiable with a neural event, it simply doesn't appear to be the case that events *of the same kind* can't occur in the same place and the same time. Events aren't like material objects in this respect—they don't exclude others of their kind from their space-time locations. They aren't 'impenetrable'. For instance, three armies could be fighting three different battles in the same place at the same time, each participating pairwise in two battles with each of the other two, A with B, B with C, and C with A. This is quite different, for example, from the case in which A and B are fighting together in an alliance against C. Here we see that the battles occurring in a given space-time location can only be individuated in terms of the *armies* that are fighting them. The same applies, *mutatis mutandis*, to all events and hence to thoughts in particular. They are individuated in terms of their *subjects*—the things *having* those thoughts. Two different subjects can't have numerically the same thought. So we can't deny the existence of subjects of thought—things occupying the role of 'self'—without denying the distinctness and thus the very existence of individual thoughts.

5. NARROWING DOWN THE POSSIBLE CANDIDATES

So *nihilism* with regard to the self, and *myself* in particular, seems not to be a coherent option (though this is an issue that I shall return to later, when I discuss the idea that the self is a 'fiction' created by the brain). I am *something*—and so a thing of *some* kind. But suppose, again, that I can discover no independently acknowledged kind of thing that is capable of occupying the 'self' role in my case. Suppose, for example, I can rule out the possibility that my *organism*, or my *brain*, or my putative *immaterial spirit*, and so on could be the thing that does my thinking: What then should I conclude concerning *what I am*? I think I would have to conclude that I am just *fundamentally* a self or person: that these terms must after all denote a fundamental ontological category, to which I belong.

Now, obviously, to argue conclusively in this fashion I would have to first identify every possible independently acknowledgeable ontological category and rule it out as one to which I could belong—and this is, to say the least, a very tall order. First of all, I don't know what the complete inventory of such categories is, since there may be kinds of things that have never yet been dreamt of in my philosophy, or anyone else's. So I am going to try to make things easier for myself by assuming that the most likely candidates for identity with *me*, amongst those things that we independently acknowledge to exist, are all going to be *bodily* entities of some kind. For—setting aside external world scepticism and idealism—we are pretty confident that bodily entities *do* exist and indeed that *we* have bodies. We also take ourselves—or, at least, scientists—to know quite a lot about these bodies and how they function. We know, for instance, that *our* bodies are living organisms composed of organic matter, organized in various ways into various parts and systems, including organs (such as the liver and brain) and cells (such as blood cells and nerve cells). What I want to rule out, then, is my identity with anything of any of *these* kinds—organisms, their organs, their cells, or various assemblies of such cells into systems of various kinds, such as central nervous systems.

In taking this approach, I admit that I am being somewhat unfair to those who believe that we are, or are at least partly composed of, *immaterial souls or spirits*. But the fact is that I don't have a clear enough grasp of what such an entity is supposed to *be* in order to get to grips adequately with this view. Furthermore, it is certainly *not* uncontentious that such things exist. If we did know clearly what they are and were reasonably confident that they do exist, then, certainly, it would be incumbent on me to take seriously the possibility that I am an immaterial soul or spirit. But as matters presently stand, I don't think it is.

6. SOME ARGUMENTS THAT WILL NOT SERVE OUR PURPOSE

So I take it that the challenge before me is to show that I am not identifiable with anything that we may reasonably categorize as *bodily* in nature. Now, prior to trying to rise to this challenge, I want to rule out certain other attempts to establish this conclusion. First of all, there are Descartes's own arguments to this effect, of which there are basically two: his *conceivability* argument and his *divisibility* argument. The conceivability argument proceeds from the premise that my existence without a body of any kind is at least *conceivable* and so (he thinks) possible, to the conclusion that I am not identifiable with anything bodily. This falls foul of the objection that what is conceivable is not necessarily really possible—unless one simply uses 'conceivable' as a synonym for 'possible', in which case the argument is question-begging. The divisibility argument proceeds from the premise that all bodily things are *divisible* but I am not. However, the claim that I am not divisible again seems question-begging in this context and, in any case, needs to be supported by some sort of argument. For my own part, I am in fact strongly inclined to think that I am indivisible, but I don't think that this claim can be supported without an independent argument that I am not identifiable with anything bodily (see Lowe 2001).

One other argument that I shall not appeal to here is one that I have elsewhere defended and called the *replacement* argument (see Lowe 2009; Baker 2000: 122–123). This argument proceeds from the premise that I could survive even if all the parts of my existing, biological body were to be replaced—gradually, of course—by non-biological substitutes, provided that this could be done without destroying my capacity for self-reflective thought. However, the trouble with this argument is, first, that it makes an empirical claim for which, at present, we have no firm corroborative evidence, however much it might seem to be borne out by examples from science fiction literature. Even more fundamentally, though, the problem with this argument is that it can't rule out the possibility that I am something 'bodily' in a more extended sense of the term. It would show at best that I could not be identified with a particular living organism or living organic part of one, such as my current living brain—where by 'living' I mean 'alive' in the biological sense of the term. But it wouldn't rule out the possibility that I am some kind of *bodily system*, such as my central nervous system, since it may be argued that the identity of such a system is not necessarily tied to its having a specifically *biological* constitution. Indeed, there is even a sense of 'brain', perhaps, in which we could talk of the same 'brain' surviving a change from being composed of organic cells to being composed of silicon-based electronic circuits, provided that it *functioned* in the same way (although I suspect that this is, really, to think of the brain as being a kind of *system* rather than a kind of *object*). So, while I think that the replacement argument is not entirely without merits, it does not really serve the purpose I now have of showing that I am not to be identified with *anything* that can deservedly be said to be 'bodily' (excluding, of course, that uncontentious sense of 'bodily' in which I am a 'bodily' thing in virtue of *having* a body, or being 'embodied').

7. THE UNITY ARGUMENT: PRELIMINARY CONSIDERATIONS

The argument that I think will serve this purpose better than any other is what I call the *unity* argument, so let us now proceed to examine it.[5] The key premise of the unity argument appeals to a thesis that I defended a little while ago. This is that each of my thoughts has just *one* subject and all of them have the *same* subject—that subject being, of course, *me*, whatever I am. Moreover, no thought that is *not* a thought of mine can have this same subject—it must be a thought of a numerically distinct subject, *someone else*. In sum, all and only *my* thoughts have just one thing, *me*, as their unique subject. Furthermore, in having me as their subject, all of these thoughts *depend upon* me for their very existence—they do so because they depend upon me for their *identity*, and any thing's identity is obviously essential to it.

In saying that each of my thoughts *depends upon me for its identity*, I am simply appealing once more to the fact that thoughts are individuated, at least in part, by their subjects—*which* thought a particular thought is being determined, at least in part, by *whose* thought it is. Of course, a thought's subject doesn't *completely* determine the identity of the thought, since the same subject may have many different thoughts, both over time and at the same time. Plausibly, however, a thought's identity *is* completely determined by its *subject*, *time*, and *content*. Its *place* doesn't seem to play a significant role in this respect, if indeed thoughts can really be said to have spatial locations at all. I am inclined to say that a thought's place, *if any*, is just to be identified with the place of its subject. Thus, my present thoughts are located, if anywhere, wherever it is that I am presently located. No finer-grained spatial location can be assigned to a thought than this. Some will perhaps object that my thoughts must at least be located in my *brain*—but *why*, unless indeed I *am* my brain? If I am *not* my brain, then my brain is not the subject of my thoughts—and, while it may nonetheless be agreed that I *need* a brain in order to have thoughts, *that* doesn't imply that my thoughts are *in* my brain, any more than the fact that I need legs in order to run implies that my running is *in* my legs.

Now, having agreed, for the foregoing reasons, that all and only *my* thoughts depend upon *me* for their very existence—that is, that without *my* existence *they* wouldn't exist—we can proceed to ask whether *bodily* things of various specifiable kinds are such that all and only *my* thoughts couldn't exist without a unique thing of one of *those* kinds existing. Let X be a candidate thing of one of these kinds. If we can establish that it is *not* the case that all and only *my* thoughts depend for their existence on X, then we have ruled out the possibility that I *am* X. So, what are the candidate things of these putative kinds? What kinds of 'bodily' thing might we hope to identify a person or self—and, more particularly, *me*—with? One obvious possibility is *whole living organisms*, that is, individual *animals*. (I assume that *plants* may be ruled out and, in any case, I surely couldn't be identified with any plant, since there seems to be none in my vicinity that is even a *possible* candidate.) Another possibility is some kind of bodily *organ* of an animal, such as, most obviously, animal *brains*—hence, in my case, a certain *human* brain. Another possibility is some distinguished *part* of such an organ, such as a human *cerebral cortex*. Yet another is some bodily *system* of an animal, such as a human central nervous system.

However, we have to be careful about how, exactly, we understand and talk of a 'system' in this sense. It would seem that a *subject* of thoughts must be a *thing* of some kind, by which I mean a concrete *object* of some kind—for it has to be something that has *properties* and exists in *time* (and probably in space too) and that can participate in *events*. It cannot, therefore, be a purely *abstract* entity. Often, when we talk of 'systems', we do mean to talk about purely abstract entities—for instance, the Dewey decimal system of library cataloguing. An example of a *concrete* system, in contrast, would be our *solar system*, consisting of the sun and the various planetary and other bodies orbiting it. A concrete system in this sense must certainly *consist of* concrete objects or things, even if it is not just the *sum* of those things, since it is necessary also for the existence of the system that the things in question should be *related* or *interact* in certain characteristic and relatively stable ways. If all the planets of the solar system were to be attracted away from the sun by other stars, then our *solar system* would no longer exist. It is an open question, perhaps, whether we should really call such a concrete system a concrete *object* in its own right, but I am not averse to saying precisely this and will assume for present purposes that it is legitimate to do so. Here, however, I just want to emphasise that a concrete system must certainly have various concrete objects amongst its *parts*. Thus, a human central nervous system will include many billions of nerve cells amongst its parts, just as a human brain and cerebral cortex do. If we call brains concrete *objects* rather than concrete *systems*, then this might either be a distinction without much of a real difference or else, perhaps, we do so because the parts of a *system* are restricted to things which play some *systemic role* in the system, whereas the parts of an *object* need not be. For instance, it might be held that the only cells involved in a human central nervous system are nerve cells which play a systemic role in such a system, whereas a human brain can include as genuine proper parts cells which are not crucial to the *functioning* of the brain as such.

8. RULING OUT THE 'ANIMAL' ANSWER

Anyway, we have now narrowed down the kinds of 'bodily' things that might, with any degree of plausibility, be identified with *me*. So let us see whether any one of them passes the crucial test of being such that all and only *my* thoughts depend upon *it* for their existence. We can begin with the whole living organism or animal body that I call 'mine'. Call it A. Do all and only *my* thoughts depend for their existence upon A? Of course, Descartes would answer emphatically 'No', because he believes that I and all my thoughts could exist without my having any animal body *at all*—that I could survive complete disembodiment—basing this on the alleged conceivability of such an eventuality. But we are not easily persuaded of the truth of this. Let us then concede, at least for the sake of argument, that I could *not* exist without a body of any kind. And, since A *is* a body of some kind, let us again ask whether it passes the test for being identical with *me*.

It seems *not*, for the following reason. If even just *one* of my thoughts, call it T, could exist without A existing, then A is not identical with me—since T couldn't exist without *me* existing—and yet it does seem that at least some of my thoughts meet this condition. Remember that A is supposed to be an *entire human animal*, which I take to be something that is not only *living* but which has, of necessity, certain distinctive kinds of bodily organs and a certain distinctive structure or 'body-plan'. A human *heart*, for instance, cannot qualify as an entire human animal, even if it is kept alive by some sort of life-support machine, nor is the concrete system consisting of the living heart attached to and supported by the machine an *entire human animal*. Now, is it the case that *none* of my thoughts could exist without a certain *entire human animal* existing? Surely not. Very plausibly, for instance, a great many of my thoughts could exist even if all that were left of my animal body, following some horrible accident, were my *head*, kept alive by a life-support machine. A living human head, whether or not attached to a life-support machine—and, indeed, whether or not attached to the rest of an entire human animal—cannot by any reasonable standard be said to *be* an entire human animal.

At this point, philosophers who favour the answer that I am indeed identical with A are sometimes prone to argue as follows.[6] They sometimes urge that, while perhaps a living human head which had *never* been 'attached' to the rest of a normal human animal body might not qualify as an 'entire human animal', nonetheless, in the dreadful circumstances just envisaged, *my* human animal, A, would *continue* to be an 'entire human animal', and so continue to *exist*, but simply be radically reduced in size and radically mutilated in form and structure. If that were so, of course, then we couldn't conclude, from the possibility of such an accident, that some of my thoughts could exist without A existing—for A *would* still exist in the envisaged scenario. Now, this looks very much like a purely *ad hoc* manoeuvre to save the favoured thesis. Such philosophers do, however, have a supplementary line of argument in support of their position. They tend to say that a normal, entire human animal does not literally *have* a 'head', conceived as a real part of that animal and thus as something which could survive the destruction of the animal. What they deny is that things like animals really have any 'undetached parts', with things like heads, arms, and various bodily organs, such as the heart and liver, being examples of such supposed parts.[7] If that is so, of course, then my animal cannot cease to exist while just its *head* carries on existing, because there is literally *no such thing* as my animal's head. Hence, if anything bodily goes on existing after my dreadful accident, it seems that it must just be *my animal*, A, albeit in a horribly reduced and mutilated form.

Now, I have *some* sympathy for the idea that it is a mistake to identify one of the 'parts' of a living human animal as being its 'head', if only because it seems to be rather arbitrary how we delineate the boundaries of such a thing. Where, for instance, does my *head* stop and my *neck* begin? On the other hand, this kind of worry is rather less pressing in the case of human *organs*, such as the heart and liver, whose boundaries seem less arbitrary, because those organs are associated with specific biological functions, unlike the 'head' and the 'neck'. Be that as it may, however, it still seems to me utterly compelling that, whether or not the bodily thing that survives my dreadful accident can properly be called my 'head', this thing, *whatever* it is—and it surely is *something*—is not by any reasonable standard *an entire human animal*. The accident surely brings about the *destruction* of my human animal, A, even though it does not necessarily bring about *my* destruction—because some of *my* thoughts can still exist in these circumstances. Hence, I cannot be identical with A. It really doesn't matter precisely how we categorize the bodily thing that survives the accident, so long as we recognize that we can by no stretch of the imagination categorize it properly as being an *entire human animal*, which is what A is. Hence, A does not survive the accident and, consequently, cannot be identical with *me*.

9. RULING OUT THE 'BRAIN' ANSWER: A FIRST ATTEMPT

We seem, then, to have eliminated *one* candidate answer to the question 'What am I?'. I am *not* my 'entire human animal', A, because it is not the case that all and only *my* thoughts depend for their existence on A.

However, many 'scientifically' minded people would not profess to be at all surprised by this conclusion, because they think that there is a much better bodily candidate for identity with me, namely, *my brain*. After all, they may point out, it seems clear as a matter of empirical fact that one *needs* a brain to be able to think, whereas one does not need a heart or a liver or arms or legs—because, they may say, it is the *function* of the brain to be the 'organ' of thought, whereas the heart and liver have quite different functions and the arms and legs, which serve several different purposes, are certainly not essentially involved in thinking. Very well, but is it then the case that all and only *my* thoughts depend for their existence on my *brain*—call it B? If they don't, then I am not *identical* with B, for now familiar reasons.

Now, even if the boundaries of the brain are easier to identify in a principled way than the boundaries of the 'head' or the 'neck', it is still true that there is some vagueness involved in specifying them. Consequently, there may be, perhaps, in at least some cases, 'no fact of the matter' as to whether a certain nerve cell really is a *part* of my brain. In other cases, there will be no question about this. A nerve cell in my *foot* is certainly not a part of my brain, whereas a functioning nerve cell in the middle of my cerebral cortex almost certainly *is* (setting aside bizarre cases such as, perhaps, one involving the recent transplant of a nerve from my foot into my brain). However, I don't want—here, at least—to try to capitalize on such vagueness in order to argue that I am not identical with B: a strategy which, if it worked, could equally be applied in the case of A, of course. There may well be some philosophical mileage in this sort of consideration, since it seems highly questionable that there is any vagueness about the identity of the *self* (cf. Unger 2006: ch.7). But let us set that consideration aside for present purposes. Let us agree that my brain, B, definitely exists and pretend, at least, that there is no indeterminacy regarding *which* bodily thing B is. Let us also agree that if I had *no brain at all*, none of my thoughts would exist.

Does this imply that all and only *my* thoughts depend for their existence on my brain, B, as they need to if I am to be *identified* with B? I am going to disregard here any appeal to science fiction scenarios involving 'teletransportation' and the like, for one of the reasons that I set aside the replacement argument earlier—they are simply too speculative at present. But can we perhaps construct an argument regarding B's candidacy for identity with me along the same lines as the argument used earlier to rule out A's candidacy? In other words, can it be argued that at least some of my thoughts could still exist even if B didn't exist, on the grounds that it would be enough for these thoughts to exist that some *part* of B—such as, very plausibly, the cerebral cortex, call it C—still existed (aided by a life-support machine, if need be) and that C could not be regarded as being identical with B itself in a much reduced and mutilated form? I think that this *is* fairly plausible, in fact. Thought does seem to be associated in particular with the cortex and by no reasonable standard can a human cortex on its own be described as an entire human brain. However, it should be clear that this manner of ruling out bodily candidates for identity with me cannot be reiterated indefinitely. A single neuron, for example, or even an assembly of several hundred neurons, cannot plausibly be claimed to be sufficient to support thought of any kind at all. Moreover, once we get down, say, to the level of individual lobes of the cortex, there comes a point at which further reduction in size does not plausibly leave us with some functionally distinct part of a human brain which cannot be regarded as being just a reduced and mutilated version of some higher-level part. With that fact in mind, we would perhaps be wise not even to pursue the current strategy for eliminating potential bodily candidates even as far as C, but leave it at B, my brain as a whole.

10. A NEW STRATEGY: PRELIMINARY CONSIDERATIONS

So we are now left looking for some new strategy to rule out the candidacy of B for identity with me. Here two further pertinent facts may be called upon. The first is that, as far as we know, our thoughts do not depend on our brains in a completely holistic fashion, with *every* thought depending on the *whole* brain. Rather, *different* thoughts very often depend on *different* parts of the brain. This is particularly clear in the case of commissurotomy patients, whose severed cerebral hemispheres fairly evidently support different thought processes—a fact that is further confirmed by patients who have undergone hemispherectomy, leaving them with just one hemisphere but still with a capacity for thought. Secondly, we should not lose sight of the kind of *dependency* that we are really concerned with at present—the ontological dependency of a thought upon its subject, which arises because thoughts are partly individuated by their subjects and thus have their identity determined by those subjects. But is this the kind of dependency that is involved when thoughts are said to be *dependent* on the brain, or on various parts of the brain? Very plausibly *not*. The most we can say, it seems, is that without a brain there can be no *capacity* for thought and hence no individual thoughts. This doesn't imply that the brain, or any part of it, is something that serves in any way to *individuate* a thought, in the sense in which the thought's subject does. Moreover, another thing that we know about human brains is that they are fairly plastic or flexible, being capable of large-scale 're-wiring', particularly in response to damage. Thoughts which might be supported by one area of the brain prior to such damage may later be supported by another. All of these considerations suggest that the kind of 'dependency' that my thoughts have upon my brain is quite different in structure and character from the ontological dependency that all my thoughts have upon *me*, as their unique *subject*.

However, I concede that this line of argument, as it stands, may appear to be less than fully compelling to someone favourable to the hypothesis that I *am* my brain, B—so let us take another track, albeit one that draws in part upon the same considerations. This new line of argument will require me to reject the view that things like B have no 'undetached parts'.

Why My Body Is Not Me 257

However, this rejection is something that I am already strongly committed to and find extremely plausible. B surely has, as undetached parts, at least such parts as individual *neurons* and various assemblies of these. Indeed, B itself, let us suppose, is wholly composed of individual neurons (ignoring, for the purposes of argument, the various other kinds of cell that we actually find within human brains). There may be some indeterminacy regarding *which* individual neurons belong to B, even though there is no such question concerning the vast majority of them. For instance, it might be debatable whether a certain neuron belonged properly to B or was one of the optic nerves. But let us, once more, ignore such issues of vagueness here, and pretend that B is composed of a perfectly determinate set of neurons—a very large set, of course. Then we can proceed to argue as follows.

11. THE NEW STRATEGY FOR IMPLEMENTING THE UNITY ARGUMENT

Allowing as we are that B has undetached parts, we can surely identify some *small* part of B, call it D, which is wholly composed by some small subset of the neurons composing B. By the same token, we can identify a much larger part of B, call it E, which is D's 'complement' in B—that is to say, E is composed by all and only the neurons in B that do *not* help to compose D. (If it is worried that a 'complement' of one object in another is somehow a less than fully *bona fide* object, then we could instead take D to be the complement of E in B, thereby forestalling any objection to the ensuing argument that might be made on the grounds that E is somehow inferior to B with regard to its status as an 'object'. Since we have this move to fall back on if required, however, I shall not in fact make it in the argument that follows.) Furthermore, let us select D on the following basis. First, D should be a part of B which is such that it is *not* the case that *all* of my thoughts depend upon it. Since—as was remarked earlier—my thoughts, to the extent that they depend on B, very plausibly do not depend on it in an entirely *holistic* way, with *every* thought depending on the *whole* of B, we have every reason to believe that a small part of B, such as D, *can* meet this condition. (Later, however, we shall consider the repercussions of denying this assumption.) Second, let us suppose D to be small enough that *no* thought of mine depends on D but *not* on D's complement in B, E. Again, we have every reason to suppose that a small part of B, such as D, which is composed by only a small subset of B's neurons, *can* satisfy this condition, since it is very plausible to suppose that a small assembly of neurons—say, a few hundred of them—is not sufficient on its own to support thought of any kind. (Again, however, we shall later consider the consequences of denying this assumption.)

With these assumptions in place, we can conclude, first of all, that every thought of mine that depends on B *also* depends on E. Why? Because the only material difference between B and E consists in B's inclusion of D—and we have assumed, as we are plausibly entitled to, that no thought of mine that depends on *D* does not *also* depend on *E*. Hence, there can be no thought of mine that depends on *B* but *not* on *E* in virtue of depending on *D*—and also no thought of mine that depends on *B* but *not* on *E* for any other reason, because *B*'s inclusion of *D* is the only material difference between *B* and *E*. Thus, as I say, every thought of mine that depends on *B* *also* depends on *E*. Equally, however, every thought of mine that depends on *E* very plausibly *also* depends on *B*, simply because *E* is a *proper part* of *B*. (In any case, since we are arguing against philosophers who hold that *all* my thoughts depend on *B*—since they contend that I *am B*—we are dialectically entitled to make this assumption here.) Hence, in particular, if *all* my thoughts depend on *B*, then it is *also* true that *all* my thoughts depend on *E*, and vice versa. *That* being so, however, it seems clear that *dependency* considerations do not favour *B*'s candidacy for identity with me any *more* than they favour *E*'s candidacy. In respect of such considerations, *B* and *E* are in fact *equally good* candidates for identity with me, to the extent that either of them is a candidate at all. The mere facts that *B* is *bigger than* and *includes E* cannot be deemed at all relevant in this regard, for these facts have nothing to do with the *dependency* relations between the thoughts in question and the objects *B* and *E*. If those other facts concerning size and parthood relations *were* relevant, they would equally count against the candidacy of *B* for identity with me, at least while *B* is an undetached part of *A*—for they would count in favour of the candidacy of *A*, my entire human animal. However, we have already ruled out *A*'s candidacy, which shows that those facts are indeed irrelevant for present purposes.

Might it not be objected here that a relevant difference between *B* and *E* is the following? *B* includes a part, *D*, on which, we have allowed, *some* of my thoughts depend, even if all of those thoughts *also* depend on *E*—whereas *E*, of course, does not include that part. But this objection, if sound, would imply that the best candidate for identity with me would in fact be the *largest* object, *O*, *every* part *P* of which is such that some thoughts of mine depend on *P*, even if *P* is a part of *O* on which no thoughts of mine depend without *also* depending on *P*'s complement in *O*. In that case, however, *B* itself would be ruled out as the best candidate for identity with me. Consider, for instance, the object *O* that includes as proper parts *B* and some blood vessel, *V*, leading into *B*. Very plausibly, *some* of my thoughts depend on *V*, since if the blood-flows that it carries were cut off, my thought-capacity would be diminished—and yet *V* is not the sort of thing on which any thought of mine can depend without *also* depending on *B*, since *V* is obviously not sufficient on its own to support thought of any kind. So, in this regard, *V* stands to *B* just as *D* stands to *E*. Consequently, if *B* trumps *E* on account of including *D*, so too does *O* trump *B* on account of including *V*. Indeed, this method of argument is quite likely to reinstate *A*, my entire human animal, as the best candidate for identity with me. But, once more, we have already ruled out *A*, so this method of argument must be flawed and cannot be used to prefer the candidacy of *B* over that of *E*.

Now, clearly, if *B* and *E* are *equally* good candidates for identity with me, then they rule *each other* out for identity with me. For *B* and *E* are numerically distinct objects, being composed of different sets of neurons and having different shapes and sizes, whereas I am just *one* thing. So *B* and *E* cannot *both* be identical with me. But neither can we with any good reason say that *B rather than E*, nor that *E rather than B*, is identical with me, for that would be to ignore the fact that they are *equally good* candidates, so that it would be arbitrary to favour one over the other. The only remaining option available, however, is to say that *neither B nor E* is identical with me. It is no good contending that *B* and *E* are *both* subjects of my thoughts, for this would deprive those thoughts of a unique subject and thereby deprive them of their identity and hence of their existence. If *B* and *E* are subjects of thoughts *at all*, then they are subjects of *numerically distinct* thoughts, since *B* and *E* are numerically distinct objects.

12. HOW THE NEW STRATEGY MAY BE REITERATED

We are now in possession of an argumentative strategy which *can* be reiterated, if need be, as often as is desired. Suppose, for instance, that it were contended—contrary to our earlier assumptions—that there *is* in fact some small part of my brain, *D*, composed perhaps of just a few hundred neurons, which is such that *all* of my thoughts depend upon *it* and, indeed, that *no* thought of mine depends on *D*'s complement in *B*, *E*. Thus, *D* would apparently be a part of my brain such that, *if it were entirely destroyed*, I would lose my capacity for thought altogether. (Of course, this is a highly implausible hypothesis, but let us set that fact aside for the purposes of argument.) Could it then be plausibly contended that I am identical with *D*? Certainly not: for *D*, even though it contains just a few hundred neurons, is still a very complex object, compositionally speaking. Each neuron in *D* is composed of many subcellular objects, such as mitochondria, and these in turn are composed of complex organic molecules, which in turn are composed of many subatomic particles. It is utterly implausible to suppose that there is no *small part* of *D*, call it *F*, whose complement in *D*—call it *G*—is not just as good a candidate as *D* itself for identity with me, in terms of the dependency relations that obtain between my thoughts and *D* and *G*, respectively. For even supposing that if *D* were *entirely* destroyed, then so too would be my capacity for thought, it cannot plausibly be supposed that the destruction of *D*'s small part, *F*, would have this consequence. Furthermore, even if this *were* supposed, we could then run again the same line of argument with respect to *F* itself and some small part of *it*. Sooner or later we shall have to arrive at some small part of my brain, such as a certain individual neuron, *N*, which is such that it would be *completely* implausible to suppose that the entire destruction of *that* object is both necessary and sufficient for the complete destruction of my capacity for thought.

What all of this brings out is simply the fact that my capacity for thought, and hence my thoughts themselves, do not depend *collectively* on any *single* bodily object, neither my brain as a whole, *B*, nor any distinguishable part of it, such as *D*, *F* or *N*. Rather, my thoughts depend in a *distributive* fashion on various different and overlapping parts of my brain. But this simply isn't the way in which my thoughts all depend upon *me*, as their subject. Rather, they all depend *collectively* on me, such that were I to cease to exist, then so would *they*—each and every one of them. This is why I call the present line of argument the *unity* argument, because it appeals to the *unified* way in which all of my thoughts depend upon *me* as their subject, in contrast with the thoroughly *disunified* way in which they depend *individually* on different parts of my brain. This fundamental structural difference in the nature of the dependency relations involved is sufficient to establish the nonidentity of me with *any* of these bodily things, even if we abstract from the distinction between 'causal' and 'ontological' dependency.

This, then, is a strategy which can be used to argue against the identification of *any* part of my body with me—including, indeed, its sole 'proper' part, my entire human animal, *A* (even though we are already in possession of another argument against my identity with *A*). Now, I mentioned earlier certain *other* bodily candidates for identity with me, namely, certain bodily *systems*, such as my central nervous system (CNS). However, the same strategy can be deployed once again with respect to these, given that, for reasons provided earlier, we are regarding such systems as *concrete* ones, possessing various bodily objects as parts—in the case of my CNS, obviously, *nerve cells*. For, just as we can consider large proper 'undetached' parts of complex bodily parts—for instance, *E* as a large proper part of my brain, *B*—so, similarly, we can consider large *subsystems* of any given bodily system, such as my CNS. And, once again, since it is surely not the case that all of my thoughts depend holistically on the *whole* of any such system, it will follow that all of my thoughts in fact depend on various large *sub*systems of such a system just as much as they do upon the whole system. From this it will follow, once more, that the whole system and such a subsystem are equally good candidates for identity with me and so in fact also equally *bad* ones, for they rule each other out. Thus, the distinction between bodily *parts* and bodily *systems* is not really relevant as far as the applicability of the unity argument is concerned. Given that, between them, bodily parts and bodily systems exhaust all the possible bodily candidates for identity with me, we can conclude that I am *nothing* bodily at all. This isn't to say that I am something that could, even in principle, be *disembodied*, just that I am not *myself* a body, nor a part of a body, nor a bodily system, nor a part of such a system.

13. AN EMERGENTIST ANSWER TO THE QUESTION

What, then, *am* I? I am just a *self* or *person*—a subject of thought and agent of actions. It seems that we must regard this as a *basic ontological category*, not just a 'functional role' which can be occupied by things of various more fundamental kinds. We can neither *identify* any particular self with an entity of some more fundamental kind, nor *reduce* selves to such entities by showing that they can occupy the 'functional role' of the self. Indeed, we may usefully compare these positions concerning the ontological status of selves with analogous positions in the metaphysics of mental *properties*—identity theories, psychophysical reductionism, and dualism, this last position maintaining that mental properties are *distinct from* and *irreducible to* physical ones (cf. Beckermann 2009). Analogously, then, I am saying that selves are *distinct from* and *irreducible to* bodies and bodily systems. So this is a *dualism* of self and body.

But nothing that I have said in defense of it supports a *Cartesian* dualism of self and body, which maintains that selves are not only distinct from and irreducible to bodies and bodily systems, but in addition that selves are *ontologically separable* from bodies and bodily systems, in the sense that selves can exist in a completely disembodied state. The analogous position in the metaphysics of mental properties would be to say that these can be exemplified quite independently of the exemplification of any physical properties—a claim to which the Cartesian substance dualist is in fact obviously committed. But my arguments in favour of self–body dualism leave open the possibility that mental properties can only be exemplified at all if they are *co*-exemplified with suitable physical properties.

This suggests a position regarding the ontological status of the self which deserves to be called *emergentist*. And, indeed, I am happy to call my view of the self an emergentist one, provided that we understand that such a view can be called 'physicalist' at best only in a rather anodyne and misleading sense. Certainly, though, I am happy to concede that it is very probably the case that selves can come into existence only in certain complex physical circumstances, in the absence of which they very probably cannot continue to exist. *Selves* and their exemplifications of *mental* properties may, then, very well depend ontologically upon the existence of *bodies* and their exemplifications of *physical* properties, but *not* in a way that implies that the former are identical with or reducible to the latter. Furthermore, this kind of ontological dependency need not exclude the possibility that the *causal powers* of selves, as agents of actions and subjects of perception, are also neither identical with nor reducible to the causal powers of bodies or bodily systems of any kind. Indeed, I think there are strong arguments in favour of the *causal autonomy* of selves—by which I mean their possession of distinct and irreducible causal powers—although I shall not go into them here (see Lowe 2008).

14. FICTIONALISM CONCERNING THE SELF DEFEATED

Now, I anticipate that scepticism regarding self-body dualism, even of my non-Cartesian kind, will not have been entirely dissipated by my preceding arguments and elucidations. Some 'hard-nosed' physicalists will urge that the 'self' is just a *fiction*—one that the brain itself somehow creates. The suggestion is that thoughts *present themselves* as belonging to, or being thought by, a person or self, often because reference to such an 'owner' is explicit or implicit in the *content* of a thought. Certain thoughts present themselves as 'me'-thoughts, such as the thought that I now feel hungry—which is quite different from the impersonal thought that *there exist now feelings of hunger*. It may be maintained that it has proved advantageous, in evolutionary terms, for the brains of certain animals to generate such personal or 'me'-thoughts, perhaps because they prompt more immediate and appropriately focussed action—for instance, a brain that creates an *I-feel-hungry-now* thought is perhaps more likely to receive rapid sustenance than one that merely creates a *there-now-exist-feelings-of-hunger* thought.

However, this sort of theory comes up once more against the difficulty of explaining how thoughts are *individuated*, if not at least partly in terms of their *subjects*. It will not do to say that they are individuated in terms of their *causes and effects*, because at least some, and in fact very many, of the causes and effects of any given thought will be *other thoughts*—for the most part, other thoughts *of the same subject*. Hence, this proposal falls victim to an implicit circularity in its account of the individuation of thoughts (see Lowe 1996: 27–30). In fact, the notion of a thought *without* a thinker seems, on reflection, to be barely coherent. To regard *thinkers* as fictions really requires one to regard *thoughts* as fictions too—and this way lies manifest absurdity for the theory being propounded. For the very notion of a *fiction* presupposes the genuine applicability of the notion of *thought*: a fiction just *is* something that is merely *thought of* as existing or being the case, when really it does not or is not. Thus, the Land of Oz is a fiction, because it is thought of—by readers of the book or viewers of the film—as existing, when in reality it does not exist. To say that *thoughts* are fictions is, correspondingly, to say that they are *thought of* as existing, when really they do not—but then at least the *thoughts* of their existing must exist, whence it is false to say that thoughts are just fictions. A fictionalist theory of thoughts is a contradiction in terms. And, as I say, a fictionalist theory of *thinkers* is committed, ultimately, to a fictionalist theory of thoughts, whence it too is inadmissible on pain of contradiction.

15. THE PHENOMENON OF 'THOUGHT-INSERTION': NO OBJECTION

Another kind of challenge that I anticipate is this: it may be urged that there is a good sense in which, paradoxical though it may sound, it simply isn't true that all and only *my* thoughts necessarily have the same subject—*me*. For some individuals who are suffering from certain psychopathological conditions report that *other people's* thoughts are somehow intruding into their own minds—a phenomenon known as 'thought-insertion' (see Stephens and Graham 2000). Of course, it is surely never literally *true* that someone else is thinking a thought in *my* mind, through some sort of process of telepathy. The phenomenon of thought-insertion is, after all, a *delusional* one. But doesn't the fact that the delusion can even *arise* tell us something important about how we conceive of the relationship between thoughts and thinkers? Doesn't it show that it at least makes sense to dissociate the *subject* of a thought—the person whose thought it is, or who is *thinking* the thought—from the person in whose consciousness the thought arises? And if so, doesn't that imply that the thesis that all and only 'my' thoughts must have *me* as their subject is not quite as self-evidently true as might be supposed? For if a thought could, at least in principle, arise in *my* consciousness but have *another person* as its subject or thinker, then there would be a perfectly good sense in which this thought would be one of 'my' thoughts—in virtue of manifesting itself in *my* consciousness—and yet not be a thought of *mine*, that is, not be thought *by me* and therefore not be individuated by *me* as its subject.

Well, I confess that I can really make no clear sense of this suggestion. I think we have to say that someone suffering from the delusion of thought-insertion really is not just *mistaken* about their condition but radically *confused* concerning it. A thought which manifests itself in *my* consciousness is *ipso facto* a thought of *mine*, which is thought *by me* as its subject. I suspect that what sufferers from this delusion are trying to report, in an incoherent fashion, is a lack of conscious *control* that they feel they have over their trains of thought. We all experience this from time to time, when thoughts 'pop' into our consciousness unbidden and often unwanted, having no apparent connection with the train of thought that we are endeavouring to pursue. We might, for instance, be trying to plan a holiday trip when, quite 'out of the blue', a thought about a sick relative springs into our mind and disrupts our train of thought. It seems likely that the delusion of thought-insertion is an exaggerated and much more debilitating version of this kind of everyday experience (see Lowe 2006b).

16. THE UNITY OF CONSCIOUSNESS: AN IRRELEVANCE

Yet another clarificatory point I should make is that when I speak, in connection with the unity argument, of the *unified* way in which all my thoughts depend upon *me* as their unique subject, I am not in any way appealing to the philosophical notion of the so-called 'unity of consciousness'. The thesis of the unity of consciousness is a phenomenological one, alleging that a subject's states of consciousness at any given time are 'unified', in the sense that they all belong to one 'stream' of consciousness, rather than being split into separate 'parallel' streams. The implication is that if a subject, S, is aware of one content of consciousness, X, and simultaneously aware of another content of consciousness, Y, then S must also be aware of X and Y *together*, as a *unified* content of consciousness. For example, according to this thesis, it would be impossible for S to be aware of a certain pain in his foot and simultaneously be aware of a certain taste in his mouth, without being aware of that pain *conjoined with* that taste.

Whether this thesis is true seems to me to be very much an open question. Obviously, it is difficult if not impossible to *test* the thesis directly, by means of introspection, for one could not notice that one was *not* aware of the pain and the taste *together*, but only *separately*, since the putative act of noticing that one was aware of them only *separately* would imply that one was in fact aware of them *together*. However, the fact that the thesis cannot be directly falsified through introspection doesn't mean that it must be *true*—although, of course, its unfalsifiability by these means may go a long way towards explaining why it may be an intuitively compelling thesis. I strongly suspect, indeed, that it is false (see Lowe 2006b). But, in any case, it is irrelevant to my present concerns, because I make no appeal to it in support of my contention that all of my thoughts depend upon *me* as their subject. My argument for the latter thesis, which is a *metaphysical* one, appeals entirely to considerations concerning the *individuation* of thoughts, as I made clear earlier. This argument will consequently still stand even if the thesis of the unity of consciousness needs to be discarded.

17. A FINAL SUMMING UP

Now it is time for me to sum up my findings. I think that there are compelling arguments in favour of the real existence of selves or persons, conceived as subjects of thought, and also compelling arguments for regarding selves as constituting a fundamental ontological category of things, distinct from and irreducible to anything bodily, whether that be an entire living organism or animal, or a part of such an animal, or even a bodily system of some sort. It is simply incoherent to regard selves as fictions created by the brains of certain animals. They are perfectly real and, as far as I can see, ontologically basic. They are what *we* are, in the most fundamental sense. This does *not* mean that we are something wholly immaterial or non-physical, in the sense of being capable of existing quite apart from bodies and their exemplifications of physical properties, as Descartes believed. But it does mean that we should reject as utterly extravagant and indefensible the views of those physicalists who say that we are 'nothing but' animals of a certain kind, or 'nothing but' our brains. A rejection of Cartesian dualism does not compel us to embrace such a physicalist position as the only tenable alternative that is consistent with the findings of empirical science. An *emergentist* view of the self, in the sense explained earlier, is not only consistent with those findings but, it seems, is the only coherent option open to us from a metaphysical point of view.[8]

NOTES

1. See Descartes (1984–1991), volume 2, *Second Meditation*. For a recent study of the plural form of the question, see Olson (2007).
2. For more on ontological categories in general, see Lowe (2006a).
3. But see further Lowe (2008).
4. For more on individuation in general, in both of these senses, see Lowe (2003).
5. For an earlier and much briefer version of the argument, see Lowe (2008: 95–99). The present paper is designed to strengthen that version in various respects.
6. Such philosophers include, prominently, Eric T. Olson: see Olson (1997).
7. For an important and influential instance of this line of thought, see van Inwagen (1981).
8. I am grateful for comments received when earlier versions of this paper were delivered at Davidson College and at Washington University, St. Louis. This paper was previously published in A. Corradini and T. O'Connor (eds.) (2010), *Emergence in Science and Philosophy*, London: Routledge.

Contributors

Martina Fürst
University of Graz, Austria

William Hasker
Huntington University, USA

Andrea Lavazza
Centro Universitario Internazionale, Italy

E.J. Lowe
Durham University, GB

David Lund
Bemidji State University, USA

Riccardo Manzotti
Iulm University, Italy

Uwe Meixner
University of Augsburg, Germany

Paolo Moderato
Iulm University, Italy

Howard Robinson
Central European University, Hungary

Henry P. Stapp
University of California at Berkeley, USA

David Skrbina
University of Michigan-Dearborn, USA

Richard Swinburne
Oxford University, GB

Charles Taliaferro
St. Olaf College, USA

Ralph C. S. Walker
Oxford University, GB

References

Aizawa, K. (2007), "The Biochemistry of Memory Consolidation", *Synthese*, 155: 65–98.
Allen, J. (2005), *The Ancient Egyptian Pyramid Texts*, Atlanta: Society of Biblical Literature.
Alter, T. and Walter, S. (eds) (2007), *Phenomenal Concepts and Phenomenal Knowledge*, Oxford: Oxford University Press.
Ananthanarayanan, R., Esser, S.K., Simon, H.D. and Modha, D.S. (2009), "The Cat Is Out of the Bag: Cortical Simulations with 109 Neurons, 1013 Synapses", in *ACM/IEEE SC2009 Conference on High Performance Networking and Computing*, Portland, OR: 14–20.
Andrews, T.J., Schluppeck, D., Homfray, D., Matthews, P. and Blakemore, C.B. (2002), "Activity in the Fusiform Gyrus Predicts Conscious Perception of Rubin's Vase-Face Illusion", *Neuroimage*, 17: 890–901.
Antonietti, A., Corradini, A. and Lowe, E.J. (eds) (2008), *Psycho-Physical Dualism Today: An Interdisciplinary Approach*, Lanham, MD: Lexington (Rowman and Littlefield).
Aristotle ([ca. 340 BC] 1984), *Metaphysics*, in J. Barnes (ed.), *The Complete Works of Aristotle*, Princeton, NJ: Princeton University Press.
Armstrong, D. (1968), "The Headless Woman Illusion and the Defense of Materialism", *Analysis*, 29: 48–49.
Assmann, J. (1997), *Moses the Egyptian*. Cambridge, MA: Harvard University Press.
Audi, P. (2011), "Primitive Causal Relations", *Ratio*, XXIV: 1–16.
Averill, E.W. and Keating, B. (1981), "Does Interactionism Violate a Law of Classical Physics?", *Mind*, 90: 102–107.
Baker, L.R. (2000), *Persons and Bodies: A Constitution View*, Cambridge, UK: Cambridge University Press.
Balog, K. (2009), "Phenomenal Concepts", in B. McLaughlin, A. Beckermann and S. Walter (eds), *Oxford Handbook in the Philosophy of Mind*, Oxford: Oxford University Press, 292–312.
———. (2012a), "Acquaintance and the Mind-Body-Problem", in C. Hill and S. Gozzano (eds), *New Perspectives on Type Identity*, Cambridge, UK: Cambridge University Press.
———. (2012b), "In Defense of the Phenomenal Concept Strategy", *Philosophy and Phenomenological Research*, 84: 1–23.
Barnett, B. (2010), "You Are Simple", in R.C. Koons and G. Bealer (eds), *The Waning of Materialism*, Oxford: Oxford University Press, 161–174.
Barsalou, L.W. (2005), "Situated Conceptualizations", in H. Cohen and C. Lefebvre (eds), *Handbook of Categorization in Cognitive Science*, Amsterdam: Elsevier, 619–650.

Bateson, G. (1972), *Steps to an Ecology of Mind*, New York: Ballantine.
Beckermann, A. (2009), "What Is Property Dualism?", in B.P. McLaughlin, A. Beckermann and S. Walter (eds), *The Oxford Handbook of Philosophy of Mind*, Oxford: Oxford University Press, 152–172.
Beckner, M.O. (1967), "Vitalism", in P. Edwards (ed.), *The Encyclopedia of Philosophy*, Vol. 8, New York: MacMillan.
Beilby, J.K. (ed.) (2002), *Naturalism Defeated? Essays on Plantinga's Evolutionary Argument Against Naturalism*, Ithaca, NY: Cornell University Press.
Bennett, M.R. and Hacker, P.M.S. (2003), *Philosophical Foundations of Neuroscience*, Malden, MA: Blackwell.
Bergson, H. ([1911] 1920), *Mind Energy*, New York: Holt.
Bickle, J. (2011), "Memory and Neurophilosophy", in S. Nalbantian, P.M. Matthews and J.L. McClelland (eds), *The Memory Process*, Cambridge, MA: The MIT Press, 195–215.
Blakemore, C.B. (1988), *The Mind Machine*, London: BBC Books.
Block, N. (1980), "Are Absent Qualia Impossible?", *The Philosophical Review*, 89: 257–274.
———. (2006), "Max Black's Objection to Mind-Body Identity", in D. Zimmerman (ed.), *Oxford Studies in Metaphysics*, 2: 3–78. Reprinted in T. Alter and S. Walter (eds), *Phenomenal Concepts and Phenomenal Knowledge: New Essays on Consciousness and Physicalism*, Oxford: Oxford University Press.
———. (2007), "Consciousness, Accessibility, and the Mesh between Psychology and Neuroscience", *Behavioral and Brain Sciences*, 30: 481–499.
Block, N. and Stalnaker, R. (1999), "Conceptual Analysis, Dualism, and the Explanatory Gap", *Philosophical Review*, 108: 1–46.
Bohm, D. (1980), *Wholeness and the Implicate Order*, London: Routledge.
———. (1982), "Nature as Creativity", *ReVision*, 5: 35–40.
———. (1986), "A New Theory of the Relationship of Mind and Matter", *Journal of the American Society of Psychical Research*, 80: 113–135.
Bohr, N. (1934), *Atomic Theory and the Description of Nature*, Cambridge, UK: Cambridge University Press.
Bonjour, L. (2010), "Against Materialism", in R.C. Koons and G. Bealer (eds), *The Waning of Materialism*, Oxford: Oxford University Press, 3–23.
Boscovich, R.G. ([1758] 1922), *A Theory of Natural Philosophy*, Chicago-London: Open Court.
Braine, D. (1992), *Human Person: Animal and Spirit*, Notre Dame, IN: University of Notre Dame Press.
Brentano, F. (1874), *Psychologie vom empirischen Standpunkt*, Bd.1, Leipzig: Duncker & Humblot.
Brower, J.E. (forthcoming), "Matter, Form, and Individuation", in B. Davies and E. Stump (eds), *The Oxford Handbook to Aquinas*, Oxford: Oxford University Press.
Brown, J.R. (1991), *The Laboratory in the Mind: Thought Experiments in the Natural Sciences*, London: Routledge.
Calcagno, A. (1998), *Giordano Bruno and the Logic of Coincidence*, New York: P. Lang.
Carnap, R. (1935), *Philosophy and Logical Syntax*, London: Paul, Trench, Trubner, and Co.
Carruthers, P. and Veillet, B. (2007), "The Phenomenal Concept Strategy", *Journal of Consciousness Studies*, 14: 212–236.
Chalmers, D.J. (1995), "Facing Up to the Problem of Consciousness", *Journal of Consciousness Studies*, 2/3: 200–219.
———. (1996), *The Conscious Mind: In Search of a Fundamental Theory*, New York: Oxford University Press.

_____. (1997), "Moving Forward on the Problem of Consciousness", *Journal of Consciousness Studies*, 4: 3–46.
_____. (2003), "The Content and Epistemology of Phenomenal Belief", in Q. Smith and A. Jokic (eds), *Consciousness: New Philosophical Perspectives*, Oxford: Oxford University Press, 220–272.
_____. (2004), "Phenomenal Concepts and the Knowledge Argument", in P. Ludlow, Y. Nagasawa and D. Stoljar (eds), *There's Something about Mary: Essays on Phenomenal Consciousness and Frank Jackson's Knowledge Argument*, Cambridge, MA: The MIT Press.
_____. (2007), "Phenomenal Concepts and the Explanatory Gap", in T. Alter and S. Walter (eds), *Phenomenal Concepts and Phenomenal Knowledge*, Oxford: Oxford University Press, 167–154.
_____. (2010), *The Character of Consciousness*, New York: Oxford University Press.
Chalmers, D.J. and Jackson, F. (2001), "Conceptual Analysis and Reductive Explanation", *Philosophical Review*, 110: 315–361.
Changeux, J.-P. (2001), "Cajal on Neurons, Molecules, and Consciousness", *Annals of the New York Academy of Sciences*, 929, 147–151.
Chemero, A. (2009), *Radical Embodied Cognitive Science*, Cambridge, MA: The MIT Press.
Churchland, P.M. (1984), *Matter and Consciousness*, Cambridge, MA: The MIT Press.
_____. (1986), "Some Reductive Strategies in Cognitive Neurobiology", *Mind*, 95: 279–309.
Churchland, P.S. (1986), *Neurophilosophy*, Cambridge, MA: The MIT Press.
_____. (2002), *Brain-Wise. Studies in Neurophilosophy*, Cambridge, MA: The MIT Press.
Clark, R. (1955), *Herder: His Life and Thought*, Berkeley, CA: University of California Press.
Clarke, D. (2003), *Panpsychism and the Religious Attitude*, Albany, NY: SUNY Press.
Cleve, F. (1969), Vol. 2 of *The Giants of Pre-Sophistic Greek Philosophy*, The Hague: Martinus Nijhoff.
Cochran, A. (1971), "The Relationship between Quantum Physics and Biology", *Foundations of Physics*, 1: 235–250.
Coliva, A. (2003), "The First Person: Error through Misidentification, the Split Between Speaker's and Semantic Reference, and The Real Guarantee", *Journal of Philosophy*, 100: 416–431.
Collins, R. (2011), "The Energy of the Soul", in M. Baker and S. Goetz (eds), *The Soul Hypothesis*, London: Continuum, 123–133.
Coyne, J.A. (2009), *Why Evolution Is True*, New York: Viking Penguin.
Crane, T. (2003), "The Intentional Structure of Consciousness", in Q. Smith and A. Jokic (eds), *Consciousness. New Philosophical Essays*, Oxford: University Press, 33–56.
Crick, F. (1994), *The Astonishing Hypothesis: the Scientific Search for the Soul*, New York: Touchstone.
Crick, F. and Koch, C. (1990), "Toward a neurobiological theory of consciousness", *Seminars in the Neurosciences*, 2: 263–275.
Dardis, A. (2002), "A 'No Causal Rivalry' Solution to the Problem of Mental Causation", *Acta Analytica*, 17: 69–77.
Davidson, D. ([1970] 1980), "Mental Events", in D. Davidson, *Essays on Actions and Events*, Oxford: Clarendon Press, 207–229.
_____. ([1974] 2001), "On the Very Idea of a Conceptual Scheme", *Proceedings and Addresses of the American Philosophical Association*, 47. Reprinted in

D. Davidson, *Inquiries into Truth and Interpretation*, Oxford: Clarendon Press, 183–198.
———. (1980), *Essays on Actions and Events*, Oxford: Clarendon Press.
———. (1993), "Thinking Causes", in J. Heil and A. Mele (eds), *Mental Causation*, Oxford: Clarendon Press, 3–17.
Dennett, D.C. (1987), *The Intentional Stance*, Cambridge, MA: The MIT Press.
———. (1991), *Consciousness Explained*, Boston, New York and London: Little, Brown and Company.
———. (1997), "True Believers: The Intentional Strategy and Why It Works", in J. Haugeland (ed.), *Mind Design II*, Cambridge, MA: The MIT Press, 57–79. First published 1981.
———. (2007a), "What RoboMary Knows" in T. Alter and S. Walter (eds), *Phenomenal Concepts and Phenomenal Knowledge*, Oxford: Oxford University Press, 15–31.
———. (2007b), "Who's On First?", in B. Gertler and L. Shapiro (eds), *Arguing about the Mind*, London and New York: Routledge.
Dennett, D.C. and Kinsbourne, M. (1992), "Time and the Observer: The Where and the When of Consciousness in the Brain", *Behavioral and Brain Sciences*, 15: 183–247.
de Quincey, C. (2002), *Radical Nature*, Montpelier, VT: Invisible Cities.
Descartes, R. (1964–1976), *Oeuvres de Descartes*, C. Adam and P. Tannery (eds), Rev. ed., Paris: Vrin/CNRS.
———. (1972), *Discourse on the Method*, trans. E.S. Haldane and G.R.T. Ross, *Collected works of Descartes*, Vol. I., Cambridge, UK: Cambridge University Press.
———. (1984–1991), *The Philosophical Writings of Descartes*, 3 vols, J. Cottingham, R. Stoothoff, D. Murdoch and A. Kenny (trans.), Cambridge, UK: Cambridge University Press.
Dewey, J. (1916), *Democracy and Education: An Introduction to the Philosophy of Education*, New York: Free Press.
Diaz, J.-L. (2000), "Mind-Body Unity, Dual Aspect, and the Emergence of Consciousness", *Philosophical Psychology*, 13: 393–403.
Dretske, F. (1981), *Knowledge and the Flow of Information*, Cambridge, MA: The MIT Press.
Dyson, F. (1979), *Disturbing the Universe*, New York: Harper and Row.
Eccles, J.C. (1989), *Evolution of the Brain: Creation of the Self*, London: Routledge.
———. (1994), *How the Self Controls Its Brain*, Berlin: Springer.
Edelman, G.M. (1989), *The Remembered Present: A Biological Theory of Consciousness*, New York: Basic Books.
———. (2006), *Second Nature: Brain Science and Human Knowledge*, New Haven and London, Yale University Press.
Feigl, H. (1958), *The Mental and the Physical*, Minneapolis: University of Minnesota Press.
Feynman, R. (1965), *The Character of Physical Law*, Cambridge, MA: The MIT Press.
Floridi, L. (ed.) (2004), *The Blackwell Guide to the Philosophy of Computing and Information*, London: Blackwell.
Fodor, J. (1974), "Disunity of Science as a Working Hypothesis", *Synthese*, 28: 97–115.
———. (1997), "Special Sciences: Still Autonomous after All These Years", *Philosophical Perspectives*, 11: 149–163.
Foster, J. (1991), *The Immaterial Self*, London: Routledge.
Freeman, K. (1948), *Ancilla to the Pre-Socratic Philosophers*, Cambridge, MA: Harvard University Press.
Fürst, M. (2012), "Exemplarization—A Solution to the Problem of Consciousness?", *Philosophical Studies*, 161: 141–151.

Galilei, G. ([1623] 1960), "The Assayer", in S. Drake and C.D. O'Malley (trans.), *The Controversy on the Comets of 1618*, Philadelphia, University of Pennsylvania Press, 151–336.
Gallois, A. (1998), *Occasions of Identity*, Oxford: Clarendon Press.
Gazzaniga, M.G. (1998), *The Mind's Past*, San Francisco: University of California Press.
Gazzaniga, M.G., Mangun, G.R. and Ivry, R.B. (1998), *Cognitive Neuroscience: The Biology of the Mind*, New York: Norton.
Gibson, J.J. (1979), *The Ecological Approach to Visual Perception*, Boston: Houghton Mifflin.
Göcke, B.P. (ed.) (2012), *After Physicalism*, Notre Dame, IN: Notre Dame University Press.
Goetz, S. and Taliaferro, C. (2011), *A Brief History of the Soul*, Oxford: Wiley Blackwell.
Gozzano, S. and Hill, C. (eds) (2012), *New Perspectives on Type Identity*, Cambridge, UK: Cambridge University Press.
Griffin, D. (1997), *Unsnarling the World Knot*, Berkeley, CA: University of California Press.
Haeckel, E. ([1868] 1876), *The History of Creation*, London: Routledge.
———. ([1899] 1929), *The Riddle of the Universe*, London: Watts.
Haggard, P. (2002), "Voluntary Action and Conscious Awareness", *Nature Neuroscience*, 5: 382–385.
———. (2004), "Seeing Through the Stream of Consciousness", *Science*, 304: 52–53.
Haldane, J.J. (2013), "Response to William Hasker's 'The Dialectic of Soul and Body'", *American Catholic Philosophical Quarterly*, 87 (3).
Haldane, J.B.S. (1934), "Quantum Mechanics as a Basis for Philosophy", *Philosophy of Science*, 1: 78–98.
Hameroff, S. (1998), "Funda-mentality: Is the Conscious Mind Subtly Linked to a Basic Level of the Universe?", *Trends in Cognitive Science*, 2: 119–127.
———. (2009), "The Conscious Connection: A Psycho-physical Bridge Between Brain and Pan-Experiential Quantum Geometry", in D. Skrbina (ed.), *Mind That Abides*, Amsterdam: Benjamins.
Hampshire, S. (1971), *Freedom of Mind*, Princeton, NJ: Princeton University Press.
Harman, G. (1990), "The Intrinsic Quality of Experience", in J. Tomberlin (ed.), *Philosophical Perspectives 4*, Atascadero, CA: Ridgeview, 31–52.
Hasker, W. (1999), *The Emergent Self*, Ithaca, NY: Cornell University Press.
———. (2011), "Souls Beastly and Human", in M.C. Baker and S. Goetz (eds), *The Soul Hypothesis: Investigations into the Existence of the Soul*, New York: Continuum, 202–217.
———. (2012), "The Emergence of Persons", in J. Stump and A. Padgett (eds), *A Companion to Christianity and Science*, London: Blackwell.
Haynes, J.-D. (2009), "Decoding Visual Consciousness from Human Brain Signals. *Trends in Cognitive Sciences*, 13: 194–202.
Haynes, J.-D. and Rees, G. (2006), "Decoding Mental States from Brain Activity in Humans", *Nature Reviews Neuroscience*, 7: 523–534.
Hill, C. (forthcoming), "Visual Awareness and Visual Qualia", in M. Sabates and D. Sosa (eds), *Supervenience in Mind*, Cambridge, MA: The MIT Press.
Hill, C. and McLaughlin, B. (1999), "There Are Fewer Things in Reality Than Are Dreamt of on Chalmers Philosophy", *Philosophy and Phenomenological Research*, 59: 445–454.
Himma, K.E. (2005), "What Is a Problem for All Is a Problem for None: Substance Dualism, Physicalism, and the Mind-Body Problem", *American Philosophical Quarterly*, 42: 81–92.

Hobbes, T. ([1655] 1981), *De Corpore*, A.P. Martinich (trans.), New York: Abaris Books.
Hodgson, D. (1991), *The Mind Matters: Consciousness and Choice in a Quantum World*, Oxford: Oxford University Press.
Hoffman, J. and Rosenkrantz, G. (1991), "Are Souls Intelligible?", in J.E. Tomberlin (ed.), *Philosophical Perspectives: Philosophy of Religion*, Vol. 5, Atascadero, CA: Ridgeview, 183–212.
Holt, E.B. (1914), *The Concept of Consciousness*, New York: MacMillan.
Honderich, T. (2006a), "Consciousness as Existence, Devout Physicalism, Spiritualism", *Mind and Matter*, 2: 85–104.
———. (2006b), "Radical Externalism", *Journal of Consciousness Studies*, 13: 3–13.
Horgan, T. (1984), "Jackson on Physical Information", *Philosophical Quarterly*, 34: 147–183.
Hornung, E. (1995), *Akhenaten and the Religion of Light*, Ithaca, NY: Cornell University Press.
Horwich, P. (2006), "The Value of Truth", *Noûs*, 40: 347–360.
Hughes, G.E. and Cresswell, M.J. (1985), *An Introduction to Modal Logic*, London: Methuen.
Hull, C. (1943), *Principles of Behavior*, New York: Appleton.
Hume, D. ([1739] 1888), *A Treatise of Human Nature*, L.A. Selby-Bigge (ed.), Oxford: Oxford University Press.
Hurley, S.L. and Noë, A. (2003), "Neural Plasticity and Consciousness", *Biology & Philosophy*, 18: 131–168.
Husserl, E. ([1907] 1999), *The Idea of Phenomenology*, L. Hardy (trans.), Berlin: Springer.
———. (1982), *Ideas Pertaining to a Pure Phenomenology and to a Phenomenological Philosophy, First Book*, F. Kersten (trans.), The Hague, Boston and London: Nijhoff.
———. (1989), *Ideas Pertaining to a Pure Phenomenology and to a Phenomenological Philosophy, Second Book*, R. Rojcewicz and André Schuwer (trans.), Dordrecht, Boston and London: Kluwer.
Huxley, J. (1942), "The Biologist Looks at Man", *Fortune*, (December): 139–148.
Inwood, M. (2009), "Plato's Eschatological Myths", in C. Partenie (ed.), *Plato's Myths*, Cambridge, UK: Cambridge University Press, 28–50.
Itano, W.M., Heinzen, D.J., Bollinger, J.J. and Wineland, D.J. (1990), "Quantum Zeno Effect", *Physical Review A*, 41: 2295–2300.
Jackson, F. (1982), "Epiphenomenal Qualia", *Philosophical Quarterly*, 32: 127–136.
James, W. ([1890] 1950), *The Principles of Psychology*, New York: Dover.
Jennings, C. (2000), "In Search of Consciousness", *Nature Neuroscience*, 3: 1.
John, E.R. (1976), "A Model of Consciousness", in G. Schwartz and D. Shapiro (eds), *Consciousness and Self-Regulation*, New York: Plenum Press.
Kandel, E.R., Schwartz, J.H. and Jessel, T.M. (1991), *Principles of Neuroscience*, Amsterdam: Elsevier.
Kant, I. ([1787] 2003), *Kritik der Reinen Vernunft*, N. Kemp Smith (trans.), London: Palgrave Macmillan.
———. (1900–), *Kant's gesammelte Schriften*, the Kgl. Preussische Akademie der Wissenschaften and its successors (eds.), Berlin: G. Reimer/W. de Gruyter.
———. ([1929] 1965), *The Critique of Pure Reason*, N.K. Smith (trans.), New York: Macmillan. Reprint, New York: St. Martin's Press.
———. (1948), *The Moral Law*, H.J. Paton (trans.), London, Hutchinson.
———. (1992), *Theoretical Philosophy 1755–1770*, D. Walford and R. Meerbote (trans.), Cambridge, UK: Cambridge University Press.
Kanwisher, N. (2001), "Neural Events and Perceptual Awareness", *Cognition*, 79: 89–113.

Kay, K.N., Naselaris, T., Prenger, R.L. and Gallant, J.L. (2008), "Identifying Natural Images from Human Brain Activity", *Nature*, 452: 352–355.
Kenny, A. (2012), "True Believers", *Times Literary Supplement*, 5699: 24–40.
Kim, J. (1995), "Mental Causation: What? Me Worry?", *Philosophical Issues*, 6: 123–151.
———. (1996), *Philosophy of Mind*, Boulder, CO: Westview.
———. (1998), *Mind in a Physical World*, Cambridge, MA: The MIT Press.
———. (1999), "Making Sense of Emergence", *Philosophical Studies*, 95: 3–36.
———. (2005), *Physicalism, or Something Near Enough*, Princeton, NJ: Princeton University Press.
Koch, C. (2004), *The Quest for Consciousness: A Neurobiological Approach*, Englewood, CO: Roberts & Company Publishers.
———. (2012), *Consciousness. Confessions of a Romantic Reductionist*, Cambridge, MA: The MIT Press.
Koons, R. and Bealer, G. (eds) (2010), *The Waning of Materialism*, Oxford: Oxford University Press.
Kriegel, U. (2009), *Subjective Self-Consciousness. A Self-Representational Theory*, New York: Oxford University Press.
Kriegel, U. and Williford, K. (eds) (2006), *Self-Representational Approaches to Consciousness*, Cambridge, MA: The MIT Press.
Kripke, S. (1980), *Naming and Necessity*, Cambridge, MA: Harvard University Press.
Landauer, R. (1992), "Information is Physical", Los Alamitos: IEEE Comp. Sci. Press, 1–4.
Lange, A., Meyers, E.M., Reynolds III, B.H. and Styers, R. (eds) (2011), *Light Against Darkness. Dualism in Ancient Mediterranean Religion and the Contemporary World*, Gottingen: Vandenhoeck and Ruprecht.
Larmer, R. (1986), "Mind-Body Interactionism and the Conservation of Energy", *International Philosophical Quarterly*, 26: 277–285.
Lehrer, K. (2004), "Representation in Painting and Consciousness", *Philosophical Studies*, 117: 1–14.
———. (2006), "Consciousness, Representation and Knowledge", in U. Kriegel and K. Williford (eds), *Self-Representational Approaches to Consciousness*, Cambridge, MA: Harvard University Press, 409–420.
———. (2011), "What Intentionality Is Like", *Acta Analytica*, 26: 1–13.
———. (2012), *Art, Self and Knowledge*, Oxford: University Press.
Leibniz, G.W. (1989), *Philosophical Essays*, R. Ariew and D. Garber (eds). Indianapolis: Hackett.
———. ([1720] 1991), *Monadology*, in N. Rescher (ed.), *G.W. Leibniz's Monadology: An Edition for Students*, Pittsburgh: University of Pittsburgh Press.
Leibniz, G.W. and Clarke, S. (1717), *A Collection of Papers...between... Mr Leibnitz and Dr Clarke*, London: James Knapton.
Levin, J. (2007), "What is a Phenomenal Concept?", in T. Alter and S. Walter (eds), *Phenomenal Concepts and Phenomenal Knowledge*, Oxford: Oxford University Press, 87–111.
Levine, J. (1983), "Materialism and Qualia: The Explanatory Gap", *Pacific Philosophical Quarterly*, 64: 354–361.
———. (2006), "Conscious Awareness and (Self-)Representation", in U. Kriegel and K. Williford (eds), *Self-Representational Approaches to Consciousness*, Cambridge, MA: Harvard University Press, 173–197.
———. (2007), "Phenomenal Concepts and the Materialist Constraint", in T. Alter and S. Walter (eds), *Phenomenal Concepts and Phenomenal Knowledge*, Oxford: Oxford University Press, 145–166.
Lewis, D. (1986), *On the Plurality of Worlds*, Oxford and New York: Blackwell.

———. (1988), "What Experience Teaches", *Proceedings of the Russellian Society,* 13: 29–57.
Li, Z. (2002), "A Saliency Map in Primary Visual Cortex", *Trends in Cognitive Sciences,* 6: 9–16.
Libet, B. (2004), *Mind Time. The Temporal Factor in Consciousness.* Cambridge, MA: Harvard University Press.
Libet, B., Gleason, C. A., Wright, E. W. and Pearl, D. K. (1983), "Time of Conscious Intention to Act, In Relation to Onset of Cerebral Activity (Readiness Potential)", *Brain,* 106: 623–642.
Liddell, H. G. and Scott, R. (1940), A *Greek-English Lexicon,* 9th ed., Oxford: Oxford University Press.
Lingnau, A., Benno G. and Caramazza, A. (2009), "Asymmetric fMRI Adaptation Reveals No Evidence for Mirror Neurons in Humans", *Proceedings of the National Academy of Sciences of the United States of America,* 106: 9925–9930.
Loar, B. (1990), "Phenomenal States", Philosophical Perspectives, 4: 81–108.
———. (1997), "Phenomenal States" (2nd ed.), in N. Block, O. Flanagan and G. Güzeldere (eds), *The Nature of Consciousness,* Cambridge, MA: The MIT Press, 597–616.
Locke, J. ([1689] 1975), *An Essay Concerning Human Understanding,* Oxford: Clarendon Press.
Loewer, B. (2007), "Mental Causation or Something Near Enough", in B. McLaughlin and J. Cohen (eds), *Contemporary Debates in Philosophy of Mind,* Oxford: Blackwell, 243–264.
———. (2008), "Why There *Is* Anything Except Physics", in J. Hohwy and J. Kallestrup (eds), *Being Reduced: New Essays on Reduction, Explanation, and Causation,* Oxford: Oxford University Press.
———. (2009), "Why Is There Anything Except Physics?", *Synthese,* 170: 217–233.
Long, A. A. (1996), "Parmenides on Thinking Being", *Proceedings of the Boston Area Colloquium in Ancient Philosophy,* 12: 125–151.
Lotze, R. ([1856–1864] 1971), *Microcosmos,* Edinburgh: T. & T. Clark.
Lowe, E. J. (1996), *Subjects of Experience,* Cambridge, UK: Cambridge University Press.
———. (2001), "Identity, Composition, and the Simplicity of the Self", in K. J. Corcoran (ed.), *Soul, Body, and Survival: Essays on the Metaphysics of Human Persons,* Ithaca, NY: Cornell University Press, 139–158.
———. (2003), "Individuation", in M. J. Loux and D. W. Zimmerman (eds), *The Oxford Handbook of Metaphysics,* Oxford: Oxford University Press, 75–95.
———. (2006a), *The Four-Category Ontology: A Metaphysical Foundation for Natural Science,* Oxford: Oxford University Press.
———. (2006b), "Can the Self Disintegrate? Personal Identity, Psychopathology, and Disunities of Consciousness", in J. C. Hughes, S. J. Louw and S. R. Sabat (eds), *Dementia: Mind, Meaning, and the Person,* Oxford: Oxford University Press.
———. (2008), *Personal Agency: The Metaphysics of Mind and Action,* Oxford: Oxford University Press.
———. (2009), "Dualism", in B. P. McLaughlin, A. Beckermann and S. Walter (eds), *The Oxford Handbook of Philosophy of Mind,* Oxford: Oxford University Press, 66–84.
Lund, D. (1994), *Perception, Mind and Personal Identity: A Critique of Materialism,* Lanham University Press of America.
———. (2005), *The Conscious Self,* Amherst and New York: Humanity Books.
Lycan, W. G. (1997), "Consciousness as Internal Monitoring", in N. Block, O. Flanagan and G. Güzeldere (eds), *The Nature of Consciousness,* Cambridge, MA: The MIT Press, 754–771.

———. (2013), "Is Property Dualism Better Off than Substance Dualism?" *Philosophical Studies*, 164: 533–542.
Mach, E. ([1886] 1959), *The Analysis of Sensations*, New York: Dover.
Mackie, P. (2011), "Mind-Body Dualism: Property Dualism and Substance Dualism", *Proceedings of the Aristotelian Society*, 111: 181–199.
Madell, G. (1981), *The Identity of the Self*, Edinburgh: Edinburgh University Press.
———. (1988), *Mind and Materialism*, Edinburgh: Edinburgh University Press.
Manzotti, R. (2006), "A Process Oriented View of Conscious Perception", *Journal of Consciousness Studies*, 13: 7–41.
———. (2009), "Does Process Externalism Support Panpsychism?", in D. Skrbina (ed.), *Mind That Abides*, Amsterdam: Benjamins.
———. (2011), "The Spread Mind: Seven Steps to Situated Consciousness", *Journal of Cosmology*, 14: 4526–4541.
———. (2012), "The Computational Stance Is Unfit for Consciousness", *International Journal of Machine Consciousness*, 4: 401–420.
Manzotti, R. and Moderato, P. (2010), "Is Neuroscience the Forthcoming 'Mindscience'?", *Behaviour and Philosophy*, 38: 1–28.
Marconi, D. (2009), "Wittgenstein and Necessary Facts", in P. Frascolla, D. Marconi and A. Voltolini (eds), *Wittgenstein: Mind, Meaning and Metaphilosophy*, Palgrave: MacMillian.
Marijuàn, P.C. (2001), "Cajal and Consciousness. Introduction", *Annals of the New York Academy of Sciences*, 929: 1–10.
Mashour, G.A. and LaRock, E. (2008), "Inverse Zombies, Anesthesia Awareness, and the Hard Problem of Unconsciousness", *Consciousness and Cognition*, 17: 1163–1638.
McDowell, J. (2008), "Responses", in J. Lingaard (ed.), *John McDowell: Experience, Norm, and Nature*, Oxford: Blackwell, 200–267.
Meinong, A. (1899), "Über Gegenstände höherer Ordnung und deren Verhältnis zur inneren Wahrnehmung", in R. Haller, R. Kindinger and R. Chisholm (eds), *Alexius Meinong Gesamtausgabe* (Band 2), Graz: Akademische Druck- und Verlagsanstalt, 377–480.
Meixner, U. (2001), *Theorie der Kausalität. Ein Leitfaden zum Kausalbegriff in zwei Teilen*, Paderborn: Mentis.
———. (2002), "Change and Change-*Ersatz*", in A. Bottani, M. Carrara and P. Giaretta (eds), *Individuals, Essence and Identity. Themes of Analytic Metaphysics*, Dordrecht: Kluwer, 427–449.
———. (2004), *The Two Sides of Being. A Reassessment of Psycho-Physical Dualism*, Paderborn: Mentis.
———. (2006a), *The Theory of Ontic Modalities*, Frankfurt: Ontos.
———. (2006b), "Classical Intentionality", *Erkenntnis*, 65: 25–45.
———. (2008), "The *Reductio* of Reductive and Non-reductive Materialism—and a New Start", in A. Antonietti, A. Corradini and E.J. Lowe (eds), *Psycho-Physical Dualism Today: An Interdisciplinary Approach*, Lanham, MD: Lexington Rowman and Littlefield, 143–166.
———. (2009), "Three Indications for the Existence of God in Causal Metaphysics", *International Journal for Philosophy of Religion*, 66: 33–46.
———. (2010), "Materialism Does Not Save the Phenomena—and the Alternative Which Does", in R.C. Koons and G. Bealer (eds), *The Waning of Materialism*, Oxford and New York: Oxford University Press, 417–437.
———. (2012), "A Cosmo-Ontological Argument for the Existence of a First Cause—Perhaps God", *European Journal for Philosophy of Religion*, 4: 169–178.
Melzack, R. (2001), "Pain and the Neuromatrix in the Brain", *Journal of Dental Education*, 65: 1378–1382.

———. (2005), "Evolution of the Neuromatrix Theory of Pain", *Pain Practice: The Official Journal of World Institute of Pain*, 5: 85–94.
Melzack, R., Israel, R., Lacroix, R. and Schultz, G. (1997), "Phantom Limbs in People with Congenital Limb Deficiency or Amputation in Early Childhood, *Brain*, 120: 1603–1620.
Merricks, T. (2001), *Objects and Persons*, Oxford: Clarendon Press.
Metzinger, T. (2003), *Being No One: The Self-Model Theory of Subjectivity*, Cambridge, MA: The MIT Press.
———. (2009), *The Ego Tunnel: The Science of the Mind and the Myth of the Self*, New York: Basic Books.
Miller, G. (2005), "What is the Biological Basis of Consciousness?", *Science*, 309: 79.
Misra, B. and Sudarshan, E. C. G. (1977), "The Zeno's Paradox in Quantum Theory", *Journal of Mathematical Physics*, 18: 756–763.
Mitchell, T. M., Shinkareva, S. V., Carlson, A., Chang, K.-M., Malave, V. L., Mason, R. A. and Just, M. A. (2008), "Predicting Human Brain Activity Associated with the Meanings of Nouns", *Science*, 320: 1191–1195.
Modha, D. S., Ananthanarayanan, R., Esser, S. K., Ndirango, A., Sherbondy, A. J. and Singh, R. (2011), "Cognitive Computing", *Communications of the ACM*, 54: 62–71.
Moreland, J. P. (ed.) (1994), *The Creation Hypothesis: Scientific Evidence for an Intelligent Designer*, Downers Grove: InterVarsity Press.
Moreland, J. P. and Rea S. B. (2000), *Body and Soul: Human Nature and the Crisis in Ethics*, Downers Grove: InterVarsity Press.
Morimoto, Y., Nogami, Y., Harada, K., Tsubokawa, T. and Masui, K. (2011), "Awareness during Anesthesia: The Results of a Questionnaire Survey in Japan", *Journal of Anesthesia*, 25: 72–77.
Nagel, T. (1974), "What Is It Like to Be a Bat?", *The Philosophical Review*, 83: 435–450.
———. (1979), *Mortal Questions*, Cambridge, UK: Cambridge University Press.
———. (1986), *The View from Nowhere*, New York: Oxford University Press.
———. (2002), *Concealment and Exposure*, New York: Oxford University Press.
———. (2012), *Mind and Cosmos: Why the Materialist Neo-Darwinian Conception of Nature Is Almost Certainly False*, New York: Oxford University Press.
Naselaris, T., Stansbury, D. E. and Gallant, J. L. (2012), "Cortical Representation of Animate and Inanimate Objects in Complex Natural Scenes", *Journal of Physiology*, 106: 239–249.
Nemirow, L. (2007), "So This Is What It's Like: A Defense of the Ability Hypothesis", in T. Alter and S. Walter (eds), *Phenomenal Concepts and Phenomenal Knowledge*, Oxford: University Press, 32–51.
Nida-Rümelin, M. (2010), "Qualia: The Knowledge Argument", in E. Zalta (ed.), *The Stanford Encyclopedia of Philosophy*, Retrieved from http://plato.stanford.edu/archives/sum2010/entries/qualia-knowledge.
Nietzsche, F. ([1886] 1973), *Beyond Good and Evil*, New York: Penguin.
———. ([1906] 1967), *Will to Power*, New York: Random House.
Nishimoto, S., Vu, A. T., Naselaris, T., Benjamini, Y., Yu, B. and Gallant, J. L. (2011), "Reconstructing Visual Experiences from Brain Activity Evoked by Natural Movies", *Current Biology*, 21: 1641–1646.
Noë, A. (2009), *Out of the Head. Why You Are Not Your Brain*, Cambridge, MA: The MIT Press.
Noë, A. and Thompson, E. (2002), *Vision and Mind: Selected Readings in the Philosophy of Perception*, Cambridge, MA: The MIT Press.
O'Connor, T. and Jacobs, J. (2003), "Emergent Individuals", *The Philosophical Quarterly*, 53: 540–555.

O'Craven, K. M. and Kanwisher, N. (2000), "Mental Imagery of Faces and Places Activates Corresponding Stimulus-Specific Brain Regions", *Journal of Cognitive Neuroscience*, 12: 1013–1023.
O'Leary-Hawthorne, J. and Cover, J. A. (1997), "Framing the Thisness Issue", *Australasian Journal of Philosophy*, 75: 102–108.
Olson, E. T. (1997), *The Human Animal: Personal Identity without Psychology*, New York: Oxford University Press.
———. (2007), *What Are We? A Study in Personal Ontology*, New York: Oxford University Press.
O'Shaughnessy, B. (1980), *The Will*, Cambridge, UK: Cambridge University Press.
O'Sullivan, B. (2008), "Through Thick and Thin with Ned Block", *Philosophia*, 36: 531–544.
Pallier, C., Devauchelle, A. D. and Dehaene, S. (2011), "Cortical Representation of the Constituent Structure of Sentences", *Proceedings of the National Academy of Sciences of the United States of America*, 108: 2522–2527.
Papineau, D. (2002), *Thinking about Consciousness*, Oxford: Oxford University Press.
———. (2007), "Phenomenal and Perceptual Concepts", in T. Alter and S. Walter (eds), *Phenomenal Concepts and Phenomenal Knowledge*, Oxford: University Press, 111–145.
Parfit, D. (1984), *Reasons and Persons*, Oxford: Oxford University Press.
Paulsen, F. ([1892] 1895), *Introduction to Philosophy*, New York: Holt.
Peirce, C. ([1891] 1992), "The Architecture of Theories", *Monist*, 1: 161–176. Reprinted in N. House and C. W. Kloessel (eds), Vol. 1 of *The Essential Peirce*, Bloomington, IN: Indiana University Press.
———. ([1892] 1992), "Man's Glassy Essence", *Monist*, 3: 1–22. Reprinted in N. House and C. W. Kloesel (eds), Vol. 1 of *The Essential Peirce*, Bloomington, IN: Indiana University Press.
Penrose, R. (1989), *The Emperor's New Mind*, Oxford: Oxford University Press.
Pereboom, D. (2011), *Consciousness and the Prospects of Physicalism*, Oxford: Oxford University Press.
Plantinga, A. (1993), *Warrant and Proper Function*, New York and Oxford: Oxford University Press.
Plantinga, A. and Tooley, M. (2008), *Knowledge of God*, Oxford: Blackwell.
Platts, M. (1991), *Moral Realities*, London: Routledge.
Popper, K. R. and Eccles, J. C. (1977), *The Self and Its Brain: An Argument for Interactionism*, London: Springer International.
Price, H. (2004), "Naturalism without Representationalism", in M. De Caro and D. Macarthur (eds), *Naturalism in Question*, Cambridge, MA: Harvard University Press, 71–88.
———. (2011), *Naturalism Without Mirrors*, New York: Oxford University Press.
Priestley, J. ([1777] 1972), "Disquisitions Relating to Matter and Spirit", in J. Rutt (ed.), *The Theological and Miscellaneous Works of Joseph Priestley*, New York: Kraus. Reprint.
Prinz, J. (2012), *The Conscious Brain. How Attention Engenders Experience*, New York: Oxford University Press.
Pusey, M. F., Barrett, J. and Rudolf, T. (2012), "On the Reality of the Quantum State", *Nature Physics*, 8: 476–479.
Putnam, H. (1983), "Computational Psychology and Interpretation Theory", in H. Putnam, *Realism and Reason. Philosophical Papers*, Vol. 3, Cambridge, UK: Cambridge University Press.
———. (1995), "Why There Isn't a Ready-Made World", in P. K. Moser and J. D. Trout (eds), *Contemporary Materialism: A Reader*, London: Routledge.

——. (2003), "For Ethics and Economics without the Dichotomies", *Review of Political Economy*, 15: 395–412.
Quine, W. V. O. (1963 [2nd ed.]), "Two Dogmas of Empiricism", in W. V. O. Quine, *From a Logical Point of View*, New York and Evanston: Harper and Row, 20–46.
——. (1969 [2nd ed.]), "Epistemology Naturalized", in W. V. O. Quine, *Ontological Relativity and Other Essays*, New York and Evanston: Harper and Row, 69–90.
Reppert, V. (2003), *C. S. Lewis's Dangerous Idea: In Defense of the Argument from Reason*, Downers Grove: InterVarsity Press.
Revonsuo, A. (2010), *Consciousness. The Science of Subjectivity*, Hove: Psychology Press.
Rey, G. (1983), "Concepts and Stereotypes", *Cognition*, 15: 237–262.
Robb, D. (1997), "The Properties of Mental Causation", *The Philosophical Quarterly*, 47: 178–190.
Robinson, D. (2008), *Consciousness and Mental Life*, New York: Columbia University Press.
Robinson, H. (1982), *Matter and Sense*, Cambridge, UK: Cambridge University Press.
——. (1989), "A Dualist Account of Embodiment", in J. R. Smythies and J. Beloff (eds), *The Case for Dualism*, Charlottesville: University of Virginia Press, 43–57.
——. (1994), *Perception*, New York: Routledge.
——. (2001), "Donald Davidson and Non-Reductive Physicalism: A Tale of Two Cultures", in K. Gillett and B. Loewer (eds), *Physicalism and Its Discontents*, New York: Cambridge University Press.
——. (2011), "Dualism", in E. Zalta (ed.), *The Stanford Encyclopedia of Philosophy*, Retrieved from http://plato.stanford.edu/ entries/dualism.
——. (2012a), "Qualia, Qualities, and Our Conception of the World", in B. Göcke (ed.), *After Physicalism*, Notre Dame, IN: University of Notre Dame Press.
——. (2012b), "'Are There Any Fs?': How Should We Understand This Question?", *Hungarian Philosophical Review*, 4: 55–68.
Rockwell, T. (2005), *Neither Ghost nor Brain*, Cambridge, MA: The MIT Press.
Roe, A. W., Pallas, S. L., Hahm, J. O. and Sur, M. (1990), "A Map of Visual Space Induced in Primary Auditory Cortex", *Science*, 250: 818–820.
Rorty, R. (1965), "Mind-Body Identity, Privacy, and Categories", *Review of Metaphysics*, 19: 24–54.
——. (2010), "Naturalism and Quietism", in M. De Caro and D. Macarthur (eds), *Naturalism in Question*, Cambridge, MA: Harvard University Press, 55–68.
Rosenberg, A. (2011), *The Atheist's Guide to Reality: Enjoying Life without Illusions*, New York: W. W. Norton.
Royce, J. ([1892] 1955), *Spirit of Modern Philosophy*, New York: Houghton Mifflin.
——. ([1898] 1915), *Studies in Good and Evil*, New York: Appleton.
Russell, B. ([1912] 1959), *The Problems of Philosophy*, Oxford: Oxford University Press.
Schiller, F. (1891), *Riddles of the Sphinx*, London: Sonnenschein.
Schneider, S. (2012), "Why Property Dualists Must Reject Substance Physicalism", *Philosophical Studies*, 157: 61–76.
Schopenhauer, A. ([1819] 1995), *The World as Will and Idea*, London: J. M. Dent.
——. ([1851] 1974), *Essays and Aphorisms*, New York: Penguin.
Schwinger, J. (1951), "The Theory of Quantized Fields", *Physical Review*, 82, 914–927.
Searle, J. R. (1980), "Minds, Brains, and Programs", *Behavioral and Brain Sciences*, 1: 417–424.
——. (1992), *Rediscovery of the Mind*, Cambridge, MA: The MIT Press.
——. (2002), "Why I Am Not a Property Dualist", *Journal of Consciousness Studies*, 9: 57–64.

Shaffer, J. (1961), "Could Mental States Be Brain Processes?", *Journal of Philosophy*, 58: 813-822.
Shagrir, O. (2012), "Computation, Implementation, Cognition", *Minds and Machines*, 22: 137-148.
Shoemaker, S. (1966), "On Knowing Who One Is", *Common Factor*, 4: 49-56.
———. (1994), "Introspection and the Self", in Q. Cassam (ed.), *Self-Knowledge*, Oxford: Oxford University Press.
Shoemaker, S. and Swinburne, R. (1984), *Personal Identity*, Oxford: Blackwell.
Skolimowski, H. (1994), *The Participatory Mind*, New York: Penguin/Arkana.
Skrbina, D. (2005), *Panpsychism in the West*, Cambridge, MA: The MIT Press.
———. (2009), "Minds, Objects, and Relations: Toward a Dual-Aspect Ontology", in D. Skrbina (ed.), *Mind That Abides*, Amsterdam: Benjamins.
———. (2010), "Whitehead and the Ubiquity of Mind", *Chromatikon*, VI: 181-189.
———. (ed.) (2009), *Mind That Abides: Panpsychism in the New Millennium*, Amsterdam: Benjamins.
Smart, J.J.C. (1959), "Sensations and Brain Processes", *Philosophical Review*, 68: 141-156.
Smart, J.J.C. and Haldane, J.J. (2003 [2nd ed.]), *Atheism and Theism*, Oxford: Blackwell.
Sober, E. (2000 [2nd ed.]), *Philosophy of Biology*, Boulder, CO: Westview.
Sperry, R.W. (1969), "A Modified Concept of Consciousness", *Psychological Review*, 70: 532-536.
Spinoza, B. ([1677] 1994), *Ethics*, in E. Curley (ed.), A *Spinoza Reader*, Princeton, NJ: Princeton University Press.
Sporns, O. (2011), "The Human Connectome: A Complex Network", *Annals of the New York Academy of Sciences*, 1224: 109-125.
Sporns, O., Tononi, G. and Kötter, R. (2005), "The Human Connectome: A Structural Description of the Human Brain", *PLoS Computational Biology*, 1: e42.
Stapp, H.P. (1977), "Are Superluminal Connections Necessary?", *Nuovo Cimento*, 40B: 191-204.
———. (2005), "Quantum Interactive Dualism: An Alternative to Materialism", *Journal of Consciousness Studies*, 12: 43-58.
———. (2013), "On the Nature of Things", Retrieved from http://www-physics.lbl.gov/~stapp/stappfiles.html.
Steeves, J.K., Culham, J.C., Duchaine, B.C., Cavina Pratesi, C., Valyear, K.F., Schindler, I., Humphrey, G.K., Milner, A.D. and Goodale, M.A. (2006), "The Fusiform Face Area is Not Sufficient for Face Recognition: Evidence from a Patient with Dense Prosopagnosia and No Occipital Face Area", *Neuropsychologia*, 44: 594-609.
Stephens, G.L. and Graham, G. (2000), *When Self-Consciousness Breaks: Alien Voices and Inserted Thoughts*, Cambridge, MA: The MIT Press.
Stoljar, D. (2005), "Physicalism and Phenomenal Concepts", *Mind and Language*, 20: 469-494.
Strawson, G. (1994), *Mental Reality*, Cambridge, MA: The MIT Press.
———. (2006), "Panpsychism? Reply to Commentators with a Celebration of Descartes", *Journal of Consciousness Studies*, 13: 184-280.
———. (2009), "Realistic Monism", in D. Skrbina (ed.), *Mind That Abides*, Amsterdam: Benjamins.
———. (2010 [2nd ed.]), *Mental Reality*, Cambridge, MA: The MIT Press.
Strawson, P.F. (1959), *Individuals*, London: Methuen.
———. (1966), *Bounds of Sense*, London: Methuen.
Stroud, B. (1984), *The Significance of Philosophical Scepticism*, Oxford: Oxford University Press.
Stump, E. (2003), *Aquinas*, London: Routledge.

Sutherland, S. (1989), *Dictionary of Psychology*, London: MacMillan.
Swinburne, R. (1986), *The Evolution of the Soul*, Oxford: Oxford University Press.
———. (1995), "Thisness", *Australasian Journal of Philosophy*, 73: 389–400.
———. (1997), *The Evolution of the Soul*, Oxford: Clarendon Press.
———. (2007), "From Mental/Physical Identity to Substance Dualism", in P. van Inwagen and D. W. Zimmermann (eds), *Persons: Human and Divine*, Oxford: Oxford University Press, 142–165.
———. (2008), *Was Jesus God?*, Oxford: Oxford University Press.
———. (2013), *Mind, Brain, and Free Will*, Oxford: Oxford University Press.
Szabó Gendler, T. and Hawthorne, J. (eds) (2002), *Conceivability and Possibility*, Oxford: Clarendon Press.,
Taliaferro, C. (1994), *Consciousness and the Mind of God*, Cambridge, UK: Cambridge University Press.
———. (2001), "The Virtues of Embodiment", *Philosophy*, 76: 111–125.
Taliaferro, C. and Evans, J. (2010), *The Image in Mind: Theism, Naturalism, and the Imagination*, London and New York: Continuum.
Taliaferro, C. and Goetz, S. (2008), "The Prospects of Christian Materialism", *Christian Scholars Review*, 37: 303–321.
Tallis, R. (2011), *Aping Mankind. Neuromania, Darwinitis and the Misrepresentation of Humanity*, Durham: Acumen.
The Human Brain Project (2011), *Human Brain Project—State of the Art. A review*, Brussels.
Tomonaga, S.-I. (1946), "On a Relativistically Invariant Formulation of the Quantum Theory of Wave Fields", *Progress of Theoretical Physics*, 1: 27–42.
Tononi, G. (2004), "An Information Integration Theory of Consciousness", *BMC Neuroscience*, 5: 1–22.
———. (2008), "Consciousness as Integrated Information: A Provisional Manifesto", *The Biological Bulletin*, 215: 216–242.
Tononi, G. and Koch, C. (2008), "The Neural Correlates of Consciousness: An Update", *Annals of the New York Academy of Sciences*, 1124: 239–261.
Tye, M. (2002), "Representationalism and the Transparency of Experience", *Noûs*, 36: 137–151.
———. (2009), *Consciousness Revisited. Materialism Without Phenomenal Concepts*, Cambridge, MA: The MIT Press.
Tyndall, J. (1874), "Belfast Address, 1874", *Nature*, 10: 309–319.
Unger, P. (2006), *All the Power in the World*, New York: Oxford University Press.
Uttal, W. R. (2001), *The New Phrenology: The Limits of Localizing Cognitive Processes in the Brain*, Cambridge, MA: The MIT Press.
———. (2004), *Dualism. The Original Sin of Cognitivism*, Mahwah: Lawrence Erlbaum Associates.
van Inwagen, P. (1981), "The Doctrine of Arbitrary Undetached Parts", *Pacific Philosophical Quarterly*, 62: 123–137.
———. (1990), *Material Beings*, Ithaca, NY: Cornell University Press.
Varela, F. J., Thompson, E. and Rosch, E. (1991), *The Embodied Mind: Cognitive Science and Human Experience*, Cambridge, MA: The MIT Press.
Velmans, M. (2000), *Understanding Consciousness*, London: Routledge.
Velmans, M. (2009 [2nd ed.]), *Understanding Consciousness*, London: Routledge.
Vision, G. (2012), *Re-Emergence: Locating Conscious Properties in a Material World*, Cambridge, MA: The MIT Press.
von Neumann, J. ([1932] 1955), *Mathematische grundlagen der quantenmechanik*, Berlin: Springer. Reprinted in R. T. Beyer (trans.), *Mathematical Foundations of Quantum Mechanics*, Princeton, NJ: Princeton University Press.
Walker, R. C. S. (1978), *Kant*, London: Routledge & Kegan Paul.

———. (1993), "Transcendental Arguments against Physicalism", in H. Robinson (ed.), *Objections to Physicalism*, Oxford: Oxford University Press, 61–80.
———. (1998), *Kant and the Moral Law*, London: Phoenix.
Wandell, B.A. and Winawer, J. (2011), "Imaging Retinotopic Maps in the Human Brain", *Vision Research*, 51: 718–737.
Watkins-Pitchford, M. and Brull, S.J. (1997), "Patient Awareness during General Anesthesia: A Shocking Outcome", *Journal of Clinical Monitoring*, 13: 51–52.
Watson, J.B. (1913), "Psychology as the Behaviourists Views it", *Psychological Review*, 20: 158–177.
White, S. (2007), "Property Dualism, Phenomenal Concepts, and the Semantic Premise", in T. Alter and S. Walter (eds), *Phenomenal Concepts and Phenomenal Knowledge*, Oxford: Oxford University Press.
Williamson, T. (2007), The Philosophy of Philosophy, Oxford: Blackwell.
Whitehead, A.N. (1925), *Science and the Modern World*, New York: Free Press.
———. (1926), *Religion in the Making*, New York: Macmillan.
Win, M.N. and Smolke, C.D. (2008), "Higher Order Cellular Information Processing with Synthetic RNA Devices", *Science*, 322: 456–460.
Zimmerman, D. (2010), "Mind-Body Dualism: From Property Dualism to Substance Dualism", *Proceedings of the Aristotelian Society Supplementary Volume*, 84: 119–150.
Zohar, D. (1990), *The Quantum Self*, London: Bloomsbury.

Index

Aboutness *see* intentionality
action at a distance 100, 104, 105, 106
Aizawa, K. 84
Akhenaten 221
Allen, J. 242
Ananthanarayanan, R. 84
Andrews, T.J. 87
anomalous monism 53, 61, 203
Anscombe, G.E.M. 198
anti-realism 194
antireductionism 212
Antonietti, A. 33
anthropic-logical principle 54
a posteriori necessary truth 42–43
Aquinas, T. 204–208, 209–211, 213, 216
argument from reason 216
argument from illusion 30
argument from perspective 31
argument of the conceptual super-scheme 52
Aristotle 48, 162, 174, 178, 204, 246
Armstrong, D. 127, 134, 152, 166
artificial intelligence 1
Assmann, J. 221
Audi, P. 202
Augustine 195, 221
Averill, E.W. 8
awareness 5, 63–71, 74, 77, 90, 93, 123–124, 173, 175, 194, 216–17

Baker, L.R. 250
Balog, K. 112–113, 115, 116, 125, 131, 132, 133
Barnett, B. 219
Barrett, J. 99
Barsalou, L.W. 53
Bateson, G. 234, 235

Bealer, G. 4, 33, 219, 242
Beckermann, A. 261
Beckner, M.O. 215, 219
behavioral pattern 156
Beilby, J.K. 55
Bennett, M.R. 81
Benno, G. 86
Bergson, H. 233
Berkeley, G. 222, 231
Bickle, J. 4
bifurcation problem 7
biology 12, 47, 105, 154, 165, 207
Blakemore, C.B. 87, 201
Block, N. 43–44, 88, 112, 113, 126, 128–129, 133, 228–229
Bohm, D. 53, 234–235
Bohr, N. 98–99, 106
Bollinger, J.J. 108
Bonjour, L. 3
Boscovich, R.G. 231, 243
Brain Activity Map 1
Braine, D. 218
Brentano, F. 133
Brower, J.E. 206
Brown, J.R. 53
Brull, S.J. 89
bundle view/theory 9, 10, 146–148, 187, 225, 228, 229

C fiber 43
Calcagno, A. 230
Caramazza, A. 86
Carnap, R. 42, 168, 223
Cartesian modal argument 11, 21, 23–25
Carruthers, P. 114
causal argument 26
causal closure 29, 77, 216, 224, 226, 229, 240

286 Index

causal autonomy of self 261
causation 6–8, 31, 76–77, 89, 166, 191, 193, 201, 220, 229, 231, 240
cerebral state 43, 44
Chalmers, D.J. 11, 25–26, 34, 36, 44, 95, 113, 116, 121–122, 125, 132, 133, 226, 228, 235, 238–239
Chalmers-Descartes modal argument 25
Changeux, J.-P. 83
Chemero, A. 84
Churchland, P.M. 169, 191, 199–200, 241
Churchland, P.S. 36, 61
Clark, R. 243
Clarke, D. 243
Clarke, S. 183
Cleve, F. 222
Cochran, A. 234
Cogito 156, 170, 177
choice 12, 29, 30, 82, 86, 95, 101–104, 109–111, 172
Coliva, A. 153
Collins, R. 8
conceivability 37, 49, 76, 151
  ideal 48, 50
conceivability argument 112, 113, 250
conceptual analysis 43, 181
conceptual scheme 36, 38–41, 45–47
conceptual super-scheme, 39, 52
conditional incompatibility 28
conscious control 107, 263
conscious self 63, 69, 73
conscious state 5, 6, 56–71, 77, 85, 124, 201, 209, 217
consciousness 3–8, 21, 26, 36, 40, 58–62, 64, 66, 70–72, 82, 85–90, 92, 99, 107, 124, 158, 167, 183, 203, 208–09, 220, 223, 226–27, 233, 239, 241, 263–64
  causal role of 226
  intentional 77
  perceptual 66–67
  phenomenal 1–3, 112
  reflective 77
  unity of 217, 263–264
conservation of energy 8
contingency 36, 41, 44, 46, 47, 48, 49, 120
continuity 72–74, 145–146, 149, 184–186
Corradini, A. 33, 265

correlation 42, 46, 86, 87, 169, 203, 230
Cover, J.A. 152
Coyne, J.A. 36
Crane, T. 133
cranialism 81
creationism 209
Cresswell, M.J. 33
Crick, F. 83, 86

Dardis, A. 224
Davidson, D. 38–41, 47, 53, 61, 163, 169, 170, 228, 265
de Quincey, C. 243
Dehaene, S. 47
Democritus 195
Dennett, D.C. 12, 19, 61, 86, 96, 131, 154–157, 168, 169, 192–195, 197–199, 202
dependence/dependency 18, 19, 60, 105, 256
Descartes, R. 4, 7, 11, 13, 14, 19, 21, 34, 82, 96, 149–150, 151, 170, 171, 177–182, 187, 195, 204, 222, 225, 243, 245–248, 250, 253, 264, 265
designator
  informative 140–143, 146, 150
  rigid 43, 140–143
  uninformative 150
Devauchelle, A.-D. 47
Dewey, J. 81, 252
diachronic unity 72
Diderot, D. 231
disembodiment 76, 253
disposition 57–59, 66–68, 210
divisibility argument 250
Dretske, F. 132
dual-aspectism 227–230, 234, 238
dualism 4, 5, 7, 17, 19, 26, 44, 49, 62–64, 81, 85, 90, 95–97, 126, 143, 163, 183, 192, 195, 220–22, 232
  bundle 9
  Cartesian 81, 207
  emergent 213–217
  Fregean 53
  integrative 197–98, 202–03
  naturalistic 235; *see also* dual-aspectism
  non-ontological 59
  of particulars 62
  Platonic 207
  property 17, 129, 158, 163, 224–27, 236

substance 4, 9, 56, 165, 171, 201, 204, 225, 229, 236
  Thomistic 209–13, 216
Dyson, F. 235

Eccles, J.C.
Edelman, G.M. 36, 86
eliminativism 86, 90, 95, 168–69, 223, 225
emergence/emergentism 9, 51, 82, 94–95, 154, 213–17, 225, 227, 237–38, 260–61
Empedocles 221
endurer 69
epiphenomenalism 3, 51, 112, 158, 216, 224, 226, 229, 240
epistemic access 59, 60, 61, 63, 65, 67, 69
epistemic entity 92–95
epistemic gap 113
Esser, S.K. 84
Evans, J. 203
event 6, 24, 28, 31, 56–58, 73, 107, 139–143, 158, 161–163, 192–193, 227, 230, 248–249
  brain/cerebral 43, 200
  intentional 143
  mental 4, 61, 140, 143, 147–148, 151, 227, 240
  microphysical 43
  neural/neuronal/neurological 51, 83, 195, 203, 240
  pain- 18
  phenomenal 43
  physical 4, 21, 26–27, 29–30, 103, 107, 140, 143, 147, 200, 203, 240
evolution/evolutionism 36, 39–41, 46, 50–52, 101, 105, 167, 176, 200, 212–213, 215, 234, 238, 262
evolutionary argument against naturalism 50
exclusion principle 154, 158, 162, 163
explanatory gap 113
explanatory gap argument 112

Feigl, H. 85
fetus 205–208, 238
Feynman, R. 99
fictionalism 261–262
first-person 6, 9, 63, 65, 66, 70–71, 73, 75, 76, 89, 90, 97, 117, 245
  experience 194
  perspective 5, 57–60, 128, 191
  phenomena 4
Flew, A. 197

Floridi, L. 92
Fodor, J. 12, 159–161
form
  subsistent 205–206
  substantial 205–208
Foster, J. 78, 183
Frege, G. 46–49, 52, 54, 114, 116
Freeman, K. 243
freedom 101, 110, 165, 171, 242
free will 87, 103, 169, 172, 242
functional role 247, 261
functionalism 50, 58, 59, 66, 67, 203, 223
Fürst, M. 33

Galilei, G. 89
Gallant, J.L. 93, 96
Galois, A. 152
Galvani, L. 84
Gazzaniga, M.G. 83
generalization argument 158
Gibson, J.J. 81
Gleason, C.A. 109
Göcke, B.P. 33, 242
Goetz, S. 198
Gozzano, S. 225, 243
Graham, G. 51, 263
Griffin, D. 243

Hacker, P.M.S. 81, 197
Haeckel, E. 232
Haggard, P. 93, 96
Hahm, J.O. 93
Haldane, J.B.S. 234
Haldane, J.J. 218, 219
half-brain transplant 148
Hameroff, S. 235
Hampshire, S. 228
Harada, K. 89
hard problem of consciousness 208
Harman, G. 133
Hasker, W. 219
Hawthorne, J. 37, 53
Haynes, J.-D. 93, 96
Heinzen, D.J., 108
Herder, J. 231, 232
heterophenomenology 193
Hill, C. 115, 126, 134, 135, 235, 243
Himma, K.E. 201
Hobbes, T. 182, 184, 195, 243
Hodgson, D. 9
Hoffman, J. 78
Holt, E.B. 81
Homfray, D. 87

Index

Honderich, T. 81
Horgan, T. 112, 117
Hornung, E. 221
Hughes, G.E. 33
Hull, C. 84
Human Brain Project 1, 84
Hume, D. 9, 69–70, 147, 151, 152, 166, 176, 182, 186, 225
Hurley, S.L. 81
Husserl, E. 33
Huxley, J. 234
hylonoism 239

idealism 26, 195, 222, 231, 233, 246, 249
identity 6, 9, 18, 19, 21, 36, 42–44, 57, 63, 67, 69, 72, 82, 85–86, 142–145, 147, 151, 169, 182–184, 195, 201, 222, 224–225, 236, 245, 249, 251, 255, 258–261
  cross-time 184
  diachronic 3, 12–13, 75–76
  intrinsic 185
  mind-brain 36–37, 42, 66
  numerical 184
  personal 9, 73–74, 184
  synchronic 75
  token 18, 58
  type 57
identity criterion 142, 144
identity theory 42, 57–58, 85–86, 242
immunity to the error 73, 75
implicate order 53, 234
incommensurability 37, 38, 40, 41, 45, 47
information 2, 6, 35, 63, 72, 86, 91–95, 100, 110, 115, 119, 120–122, 125–126, 150, 155, 186, 186, 198, 234–235
intentionality 1–6, 59, 69, 89–90, 97, 167, 173, 208–211, 223–224, 238–241
intentional content 6, 67, 68
intentional stance 154–156
interactionism 7–8, 95
internalism 82, 84, 90–91
interpretation 59, 61, 62, 93, 113, 119, 123, 127, 160, 162, 222, 235
  Copenhagen 99 102
intrinsic property 6, 58, 63, 66–68
introspection 58, 152, 264
Inwood, M. 183
irrationality 52, 176

irrealism 41
Israel, R. 96
Itano, W.M. 108
Ivry, R.B. 83

Jackson, F. 44, 112–114, 130, 133, 166
Jacobs, J. 219
James, W. 107, 139
Jennings, C. 86
Jessel, T.M. 83
John, E.R. 86

Kandel, E.R. 83
Kant, I. 42–43, 72, 78, 171–175, 177–179, 186, 187, 225, 243
Kant's arguments 42
Kanwisher, N. 87
Kay, K.N. 93, 96
Keating, B. 8
Kenny, A. 196–197
Kim, J. 12, 84, 95, 154, 158–159, 162–163, 168, 191–193, 194, 202
Kinsbourne, M. 96
knowledge argument 112–115, 120, 130
knowledge by acquintance 65, 66, 69, 72, 115
Koch, C. 82, 83, 85, 87, 244
Koons, R.C. 4, 33, 219, 242
Kötter, R. 84
Kriegel, U. 124, 133
Kripke, S. 42–43, 112
Kripke's arguments 42

Lacroix, R. 96
Landauer, R. 92
La Mettrie, J.O. de 231
Lange, A. 242
Larmer, R. 8
LaRock, E. 89
Lehrer, K. 122, 130, 131, 133
Leibniz, G. 3, 7, 45, 183, 195, 217, 230–232, 239, 240, 243
Levin, J. 112, 116
Levine, J. 112, 124, 132, 115, 131, 166
Lewis, C.I. 42
Lewis, D. 27–28
Li, Z. 93
Libet, B. 82, 109
Libet's experiment 109–110
Liddell, H.G. 184
Lingnau, A. 86
Loar, B. 113, 115, 126, 135

Locke, J. 184–185, 225
Loewer, B. 12, 159–161, 170
logical incompatibility 28
logical law 1, 45–49
Long, A.A. 19, 222, 243
Lotze, R. 232
Lowe, E.J. 33, 250, 261, 262, 263, 264, 265
Lund, D. 6, 14, 68, 74, 76, 78
Lycan, W.G. 134, 243

Mach, E. 232–233, 239
Mackie, P. 243
Madell, G. 78
malin génie hypothesis 177
Mangun, G.R. 83
Manzotti, R. 83, 84, 92, 244
Marconi, D. 42
Marijuàn, P.C. 83
Mashour, G.A. 89
Masui, K. 89
materialism 2–3, 5–7, 51, 56–57, 59–64, 68–69, 107, 113, 168, 195, 208, 211, 216, 236; *see also* pysicalism
  anti- 26
  Cartesian 82, 85
  eliminative 3, 59
  non-reductive 59, 226–227
  promissory 105
  reductive, 59
  supervenience 60
  vitalistic 231
Matthews, P. 87
maximal body 20
McDowell, J. 163–166, 168, 169–170
McLaughlin, B. 115, 126
meaning 2–3, 38–39, 48, 106, 166, 193
mechanism 4, 25, 36, 51, 83, 88, 89, 182, 202, 213
Meinong, A. 133
Meixner, U. 33, 34
Melzack, R. 93, 96
memory 1, 4, 36, 72–73, 76, 147, 186, 231
mental content 3, 51, 88, 93
mental phenomenon 4, 7, 57, 63, 82, 93, 97, 192, 194
mental property 3, 7, 38, 90, 139–40, 144, 147–49, 151, 158, 171, 187, 216–217, 224–25, 227–29, 236
mental state 3, 38, 42, 57, 66, 93, 129, 158, 169, 182, 186, 199, 201, 224, 230, 238–240

mental unity 240
Merricks, T. 152, 197, 198
Metzinger, T. 41, 93, 94
Miller, G. 86
mind-body problem 5, 8, 65, 86, 94, 169, 201, 220, 231, 236
minimal body 20
Misra, B. 108
Mitchell T.M. 278
mode of presentation 124–125
  cognitive 128–129
  descriptive 119
  metaphysical 128, 129
  phenomenal 116, 117, 119–120, 126, 129
  physical 119
Moderato, P. 83
Modha, D.S. 83, 84
monism 35, 40, 45, 48, 49, 50, 61, 195, 203, 221–223, 225–230, 235–237
morality 172
Moreland, J.P. 13, 209–219
Morimoto, Y. 89

Nagel, T. 5, 39, 54, 55, 128, 168, 197, 228, 229, 236, 238
Naselaris, T. 93, 96
naturalism 2, 4, 7, 36, 51–52, 63, 156, 158, 163–167, 227–231
necessary property 42
necessity 4, 6, 36, 39, 41–43, 45–50, 125, 128, 131, 139–149, 149, 156, 159, 161, 181–182, 217, 229, 237, 250, 253, 262
Nemirow, L. 115
neural activity 83, 86–89, 93
neural chauvinism 85
neural phenomenon 85
neural process 87–88
neurobiology 36
neurophilosophy 36
neuroscience 3, 10, 41, 50, 81–90, 95, 200
Nida-Rümelin, M. 113
Nietzsche, F. 166, 232
nihilism 248
Nishimoto, S. 93, 96
Noë, A. 81, 85, 96
Nogami, Y. 89
nomological reduction 168
non-abstract individual 17–18, 22, 27, 28, 31–32

290   Index

O'Connor, T. 219, 265
O'Craven, K.M. 87
O'Leary-Hawthorne, J. 152
O'Shaughnessy, B. 228
Olson, E.T. 265
ontological promissory note 92–94
ontological status of the self 247
ontology 5, 60, 61, 63, 64, 69, 91, 92, 95, 160, 167, 169, 225, 232, 243

Pallas, S.L. 93
Pallier, C. 46
panpsychism 226, 237–239
Papineau, D. 112, 113, 115, 117–120, 125–126, 129, 132, 134
Parfit, D. 36, 185
Parmenides 222
Paulsen, F. 232
Pearl, D.K. 109
Peirce, C. 233
Penrose, R. 86
perceptual content 67–68
perdurer 69
personal identity 9, 36, 73–74, 151, 184
phenomenal character 112, 113, 115–117, 120–126
phenomenal concept 44, 112–115, 129–130
    causal-recognitional account of 116
    conceptual role account of 126
    constitutional account of 125–128, 134
    demonstrative account of 113, 116, 117, 125, 126
    direct recognitional account of 115, 126
    encapsulation account of 122–125
    physicalist account of 115–117
    physicalist constitutional account of 113, 116, 117 126, 128
phenomenal concept strategy 112, 117–122
phenomenic aspect 36
phenomenic color 41, 72
phenomenology 21, 39, 44, 72, 77, 119, 120, 121, 193, 208, 263
physical event 4, 21, 26, 27–31, 43, 103, 107, 140, 143, 147, 200, 202, 228, 220
physical law 8, 47, 48, 104, 107, 192, 193, 236
physical phenomenon 8, 84, 86, 90, 95, 192
physical process 66, 86–87, 210

physical property 3, 7, 38, 58, 82, 92, 103, 104, 105, 115, 117, 139–140, 147–148, 171, 216–217, 224–225, 229, 239
physicalism 3, 17–19, 22, 26–30, 36, 39, 42–43, 48–49, 52, 57, 81, 84, 89–90, 112–113, 115, 126, 130, 154, 163, 166, 195, 223–225, 237–238, 261, 264
    non-reductive 159–160, 224
    token-identity 58, 66
Plantinga, A. 6, 51–52, 55
Platts, M. 175
Popper, K.R. 9, 12, 105
possibility
    conceptual 227
    de dicto 24–25, 33
    de re 24–25, 33
    epistemic 76
    logical 149, 226
    metaphysical 74, 182
possible world 22, 36, 37, 42, 44–45, 47–48, 120–121, 124, 140, 142
Prenger, R.L. 93, 96
Price, H. 166–168, 170, 192
Priestley, J. 231
primacy of the mental 191
principle of sufficient cause 28–29
principle of sufficient reason 28
Prinz, J. 83, 87, 89
privileged access 139–140, 143
probing process 103
problem of embodiment *see* bifurcation problem
progressive creation 213
property 2, 9, 17, 22, 56, 95, 103, 117, 128–129, 139–143, 163, 180, 183–184, 222, 252
    causal 58, 144
    causal-relational 5, 63, 66, 67
    conceptual 105
    contingent 22
    empirical 100
    essential 42, 58, 76, 89, 140, 146
    functional 44, 58
    fundamental 82, 161, 223
    genuine 161
    intrinsic 6, 58, 63
    mathematical 44
    mental 3, 7, 8, 38, 90, 140, 147, 151, 158, 171, 216–217, 224, 227, 237, 261
    modal 76
    monadic 139, 145

neurophysiological 51
noncausal 77
non-physical 114, 117
phenomenal 44, 115, 123
physical 3, 7, 38, 58, 82, 92, 103, 140, 147, 171, 216, 224, 227, 239
proto-mental 236
psychological 157, 158
qualitative 66
quantitative 89
reference-fixing 116
relational 58, 66, 67, 139
second-order 58
self-identifying 71
thick 44
thin 44
psychophysical law 88
psychophysical parallelism 230, 239, 241
Pusey, M.F. 99
Putnam, H. 61, 159, 194–195
Pythagoras 221

qualia 4, 84, 211, 224, 230, 239, 241
qualitative phenomenality 68
Quine, W.V.O. 36, 169–170, 174, 176, 187, 195
quantum effect 98, 108
quantum mechanics/physics/theory 28, 40, 98–103, 105, 108, 110, 221, 234
quantum indeterminacy 9
quantum logic 46
quantum Zeno effect 108

rationality 30, 48, 101, 165, 172, 177, 208, 214, 216
Rea, S.B. 209, 214, 218, 219
realism 72–75, 104, 158–59, 160, 162, 169, 225
reason/reasoning 6, 23, 30, 35, 55, 64, 171–177, 179–180, 187
reductionism 4, 6, 48, 57, 58, 82, 159, 164, 212, 261
Rees, G. 93, 96
replacement argument 250
Reppert, V. 219
Revonsuo, A. 86
Rey, G. 39
Robb, D. 243
Robinson, D. 202
Robinson, H. 4, 7, 10, 55, 78, 130, 170
Rockwell, T. 81–82, 84, 85

Roe, A.W. 93
Rorty, R. 61, 166–168, 170
Rosch, E. 81
Rosenberg, A. 196–197
Rosenkrantz, G. 78
Royce, J. 228, 233–234
Rudolf, T. 223
Russell, B. 65, 131
Ryle, G. 197, 199

Schiller, F. 231
Schluppeck, D. 87
Schneider, S. 224
Schopenhauer, A. 231–232, 240
Schultz, G. 96
Schwartz, J.H. 83
Schwinger, J. 107
Scott, R. 184
Searle, J.R. 54, 92, 226–227, 243
second nature 163–164
self-awareness 63, 69, 70, 71, 73, 194
self-consciousness 58, 71, 186
self-reflective subject of thought 246
semantics 1, 2, 53, 89
Shagrir, O. 93
Shoemaker, S. 78, 150, 153, 185
Simon, H.D. 84
singularism 202
Skolimowski, H. 243
Skrbina, D. 241, 242, 243
Smart, J.J.C. 57–58, 85, 89, 90, 218
Smolke, C.D. 54
Sober, E. 192–194, 201
Socrates 185, 205, 221, 242
soul 81–82, 139, 151, 183, 185, 192, 198, 202, 204, 205–217
Sosa, E. 202
special science 6, 154–158, 163, 168–169
Sperry, R.W. 86, 243
Spinoza, B. 230, 231, 239, 240, 243
Sporns, O. 84
Stalnaker, R. 43, 44
Stansbury, D.E. 96
Stapp, H.P. 9, 100, 104
Steeves, J.K. 87
Stephens, G.L. 263
Stoljar, D. 112
Strawson, G. 222, 235–236, 237–238, 243
Strawson, P.F. 186, 228
Stroud, B. 187
Stump, E. 13, 205–206, 208, 216, 218
subjectivity 5, 56, 69, 82, 192, 230

substance 8, 49, 56, 139–142, 145–146, 171, 180, 210, 212, 217, 221, 225, 226, 229–230, 232
  immaterial 192
  material 182, 208, 225
  mental 97, 140, 146–149, 187, 217
  non-physical 180
  non-spatial 145
  pure mental 149–151
  physical 140, 145–149, 182
  simple 9, 82, 217
  spiritual 185
subsumption 18, 19
Sudarshan, E.C.G. 108
supernaturalism 33, 165
Sur, M. 93
Sutherland, S. 86
Swinburne, R. 152, 153, 185, 198, 203
synchronic unity 70–72, 75
Szabó Gendler T. 37, 53

Taliaferro, C. 192, 198, 199, 203
Tallis, R. 197
teleology 208
theological argument 208
Theophrastus 222
third-person 6, 56, 60, 64, 69, 70, 191, 193, 203, 241
thisness 145–146, 148, 150, 151
Thompson, E. 81, 85
thought experiment 36–37, 45, 52, 113, 114, 148, 149, 150
thought-insertion 262–263
Tomonaga, S.-I. 107
Tononi, G. 84, 85, 88, 95, 96, 241, 244
Tooley, M. 55
traducianism 209

translation reduction 168
transcendence argument 6, 164–165
transparency thesis 132–133
trope 20
Tsubokawa, T. 89
Turing test 2
Tye, M. 115–116, 132, 133
Tyndall, J. 98

Unger, P. 155
unity argument 251–252, 257–258
universal 17, 20, 139, 237
Unnoticed Subject-Switching hypothesis 72, 73
Uttal, W.R. 81

van Inwagen, P. 152, 192, 193, 195, 265
Varela, F.J. 81
Veillet, B. 114
Velmans, M. 226, 235
Vision, G. 243
vitalism 211–212, 215, 216, 217
von Neumann, J. 99, 101–103, 105–106, 109, 111

Walker, R.C.S. 187
Wandell, B.A. 93
Watkins-Pitchford, M. 89
Watson, J.B. 84
White, S. 243
Whitehead, A.N. 81, 227, 243
Williford, K. 133
Win, M.N. 54
Winawer, J. 93
Wineland, D.J. 108
Wright, E.W. 109

Zimmerman, D. 223, 224, 225, 229
Zohar, D. 235